D1738938

THE PERFORMATIVE STATE

THE PERFORMATIVE STATE

Public Scrutiny and Environmental Governance in China

Iza Ding

CORNELL UNIVERSITY PRESS   ITHACA AND LONDON

First published 2022 by Cornell University Press

Library of Congress Cataloging-in-Publication Data

Names: Ding, Iza, 1985– author.
Title: The performative state : public scrutiny and environmental governance in China / Iza Ding.
Description: Ithaca [New York] : Cornell University Press, 2022. | Includes bibliographical references and index.
Identifiers: LCCN 2021052214 (print) | LCCN 2021052215 (ebook) | ISBN 9781501760372 (hardcover) | ISBN 9781501760389 (epub) | ISBN 9781501760396 (pdf)
Subjects: LCSH: Environmental policy—China—Public opinion. | Local government and environmental policy—China—Public opinion. | Environmental protection—China—Public opinion. | Communication in politics—China. | China—Environmental conditions—Public opinion. | China—Politics and government—2002–
Classification: LCC GE190.C6 D55 2022 (print) | LCC GE190.C6 (ebook) | DDC 333.720951—dc23/eng20220228
LC record available at https://lccn.loc.gov/2021052214
LC ebook record available at https://lccn.loc.gov/2021052215

Contents

Acknowledgments

Not until the end of this journey did I begin to grasp the meaning of "It takes a village." "It" is a little manuscript, under three hundred pages light. Like most books, odds are it will eventually disappear into the stacks of many a library, words dissolving in the torrent of time. But the years of its making have changed its author in ways that even she cannot fully fathom. They lured its author into a labyrinth of knowledge—sometimes traversing an enchanting forest, other times crossing an engulfing sea storm; here an ecstatic epiphany, there a disappointing dead end. They also pulled her into a web of human relationships that shaped every letter, space, and pixel. To its author it is no longer a book, but a gift of enormous generosity from her fellow travelers on this wonderful journey of a decade long.

I started this project at Harvard University, where I received generous financial support from the Fairbank Center for Chinese Studies, the Ash Center for Democratic Governance and Innovation, and the Institute of Quantitative Social Sciences. Funding from the Department of Political Science and Asian Studies Center at the University of Pittsburgh, where I have served as a faculty member since 2016, helped me bring this project to fruition.

I owe deep debts to my dissertation committee. I was fortunate to have Liz Perry as my advisor. Her candor and kindness propelled me forward. Her way of scholarship gives all her students the best role model they could ever ask for.

I appreciate the unequivocalness of Grzegorz Ekiert, whose jocular cynicism and penchant for Weber proved equally infectious. I will never forget his admonition that "erudition means more than reading the last five issues of the *APSR*."

Susan Pharr's guidance on scholarship and professional development have stuck with me. She supported my never-materialized ambition to study spearfishing societies, for which I am grateful.

Tony Saich's wisdom, wit, and work ethic shaped my understanding of a scholar's purpose.

I first met Yuhua Wang in Ann Arbor, Michigan, where he witnessed my awkward undergraduate phase of radical devotion to rational-choice theory. I'm glad I've since evolved, and I'm grateful for all of Yuhua's wisdom and support.

Peter Hall gave me as much time and advice as a dissertation committee member would. His office—a medieval library, more like it—must have been the incubator of countless dissertation ideas. I remain in awe of his erudition.

I thank Mary Gallagher, Michael Kennedy, John Jackson, and the dearly missed Ron Inglehart for endorsing my nosedive into graduate school.

I cherish the compassion and company of friends I met in Cambridge. Meina Cai, Chris Carothers, Huirong Chen, Ling Chen, Joan Cho, Kyle Jaros, Saul Wilson, Liang Xu, and Yanhua Zhou patiently commented on disoriented early drafts of this project.

Emily Clough, Alex Hertel-Fernandez, Shelby Grossman, Amanda Pinkston and others in the graduating class of 2016 were wonderful job-market companions and helped shape this project. Shelby is always one step ahead of me, and she has always helped me when I'm finally ready to take my own step.

I have many fond memories from Cambridge days with Tim Beaumont, Mark Bell, Volha Charnysh, Jiaxi Chen, James Evans, Adam Frost, Viral Gandhi, Hollie Gilman, Noam Gidron, Jingkai He, Marek Hlavec, Yue Hou, Larissa Hsie-Hwang, Kostya Kashin, Tae-Yeoun Keum, Carly Knight, Dan Koss, John Liu, Yinan Luo, A. Greer Meisels, Sara Newland, Ouyang Bin, Jen Pan, Ruxy Paul, Andrew Mac-Donald, Molly Roberts, Andrei Roman, Rory Schacter, Rachel Stern, Yeling Tan, Jesse Turiel, Peter Volberding, Guoqin Wang, Yiqing Xu, Hannah Waight, Anna Weisfeiler, L-T Zhang, Fangshen Zhu, and others.

Jeff Javed became my closest friend in graduate school. He was my cheerleader, workout buddy, travel companion, loyal confidant, and savvy critic. In a life full of performativities on the front stage, I am lucky that Jeff is always there after the curtain falls.

I am filled with gratitude for colleagues at the University of Pittsburgh. Michaël Aklin, Barry Ames, Dan Berkowitz, Danny Choi, Mike Colaresi, Daniela Donno, Steve Finkel, Michael Goodhart, Max Goplerud, Doug Hanley, Jon Harris, Colin Johnson, George Krause, Andrew Lotz, Scott Morgenstern, Jennifer Murtazashivili, Ilia Murtazashivili, Laura Paler, Guy Peters, Jessica Pickett, Mike Poznansky, Burcu Savun, Kay Shimizu, William Spaniel, and Jae-Jae Spoon all offered helpful comments on this project among other forms of support.

The Asian Studies Center and the East Asian Library at Pitt have always had my back. I'm especially grateful to Joe Alter, Jim Cook, Rachel Jacobson, Lynn Kawaratani, Emily Rook-Koepsel, and Haihui Zhang.

Many thanks to the graduate and undergraduate students at Pittsburgh who have inspired me. I thank Ignacio Mamone, Amaury Perez, and Louis Wilson for their excellent research assistance. I especially owe Qing Chang, Huseyin Zengin, Shuli Zhang, Yixuan Zhang, Andy Zhao, and Deyu Zhou for their assistance in the last stages of this project.

I also thank my wonderful undergraduate research assistants: Qianru Du, Silang Huang, Zhaocheng Li, and Wilson Liu.

I received essential support from Pitt's Asian Studies Center to host a manuscript conference. Many important decisions I made for this book were born then and there. I am grateful for my departmental colleagues who attended, especially Anibal Perez-Linan for serving as a formal discussant, Daniela Donno for moderating, and Amaury Perez for taking notes, as well as colleagues who traveled from afar: Martin Dimitrov, Anna Grzymala-Busse, Pierre Landry, Andy Mertha, and Erica Simmons.

Many thanks to the many others who have suffered through various drafts and segments of this book: Jeffrey Alexander, Daniel Armanios, Adam Casey, Charlotte Cavaille, Matthew Cebul, Marilia Correa, Natalia Forrat, Mary Gallagher, Yuequan Guo, Peter Hall, Mary Alice Haddad, Hanisah Abdullah Sani, Steve Harrell, Guoer Liu, Jundai Liu, Sida Liu, Eddy Malesky, Chris Marquis, Reo Matsuzaki, Dan Mattingly, Brendan McElroy, Kevin O'Brien, Steven Oliver, Dan Slater, Dorie Solinger, Mike Thompson-Brusstar, Minh Trinh, Denise van der Kamp, Sasha de Vogel, Rebecca Wai, Hannah Waight, Yuhua Wang, Nicole Wu, Xiaohong Xu, John Yasuda, Yun Zhou, and others I may have inadvertently omitted.

Much appreciation to Xun Cao, Xiang Gao, Tianguang Meng, and Zeng Yu for sharing their data.

Versions of this project were presented at the Environment and Environmentalism in East Asia Conference in Banff, AAS in Kyoto, China and the Environment in the Social Sciences Conference in Vienna, Global Politics Seminar at Pitt, Shanghai Jiao Tong University, Southwest Workshop on Mixed Methods Research at UC Santa Cruz, Workshop on East Asian Policymaking at Wesleyan University, Tulane University, National University of Singapore, Chinese University of Hong Kong, Yale University, University of Michigan, University of Cambridge, University of Oxford, and London School of Economics. I thank Martin Dimitrov, Fabian Drixler, Ashley Esarey, Mary Gallagher, Mary Alice Haddad, Pierre Landry, Egor Lazarev, Reo Matsuzaki, Alfred Wu, Zhong Yang for their invitations, and for participants in these workshops for their feedback.

Many thanks to the editorial team at Cornell University Press, especially Roger Haydon, Clare Jones, Jim Lance, and Karen Hwa, for their support. They gave me both incredibly helpful suggestions and much-appreciated leeway.

I thank two reviewers for trusting in the manuscript this book was still in the process of becoming. I also thank the three anonymous reviewers of my article "Performative Governance" that is based on a part of this book.

I thank Colleen Berry, Barbara Peck, and Jack Rummel for their expert and sensitive copyediting.

I'm indebted to all my coauthors for their patience as I juggled book-writing and other projects.

Over the years I've learned and gained so much from many friends outside my home institutions. Reunions with Dimitar Gueorguiev, Bill Hurst, Pierre Landry, Lynette Ong, Wenfang Tang, Zhong Yang, and others at Shanghai Jiao Tong University became something I looked forward to every summer. I've been the lucky beneficiary of Lizhi Liu's acumen and camaraderie. I've enjoyed Martin Dimitrov's great humor, and Xiaojun Li's great company. I adore Blake Miller's gaiety, Sasha de Vogel's tenacity, and Mike Thompson-Brusstar's vivacity. I admire Denise van der Kamp's thoughtfulness and Debbi Seligsohn's invincibility. I've always appreciated Jingkai He's bonhomie and Junyan Jiang's acuity. Ben Read was generous with his advice on navigating both fieldwork and flight paths. I'm grateful for Dan Slater's unswerving confidence and generative collaborations. In my fieldwork for the book's quarter-chapter on Vietnam, Nguyen Thuy Chi, Tran Chi Trung, Minh Trinh, Phan Tuan Ngoc, and Annika Yates introduced me to the great city of Hanoi in style.

During some of my tougher moments as junior faculty on the ever-moving ticker of the tenure clock, a number of people lifted me up. Jeff Javed played the brother I never had. Hannah Waight became my sociological soul sister. Yuhua Wang always made time for my questions. Christian Sorace was never short of encouragement. Maria Repnikova took me dancing. Xiang Gao's pep talks rallied me. Sparring with Yang Zhang spurred me. Diana Fu memorably reassured me of the obvious: "Eggs must incubate before they hatch." Walking, thinking, and laughing with Danny Choi and Max Goplerud became an indispensible ritual. I owe my gratitude to all who ever told me in one way or another: you are doing just fine.

A wise man once said, "You never finish a book. They just finally take it away from you." As I was desperately clinging to this manuscript on the cusp of its completion, thanks to those who told me to let go. Xiang Gao, Zhenhuan Lei, Lizhi Liu, Fengming Lu, Xiao Ma, Lachlan McNamee, Christian Sorace, Minh Trinh, Hannah Waight, Erik Wang, Juan Wang, Yang Zhang, and Ying Zhang helped go over "final-final" drafts.

All my life I've been blessed with female mentors and role models. My mother exemplified female leadership as a normal way of life. Mary Gallagher and Anna Grzymala-Busse showed me how to simultaneously take things seriously and not seriously. Jae-Jae Spoon showed me how much can be accomplished in a single day. Nara Dillon and Daniela Donno prove that a person can be terrifyingly smart and extraordinarily kind at the same time. Liz Perry taught me to never go with the flow, and to always forge my own path. All of them taught me the absolute futility of conformity.

Finally, I'm blessed with people who remind me that there is a bigger world outside academia. I shall skip most of their names because by definition they will never read this book. Charlie Tian, Yichen Guan, and Taiyi Sun are lovely island-hopping companions. Will Moon shows me how to work hard and play harder. Eric Qian shows me how to live with inspiration and introspection. Jeff Javed shows me every day that a better version of myself is possible. Will McManus's love and care have provided me with the steadiest of foundations. My childhood friends—Annie, Charlie, Emily, Lili, Michael, Rita, Sara, Vanessa, Vivian—still meet me at the mall like we would when we were kids.

We have arrived at the space conventionally reserved for parents, grandparents, aunts, uncles, cousins, second cousins, distant cousins, and the rest. I shall again skip their names because most of them don't speak English. But without them I wouldn't have walked this beautiful earth, traversed these glorious continents, and lived this privileged life. So, thank you, my village.

STATECRAFT AS STAGECRAFT

The best fortress there is, is not to be hated by the people.

—Niccolò Machiavelli

On an unrecorded date in 77 BC, a first-time prosecutor named Gaius Julius Caesar brought charges of corruption against Gnaeus Cornelius Dolabella, eminent Roman consul under Sulla, former proconsul of Macedonia, and governor of Thracians.[1] The use of public office for personal enrichment was commonplace among Roman magistrates like Dolabella, but Caesar, twenty-three years of age and "of little achievement and from a poorly connected family," decided to pursue him in what seemed certain to be a futile chase.[2] Facing up against two of Rome's ablest and most seasoned orators, Quintus Hortensius and Caius Aurelius Cotta, the young Caesar perorated against corruption in front of a crowd of spectators. His elocution was lyrical, his moralism impeccable, his comportment immaculate, his stance steadfast.

The trial ended with Dolabella's exoneration—an outcome Caesar himself must have anticipated and "may have wished for."[3] For it was not justice that Caesar was after. The dictator-to-be had an astute understanding of his audience, both in the Senate and on the Roman street. By targeting a prominent politician, Caesar drew the limelight to himself, and with limelight came the opportunity for power—what the ambitious young civil servant truly sought.[4]

There are many kinds of power—some secured by fear, others born out of love. Sixteen hundred years after the Dolabella trial, a political cognoscente from Florence advised a prince that when you cannot have both, it is better to be feared than loved.[5] But before Caesar could be feared, he set out on a journey to amass the public's love.[6]

Not many details of the Dolabella trial survive, but few of its chroniclers failed to mention that Caesar's theatrical performance commanded the crowd's attention and assent, despite its failure at obtaining a conviction.[7] Although his prosecution failed—and was doomed to fail—Caesar's performance smoothed his path to political power.

Upon his speech's popular success, Caesar published it for circulation. In the years to come he repeated similar spectacles—in court, in the senate, at funerals—whose outcomes were "less important for his own career than his personal performance."[8] It wasn't just any performance that won Caesar his fame. It was by consciously casting himself as "a politician working for the best interests of the people" that Caesar became "a friend of the people."[9] The theatrical quality of Caesar's political performances inspired Cicero to compare great orators to great actors.[10]

From Politicians to Bureaucrats

Political leaders like Julius Caesar who master the art of theatrical performance in pursuit of mass support can be found throughout history and in every corner of the world. Some, like Martin Luther King Jr., have put their charisma to noble purposes; others have taken history down dark paths.

Max Weber famously called this kind of power "charismatic authority."[11] Passion and wonder are its main elements, discipline and routine are its main enemies. It promises its followers spiritual salvation even when it cannot provide material progress. It turns its willing audience into believers of the unbelievable. It reduces statecraft into stagecraft, giving birth to what Weber once critiqued, in his well-known lecture on "Politics as a Vocation," as the "mere 'power politician,'" who is "constantly in danger of becoming an actor . . . and of being concerned merely with the 'impression' he makes."[12]

The same is not typically said of bureaucrats, another object of Weber's fascination. Bureaucrats have long been considered a very different kind of beast than politicians—even the opposite kind of beast. If charisma enchants, bureaucracy disenchants. If charisma improvises, bureaucracy plans. If charisma knows no discipline and follows no rules, bureaucracy knows only discipline and rules. If charisma offers marvel and transcendence, bureaucracy erects a "permanent structure" that is "oriented toward the satisfaction of calculable needs with ordinary, everyday means."[13] If charismatic authority feeds off the emotions of its followers, bureaucratic authority rests on "the belief in the validity of legal statute and functional 'competence' based on rationally created rules."[14]

This is why a "Weberian bureaucracy," in present-day social science language, refers to an organization—be it an economic enterprise or administrative agency—with distinctly "rational" features.[15] Its most distinct markers include an official mission, hierarchy of authority, division of labor, esteem for technical expertise, and impersonal execution of rules. Unlike elected politicians, whose success rests on popularity, modern bureaucrats' success is ostensibly measured by their ability to execute the responsibilities associated with their position. It therefore stands to reason that politicians frequently rely on the method of theatrical performance, while bureaucrats' performance is geared toward the substantive.[16]

A critical assumption underlies these differences between what "performance" means for a pure politician and a pure bureaucrat: their main audience is different. For a politician it is the public, whereas for a bureaucratic "agent" it is their "principals." Politicians derive their positions "from below," and care for no prize more than the prize of popular support; bureaucrats derive their positions "from above," and care for no audience more than the audience of their superior.[17] According to this view, politicians need a stage like a fish needs water, whereas bureaucrats are but "a small cog in a ceaselessly moving mechanism," "an appendage of the machine," tucked away in a "shell as hard as steel" from the spotlight of public acclaim and acrimony.[18]

But what if this assumption does not always hold true? What happens when the bureaucratic apparatus of officialdom is captured in the light of public scrutiny? A theoretical possibility therefore presents itself: perhaps bureaucrats are not always the antithesis of performative politicians; perhaps their route of march is not so essentially fixed.

"Airpocalypse"

The theoretical prospect above came to empirical life when I began conducting fieldwork on China's environmental governance in 2013. China presents itself as a land of bureaucrats: its leaders do not submit themselves to the popularity test of competitive elections, making its political system formally authoritarian. It can be said that bureaucracy and authoritarianism are natural bedfellows, given their shared hallmark of hierarchy.[19] Bureaucracies typically operate in authoritarian fashion, with neither their top leaders popularly elected nor their decisions made by majority rule. This is why the terms *bureaucratic* and *authoritarian* are often used interchangeably as monikers for the Chinese state—in both its modern and imperial guises.[20]

For all its bureaucratic and authoritarian features, China paradoxically also presents an array of ideas and practices that stand opposed to bureaucracy and authoritarianism. A polity devoid of Schumpeterian democracy (as defined by competitive elections for peak political office) can nevertheless exhibit considerable responsiveness to the public. This has been expressed inside China through Rousseauian theories of participatory democracy, Marxist theories of substantive democracy, Maoist notions of antibureaucratism, and the concept of deliberative democracy.[21] Attempts to realize these ideals fall short of democracy in practice.[22] But the idea that the Chinese system selectively tolerates and even invites public participation is undeniable.[23]

Public pressure was especially pronounced and influential on the issue of environmental pollution in 2013, around the time I began fieldwork for this study. It was a year when pollution in China reigned in the headlines, making it a problem the party-state could not easily ignore.

Although environmental concerns have always existed in China, and environmental governance has never been absent, multiple events have pushed pollution to the foreground of public attention in recent decades.[24] At the 2008 Beijing Summer Olympics, some foreign athletes reported respiratory complaints.[25] That same year, the American Embassy in Beijing installed a rooftop air quality monitor and tweeted out hourly updates of Particulate Matter 2.5 ($PM_{2.5}$) levels.[26] (Twitter was not yet blocked in China.) Beijing's longstanding mysterious fog was henceforth recognized by the wider public as "smog" (wumai), which could now be discerned and measured with concrete numbers.[27] News reporting ramped up in subsequent years, culminating in another critical event: headlines in January 2013 announcing the arrival of an "airpocalypse" in Beijing after pollution blasted through the upper limits of air quality meters.[28]

Less than two months later, a story about "rivers of blood" stunned the citizenry. Images of dead pigs floating down the Huangpu River, which runs through Shanghai and supplies the city's tap water, dominated the news cycle.[29] It was soon discovered that farmers in upstream provinces had been dumping disease-ridden hog carcasses into the river. That March, authorities fished out more than ten thousand dead pigs from the Huangpu.

In the following years, news agencies inside and outside China churned out headline after headline about "cancer villages," "toxic running tracks," and "poisonous rice," with no end in sight.[30]

Pollution exacts palpable damage on public health. A widely cited 2010 Global Burden of Disease study found that air pollution was contributing to about a million premature deaths in China each year.[31] A 2017 University of Chicago study found that air pollution had reduced the life expectancy of Chinese citizens by an average of 3.5 years.[32]

The public outcry over pollution was loud and clear. In the first decade of the twenty-first century, the number of environmental complaints nationwide increased by 53 percent, and the number of environmental protests increased by 29 percent annually.[33] In my own 2015 national urban survey (covered in chapter 4), 79 percent of respondents reported that they would choose pollution control over economic development if the two desiderata were to come into conflict, and about two-thirds of the respondents expressed a willingness to join environmental protests. When *Under the Dome*, a documentary about air pollution, was released online in 2015, it was played more than a billion times in a single day, unleashing a perfect storm of Internet clamor. Pundits called it China's "Silent Spring" moment.[34]

China's Environmental State

This gathering outcry dragged an introverted bureaucracy and its street-level bureaucrats into the spotlight. Facing an environmentally conscious and contentious public willing to challenge the "mandate of heaven," how does the state cope? Can the state redeem itself on one of the hardest public policy problems it has ever faced? To answer these questions, I traveled to the belly of China's environmental state and participated in the organizational life of a municipal environmental protection bureau (EPB).

The Chinese EPB is one of the many agencies that form the organs and limbs of China's bureaucratic state. This agency consists of a national-level ministry—called the Ministry of Environmental Protection (MEP) when this study started, and renamed the Ministry of Ecology and Environment (MEE) in 2018—and subordinate EPBs (renamed the Ecology and Environment Bureau in 2018) at the provincial, municipal, and county levels. Authority emanates downward from the national ministry to the provincial agencies, and from the provincial agencies to municipal and county bureaus. The MEP/MEE's main organizational mission is to establish rules and practices for environmental protection and to implement environmental policies, laws, and regulations.[35]

My main research site was Lakeville, a city in the Yangtze River Delta.[36] Given the city's relative wealth compared to the national average, and overall reputation for good governance, I expected to find best practices in the form of strict enforcement of environmental regulations there. But as I will detail in chapter 3, my initial expectations quickly fell apart once I entered the field. Day in and day out, my participant observation at the Lakeville EPB revealed that best practices were hard to come by. Despite its very Weberian appearance—and to some extent, substance—the EPB was incapable of performing its primary mandate, that is, to enforce environmental regulations on the city's thousands of polluting enterprises.

This realization was at first puzzling. After all, China is not only known for its environmental pollution but also for the bold strides it has taken in pollution control in recent years. From the "blunt-force" closure of factories to massive investment in renewable energy, to the ambitious rollout of a national cap and trade system, to the dramatic blanket ban on coal furnaces in northern regions (a policy that was quickly reversed), China's state-led environmentalism has been as pronounced as its pollution problems.[37] Some have even critiqued China's recent environmental advances as "coercive environmentalism."[38]

Paradoxically, authority over environmental policies is beyond the reach of street-level bureaucrats. Working under every potential "policy entrepreneur," who tirelessly advocates for improving environmental regulations, is a throng of "policy proletarians," whose energy is devoted toward operating rather than changing the system.[39] Behind every dramatic enforcement campaign and substantive policy change lies the less visible reality of everyday governance. Since economic growth still relies on many polluting industries and energy-intensive consumption, environmental concerns usually take a back seat to accommodate more pressing economic needs. Street-level bureaucrats responsible for everyday governance thus find themselves in a situation where they are accountable for something largely outside their control.

If street-level bureaucrats have little control over either making environmental policies or fixing environmental damage, we should naturally expect to see inaction. But bureaucrats at the Lakeville EPB were not dragging their feet, sitting back, or muddling through, as beleaguered bureaucrats are commonly expected to while away their hours on the clock.[40] The dearth of substantive governance manifested not as *inactivity* but, surprisingly, as *hyperactivity*.

Moreover, their actions deviated from the archetype of modern bureaucrats and started to resemble those of elected politicians, even in a political regime that is by definition bereft of them. After all, as Weber himself emphasized, ideal types are starting points rather than stopping points.[41] They are methodological anchorages from which our analysis departs, with the very purpose of observing how "actual action[s]" deviate from them.[42] And indeed, the theoretical distinctions between the two pure types of officialdom were coming undone before my eyes, at the street level.

Performative Governance

Pushed to the front of public attention but armed with little authority, bureaucratic behavior takes on an underappreciated dimension—a *performative* dimension. Instead of being inert, environmental bureaucrats were constantly on the move. But instead of punishing violations and substantively improving the environment, bureaucratic behavior was mostly devoted to maintaining the bureaucracy's public image of responsiveness, benevolence, and effectiveness.

I call this "performative governance"—the state's deployment of visual, verbal, and gestural symbols of good governance for the audience of citizens. Performative governance's main alternative is substantive governance—governance that is geared toward delivering the fruits of effective rule that people demand and deserve.

Understanding what performative governance looks like and how it differs from substantive governance is normatively important and theoretically interesting. For every citizen, knowing whether their government is behaving performatively or substantively is the crucial beginning to holding the state accountable for its actions and inactions. The real-life stakes involved in distinguishing the two types of governance is thus quite high.

As a matter of social science inquiry, since the intention of performative governance is to foster an impression of substantive governance, it is difficult to discern which is which with surface-level observations alone. Finding the appropriate theories and methods to tell them apart thus presents a difficult but stimulating intellectual challenge.

This book takes on this challenge by analyzing performative governance in China's environmental state, but also in other selected issue areas. In doing so I unpack the sources, properties, and outcomes of performative governance. What makes state behavior performative as opposed to substantive? Does performative governance always impress its audience? When does it improve the state's image and when does it fall flat?

The rest of this chapter offers answers to these questions, and the rest of this book provides evidence for those answers. But before delving into the conditions of performative governance and its reception by the public, let's further unpack the definition of performative governance. Although the concept contains only two words, each carries many meanings. First, what does "performative" mean? Second, what is "good governance"? In other words, what exactly is the impression the state seeks to foster?

On "Performativity"

You are more than entitled not to know what the word "performative" means. It is a new word and an ugly word, and perhaps does not mean anything very much. But at any rate there is one thing in its favour, it is not a profound word.

—J. L. Austin, "Performative Utterances"

There is much confusion and contention over the meaning of the word *performative*. *Merriam-Webster* offers three related definitions.[43] The first is "the performance of [a] specified act by virtue of its utterance." This definition stems from J. L. Austin, who coined "performative utterance" to describe speech acts—words that are "doing something rather than merely saying something."[44] For example, when an umpire says "out," when a judge says "guilty," when a couple says "I do."[45] "I do" not only reports the initiation of a legal union but also shapes the subsequent social behavior and economic outcomes of a couple. Austin distinguishes performative utterances from descriptive statements such as "the sky is blue."

Since its invention in the early twentieth century, the word has taken on two additional meanings that extend beyond speech. *Merriam-Webster's* second definition of performative is "relating to or marked by public, often artistic performance." Performative here is used to describe theatrical performance as an art form.

Merriam-Webster's third definition of performative is "made or done for show (as to bolster one's own image or make a positive impression on others)."[46] My use of "performative" mostly falls under this definition.

Performativity is of growing interest to social scientists. Economic sociologists have invoked "performativity" (in the first sense detailed above) to describe how theories about the market may purport to explain market behavior, but in fact help shape it.[47] As Albert Hirschman wisely argued, what we now assume to be the natural and rational laws of economic relations are but scripts written by market theorists to direct the beliefs and behaviors of market actors.[48] (Calling markets rational is not only saying something about markets, but doing something to markets.) Anthropologists like Victor Turner and Clifford Geertz have illustrated how symbols, rituals, and ceremonies permeate our social life—from sports to religion to politics.[49] In cultural sociology, performativity is often expressed through Pierre Bourdieu's notion of *habitus*—habits, tastes, skills, intuitions, lifestyles, and everything else that comes with an individual's class.[50]

It was Judith Butler who effectively popularized the concept of "performativity" in the United States. Butler argues that gender identities are not naturally given or inherently stable, but are repeatedly instituted through the social performance of gender conventions.[51] In defining "performative governance," I borrow from Butler's definition of performativity as "language, gesture, and all manners of symbolic social sign."[52] In theorizing "performative governance," however, I draw inspiration from sociologist Erving Goffman, who rarely used the word *performative*, but whose works became canonical in the literature on performativity.[53] In his best-known study, Goffman likens everyday social interaction to theatrical performance, arguing that when individuals appear before others they will "present [themselves] in a light that is favorable to [themselves]."[54] They will—sometimes strategically, other times subconsciously—display certain language, gestures, and symbols to influence the impressions others form of them. Goffman calls such social settings the "front stage," which is divorced from the "back stage," where actors are hidden from their audience.[55]

Although Butler and Goffman now jointly carry the banner of performativity, some important differences between them are worth clarifying. Goffman's performativity is a *strategy of impression management*; Butler's is *submission to cultural hegemony*.[56] For Goffman, there is a clear separation between the front stage and the back, between one's public "role" and private "self." For Butler, the two stages are inseparable; performativity constitutes the very identity of the performer—the "role" *is* the "self." Moreover, while Goffman's study is purely analytical, Butler is interested in persuading her reader that they have the agency to bring about performative breakdown.[57]

The upshot for our purpose here is that scholars disagree on performativity's sources, the level of its intentionality, and how it changes over time. But the larger phenomenon—the construction of social reality through the performance of visual, verbal, and gestural symbols—remains a consistent theme across different fields of observation.

In this study I use "performative" to refer to the symbolic aspect of state behavior, so as to distinguish it from the substantive outputs or outcomes of what we typically mean by "government performance." When we use the word *performance* to describe governments today, we mean the quality of their public service as measured by some objective standards, usually economic performance, but not its other, more theatrical meaning. Performative governance in this book refers instead to the state's symbolic performance of "good governance."

The idea behind performative governance is not new. The same term has been used by scholars of democracy to describe the ritualistic and theatrical nature of democratic participation.[58] As state behavior, a rainbow of concepts share a "family resemblance" with it. Higher on the ladder of abstraction sit "signaling," "credit claiming," "blame avoidance," "public relations," "audience costs," and "propaganda." Within the literature on Chinese politics, performative governance echoes "therapeutic governance," "image projects," and "symbolic legitimacy."[59] Parallel on the spectrum of organizational behavior, performative governance overlaps with notions like "symbolic implementation" and institutional "decoupling."[60] I use performative governance instead of other affinitive terms because it most exactly captures the state's enactment of visual, verbal, and gestural symbols of good governance.

If everything is performative, then nothing is performative. While performativity is everywhere in life and politics, few have considered its boundaries and alternatives. Even Goffman said that "all the world's not, of course, a stage, but the crucial ways in which it isn't are not easy to specify."[61] The intended contribution of this study is not to have discovered the existence of performativity in political processes. (I will return to the vast literature on theatrical performance in politics in the conclusion.) Instead, my intended contribution lies in analyzing a specific kind of performativity—that is, the state's theatrical performance of *good governance*—and to reveal its sources, properties, alternatives, and consequences.

Performative governance abounds in China, but not all governance, in China or elsewhere, is performative. Every state is many-handed and multifaced, capable of being responsive and repressive, redistributive and extractive, transparent and deceptive, all at the same time.[62] A central purpose of this book is to consider the ways in which state behavior *is and is not* performative.

Identifying Performativity

A key challenge in many contemporary social science investigations is the wide gulf between ontology and methodology.[63] This is especially true of performativity. That is to say, we are ontologically aware that performativity exists in all kinds of social behaviors, but the methodological predicament lies in identifying and, if one so wishes, measuring it. This predicament even plagued the concept's inventors. After J. L. Austin distinguished performative utterances from other kinds of speech, he became embroiled in debates about whether certain sentences were or were not performative, leading to his exasperated declaration that "it is not a profound word."[64] Victor Turner freely admitted that "many social scientists frown on the [term]."[65]

What perhaps alienates many empiricists from the study of performativity is that unlike, say, GDP, behavior of a theatrical nature is simply not quantifiable. Even if we could manage to construct a quantitative measure to describe a behavior as *more or less* performative, this still would not allow us to distinguish performativity from its alternatives.[66] Less performative governance does not automatically mean more substantive governance. This study does not merely seek to distinguish the presence of performative governance from its absence, but to clarify how performative governance differs from its multiple alternatives, especially substantive governance.

This leads us to the identification challenge. That is, if performative governance is intended to foster an impression of good governance, these two conceptually distinct phenomena may prove observationally equivalent on the front stage—for example, when state agents appear on TV, on the street, and in newspapers.

I overcame this challenge through ethnographic observation. This method follows a simple logic: the more time we spend with someone, the more familiar they become to us, and the better we understand them. As I spent more time with street-level bureaucrats, I learned that they were anxious about public opinion, that they were aware of the futility of their enforcement efforts, and that some were even conscious of the performative nature of their actions. Close daily observation allowed me to tell performative governance from its likely alternatives: bureaucrats were not simply "going through the motions" or coming up short at substantive governance while "doing their best." Rather, they were devoting even more effort than expected toward the very active, even creative, task of fostering an impression of good governance.

To be clear, intentionality is by no means necessary to identify performativity. Performativity can be unconscious or half-conscious. We reflexively clap when others clap, whether or not we found the performance enjoyable. We write "I hope this email finds you well" without a conscious intention to manipulate the receiver into thinking that we care about them in any meaningful way. Butler argues that gender performativity can be one's obedience to cultural hegemony, and the surreptitious power of hegemony, as Gramsci teaches, is that we don't think about it. Thus, identifying performative governance is a matter of locating its empirical properties and not simply delving into actors' conscious intentions.

Another way performative and substantive governance can be observationally equivalent is when state behavior takes on both properties at once. It is surely the case that if we look hard enough, we can find both performativity and substance in almost every single interaction, if not every action. But the two terms have more specific meanings in this book. By "performative," I do not include every action that projects a symbol or an image, and by "substantive," I do not include every action that has any impact on reality. Defined this way, every action would be both performative and substantive, rendering the conceptual distinction useless. To avoid leading the analysis down a rabbit hole of tautology, I treat performative and substantive performance as *conceptually distinct*. This in no way denies that the two phenomena can be unearthed in tandem in the real world.

On "Good Governance"

In my definition of performative governance, the state seeks to foster an impression of "good governance." But what is good governance? Since what is "good" is in the eyes of the beholder, what constitutes "good governance" can be different for me, for the reader, for an average citizen in a given country, or for the government of a given society.

As I use the term here, *good governance* refers to a broad, if never unanimous, state-society consensus on how a particular government should behave (and not my own or any particular philosopher's normative beliefs). One might question whether such state-society consensus can ever exist without the threat of coercion, especially in authoritarian regimes. But even if a consensus is forged in a top-down manner, this doesn't mean it can't become "common sense."[67]

The fuzzy contours of state-society consensus on good governance delimit the repertoire of performative governance, which may vary from place to place. To offer a prosaic example: for many people in the United States, good governance means limited governance, whereas in Scandinavia, a small government is not generally seen as intrinsically desirable. This doesn't mean that there are no significant overlaps between what different societies consider "good." To see why, let's start with some general principles before we examine what good governance has meant in China, and what it meant in the historical moment when this study took place.

When evaluating the quality of governance, we might pay attention to three aspects: *processes, outputs,* and *outcomes*. Political processes are the ways decisions are made in a polity, such as elections, consultations, deliberations, and dictates. Some desirable qualities of political processes include efficiency, transparency, openness, inclusiveness, responsiveness, freedom from coercion, and majority rule.[68] Processes generate outputs, which can be laws, policies, regulations, and the particular political leaders elected or selected to exercise power. Some desirable qualities associated with political outputs are clarity, fairness, effectiveness, competence, and benevolence. Political outcomes are the effects these outputs have on society at large. Desirable outcomes include substantive justice, political stability, improvements in individual and collective well-being, and any other outcome that can be said to advance the common good.

It is important to differentiate these different aspects of governance, because good processes do not always produce good outputs, and good outputs do not always lead to good outcomes. For example, democracy may be the most desirable political process for all its positive procedural attributes, yet democratic processes might still yield bad decisions and undesirable outputs (for example, discriminatory policies and malevolent leaders). Meanwhile, outputs that are good on paper may not lead to intended outcomes like improved well-being, such as when policies are poorly implemented, when laws are ignored, when good leaders make bad decisions, or when unforeseen circumstances cause unintended consequences.

What's said above gives us a bundle of attributes that are potential indicators of good governance. Next, we may examine what good governance means in different contexts, including what it means in China. It is commonly argued that citizens in democracies care more about political processes than citizens in authoritarian regimes, who tend to focus more on outcomes. The very legitimacy of the democratic system is believed to be upheld by the "procedural justice" of its institutions.[69] Even when citizens disagree with the system's decisions, they seem not to reject democracy itself.[70] Conversely, since authoritarian regimes are believed to lack the "procedural legitimacy" of democratic institutions, it's argued that their citizens tend to pay more attention to the outcomes of the system's substantive performance. As a result, the "performance legitimacy" of authoritarian regimes has become a popular notion in academic research and mass media.[71] It describes political support derived from outcomes—economic performance in particular.[72]

This process-versus-outcome distinction of what good governance means in democratic and authoritarian systems is helpful but incomplete. For starters, the perceived legitimacy of democratic institutions is not based on procedures alone—a government's ideological compatibility with its constituents can matter greatly, as do economic outcomes.[73] The rise of populism in recent years is partly indicative of widespread dissatisfaction with governance outcomes in democracies. By the same token, "good governance" also transcends economic performance in nondemocratic systems. For example, authoritarian regimes that pursue legal development more or less bind themselves to taking procedural justice seriously.[74]

What does good governance mean in China? It is important to dismiss at the outset the uninformed notion that that there is a single Chinese view on anything. We may nevertheless identify widely held beliefs in China and see how they evolve over time.

The Chinese state has recently become enamored with the notion of "service-oriented government" (*fuwuxing zhengfu*). This concept made its debut in 2007 at the Seventeenth National Congress of the Chinese Communist Party (CCP), where President Hu Jintao declared it an essential part of the party's political reforms.[75] At the Eighteenth Party Congress in 2012, Hu repeated the imperative to "build a service-oriented government that is based on scientific functions, structural optimization, integrity and efficiency, *and people's satisfaction.*"[76] This dictum became an integral part of President Xi Jinping's "China Dream" (*Zhongguo meng*) and was heard in his inaugural speech in 2012. Since then, "building a service-oriented government based on people's satisfaction" (*jianshe renmin manyi de fuwuxing zhengfu*) has become an echoing expression in policy documents. This much-trumpeted shift in governance orientation has been backed up by a series of governance reforms at the local level.[77]

"Service" has at least two connotations in everyday life and in politics. First, it can refer to the product rendered. In the marketplace, it means something a customer has purchased. In the case of government provision of social services, this includes policy outputs such as education, healthcare, pensions, and social security. Second, service may refer to the experience offered. In the marketplace, it literally means customer service. With government services, it includes every aspect pertaining to citizens' "user experience" when interacting with government offices and agents. Citizen experience may be affected by features of the political process mentioned earlier, such as efficiency, transparency, and responsiveness.

If the first type of service—the product, or substantive performance—has historically shaped Chinese conceptions of good governance, the second type of service—the process, and the notion of responsiveness in particular—picked up steam in the past decade, both in official discourse and in academic research.[78] During a State Council meeting in 2016, Premier Li Keqiang urged that "a modern government should respond to people's expectations and concerns in a timely manner."[79] In turn, local governance reforms blossomed, such as "immediate response to complaints" (*jie su ji ban*) reforms at the subdistrict level in many cities; the "whistleblowing on the streets, [rapid] check-in from [relevant] agencies" (*jiexiang chuishao, bumen baodao*) reform in Beijing; and one-stop shop (*zuiduo paoyici*) reforms in Zhejiang Province.[80] In academic research, "authoritarian responsiveness" has emerged as a vibrant field of study.[81]

Service-oriented government is often juxtaposed with, and discussed as a shift away from, the outdated "management-oriented government" (*guanlixing zhengfu*). The difference between the two is that a service-oriented government is focused on meeting the citizens' expressed needs, whereas a management-oriented government paternalistically defines citizens' needs for them. A service-oriented government rejects the "primacy of officials" (*guanbenwei*), and instead stresses the "primacy of citizens" (*minbenwei*), seeing itself as a service provider and its citizens as customers.[82] Service-oriented governance in contemporary China echoes the Maoist notion of "serving the people" (*wei renmin fuwu*), which has been traced even further back to Confucian notions of *minben* (that is, primacy of the people) by party theoreticians.[83]

Ergo, service-oriented governance has become a primary ingredient in contemporary China's recipe for "good governance." It concerns not only the products but also the experiences rendered by government services. Yu Keping, a prominent Chinese scholar and policy advisor, defines "good governance [*shanzhi*]" as including "legitimacy [*hefaxing*], transparency [*touming*], accountability [*zerenxing*], rule of law [*fazhi*], responsiveness [*huiying*], effectiveness [*youxiao*], participation [*canyu*], stability [*wending*], cleanliness and honesty [*lianjie*], fairness and justice [*gongzheng*]."[84] These notions of good governance are hardly unique to China.

Clarifying what good governance means helps us understand the repertoire of performative governance, because any impression a state seeks to foster will likely be based on a definition of good governance that is familiar to its audience. In this case, the Chinese state's performative governance projects an image that is distinct from another type of impression authoritarian regimes typically project—the image of awe and fear.[85] Goffman's classic 1959 study cites several examples of the state's imposing theatrical displays, including a description of a Chinese mayor's street procession at the turn of the twentieth century:

> [The] luxurious chair of the mandarin, carried by eight bearers, fills the vacant space of the street. He is mayor of the town, and for all practical purposes the supreme power in it. . . . . He is an ideal-looking official, for he is large and massive in appearance. . . . He has a stern and forbidding aspect, as though he were on his way to the execution ground to have some criminal decapitated. This is the kind of air that the mandarins put on when they appear in public. . . . I have never seen any of them, from the highest to the lowest, with a smile on his face or a look of sympathy for the people whilst he was being carried officially through the streets.[86]

Suffice it to say, if this mayor were to appear on the streets of China today, he would have a hard time remaining mayor. Modest, smiling, and sympathetic expressions are more likely to appear on officials' faces nowadays. This "man of the people" manner has emanated from the top of the bureaucratic state all the way down to the street level.[87] According to a nationally representative survey conducted in 2003, 39 percent of respondents believed that local government agencies were "warm and friendly" when executing policies; by 2011, the number climbed to 61 percent.[88] Regardless of the substantive outcomes these warm and friendly processes generate, the CCP's definition of good governance, and thus its script for performative governance, is now distinctly benevolent.[89] As the end of this book will show, even the coercive arm of the state sometimes reveals its sensitive side.

Why Performative Governance?

Having defined it, we can now move on to ask: "Why performative governance?" Under what conditions does performative governance become more or less likely? Cultural and institutional explanations are often the first to bubble to the surface. Before fleshing out my own argument, I briefly consider four propositions that might be considered alternative explanations.

The first argument emphasizes the prevalence of performativity in human interaction. As the title of Goffman's book suggests, "the presentation of self" permeates "everyday life." Since performativity is a human interactional condition, performative governance is an essential condition of human governments.

This proposition is sound, although theatrical performance can also be found in other species. In mating season, male magnificent frigatebirds of the Galápagos Islands inflate their scarlet throat pouch to the size of a balloon to impress potential mates. Before performing their mating dance, male parotias—also known as the six-plumed birds of paradise—meticulously groom and decorate a clearing on the forest floor as their stage, and polish a tree branch for a viewing platform, all to maximize the visual impact on their audience. Natural selection allows parotias that excel at their theatrical performance to pass down their genes, which preserves and augments this trait. Performativity is human, but not uniquely human.

A second argument centers on Chinese culture or East Asian culture. Some might argue that Chinese culture is known for its concern with the "face," thus performative governance may be particular to China. Any such proposition would venture too far down the path of cultural determinism and essentialism. Examples of performativity can be found around the world and throughout history. Dolabella's trial, described at the beginning of this introduction, is just one of the umpteen. Goffman's study of impression management was, after all, conducted in a Western society. Although China is the focus of my analysis, I will also refer to examples of performative governance in other parts of the world. Chapter 5, in particular, delves into two additional cases of performative governance in the United States and Vietnam.

A third argument might see performativity through the lens of principal-agent theory, and argue that the audience for performative governance is not citizens at all, but the senior officials who control street-level bureaucrats' careers. To be sure, hierarchical command is a defining trait of bureaucracy. Thus, any analysis of bureaucratic behavior, by definition, assumes that there is a fair amount of command, control, and upward accountability. But performing obsequiousness to superiors is a different phenomenon from performing responsiveness to citizens—as my description of performative governance will show.[90]

A fourth explanation zooms in on institutions and practices of communist and postcommunist regimes.[91] Specifically, it focuses on the state's proactive use of "input institutions,"[92] such as letters and complaints in the former Soviet Union,[93] as well as China's petition system and protest tradition to gauge public opinion, which reverberates back to imperial times.[94] These studies provide necessary and helpful background for the case of Chinese governance. But they pay less attention to internal variations within the state and the conditions under which these institutions serve performative or substantive purposes.

To answer "why performative governance," the first part of this book (chapters 1–3) examines the factors that foster it, while fully acknowledging that larger cultural-institutional forces are always at play. To put it in the language of political science: holding constant a general tendency for performativity to emerge in human interactions, when are we more likely to see performative governance as opposed to other types of state behavior? Why do we see performative governance by some agencies but not others? And at some times but not others?

I argue that two conditions make performative governance more likely. First, when the state or bureaucracy lacks the *capacity*—either logistical ability or political authority—to substantively fulfill its functional promises. Second, when public *scrutiny* over state behavior is strong. I use scrutiny to capture the extent to which the state, or a single bureaucracy within it, is placed under critical examination for its performance. I specifically focus on scrutiny from the wider audience of society, which is ostensibly irrelevant for bureaucrats, whose salary, promotion, and dismissal are usually determined by their superiors alone. The combination of low capacity and high scrutiny makes performative governance an especially attractive coping mechanism because audience attention is intense, yet substantive governance is unfeasible. This is indeed the situation in which the Chinese EPB found itself during my ethnographic fieldwork.

This theoretical argument about what gives rise to performative governance leads to further predictions of state behavior when the two variables—capacity and scrutiny—assume different values. I explain in chapter 1 that when capacity and scrutiny are both weak, governance is inert. When capacity is strong and scrutiny is weak, governance is paternalistic—it can be either developmental or predatory. Finally, when capacity and scrutiny are both strong, we have substantive governance. (For a visual representation of my typology see table 1 in chapter 1.)

To be sure, these pure types of state behavior are neither mutually exclusive nor jointly exhaustive. I do not propose a deterministic theory, nor do I pretend to have captured every kind of governance. As I explain in chapter 3, my top priority is to develop a theory that is internally valid to my case. Having said that, since there is reasonable belief that similar conditions (e.g., conditions of low capacity and high scrutiny) exist elsewhere—in other organizations, localities, or countries—my arguments can reasonably be expected to travel.

Furthermore, these pure types are not static. I do not argue that China's environmental bureaucracy is forever stuck in performative governance. I will show that in the decades prior to my fieldwork, the bureaucracy evolved from inertia to performativity. Several years after finishing my fieldwork, and with follow-up interviews, the last of which were conducted in 2020, I find that the bureaucracy is moving toward substantive governance. These changes are documented throughout chapters 1–3. Their causes lie precisely in the shifts over time in my theory's two key conditions: capacity and scrutiny.

Performative governance is gradually giving way to greater substantive governance in China's environmental state. This does not mean performative governance is of declining theoretical relevance, however. Even if every observation eventually becomes outdated in the grand scheme of things, the caprice of time and the ephemerality of human behavior does not render understanding a phenomenon at a specific time any less valuable, especially if the analysis illuminates practices and patterns broadly identifiable across space and time.

When answering the question "why performative governance?" one must appreciate that there are different kinds of "why" questions. This book answers the positivist version of the question, that is: When does performative governance become more likely? It does not answer normative versions of this question, such as: Are there situations in which performative governance may serve the common good, although in general it seems deceptive and thus undesirable?

To briefly engage the normative question, consider a recent example. A year into the COVID-19 pandemic, scientists had successfully developed vaccines. But many people in the United States believe that the pandemic is an elite conspiracy to impose socialist control, and that vaccines are harmful. To convince the public that the vaccine is safe, three former presidents—Barack Obama, George W. Bush, and Bill Clinton—volunteered to get their vaccinations on TV.[95] Two weeks after this announcement, Vice President Mike Pence and his wife also received televised vaccinations.

Such actions are both substantive and performative: substantive in that vaccines were indeed made available to the wider public, performative in that they were administered on TV to reassure a skeptical public. (One does not need to appear on TV to be vaccinated.) Pence getting the vaccine sent two signals to American citizens: first, the Trump administration had overseen the successful development of vaccines, and getting the vaccine on TV helped the government claim credit; second, vaccines are safe, and getting the vaccine on TV encouraged wary citizens to follow suit. The first is performative governance according to a strict version of my definition, because it's directly connected to "good governance," while the second sees the definition slightly stretched. I do not intend to stretch the concept to describe every form of performativity by authorities, but I also have no quibble with others choosing to use the concept more expansively.[96] One may argue that the second intention, the one that promotes public safety, is indeed desirable.

One might also make a normative case for performative governance by saying that dispositions of "service orientedness" are in and of themselves a virtue, even when the state is shorthanded and cannot resolve people's problems. Of course, no one is arguing for malevolently denying citizens services when resources are abundant. But as Bernardo Zacka's study of street-level bureaucrats in the United States reveals, "Frontline workers in the public services . . . are condemned to being front-row witnesses to some of society's most pressing problems without being equipped with the resources or authority necessary to tackle these problems in any definitive way."[97] In this case, "*How* one is treated is just as crucial as *what* one gets."[98]

Those who believe in the conditional necessity of the more cynical, deceptive version of performative governance may invoke Machiavelli, who argues that hoodwinking the public—such as by "appearing to be religious"— is sometimes necessary not only for the benefit of the prince but also for the benefit of the people. For example, "Although the use of fraud in every action is detestable, nonetheless in managing war it is a praiseworthy and glorious thing."[99] They might also follow Mary Dietz's exposition of *The Prince* as Machiavelli's own devious, though failed, deception to "undo Lorenzo de Medici by giving him advice that would jeopardize his power, hasten his overthrow, and allow for the resurgence of the Florentine republic."[100] This theme is beyond the scope of my book, but interested readers may refer to the archipelago of argumentation on the vices and virtues of acting (and even lying) in politics, such as the proposition that "in certain circumstances, citizens have a *right* to be lied to."[101]

This book is not about the vices and virtues of performative governance, fascinating as they may be, but about its underlying conditions and ensuing consequences.

Turning to the Audience

Real life is not an immaculately choreographed dance. While the motivation behind performative governance is to foster the impression of good governance, this does not mean it is always effective. On the one hand, since the brain intuitively links referential symbols with specific meanings—associating smiling with friendliness, for instance—we might hypothesize that the theatrical performance of good governance will persuade citizens that good governance has occurred. On the other hand, not all performances generate applause, so we might question the extent to which the public is receptive to performative governance and its intended messages, especially when theatrical display is not accompanied by substantive delivery. Like Goffman and Butler, I anticipate that "performance disruption" and "performative breakdown" will be just as commonplace, so I treat them as part of my empirical investigation.[102]

The second part of this book (chapters 4 and 5) examines the citizen audience's appraisal of performative governance. I ask when performative governance is successful at impressing this audience, and when it fails. To answer these questions, we need to zoom out from the kind of individual interactions an ethnography of the state attends to, and shift perspective from the state to its citizens, and then to the entire public sphere. Some changes in the unit of analysis are in order.

In doing so I make three analytical moves. First, I trace the mechanisms of political communication from state to society, and identify the mass media as an influential front stage on which performative governance is projected to a wider audience. Second, I take special interest in ordinary audience members, whose attention to the issue is not as ardent as that of activists, whose attitude toward the regime is not as recalcitrant as that of dissenters, and whose appraisal of performative governance can tilt in either a positive or negative direction. Third, I demonstrate that the direction in which the wind of public opinion blows depends on the information environment in which state and society interact.

Survey and interview evidence in chapter 4 shows that substantive governance does indeed matter for citizen evaluations, as expected; but so does performative governance. When performative governance is effective at persuading citizens of the state's virtue, it does so through two mechanisms. First, by lowering itself in front of the citizens, performative governance gives citizens a sense of power and efficacy, even when the state cannot substantively solve their problems. Second, the promissory nature of performative governance gives some citizens the impression that governance outcomes (in this case, air quality) are in the process of improving.

But when does performative governance cease to exist or fail to impress? I further discuss three paths to performative breakdown. First, my opening chapters explain how performative governance ends through the changing of its underlying conditions—low capacity and high scrutiny. As the Chinese EPB acquires more authority and greater autonomy from local economic and political interests, environmental governance has become more substantive. However, such change has yet to become thoroughgoing, permanent, or irreversible.

Second, the actors of performative governance (state agents, in this case) may choose to "exit" the ensemble, and in some cases use their "voice" to improve governance.[103] But as I will show, only in rare instances—when stakes are high and opportunities are ripe—do exit and voice lead from performative disruption to actual performative breakdown.

The third, related path to performative breakdown is through the state's loss of control over the domestic information environment. Specifically, when the audience acquires "destructive information" about the theatrical performance, they grow skeptical about its verisimilitude.[104] This kind of performative breakdown is of the greatest concern to a state, because it is effectively a communication breakdown between state and society. This is the key mechanism investigated in chapter 6.

Overview of the Book

This introduction has not introduced much by way of empirical evidence. Readers with a pressing need to see direct evidence of performative governance in China might turn straight to chapter 3, which is based on my participant observation at a municipal EPB. For readers who are just as interested in my theorization and secondary arguments, including my empirical investigations into the evolution of China's environmental state over time and the "causes and effects" of performative governance, the book's chapters are best read in full and sequential order.

The first part of this book, chapters 1–3, attempts to follow Richard Bonney's advice that "the study of government requires knowledge of the theory of government (i.e., of the history of political thought), knowledge of the practice of government (i.e., of the history of institutions) and finally knowledge of government personnel (i.e., of social history)."[105] Chapter 1, "Anatomy of the State," completes the introduction's unfinished job of setting the theoretical stage for the empirical analysis to come. I first clarify my level of analysis as the bureaucratic state. I dissect "the state" vertically, between the ruling regime and the bureaucratic apparatus, as well as horizontally, between its various functional organs and arms. Recognizing the state's internal complexity and variety helps us understand its multifaced interaction with the society it serves.

I then proceed in chapter 1 to argue that state-bureaucratic behavior is shaped by capacity and scrutiny, which combine to produce four types of governance: inert, when capacity and scrutiny are both weak; paternalistic, when capacity is strong but scrutiny is weak; substantive, when capacity and scrutiny are both strong; and finally, performative, when capacity is weak but scrutiny is strong. I discuss the underlying sources of capacity and scrutiny and illustrate this typology with examples globally and within the Chinese state. A central lesson is that the Chinese state is highly uneven across its many disparate bureaucracies in how much capacity it possesses, how much scrutiny it confronts, and thus how it conducts itself.

Chapter 2, "Old Woes and New Pains," provides necessary historical background on China's state environmentalism and makes three main points about environmental pollution and governance in China. First, environmental degradation existed long before its impact entered the public consciousness. Second, rising scrutiny was not merely a product of objective pollution levels, but also of international and domestic political shifts. Third, the development of contemporary China's environmental bureaucracy over the past four decades followed the predictions of my typology in chapter 1. Until quite recently, environmental governance in China was largely inert—the bureaucracy neither possessed the capacity that would allow it to govern, nor confronted the public scrutiny inciting it to act. Then, as scrutiny intensified in the mid-2000s, the state pursued a strategy of performative governance: though it lacked the capacity to meet citizen demands, it had to do *something* to appease public outcry over pollution. Finally, as capacity increased in recent years, in part due to shifting policy priorities, China's environmental state has at times switched gears toward substantive governance. However, substantive environmental governance remains sporadic for reasons that will become evident.

Chapter 3, "Beleaguered Bureaucrats," is the book's core empirical chapter. It presents an ethnographic case study of performative governance at work, based on five months of participant observation at a municipal EPB in China, as well as interviews with government officials and EPB bureaucrats in other Chinese cities. Thick description of the inner workings and public performances of the EPB distinguishes performative governance from its main conceptual alternative— substantive governance. A close look at the fears and aspirations of the EPB's street-level bureaucrats sheds light on the simultaneous rationality and irrationality of performative governance. For an irrefutably weak agency under intense public scrutiny, the agency's formal mandates must take a back seat while it polishes and preserves its public image, which directly impacts its agents' career security.

The second part of this book (chapters 4 and 5) puzzles through a natural follow-up question: How do citizens perceive performative governance? Since most Chinese citizens have never directly interacted with environmental bureaucrats, can performative governance reach and sway a wider audience? If so, how?

Chapter 4, "Audience Appraisal," extends the state's front stage to the mass media. I use interviews with EPB bureaucrats, journalists, editors, and television news producers to show how state agencies communicate with the general public, and how the media plays its "supervisory" function over state behavior. I then use a national public opinion survey to analyze citizen perception of local environmental governance, finding that exposure to performative governance in the news indeed improves public assessments of environmental governance, even as Chinese citizens clearly covet more substantive improvements in air quality. Because the substantive issue in this book is environmental pollution, my survey also generates novel insights about public perceptions of pollution. Finally, I use semistructured interviews with citizens to understand their cognitive processes when they assess pollution and evaluate government performance—positive, negative, and undecided. Even when citizens recognize pollution to be a serious problem, this does not necessarily lead them to demand policy change.

Performative governance is not always effective at impressing its audience, of course. Chapter 5, "Performative Breakdown," analyzes one case of performative success and three cases of performative breakdown. I argue that performative breakdown can result from a state's failure at information control—specifically, when *destructive informati*on about the discrepancies between the state's image and practices is revealed to the public, inducing audience cynicism. I first use a pair of "most different" cases—the Flint water crisis in Michigan and the coronavirus outbreak in Wuhan—to demonstrate the power of destructive information in bringing state malpractice to light. I then analyze two water crises in what are widely considered the "most similar" regimes of China and Vietnam, showing how variation in the level of control wielded by these two regimes over their respective information environments helps explain why performative governance was effective at appeasing public opinion in the Chinese case, but not in Vietnam.

The final chapter concludes with a reflection on the double-meaning of the word performance; how performative governance relates to the CCP's ongoing battle against bureaucratic formalism; and the potential for a collapsing together of the bureaucratic and the political in our present information age.

ANATOMY OF THE STATE

What is the government? Nothing, unless supported by opinion.
—Napoleon Bonaparte

A revolutionary party is most afraid of not hearing the voices of the people.
—Deng Xiaoping

A lesson every ruler eventually learns is that state making is not state keeping. Historically, state making often happened through the mobilization of resources and persons for war, as Charles Tilly cogently explains about Europe.[1] The CCP's victory in the middle of the twentieth century, emerging from the whirlwind violence of the Second World War and the Chinese Civil War, was ultimately a military triumph, secured through crafty strategies of mobilization and astute tactics of warfare.[2] As Chairman Mao himself remarked, "Political power grows out of the barrel of a gun."

However, conquering a territory and governing it require different skill sets, and it is the latter that has so often piqued and pained history's most adept military commanders. Napoleon Bonaparte ascended to the throne through a series of splendid military conquests, but he ultimately struggled with governance, marveling at "the impotence of force to organize anything."[3] Mao Zedong is known to have been a military strategist extraordinaire, but his insistence on bringing wartime mobilization techniques into everyday governance resulted in numerous policy failures, unnecessarily dragging the nation through famine and chaos.[4] Suffice it to say, violence can make a state, but violence alone is never enough to keep a state.

Two exigencies, in particular, confront rulers engaged in domestic governance: first, they need to develop the ability to enforce measures within their bailiwick; second, they must reckon with the voices of the governed, who demand that the state lives up to its promises. I use "capacity" to refer to the former, meaning the state's logistical ability and political authority to carry out its various domestic functions. I use "scrutiny" to refer to the latter, meaning the extent to which the state is placed under critical examination for its performance from the wider citizenry.

Capacity and scrutiny are two quintessential ingredients in the cocktail of governance. In the discussion that follows, I examine how the two interact to produce four pure types of state behavior: inert, when capacity and scrutiny are both weak; substantive, when capacity and scrutiny are both strong; paternalistic, when capacity is strong but scrutiny is weak; and, crucially for this book, performative, when capacity is weak but scrutiny is strong.

My main unit of analysis is at the level of the bureaucratic agency, understanding that different parts of the state can vary in how much capacity they enjoy and how much scrutiny they endure, and that the same part of the state can be expected to act differently when these underlying conditions change. That said, since the state is an aggregate of bureaucratic agencies, the logic of bureaucratic behavior presented here may also apply more broadly to the state as a whole.

"The State"

A theory that makes claims about "the state" can't take the definition of the state for granted. Here I briefly return to Weber as my theoretical anchor, recognizing that many others before and after him have also written about (and perhaps written even smarter things about) the state. Think of Weber as a fellow traveler on our journey of discovery, as someone to think and quibble with, and not as some ultimate authority on the state—or as a friend or foe of my arguments.

By "the state" I mean the bureaucratic apparatus responsible for making and implementing the official rules and decisions (such as laws, policies, and regulations) in a politically sovereign territory. This way of seeing the state is less holistic than Weber's oft-cited assertion that the state is "a human community that (successfully) claims the monopoly of the legitimate use of physical force within a given territory."[5] Weber said this in his famed lecture on "Politics as a Vocation," delivered in July 1919, during a revolution that overthrew the German monarchy after its defeat in World War I. In defining the state, Weber drew on Leon Trotsky's claim that "every state is founded on force."[6] Trotsky's earlier assertion that "the monopoly of brute force and repression belongs to the state power" had possibly also inspired Weber.[7] Weber's remark eventually became the most popular definition of the state in the social sciences, and is still regularly used.[8]

Perhaps because of the world-historical moment when Weber gave his lecture, his conception of the state emphasized its unmatched claim to violence.[9] To be sure, in the next sentence he immediately clarified that "force is certainly not the normal or the only means of the state—nobody says that—but force is a means specific to the state." Yet this influential definition, usually invoked in a reductive sense, has nevertheless inspired a cornucopia of visions of the state as an autonomous, dominant, and intrinsically violent force.[10]

Such images of the state are agreeable to the intellectual offspring of Adam Smith, who are ideologically inclined to suspect the state's malignant intentions and to trust the benevolence of the state's putative rivals—the market in particular. This concordance between Weberian and Smithian perspectives is quite ironic, given that their theories of the state's role in economic growth are typically portrayed as opposites.[11] (Neither devotees nor dissenters of Smith often acknowledge his critiques of the market, as much as he marveled at the invisible hand that connects us all with the butcher, the brewer, and the baker.)[12]

An image of the state as the monopolizer of violence and as the "grabbing hand" toward private property is also agreeable to aficionados of George Orwell, the literary virtuoso whose penetrating insights on totalitarianism became part of the West's ideological artillery against Marxism-Leninism during the Cold War.[13] This is also ironic, given that Orwellian images of the state are by no means in total opposition to Marxist critiques. It was Lenin after all who proclaimed that "so long as state exists there is no freedom. When there is freedom, there will be no state."[14] What it took time for Lenin to appreciate was that, instead of withering away, the socialist state would grow ever stronger and ever more expansive, through ever grander schemes of "high modernism."[15]

Conceiving the state as a violent, autonomous, and dominant monolith has its normative advantages and analytical pitfalls. The normative advantage is that it makes us watch the state—the Big Brother, the leviathan, the prince, the protection racket—with the utmost suspicion that it deserves. "For when it comes to the state, one never doubts enough."[16] The analytical pitfall is that this reductive outlook comes up woefully short at describing states today.[17] Immediately it raises the question: Exactly *who* belongs to this "human community" that claims the monopoly of the legitimate use of violence? The head of state is surely included, but is a street-level bureaucrat, who's clearly a part of the state, also a member of this power monopoly?

Consider Hauptmann Gerd Wiesler, the Stasi agent in the Oscar-winning film *The Lives of Others*. Wiesler is a mid-ranking official in the most repressive branch of one of the most repressive states that ever existed. But was he really a claimant to the monopoly of violence in East Germany? Or, considering his ignominious downfall when he refused to comply with orders from above, was he always merely a tool—and ultimately another victim—of the truly powerful?

A moralist might say that it doesn't matter: every person on the state's payroll is complicit in what the state does. (Some might even go so far as to argue that every citizen is complicit unless they engage in outright resistance.) An empiricist, however, might not paint the entire state with the same brush, but emphasize differences in color, texture, and shading. They would heed how the state's internal variation across actors and domains influences its many-faced behaviors.

Such internal variation may be of less concern for scholars of premodern or early-modern states, whose reach was limited and whose monopoly over anything at all was thus questionable.[18] Tilly records that until the sixteenth century, England's kings could only levy taxes during times of war, and had to live off their own property in periods of peace.[19] Weber observes that the historical state's limited reach was "even true of large political structures such as those of the ancient Orient, the Germanic and Mongolian empires of conquest, and of many feudal states."[20] But modern states have expanded greatly since medieval times, from the "personal trustees, table-companions, or court servants" whose "commissions and powers are not precisely delimited and are temporarily called into being for each case," to what we now call *governments*—permanent, public, and lawful bureaucratic authorities with defined, delimited, and diverse (functional and territorial) jurisdictions.[21] Weber submits that such "permanent agencies, with fixed jurisdiction, are not the historical rule but rather the exception."[22]

A careful reader of Weber will notice a contrast between his definition of the state as a monopolizer of violence in "Politics as a Vocation" and his attention to the bureaucratic machinery of the modern state in *Economy and Society*. The former is about what the state can do, and the worst it can do; the latter is about what constitutes the state—that is, functional bureaucracies. Indeed, today's states are so large and internally complex that it would be questionable or even misleading to treat a street-level bureaucrat, even in the most authoritarian system, as a member of a power monopoly. A minimalist conception of the state inspired by Weber's notion of monopoly over violence thus fails to capture the substantial size, functional specialization, and immense internal diversity of modern states.

A potential outgrowth of the modern state's expansive reach into more and more areas of social life is newly blurred boundaries between state and society.[23] States historically have held themselves together, and set themselves apart from the societies they govern, by offering "material reward and social honor" to their "executive staff."[24] But many states today do not compensate their personnel at a level allowing them to stand above and apart from their counterparts in the world of business. If we compare the earnings and prestige of public-sector and private-sector jobs around the world today—with notable exceptions such as Singapore, where state salary is famously high, and North Korea, where the state controls the entire formal economy—it is hard to conclude that the path of state employment still confers more material reward or social honor.

Take China as an example. The party-state employs more than seven million civil servants, with a total of forty million—close to 3 percent of the population—living off the state's paychecks.[25] For many Chinese citizens, especially those living in the Yangtze and Pearl River deltas, where the private sector stands tallest, civil service is at best considered a "stable" career rather than a lucrative one. During the initial years of economic reform, when petty corruption and grand graft were implicitly tolerated for the sake of economic growth, being a state official may have led some to opulence (and perhaps eventual downfall during subsequent anticorruption campaigns). Today, few in China enter the civil service for wealth, and wealth is entwined with social honor. Ultimately, it is an empirical question whether the profile and preferences of most of these seven million "state agents" align more closely with the power holders on top or with society at large.

In sum, the state is a bureaucratically organized human community that both makes and implements policy within a fixed sovereign territory. It claims the monopoly over the legitimate use of violence, but it exercises much more than violence. A modern state's functions are diverse. What these functions are and the ways in which they are exercised varies from domain to domain. The rest of this chapter unpacks the forces that drive such variations. I start with the notion of capacity, which permeates contemporary research on the state, and then introduce the notion of scrutiny, which I combine with capacity to produce my typology of state-bureaucratic behavior.

Capacity

"Uneasy lies the head that wears a crown."[26] First and foremost, rulers must fend off external threats and eliminate internal ones. Military and policing activities are crucial—or at least portrayed by rulers as crucial. But they are expensive. Of those internal competitors the ruler refrains from obliterating, some can be co-opted into the ruler's inner circle and offered a share of the pie. This also takes money. What is more, rulers have to make payments to those who carry out their orders, be it to fight a war, send a message to a foreign country, conduct a census, collect taxes, disseminate decrees, or arrest rioters. Finally, rulers must keep their citizens content by providing them protection of their persons and property, and by subsidizing their basic needs like education and healthcare. To raise money for these many purposes, and to implement these gargantuan tasks, rulers need a bureaucratic state.

I use capacity to refer to the state's logistical ability and political authority to perform its various functions: violence and order, taxation and redistribution, propaganda and education, economic development and environmental protection. When it comes to a single bureaucratic agency, capacity means the agency's physical resources, legal mandate, and political clout to carry out its defined functions. In part, this echoes Michael Mann's "infrastructural power," defined as the state's ability to "implement logistically political decisions throughout the realm."[27]

But state capacity isn't merely "infrastructural" in the plain meaning of that word; it also includes "superstructural" types of power, such as culture, ideology, norms, and beliefs that allow the state to implement most policies with limited coercion.[28] As we will see in chapter 3, without superstructural power, the state (or a single bureaucracy within it) has no influence to carry out its dictums, even if it has the necessary money, expertise, and technology, and even if its measures are legitimized by law.

State capacity is considered essential to the substantive performance of any regime. It has been used to explain successful economic development, effective governance, lasting democratic consolidation, and durable authoritarian regimes.[29] Contemporary social science research has used many different metrics to calculate state capacity. Some hold that state capacity can be approximated by a country's overall economic strength, and use GDP or GDP per capita as a proxy.[30] Others gauge state capacity with the level of education, treating human capital as an important component.[31] Scholars of state origins argue that the primary purpose of a bureaucratic state is to extract taxes, and thus, "a stable system of taxation is the precondition for the permanent existence of bureaucratic administration."[32] Following this tradition, empirical studies have estimated state capacity with measures like tax revenue as a percentage of GDP, or taxes on personal income, profits, and capital gains as a percentage of GDP (a measure of the state's capacity to tax the rich in targeted fashion).[33]

Yet others who see the state as the sum of its actual moving parts—as a collection of bureaucracies—have proposed more direct measures of state capacity as the quality of its bureaucracies and bureaucrats.[34] Devotees of Weber, who have studied his exposition on bureaucracy through and through, see no better way to appreciate a state's capacity than through its "Weberianness."[35] What is

Weberianness? The term *rational-legal* leaps to mind: rational and meritocratic in its means of recruitment, and legal in the rule-based, predictable career patterns of its employees. Weberians believe that such rational-legal rules explain economic growth, though others have challenged this contention.[36]

All of the aforementioned metrics of state capacity tend to flatten the state's internal variations. They either focus on the outcomes state capacity is supposed to produce, such as economic growth, or use the capacity of an individual bureaucracy—usually a peak economic or coercive agency—as a proxy for general state strength.[37] This focus is a natural decision for scholars interested in cross-national comparisons. It's also reasonable to assume that some features might be consistent across different bureaucratic agencies within a single country.

But writ large, the story of state capacity is a story of unevenness. Even for states commonly thought to have high capacity, significant variations exist within. In the United States, for instance, local police departments receive far more state funding than other bureaucratic agencies. Another example is the US Food and Drug Administration, which Daniel Carpenter calls "the most powerful regulatory agency in the world."[38] Agencies like the US Environmental Protection Agency are known to be significantly weaker, especially when they lose influence under Republican presidents.

Furthermore, capacity is always relative. A strong state cannot win a war with an even stronger opponent. Similarly, even a well-endowed bureaucracy can't enforce regulations if its object of enforcement or its object's bureaucratic allies within the state are even more powerful. In Chinese politics, the influential framework of "fragmented authoritarianism," first elaborated by Kenneth Lieberthal and Michael Oksenberg, remains paramount in understanding China's policy process as a product of "bureaucratic conflict."[39] The story of policymaking in China is often one of "bargaining among Ministries A, B, and C and Province D," with "[d]isgruntled Ministries E and F, losers in the deal, [pursuing] strategies to erode the agreement."[40] This fragmentation logic for policymaking also goes for policy implementation, where local bureaucratic conflicts and mismatched incentives cause policies to be unevenly implemented—overimplemented, underimplemented, or symbolically implemented.[41]

The variation in capacity between different parts of the bureaucratic state is key to our discussion here. My study is interested in a part of the state—the environmental bureaucracy—that has been of lesser concern to studies of comparative bureaucracy, which are primarily interested in the relationship between bureaucracy and economic growth.[42] But environmental protection is, in many if not most cases to date, antithetical to economic growth.[43] By the very logic of the developmental state literature, some regulatory agencies, such as those entrusted with environmental and labor protection, must be weak to allow economic agencies to exert their full strength. The renewable energy sector is an exception, as it promotes both industrial development and energy efficiency. But current methods to manufacture, deploy, and recycle renewables still generate pollution. What's more, income growth itself incentivizes greater energy consumption. So although it might be significantly offset by renewable energy, the tradeoff between economic growth and environmental protection remains painfully real.

Variation and tradeoffs in bureaucratic capacity are not limited to economic development versus environmental protection. For example, "rentier states" tend to enjoy very high coercive capacity, but their extractive and developmental capabilities may be much lower.[44] Other factors, such as historical contingencies, leadership preferences, organizational culture, and networks between state and nonstate actors can also explain why some bureaucracies acquire more capacity than others.[45]

Bureaucratic capacity does not always translate into successful policymaking or implementation, however. For the capacity to do anything at all necessarily means the capacity to engage in bad behavior. "State" and "bureaucracy" are often used as pejoratives associated with stagnation and staleness for good reason. Unchecked power threatens to corrupt its holders and prey on its followers, benefiting the few at the expense of the many.

Scrutiny

What, then, prevents a bureaucracy, or the state writ large, from engaging in foot-dragging or organized "banditry" all the time?[46] I use "scrutiny" to refer to the extent to which the state, or a single bureaucracy, is placed under critical examination for its performance.

Let's begin with two clarifying questions about scrutiny. First, who scrutinizes state agents? In other words, who is the critical audience for bureaucratic behavior? Second, what are the audience's expectations? The following discussion distinguishes between internal scrutiny that comes from within the state's own hierarchy and external scrutiny that emanates from the general public, calling attention to the potential tensions between the two, and to the ascending role that public scrutiny plays in shaping bureaucratic behavior in the information age.

In classic theoretical discussions of bureaucracy, scrutiny of bureaucratic behavior typically operates within an organization. A defining feature of bureaucracy is hierarchy: "A firmly ordered system of super- and subordination in which there is supervision of the lower offices by the higher ones."[47] The critical audience of bureaucratic behavior is thus understood to be higher-level supervisors.

In large bureaucratic systems, information asymmetry may emerge between offices at different levels, causing what's known as principal-agent problems. When the principal fails to exercise effective scrutiny over the action of their subordinate agents, bureaucrats' actions may deviate from the preferences and interests of their superiors. The hackneyed Chinese idiom "The sky is high and the emperor is far away" captures how local officials may defy the central government's mandates when they believe they are not being watched.

Bureaucracies have invented numerous methods to solve their principal-agent problems. One is "graded authority."[48] For example, most bureaucratic structures, be it a government agency, private enterprise, or guerrilla movement, use some kind of "one level down" system of supervision: each office is responsible for supervising the actions of offices one level below its rank. If the leadership suspects that lower-level agents aren't doing their jobs and midlevel agents are negligent in their supervision, they may bypass the midlevel agents and enact direct discipline over the lower-level agents. The CCP periodically uses "work teams" (*gongzuozu*) or "supervisory groups" (*duchazu*)—ad hoc cadre teams sent by the center to localities, thus circumventing midlevel authorities such as provinces—to control and guide local state behavior, from anticorruption to mass mobilization.[49] In recent years, inspection teams have been used in Chinese environmental governance to strengthen local enforcement of environmental regulations.[50]

Bureaucracies also regularly use performance evaluations to assess agent behavior. Agents learn in advance what the expectations are for their positions, sometimes including specific goals to be accomplished within a certain time period. They also learn the rules determining their salaries, bonuses, promotions, and dismissals. These rules are often called "rational-legal" because they're designed to be objective and impersonal. In extremely authoritarian bureaucracies, such as the military, discipline is exercised as "nothing but consistently rationalized, methodically trained and exact execution of the received order."[51]

Performance evaluation is almost universal in bureaucratic structures. Chinese emperors of the Ming (1368–1644) and Qing (1644–1911) dynasties conducted evaluations of local officials every few years. Officials were judged on their moral uprightness and functional capabilities, especially their ability to collect taxes.[52] China's current performance evaluation mechanism (*jixiao kaohe*) for cadres and bureaucracies dates back to the beginning of the Reform era. Its early emphasis on growth and investment has been credited for effectively incentivizing local economic development.[53] Over four decades, new indicators like environmental protection, labor protection, public health, and local government indebtedness have been added to the ever-growing list, and the weight of each indicator is subject to constant adjustment. For example, a 2013 decree from the

Central Organization Department outright forbade ranking localities based on GDP and GDP growth figures.[54]

However—coming back to the question of audience—higher-level authorities are not necessarily the only audience for bureaucratic behavior. When the audience lies outside the bureaucracy, it introduces to our analysis a more capricious driver of state behavior: external scrutiny by the public. Street-level bureaucrats such as police officers, social workers, and public hospital staff are especially exposed to public scrutiny, given their constant encounters with citizens.[55] These encounters, in turn, shape citizens' impression of the state.[56]

Internet and social media magnify public scrutiny and its potential effect on state behavior. In 2010, the mistreatment of a street vendor by the Tunisian police set off the Arab Spring protests, which spread rapidly owing to mass mobilization on social media, resulting in the toppling of several regimes and outright civil war in others.[57] (The Internet and social media will play a critical role in my analyses in chapters 4 and 5.)

When internal, hierarchical scrutiny fails to ensure that bureaucrats perform their assigned functions—that is, to engage in substantive governance—public scrutiny can fill the gap. For example, street-level police abuse often results from a lack of scrutiny within the police ranks, and public attention to the problem may improve the quality of policing.

Yet tensions may surface between internal and public scrutiny. As Michael Lipsky argues, street-level governance embodies an "essential paradox": "On the one hand, the work is highly scripted to achieve policy objectives that have their origins in the political process. On the other hand, the work requires improvisation and responsiveness to the individual case."[58] This paradox sheds light on the versatility of street-level bureaucratic behavior, which often defies the mechanical and impersonal formula of Weberian "rational bureaucracy" through the introduction of public scrutiny.

Public scrutiny does not arise out of thin air, or through mechanisms that are entirely exogenous to the political process. Scrutiny may reveal the public's pressing concerns of the moment, but it can also be engineered by influential elites inside or outside the state. As this book will show, rising scrutiny over environmental pollution in China is not only a product of pollution itself. It also results from intense media attention and public discussions that are sanctioned and sometimes even invited by the state.

In China, public scrutiny has long been part of the political process. Complaints, petitions, and protests have historically assisted the central government in both devising policies and in controlling official behavior at the local level.[59] In recent times, public satisfaction has been formally included in performance evaluations for both officials and bureaucratic agencies. A 2016 Party and State Council decree on the "comprehensive management of public safety" (*shehui zhi'an zonghe zhili*) lists "mass incidents" (protests) as a red card for local officials; others include "major criminal cases" (*zhongda xingshi anjian*) and "public security incidents" (*gonggong anquan shijian*).[60] If mass protests erupt in a locality, the "one item veto rule" (*yipiao foujue*) may be invoked to flunk the entire performance evaluation of that area's top officials. Some localities have even experimented with including "public participation" (*gongzhong canyu*) in the performance evaluation of bureaucratic agencies.[61]

As a regime that came to power through a social revolution, the CCP is keenly attuned to the destructive potential of public sentiment, which has entrapped the party since the day it came to power. As Deng Xiaoping said on the eve of economic reform: "We must believe that the vast majority of the people have the ability to judge right from wrong. A revolutionary party is most afraid of not hearing the voices of the people. Silence is the most terrifying thing."[62]

A Typology of State Behavior

Having defined and unpacked capacity and scrutiny, we can now consider and observe how they interact. Capacity and scrutiny combine to produce four pure types of state-bureaucratic behavior, as shown in table 1. First, when capacity and scrutiny are both weak, the state tends to be inert: it lacks the logistical capacity and political authority to perform its functions, and it confronts little public pressure to do so. Catherine Boone's research on West Africa shows state inertia in regions without valuable exportable commodities.[63] Jennifer Murtazashvili finds that archaic Soviet bureaucracies linger and languish in policy areas of limited public importance in Central Asia.[64]

Inert bureaucracies exist for many reasons. They may be kept on life support to provide employment, as Anna Grzymala-Busse describes in some postsocialist systems.[65] Or they may be inert because their functions are considered relatively unimportant. As the next chapter shows, China's EPB remained largely inert for decades after its establishment in the early 1980s until the mid-2000s, before public scrutiny eventually intensified.

Second, when capacity is strong but scrutiny weak, the state exhibits paternalism. When the public is not paying attention to the issue in question, or has been influenced to think the issue is not important, the state enjoys relative autonomy to use its strong capacity flexibly. Like a strict parent, a paternalistic state can use its autonomous capacity for good or ill—in social science parlance, it can be either predatory or developmental. Police departments in the United States are bureaucratic agencies whose capacities have historically outstripped limited public scrutiny over their behavior, often leading to predatory actions. Kevin O'Brien and Lianjiang Li's study of policy implementation in the Chinese countryside finds that "cadre insulation from social pressure . . . ha[s] encouraged the execution of unpopular but not of popular policies."[66] At the national level, scholars of rentier states argue that because these states rely for their revenues on the sale of natural resources rather than income taxes, their citizens tend to voice less demand for representation and are more tolerant of repression.[67] Meanwhile, the developmental state literature argues that autonomy from societal groups allows authorities to craft industrial policies that are nationally beneficial but may hurt powerful societal interests in the short term.[68] Although the outcomes may differ dramatically, these paternalistic state behaviors share the common underlying features of high capacity and low scrutiny.

Third, when capacity and scrutiny are both strong, state behavior tends to be the most substantive: the state is capable of performing its key functions, and public scrutiny will make its life miserable if it fails. Wealthy democracies are the most likely candidates for substantive governance because of their overall high state capacity and invasive public opinion. But substantive governance exists elsewhere, too, even in the poorer and less democratic corners of the world. Lily Tsai's study of public goods provision in Chinese villages is an example of substantive governance. Village leaders who were subjected to scrutiny from villagers within their "solidary groups" maintained school buildings and paved roads whenever they had the resources to do so.[69]

Last, and crucially for this study, when capacity is weak but public scrutiny strong, state behavior tends to be performative. The state or bureaucracy in question lacks the logistical capacity and political clout to deliver good governance outcomes, but it is pressured to appear responsive to appease public opinion. Performative governance is most likely to be found among resource-poor, street-level bureaucracies on the front line of state-society interaction. Chapter 3 details what performative governance looks like on the ground.

My admittedly simple yet aspirationally encompassing typology provides a way to interpret state behavior without access to its backstage. I do not claim that it is exhaustive, nor do I claim that capacity and scrutiny are the only causes of state behavior. Other important factors include culture, ideology, leadership, and interest groups: all warrant serious consideration of their own. Also vital are the specifics of individual policy design, which may independently affect bureaucratic incentives and behaviors.[70]

As pure types, these state behaviors are not mutually exclusive. My typology, deductively produced, helps predict the kind of government behavior that becomes prioritized when state capacity and public scrutiny assume different values. No single state or bureaucracy is utterly inert, implacably paternalistic, relentlessly performative, or consistently substantive. For example, it's quite plausible that public relations–savvy governments or agencies would complement the

TABLE 1 Capacity, scrutiny, and state-bureaucratic behavior

		Capacity	
		Low	High
Scrutiny	Low	*inert*	*paternalistic*
	High	*performative*	*substantive*

substantive delivery of services with performative governance if they have the resources to achieve both—an environmental bureaucracy can put on a spectacle of closing down polluters while also actually closing them down. Disaster relief is an area where performative and substantive governance often coexist.[71] In these situations, the state is under the intense scrutiny of a panicked public and must concentrate its capacity on the imperative of saving lives.

Chinese Bureaucracies

The Chinese state typically gives off an image of strong capacity. This image of strength comes largely from the fact that, after decades of breakneck growth, China has become the world's second largest economy. Since state capacity is often measured by economic figures, the Chinese state is almost universally perceived as strong by outside observers. Additionally, China's authoritarian political system is said to exhibit high levels of what Mann calls "despotic power": "the range of actions which the elite is empowered to undertake without routine, institutionalized negotiation with civil society groups."[72] High despotic power means low societal engagement in policy formulation and implementation.

However, images of power are not the same thing as power itself. Although China's overall GDP ranks second in the world, its GDP per capita in 2018 was $9,771 (in USD), just above that of Mexico ($9,673), but below Kazakhstan ($9,815) and Russia ($11,289), and significantly lower than countries commonly used as its reference points, such as the United States ($62,887). Much of China's countryside and many interior provinces are still poverty-stricken and yearning for material improvement.

Even now, China remains adamant about its status as a developing country, albeit "the largest developing country in the world."[73] During the 2020 "Two

Sessions" (plenary sessions of the People's Congress and People's Political Consultative Conference), Premier Li Keqiang remarked in a press conference that "600 million people [in China] are still only earning 1,000 yuan (US$141) a month."[74] There are clear strategic reasons for China to cling to its developing country status. It translates into "special and differential treatment" by the World Trade Organization (WTO), although in practice China's WTO commitments have been comparable to those of developed countries.[75]

Careful empirical studies have called China's image of strong state capacity into question, even in the core coercive branches of the state. For example, Sheena Greitens finds that China's per capita spending on domestic security in 2013 was only $92, compared to $489 in the United States and $393 in Russia.[76] This figure is rising, but "increased overall spending on domestic security is likely to indicate—and be motivated by—the inadequacy of China's coercive capacity rather than its repressive strength."[77]

Furthermore, any blanket assessment of overall state capacity, whether strong or weak, obscures variation across the state's bureaucratic arms and organs. This is certainly the case with China. Any government employee can confirm the massive variation in the power and status of different bureaucracies, even between offices at the same administrative level.

Within the Chinese state there are three types of bureaucratic power: power over personnel (*renshi*), power over administrative approval (*shenpi*), and power over public finance (*caizheng*).[78] In an average city, power over personnel is held by the municipal Party Committee and its Organization Department (Zuzhibu). Power over administrative approval is in the hands of the Development and Reform Commission (DRC, Fagaiwei) and the Commission of Economy and Information (Jingji he xinxihua weiyuanhui/Jingxinwei). Power over finance is in the "public finance mouth" (*caizheng kouzi*), such as the Finance Bureau (Caizhengju). Besides these, party organs like the Organization Department, Propaganda Department, and Political and Legal Affairs Commissions (Zhengfawei) are especially strong (even though they are not officially a part of the bureaucratic state). The General Office of the State Council (Guowuyuan bangongting) and its subnational counterparts are also powerful for the coordinating roles they play.

This variation in bureaucratic power can be demonstrated with numbers. One intuitive but inferior way of comparing bureaucracies is to compare their budgets. For example, the 2018 budget of China's Ministry for Environmental Protection (MEP) was a paltry 5 percent of that of the Ministry of Health, a bureaucracy that is by no means China's strongest. Budgets may be popular proxies for bureaucratic strength, but they don't provide perfect, apples-to-apples comparisons. Each ministry's annual budget includes very different spending categories.

For example, part of the Ministry of Education's budget funds seventy-five universities that are directly administered (*zhishu*) by the MOE, meaning its budget is necessarily higher than those of most bureaucracies.

Revenue is another potential measure for bureaucratic power; the more a bureaucracy brings into state coffers, the more authority it acquires. The main income source for local governments is taxation, especially value-added tax and corporate income tax. Nontax income, for instance from fines and fees, comprises less than 20 percent of state revenue. This means big corporate taxpayers in a locality can be more influential than some state bureaucracies. Although revenue converts into political power, the regime is conscious not to let it become the definitive currency in Chinese politics, and not to let major revenue generators, such as rich provinces and big businesses, become too influential.

A third way of estimating the relative strengths of national ministries and their local counterparts is by the political rank of their top officials. Ministers and deputy ministers of powerful bureaucracies often occupy seats in the Central Committee of the CCP (Zhongyang weiyuanhui) as either full members or alternate members. Figure 1 compares the number of Central Committee seats

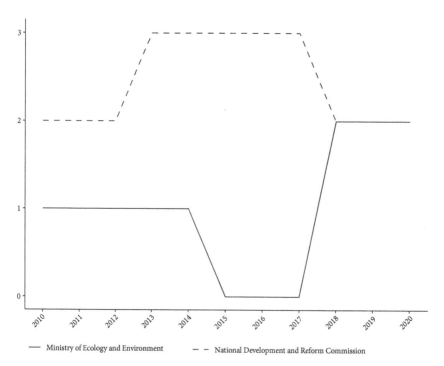

FIGURE 1. Number of full members from the MEP/MEE and the NDRC on the Party Central Committee (2010–20)

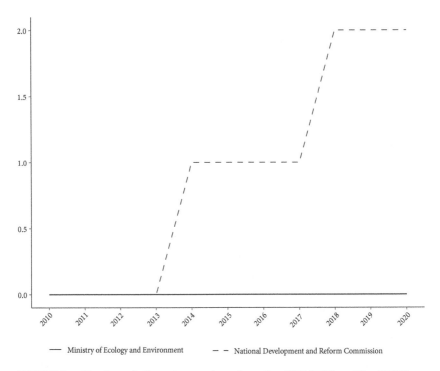

FIGURE 2. Number of alternate members from the MEP/MEE and the NDRC on the Party Central Committee (2010–20)

occupied by the MEP/MEE and National Development and Reform Commission (NDRC) between 2010 and 2020. Figure 2 does the same with alternate Central Committee members.[79]

It's clear that the NDRC has always outstripped the MEP on this measure. In 2015, for example, the NDRC had three full members and one alternate member, making it the most powerful functional bureaucracy under the State Council. By contrast, the MEP was the only bureaucracy with no seats in the Central Committee. Even though the MEE and NDRC now both have two full seats, the NDRC has more alternate members.

At the subnational level, a similar lesson obtains. For instance, it is not uncommon for the directors of municipal Public Security Bureaus (Gonganju)—a powerful bureaucracy—to simultaneously hold the position of deputy mayor. But until very recently, a dual position of deputy mayor and EPB director was unheard of.

A fourth and related way of estimating the pecking order of bureaucracies is to look at whether their ministers and local directors get promoted to more prominent positions in the regime. As Stan Hok-Wui Wong and Yu Zeng argue, bureaucratic rank alone is insufficient for capturing the political clout of

Chinese officials—an extreme example being Deng Xiaoping, who commanded the country without ever holding the highest office in the party.[80] Wong and Zeng analyzed the career trajectories of thousands of provincial-level bureau leaders in the 2000s and found that leaders of powerful bureaucracies are significantly more likely to join the Party Central Committee.[81]

Who gets to work for powerful bureaucracies is not randomly assigned. The regime cultivates cadres for leadership positions by posting them to strong bureaucracies or by sending them to govern localities that are economically important, like Shanghai, or politically sensitive, like Tibet. Before his fall from grace, Bo Xilai was first the mayor of Dalian, then governor of Liaoning, then minister of commerce, and then mayor of Chongqing—one of the four province-level municipalities directly administered by the central government.

Positions in what's known as "core bureaucracies" (*hexin bumen*) or "strong bureaucracies" (*qiangshi bumen*) like the DRC and the General Office are optimal grounds for training cadres to balance multiple tasks and priorities—thus the party's logic of assigning cadres it wishes to cultivate for higher office to these bureaucracies. Local DRCs are popularly known as "little state councils" (*xiao guowuyuan*). Meanwhile, cadres with few promotion prospects are relegated to weaker bureaucracies like the MEP and EPBs. It is a popular notion that "entering the environmental protection system means the end to one's political career [*shitu zhongjie*]."[82] A retired official told me in 2013 that being assigned the position of an EPB director is equivalent to being sent to the "cold palace" of the emperor's harem (*daru lenggong*).[83]

A fifth, coarser way of assessing the relative strength of China's many bureaucracies is by dividing them into planning agencies, informally referred to as "affairs bureaus" (*shiwu bumen*) or "staff bureaus" (*muliao bumen*), as opposed to enforcement agencies (*zhifa bumen*), informally called "implementation bureaus" (*zhixing bumen*) or "business bureaus" (*yewu bumen*). Planning agencies are considered especially powerful because they are closest to policymaking. For example, the DRC and the General Office are consummate planning agencies. The EPB is a typical enforcement agency, lying farther away from policymaking—even from environmental policymaking during the period of this study.

This difference between bureaucracies that can formulate policies and bureaucracies mainly in charge of implementing policies roughly correlates with the different levels of public scrutiny they encounter. Enforcement agencies operating at the street level naturally come into more contact with citizens. Planning agencies carrying out their functions in their offices are naturally under less public scrutiny. Having said that, the amount of scrutiny a bureaucracy endures is not entirely predicted by the bureaucracy's planning versus implementing role.

For example, around the 2008 milk scandal, the State Food and Drug Administration was subjected to unprecedented public outrage, even though its main functions don't take place in front of citizens.

An Uneven State

Taken together, the variation in the capacity of Chinese bureaucracies and the amount of public scrutiny they come under map onto the four types of state-bureaucratic behavior mentioned earlier—inert, paternalistic, performative, and substantive.

Although inertia is considered a common tendency of bureaucracy, entirely inert bureaucracies are rare in China's reform era. Reforms smashed millions of iron rice bowls. Since then, the size of the state is intentionally kept limited and salaries are kept modest to avoid waste and forestall citizen discontent. Yuen Yuen Ang finds that China's public employment per capita is a third that of the international mean.[84] Inert bureaucracies are often dissolved when the needs for their functions fade away, or upgraded if the needs for their functions increase.

Consider the remarkable fate of China's bureaucracies for heavy industry after the Mao era. On the eve of economic reform, China had no fewer than eight ministries devoted to the machine industry (*jixie gongye*) alone, from the First Ministry of Machine Industry (Diyi jixie gongyebu) to the Eighth Ministry of Machine Industry (Diba jixie gongyebu), all inclusive. The reform's initial emphasis on "light industries" such as manufacturing left many of these bureaucracies obsolete. In 1982, all eight ministries of the machine industry were merged into one—the Ministry of Machine Industry (Jixie gongyebu), which was again merged with the Ministry of Ordinance Industry (Bingqi gongyebu) in 1986, and then again with the Ministry of Electronics Industry (Dianzi gongyebu) in 1988, to form the Ministry of Machinery and Electronics (Jixie dianzi gongyebu). In 1993, the newly formed ministry was undone yet again, and five years later it was demoted to the State Bureau of Machine Industry (Guojia jixie gongyeju). Two years later, in 2000, it was phased out of the state entirely to become the China Machine Industry Association (Zhongguo jixie gongye xiehui)—a government-sponsored business association.

As of the early 1980s, China had multiple bureaucracies regulating heavy industries. But by the end of the 1990s, all had lost ministerial status and been placed under the jurisdiction of the State Economic and Trade Commission (Guojia jingji maoyi weiyuanhui), which was itself dissolved in 2003, with its key functions transferred to the newly minted State-Owned Assets Supervision and Administration Commission (Guoyou zichan jiandu guanli weiyuanhui), the NDRC, and the Ministry of Commerce (Shangwubu). For a more recent example, the State Family Planning Commission (Guojia jihua shengyu wei-yuanhui), an inert bureaucracy after the abolishment of the One Child Policy, was merged with the Ministry of Health (Weishengbu) in 2013 to become the National Health and Family Planning Commission (Guojia weisheng he jihua shengyu weiyuanhui).

For examples of paternalistic bureaucracies in China, we can look to the Ministry of State Security (Guojia anquanbu, MSS), the NDRC, and powerful state-owned enterprises (SOE). Compared to front-line bureaucracies such as the EPB and the Urban Management Bureau (Chengguan), paternalistic bureau-cracies enjoy hefty financial endowments and political clout. At the same time, they are further removed from the scrutiny of public opinion. We know little about the MSS, but descriptions of the NDRC and SOEs have indeed ranged from "predatory" to "developmental"—both of which fall under my description of state paternalism.[85]

Despite all its deficiencies, public healthcare in China might be as close as we get to substantive governance. China's National Health Commission (NHC) presides over one of the most salient and longstanding public policy issues in China. The state has effectively kept healthcare at relatively low (albeit increas-ing) costs with widening coverage.[86] In the 2000s, the rural cooperative medical insurance scheme expanded to cover 97 percent of the rural population, although the premiums and benefits varied widely based on local fiscal capacity.[87] Under powerful market pressures, inequality in healthcare has become rampant, peri-odically summoning widespread public outcry when the system underperforms. The enduring importance of healthcare to the Chinese public has made it one of the state's top priorities for capacity building.[88]

Yet the ongoing COVID-19 pandemic has pushed governments, in China and elsewhere, to their limits if not breaking points. This does not bode well for sub-stantive governance in today's world: in the face of unprecedented global chal-lenges like emergent viruses, climate change, the misinformation epidemic, and technological disruptions, substantive governance might become a rarer com-modity. Not necessarily because states don't wish to use their capacity where it counts but because they simply lack the capacity to solve these tough and com-plex problems.

If state capacity fails to catch up with public demands in these challenging issue areas, we are left with three scenarios. First, under conditions of low capac-ity, inert governance will prevail where scrutiny is also low, and performative gov-ernance will predominate where scrutiny is high. Second, as the state's coercive capacity gets strengthened by technological advancement, it may far outstrip the power of scrutiny, allowing states to respond through surveillance and repression with greater ease. Third, the incapable state could become increasingly unreliable and irrelevant to people's needs, leading them to turn to nonstate solutions.

In my search for pockets of substantive governance, I found that citizens and state bureaucrats were similarly reluctant to offer concrete examples. There appeared to be a general ethos that state bureaucracies should be critically scrutinized more than praised. Such critical scrutiny may seem contradictory with empirical findings of widespread regime support in China, but it is not. Just like democratic citizens may be critical of their government without losing trust in democracy, citizens in single-party regimes can also be critical of their government without losing trust in their political system (in part because they don't believe that multiparty elections can solve their problems).

Yet one interviewee regaled me with a locally specific example of substantive governance: the "Flatbread Bureau" (Shaobingban) of Jinyun County in Zhejiang Province. This bureaucratic agency was set up by the county government to promote and regulate Jinyun's highly sought-after flatbreads. The agency's substantive governance lies in its tireless efforts at marketing the flatbreads made in the county while ensuring that they retain their tasty and sanitary standards to withstand customer scrutiny around China. While some might consider this a whimsical example, the importance of substantive governance in income and employment-generating industries like flatbread-making in Jinyun is no joking matter across the developing world.

Finally, as I detail in chapter 3, the MEP and local EPBs have been sites for performative governance. During the time of my study, the MEP was among the weakest functional bureaucracies in China. But as a front-line enforcement agency, it confronted intense public scrutiny after pollution came to the forefront of public attention in the mid-2000s. The combination of low capacity and high scrutiny pressured the bureaucracy to engage in performative governance, because appeasing public opinion was paramount to EPB bureaucrats' career security.

Before zooming in on this recent moment in history, let's take a longer view at the remarkable evolution of China's modern environmental state, starting from day one.

OLD WOES AND NEW PAINS

Dark tides rolled in and ebbed out along the coast of Dalian, a port city in northern China. A veil of dingy foam draped over the listless waves. When the tide fully receded, just before high noon, the smoke-colored beach peered out to meet the sun. From afar, the beach seemed to be festooned with sparkling, oddly shaped flecks, which on closer examination were the bodies of dead fish. Fishermen gazing toward the ocean saw mile upon mile of the same gloomy sight. That year alone, they lost three million square meters of coastal water used for shellfish farming. To the north, the Songhua River, a tributary of the third longest river in China, had no fish left.[1]

The year was 1971. The Great Proletarian Cultural Revolution had come to an abrupt halt in Beijing. Violent street conflicts ended, at least in the cities, but confusion and nervousness still hovered over the nation. The National Day celebration was canceled in September after Marshal Lin Biao, Chairman Mao's heir apparent, died in a mysterious plane crash, reportedly after a failed coup attempt against Mao.

Across the Pacific Ocean in the United States, the voting age was lowered to eighteen. In the summer, the *New York Times* began publishing the Pentagon Papers, revealing incendiary details about the Vietnam War—or the American War, as it was called by the Vietnamese.

During this emotional and uncertain time in both the United States and China, something previously unthinkable was unfolding under the radar of public scrutiny. Escalating tensions with the Soviet Union had forced both Washington and Beijing to set aside their ideological differences and decide that, when all's said and done, the enemy of my enemy is my friend. In April, American and Chinese ping-pong teams met face to face. Soon after, President Richard Nixon lifted trade and travel restrictions on China. In July, after twenty years of severed ties, Nixon announced his plan to visit China. The People's Republic of China (PRC) joined the United Nations and its Security Council in November.

As it happened, the first major U.N. conference the PRC attended was the 1972 Conference on the Human Environment in Stockholm. That meeting produced the first international institution for environmental protection—the Stockholm Declaration, calling for "governments and peoples to exert common efforts for the preservation and improvement of the human environment."[2] The Stockholm Declaration forged the eventual path toward the Kyoto Protocol (1992) and the Paris Agreement (2016). China, lacking a bureaucracy devoted to environmental protection, sent a multiministerial delegation led by the deputy minister of Fuel and Chemical Industries (Ranliao huaxue gongye bu).[3]

After Stockholm, the term *environmental protection* (*huanjing baohu*, or the abbreviated *huanbao*) appeared in the *People's Daily*, the CCP's most authoritative publication, for the first time.[4] In August 1973, the State Council convened its first National Conference on Environmental Protection (Quanguo huanjing baohu huiyi) and passed "Some Decisions on the Protection and Improvement of the Environment" (Guanyu Baohu he Gaishan Huanjing de Ruogan Jueding).[5] Premier Zhou Enlai set up a working group to investigate pollution in the Songhua River and other bodies of water in northern China.[6]

International engagement gave birth to China's state environmentalism. But environmental concerns were soon cast aside as the nation embarked on its monumental economic reforms in the late 1970s. It would be decades before the "environmental state"—bureaucracies and institutions of environmental protection—would grow and flourish into anything more than a foundling.[7]

While China's environmental problems are not much different from those elsewhere, their sheer scale warrants an inquiry into the historical forces behind them. This chapter surveys the history of environmental change and governance in imperial, modern, and contemporary China.

The first part of the chapter presents a montage of what I consider necessary historical and philosophical background for our substantive discussion. It shows how environmental degradation existed long before the public was conscious of its impact. Without straying too far from an analysis of the state, it also dispels some common myths about environmental degradation in China—cultural explanations in particular.

The chapter's second part explains the origins of heightened environmental concerns in recent decades. It argues that public scrutiny—a key driver of state behavior in my typology presented in the previous chapter—is not just a result of objective pollution levels, but also a product of international and domestic politics.

The third part of the chapter returns the discussion to the environmental bureaucracy. It adds capacity—the other key driver of state behavior—back into the formula. I trace the development of the environmental bureaucracy since its inception in the early 1980s to now, and highlight how it has moved across cells in my typology.

Specifically, the EPB was initially inert: it neither possessed the capacity that would allow it to govern nor confronted the scrutiny that would incite it to act. Then, as public scrutiny intensified in the mid-2000s, the EPB began to pursue a strategy of performative governance: it still lacked the capacity to control pollution, but it had to do *something* to placate the raging public outcry (this will be the focus of chapter 3). Finally, as the agency acquired more capacity in recent years—due partly to an adjustment to China's development model and partly to public demand—it has switched gears to pursue more substantive modes of environmental governance. So far, however, capacity gains have been limited. The end of this chapter will explain why.

Down the River of Time

Climate change was no stranger to our ancestors. It scorched the Mayans, drenched the Khmers, parched the Akkadians, and froze the Vikings.[8] In imperial China, it shepherded dynasties through their rises and falls. A cooling of our rapidly warming planet would be welcome news today, but colder isn't always better. Scholars at Beijing Normal University found a significant correlation between low temperatures, subsequent famine, and peasant rebellions in Chinese history.[9] Mark Elvin relates the economic prosperity and demographic expansion of the Tang (618–907) and mid-Qing (1644–1911) dynasties to their warm climates, while each downturn in annual temperature coincided with a major political crisis.[10] Scholars have also attributed the Manchus' toppling of the Ming dynasty (1368–1644) to climate change during the "little ice age," a period between the sixteenth and nineteenth centuries when average global temperatures cooled significantly.[11]

Geography has fashioned variations in political and economic development around the world. It has been argued that high latitudes and coastal access are crucial historical prerequisites for economic growth.[12] It has also been argued that easier access to coal explains why Europe industrialized before China.[13] Within China, geography and climate shaped subnational variation in state-society relations. For example, Elizabeth Perry notes that the harsh ecological conditions in the Huai River Valley in northern Anhui Province were associated with the region's recurrent peasant uprisings.[14]

In turn, humans have confronted nature with extreme measures of their own—usually to nature's detriment. In a study about the environmental impacts of agricultural development and population expansion in imperial China—including the retreat of wild elephants that once inhabited the entire Middle Kingdom to its southwest border with Burma—Elvin states a cold, hard fact: "Chinese farmers and elephants do not mix."[15]

Hydraulic engineering was used extensively to aid agricultural development. In 256 BC, the governor of the Shu Shire under the Qin State ordered the construction of the Dujiangyan irrigation system. Redirecting the Min River brought water to a two-thousand-square-mile stretch of the Chengdu plain in Sichuan Province, turning the region into a breadbasket.[16] The more recent Three Gorges Dam—the world's largest dam and power station—was an engineering project first conceived by Sun Yat-sen in 1918. For almost a century it passed through the hands of the Nationalist government, the Japanese occupiers, and planners under state socialism, before eventually being realized in 2006. The controversial dam helped reduce greenhouse gas emissions, but also caused irreversible ecological damage, including a fatal blow to the Chinese river dolphin—a species that was already on the verge of extinction.[17]

When poet Du Fu bewailed the destruction of the capital Chang'an (now Xi'an) after the An Lushan rebellion (775–763), he wrote one of the most revered lines of Chinese poetry: "[My] country is destroyed, but the mountains and rivers are still here" (*guo po shan he zai*). Yet as China entered modernity, most of its forest had disappeared. Extreme weather events were frequent.[18] Wild elephants were nowhere to be found. Looking down the river of time, Elvin laments that

> it is hard for those familiar with the degraded, abraded and polluted developed parts of China at the present day, almost without wild animals or birds, to imagine the world of a millennium-and-a-half ago, when the banks of the Chang were covered as far as the eye could see with forests of sweet-gum trees, the river so clear that fish could be seen swimming along the bottom, the view eastward from the Tai Lake was one of hillocks rising from a green haze of water-chestnuts and reeds, the coasts were undyked tidal flats apart from a few salterns, and whales were so frequent on the seas that sailors had to beat drums to frighten them away.[19]

Environmental degradation at this scale is not unique to China. The following passage comes from Robert Marks's account of global environmental history:

> Wolves roamed throughout most of Europe, as can be attested by *Grimm's Fairy Tales*. . . . In China, tigers at one time inhabited most of the region and periodically attacked Chinese villages and cities, carrying away piglets and babies alike when humans disrupted their ecosystem by cutting away the forests that provided them with their favored game, deer or wild boar. Tigers remained so plentiful in Manchuria that the emperor's hunting expedition could bag sixty in one day, in addition to a thousand stags, and reports of tiger attacks on south China villages continued until 1800.[20]

Elizabeth Kolbert calls the drastic dwindling of biodiversity under the hegemony of Homo sapiens "the sixth extinction"—the first of the six to be man-made.[21]

Nature under High Socialism

Although there is abundant historical evidence of environmental degradation and climate change, scientists warn that what's occurring in the current era is unprecedented. Some call it the Anthropocene, a geological epoch believed to be new for its "rapid rising human population [that] accelerated the pace of industrial production, the use of agricultural chemicals, and other human activities."[22]

The PRC was born in the heyday of the Anthropocene. During its formative years, however, China's environmental problems seemed inconsequential when compared to all the human suffering.[23] Land Reform alone resulted in the death of more than a million "landlords" and "counterrevolutionaries."[24] More than 30 million perished during the Great Leap Forward.[25] Another 750,000 to 1.5 million passed away during the Cultural Revolution, and millions more were subjected to political persecution.[26]

Less was known about the grievous injuries quietly inflicted on nature in the high-socialist era.[27] During the Great Leap Forward, vast stretches of forest land were leveled to fuel hundreds of thousands of steel furnaces in the reckless pursuit of surpassing Great Britain in steel production.[28] Intensified agricultural production also exacerbated deforestation, as Qu Geping writes: "Regardless of topography, grain production became the all-important priority. . . . Large forested areas were either destroyed to produce grain or neglected, aggravating hydrological cycles and soil erosion."[29]

After the 1960 Sino-Soviet split, concerns arose over food security in the event of a Soviet or American nuclear attack. This led to a campaign to build an inland "Third Front" that would be both agriculturally and industrially self-sufficient.[30] In 1964, Mao selected Dazhai, a village-brigade in impoverished Shanxi province, as an agricultural production model. As the legend went, after Dazhai was decimated in a 1963 flood, the village refused outside aid and rebuilt on its own. "[They] terraced the crumbly loess soil, tunneled through hills for irrigation, and spread chemical fertilizers from a local plant on their fields; agricultural yields climbed."[31] But the fervid campaign, "In Agriculture Learn from Dazhai" (*Nongye xue Dazhai*), destroyed many of the communities that tried to turn themselves into another Dazhai through sheer physical force.

Another well-known episode was the "Exterminate the Four Pests" (*Chusihai*) campaign. Mao, who was no expert on wildlife or ecology, ordered the extermination of sparrows, mosquitoes, flies, and rats, believing that crop yields would improve as a result. The entire country mobilized to kill sparrows, and victory was declared in a 1958 *People's Daily* article: "Three million people in the capital reaped glorious fruits after an entire day's battle against sparrows. . . . According to incomplete statistics, the whole city beat, poisoned, and exhausted 83,249 sparrows to death."[32] The systematic extermination of sparrows worsened an outbreak of locusts and other insects eaten by sparrows, causing a steep drop in crop yields and aggravating the famine.[33]

Science and Culture

How do we make sense of this "sixth extinction" that is caused not by ice, not by meteoroids, but by mankind itself? Cultural explanations are often the first to bubble to the surface. In this respect, blame has been directed at all kinds of "Eastern" and "Western" cultures—that is, belief systems and their corresponding practices: capitalism, socialism, and Confucianism, to name a few.

Let's begin with the West. Both the Christian religion and the Scientific Revolution offered justifications for human hegemony over plants and animals. Religion says that this arrangement was God's design. Natural selection explains that human triumph was "the survival of the fittest"—a term coined by Herbert Spencer and later adopted by Charles Darwin as an alternative to "natural selection."

Friedrich Nietzsche, a contemporary of Darwin who eagerly (but less successfully) engaged with evolutionary theory, attempted to adapt the theory to human affairs.[34] Nietzsche argued that unlike plants and animals, the fundamental driver of human behavior is the "will to power," although his definition of power is closer to what we now mean by happiness.[35]

Nietzsche may have been fuzzy on his science, but he was onto something with his notion of "will to power." Soon, power seekers had warped Darwinism into Social Darwinism and weaponized scientific terms like *survival, competition,* and *natural selection* to post hoc justify and ad hoc promote the triumph of races, nations, industries, and markets.[36] The will to power devolved into a scramble for power. Enlightenment's epiphany marched in lockstep with its curse.[37]

By the time the West came to the gate of repentance, Social Darwinism had been stripped of its scientific façade. Carolyn Merchant argues that there is nothing natural or scientific about the exploitation of nature: if anything, she insists, the Scientific Revolution helped rationalize various forms of exploitation, not just of nature but also of fellow human beings.[38] Merchant identifies the Enlightenment as a turning point in Western culture. Capitalism, fueled by the advances in the sciences and scientific methods, in turn used science to legitimize the objectification and subjugation of nature in its aggressive pursuit of wealth and power. More broadly, the eco-feminist movement attributes the oppression of women, slaves, labor, and animals to the patriarchal culture of the West.

Interestingly, scholars of the Chinese environment have similarly blamed Chinese culture—Confucianism in particular—for its poor treatment of nature.[39] Many have singled out as evidence a famous idiom from the *Lost Book of Zhou* (*Yi Zhou Shu*), "Men will conquer nature" (*rendingshengtian*). But the actual meaning of the idiom is that perseverance can help people overcome difficult circumstances, with nature as a metaphor for forces outside one's control.

In contrast, scholars often suggest that Buddhism, Daoism, and some non-Han minority cultures advocate a more harmonious relationship between man and nature. There is much truth to this claim. But before romanticizing Daoism's charmed relationship with nature (and how can anyone who has read Zhuangzi not be enthralled?), we should recognize that some Daoist ideas are also inherently anti-intellectual.[40] This critique may in turn be countered by the argument that there is nothing inherently wrong with anti-intellectualism, especially when scientific knowledge is often used for violence and oppression, and intellectuals have proven to be as capable of evil as the less educated. (This book does not delve into such philosophical debates, as interesting as they are.)

The fact of the matter is that we can easily apply Merchant's critique of Western culture to many other cultures and recognize that patriarchy, military conquests, and developmental obsession are endemic to many societies (especially powerful ones) around the globe.

Still, it takes little effort to find Confucianism's nature-loving side. Marks documents that when the Confucian governor Lin Zexu led the fabled campaign to dump 1,188 tons of opium into the South China Sea in June 1839 at the onset of the First Opium War, he apologized to the creatures of the sea for polluting their realm and pleaded that they stay well away from the coast.[41]

We can also single out influential Confucian passages asking that men treat nature as gently as they would themselves. For example: "Use only one hook to fish, and only shoot birds that are flying" (*diaoerbugang, gebushesu*), meaning that a good person knows restraint and compassion—they shouldn't catch more fish than they need to fill their stomach, or kill baby birds in the nest.[42] In General Learning Questions (*Daxuewen*), Ming-dynasty neo-Confucian intellectual-politician Wang Yangming compares the benevolence of human nature to that of nature itself:

> A big person is he who sees everything between heaven and earth as one. . . . When they see a child fall into a well, they feel frightened and compassionate, because their benevolence is like that of a child. You might think this is because a child is of their own kind, but when a big person sees birds cry with sadness and animals tremble with fear, they cannot stand to listen or watch, because their benevolence is like that of animals. You might still think this is because animals also have consciousness, but when a big person sees flowers trod upon or tree branches broken, they feel compassionate, because their benevolence is like that of flowers and trees.[43]

Writings like this have been emphasized by contemporary Confucians as well as the party itself to make the case for the compatibility between Confucianism and environmental protection.[44] Daniel Bell, a prominent critic of democracy, said in a 2021 interview that "what drives the Confucian revival in China . . . is a concern for the environment."[45]

Accounts of environmental pollution in modern China also tend to overestimate the pride of place enjoyed by Confucianism, while neglecting the robust influence of Western ideas since the nineteenth century, including liberalism, Marxism, capitalism, and Christianity. Elvin makes this point succinctly: "There is no such thing as a 'Chinese view of nature.'"[46]

Taken together, Western eco-feminists and critics of Confucianism may both have overstressed cultural specificity. Equally misconstrued are the ideology and practices of socialism. On one hand, both "Western" and "Eastern" critics of capitalism portray socialism as being more amenable to nature. Pan Yue, an outspoken Marxist environmentalist and deputy minister of China's MEP between 2003 and 2015, writes that "naturalism is humanism, and humanism is socialism."[47] At the same time, when states put socialism into practice—as "state socialism"—economic development becomes the priority. As Stevan Harrell writes about the CCP: "From cautious imitation of Stalin through utopian fantasy and disaster, to retreat into planned economy, to adopting much of capitalism, to dreaming of a green future, development has always been at the core."[48] The Great Leap Forward, for example, was one of the grandest state-led developmental efforts—though also one of its greatest failures. For state socialists, pollution was a "necessary evil" on the road to human liberation.[49]

Therefore, ascribing environmental destruction to a particular culture or ideology is as flawed as attributing political violence to specific religions. It is not the fabric of any culture per se, but human beings' will to power—over nature and each other—that leads to the destruction of nature. Despite their superficial differences, Confucianism and various forms of Enlightenment humanism (including capitalism and developmental socialism) all share the maladies of anthropocentrism.[50] If any culture is to blame, it is human culture.

From Stockholm to Beijing

In the early days of the PRC, criticizing environmental pollution was taboo and tantamount to "smearing socialism" (*gei shehuizhuyi mohei*)—the system that could do no wrong. This began to change toward the end of the Maoist era. As the beginning of this chapter argues, the PRC's admission to the United Nations at a time when environmental awareness was rising in the West—Rachel Carson's *Silent Spring* was published in 1962—generated the political opportunity and necessity for China to join the international effort for pollution control. The Chinese delegation to the 1972 Stockholm Conference reportedly returned with "broadened horizons"; they urged that environmental protection be put on the state's agenda.[51]

But this ideational change did not take hold easily. The backlash against environmental protection was strong from the start, especially among state-owned enterprise managers under pressure to fulfill production targets.[52] Public awareness was also low (though never absent), because pollution had long been portrayed as a foreign, capitalist sin—not one a People's Republic would ever commit.

To raise public awareness and signal its newfound attention to the environment, the party-state pursued two strategies. First, state media gradually increased their use of the phrase "environmental protection" (*huanjing baohu/huanbao*), as figure 3 shows.[53] A lengthy *People's Daily* opinion piece in June 1973 spelled out the theoretical foundation for environmental protection. The article opened by referencing the writing of Friedrich Engels, who maintained that environmental pollution is a problem that first and foremost plagues capitalist societies. It then cautioned, "We cannot believe that environmental problems do not exist under socialist conditions. On the contrary, we must pay attention to environmental protection as we develop the socialist economy."[54] As a socialist country

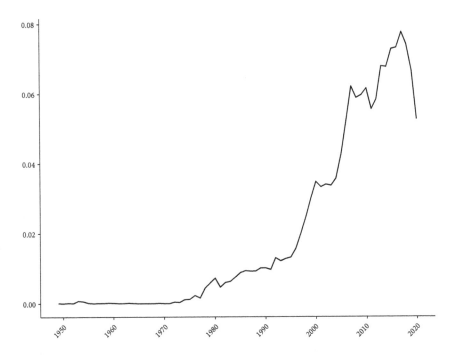

FIGURE 3. Normalized percentage of articles containing "environmental protection" (*huanjing baohu* or *huanbao*) in the *People's Daily* (1949–2020)

that "proceeds in all cases from the interest of the people" (*yiqie cong renmin liyi chufa*), the goal of socialist economic development is to improve people's welfare. Thus, the article concluded, protecting the environment while pursuing economic development is being responsible to the people and future generations.[55]

Second, state propaganda framed the urgency of pollution control as a *popular demand*, even though at the time there was little evidence of the general public's attention to environmental problems. In October 1973, *People's Daily* published a letter from two teachers in Hubei province:

> As the Socialist development enterprise flourishes, factories of all sizes blossomed like bamboo after the rain. This is a gratifying phenomenon. . . . However, some localities neglected pollution by the "three wastes" (*sanfei*). For example, a township in our locality built a sugar factory in a dense residential area, and did not seriously manage the three wastes, causing severe pollution to the local air, water, and environment. People passing by have to hold their breath and move quickly. The impact on local residents is even greater. We hope relevant departments and work units will value the principle of "being responsible to

the people," attach high importance to pollution by the three wastes, and enhance the scientific management of the three wastes.[56]

Meanwhile, the state also raised awareness of environmental protection by relating it to public health: new environmental policies were pushed through various "patriotic hygiene campaigns" (aiguozhuyi weisheng yundong).[57]

From this ideational change sprang a nascent environmental state. As mentioned before, the First National Conference on Environmental Protection convened in Beijing for two weeks in August 1973. It was reported that three hundred representatives from local governments, industries, and academia presented "shocking evidence" of the pollution of oceans, rivers, forests, grasslands, and urban environments.[58] In May 1974, the State Council set up a multiagency Environmental Protection Leading Group (Huanjing baohu lingdao xiaozu). In the continuing absence of an actual environmental protection bureaucracy, the leading group consisted of officials from bureaus for economic planning, industrial policy, agricultural policy, public health, transportation, and water resource management. Many provinces followed suit by setting up their own environmental leading groups, often called the Office for the Control and Management of Three Wastes (Sanfei kongzhi guanli bangongshi), which focused on the management of wastewater, waste air, and solid wastes generated by industrial activities.

Looking back, it's remarkable that even in the early 1970s, central authorities had already recognized the environmental pitfalls of the developmental trajectory followed by earlier industrializers. The 1973 "Some Decisions" criticized the "pollute first, clean up later" (xian wuran, hou zhili) model and instead asked for "balancing economic development and environmental protection," demanding that "whoever generates pollution manages it" (shei wuran shei zhili).[59] As a 1974 People's Daily editorial wrote: "Environmental pollution often forms quickly, yet it takes a long time to eliminate pollution. If [we] manage pollution after it forms and deteriorates, [we] will not only pay a bigger price, but will also find it difficult to achieve good results in a short time."[60] This early attention to environmental protection turned out to be insufficient for addressing the governance challenges to come. Yet this failure has not been the result of ignorance, at least since the 1970s.

From Inertia to Reform

Industrial pollution in China's reform era is a new beast that draws its energy from across the globe. Reform started in the countryside with the return to household farming, but industrial takeoff was propelled by foreign direct investment, lured by cheap labor and land and by lax regulations. In this process, the industrialized world exported much of its pollution and greenhouse gas emissions to China. But plenty of China's pollution was homegrown. Economic growth leads to increased consumption, electricity use, and transportation, all major causes of air pollution and greenhouse gas emissions.

How the Chinese economy took off is a million-dollar question beyond the scope of my little book. But one observation is important for us here: economic development, at least initially, benefited from the seamless alignment of the interests of the country's main stakeholders—the central government, local governments, businesses, and citizens. Economic development also aligned with the political incentives of local officials, since GDP growth was a valued criterion for promotion, and some corruption was implicitly tolerated.[61]

This alignment of interests falls apart in pollution control.[62] Industries keep local governments afloat by contributing taxes and providing employment; many firms stay in a locality only because of its lax environmental and labor regulations. The middle class may demand cleaner air, but few are willing to sacrifice their income or give up driving and flying. Officials responsible for the economy cannot sacrifice development. When some central officials advocated for "green GDP" in the mid-2000s, it caused so much backlash from local governments that the idea was immediately dropped.[63] A 2013 study finds that officials who invested more in environmental protection were on average less likely to receive political promotion.[64]

But these challenges did not stymie the gradual growth of China's environmental state. As early as 1978, officially the first year of Reform and Opening, the State Council included "environmental protection" in China's Constitution, declaring it part of the "four modernizations" and pledging that China would not follow the "pollute first, clean up later" path of early industrializers.[65] A year later, the state passed its first Environmental Protection Law of the People's Republic of China (Trial Implementation). In the following two decades, new environmental policies, laws, and regulations mushroomed at both national and subnational levels, including the Ocean Environmental Protection Law, the Forest Law, the Water Pollution Prevention and Management Law, the Air Pollution Prevention and Management Law, and thousands of local regulations.

New laws, regulations, and administrative rules have proliferated in every policy domain, including in environmental protection, an area that is historically minuscule. Many environmental regulations are borrowed directly from abroad—Japan, the European Union, and the United States in particular.[66] To be sure, tough regulations are often poorly enforced—but such rulemaking bespeaks intended rationalization of governance procedures, if not always substantive improvement in governance outcomes.[67]

As of now, China's main model of environmental governance can be characterized as "command and control," which bears a resemblance to the target system under the planned economy.[68] At the beginning of each year, the central government sets national emission reduction (*jieneng jianpai*) targets on each pollutant. These targets are then allocated to provinces, which divide them up among localities (municipalities and counties). Local governments then assign emission reduction targets to each polluting enterprise.

Any new infrastructural project or industrial enterprise must first pass an Environmental Impact Assessment (EIA, *huanping*) before construction or production are allowed to start. The enterprise contracts a third-party EIA firm to evaluate the potential environmental impact of the project. The enterprise then submits their EIA report (*huanping baogao*) to the local EPB, seeking approval for construction and operation.[69] Once the EPB has approved the operation, the enterprise applies for a pollution permit (*paiwu xukezheng*), which specifies the quantity of each type of pollutant the enterprise can legally discharge, the proper methods of discharge, and requirements for pollution abatement facilities. To fulfill emission reduction targets, the local government limits the number of new pollution permits issued each year.

As formal rules proliferate, so does the environmental bureaucracy. Before the 1970s, the Ministry of Health was nominally in charge of environmental policies. During the initial years of Economic Reform, the State Environmental Protection Agency (SEPA, Guojia huanjing baohu ju) was part of the Ministry of Construction (Jianshebu). In 1988, SEPA became an independent entity under the State Council. Within a decade, it was elevated to the ministerial level. Another decade later, SEPA was promoted to the MEP, reaching the highest bureaucratic level. In 2018, the MEP was renamed the MEE, incorporating many functions that had previously fallen outside its jurisdiction.

Underlying the notion of fragmented authoritarianism is the important observation that decision making under authoritarianism can exhibit pluralist features. One benefit of this fragmented decision making is that actors from different backgrounds and with different kinds of expertise can weigh in during the policy process. Environmental policy making, in particular, is an area that involves diverse stakeholders, including nonstate and international actors.[70] For example, the USEPA, Environmental Defense Fund, and the European Union all helped introduce cap and trade systems to China.

According to Andrew Mertha, "agency slack" in such a fragmented system provides "points of entry" for "policy entrepreneurs"—marginalized officials, members of the media, and NGOs—to influence the policy process and form ad hoc alliances to shape policy outputs.[71] Policy entrepreneurs also exist at higher levels. For instance, former deputy minister Pan Yue was an advocate of the Green GDP idea in the mid-2000s. Ironically, Pan's activism turned out to be a curious mismatch with the MEP at that time. In 2015, Pan left the MEP to serve as vice president of the Central Academy of Socialism.

Activism at the top of the environmental bureaucracy is not mirrored at the street level, however. When it comes to policy implementation, fragmented authoritarianism was more a bane than a boon. Ran Ran found at least thirteen stakeholders involved in the process of environmental policymaking and implementation in 2015.[72] For example, in a city, these actors could include the municipal party secretary, the mayor, the EPB, the DRC, the Public Security Bureau, the Bureau of Forestry and Landscaping, the Public Management Bureau, the Bureau of Land and Resources, the Bureau of Economy and Information Technology, the water company, the railway company, etc. Unclear delegation of responsibility leads to collective action problems. Agencies often pass pollution problems around like a hot potato.

Second, agencies in charge of economic and industrial planning, such as local DRCs, might obstruct the EPBs' enforcement efforts if polluting enterprises contribute to the local economy.[73] Ran argues that in environmental governance, the bigger the responsibility a bureaucracy bears, the less power it actually enjoys. The agency that bears the most responsibility is of course the EPB; it is also the weakest.[74]

Third, subnational EPBs are under the dual authorities of the EPB one level above them, as well as the party committee (especially the party secretary) of the locality to which they belong. For example, a municipal EPB answers to both the provincial EPB and the municipal party committee. But in practice, the municipal EPB's loyalty to the municipal leadership trumps their subordination to the provincial EPB. This is because the EPB's operations are funded by the local government, and the EPB's directors used to be appointed by the municipal party committee.[75] As one county EPB official put it, "We listen to whoever pays us."[76] And since the fulfillment of emission reduction targets is hard to verify, localities often massage the data in their reports.

Moreover, pollution's sources are both confused and diffused. Many lie outside the EPB's reach. For example, around 40 percent of urban air pollution comes from automobile exhaust, over which the EPB has almost no control: NDRC sets fuel standards and the Transportation Bureau regulates the number of cars on the road. The transregional movement of air and water pollution also hamstrings local enforcement of regulations. In the winter, sulfur dioxide generated by coal burning in northern China is carried by the wind to other parts of the country, and can even be detected in trace amounts across the Pacific. But local EPBs have no jurisdiction over distant pollution sources. These structurally embedded obstacles deepened the EPB's political weakness.[77]

What's worse, firms—the object of environmental enforcement—have plenty of crafty ways to evade regulations. The crassest method is bribery. Evidence of corruption often appeared in studies of environmental governance in the 1990s and early 2000s. Enterprises that have close relationships with the local government—such as big taxpayers (*nashui dahu*)—hold the so-called "amnesty gold medal" (*miansi jinpai*). Smaller enterprises still try to cultivate personal relationships with EPB bureaucrats, exchanging gifts for tips on upcoming inspections. Since environmental fines tend to be small, the attendant payoffs tend to be small as well, such as discounts on an enterprise's products (e.g., tires, toilet bowls). Such low-level corruption has either ceased under Xi Jinping's anticorruption campaign, or continues to operate in extreme secrecy and at major risk.

Firms are also adept at evasion. To discharge waste water directly into a lake or river, some enterprises bury "dark pipes" (*anguan*) underground. These pipes are incredibly hard to spot. To evade online monitoring (*zaixian jiankong*) of emissions, some firms hire computer engineers to write programs that change data at source points before they are synced with the EPB's monitoring system.

Not all regulatory evasion methods are illegal. For example, the owner of a cellphone hardware manufacturer told me he keeps a fish tank at the factory's main gate, and regularly replenishes it with fresh water and live fish. He believed that the fish tank primes inspectors to think that the factory is properly treating its industrial waste water.

All told, day-to-day environmental enforcement has been a mission impossible, despite the explosive rise in laws and regulations and considerable expansion of the environmental bureaucracy. A recurrent theme in the existing research on Chinese environmental governance is that rules are strong but enforcement is poor.[78] Substantive enforcement isn't entirely absent, but it usually happens only after major environmental crises (*zhongda tufa huanjing shijian*), when environmental problems become de facto matters of social stability that will affect the political future of local cadres. Elizabeth Economy summarizes this mode of environmental governance as "a game of crisis management."[79] This slapdash approach to policy implementation is also reminiscent of the campaign-style governance of the Maoist era.[80]

During early Reform, the enforcement difficulties highlighted above translated into inert governance by the EPB. As the next chapter will detail, the EPB was once known as a "clean water yamen" (*qingshui yamen*), referring to agencies that produce little revenue and are on the periphery of governance concerns.[81] A career in a clean water yamen is neither powerful nor lucrative, but it is supposed to be comfortable (*shufu*) and "idle" (*xian*). In contrast, a career in a "fat water yamen" (*feishui yamen*) or "oil yamen" (*youshui yamen*) like the DRC means more income and potential for promotion, but also more uncertainty—for example, more chances to be sacked during an anticorruption campaign.

Inert governance became less so around the mid-2000s, when the dramatic rise in the salience of pollution widened the mismatch between subpar governance and the strong public demand for cleaner water and air. The EPB became exposed to intense public scrutiny, even as the public knows little and cares even less about the constraints EPB bureaucrats face. Not yet having the ability—nor even the legal authority—to shutter or severely punish polluting enterprises, the EPB engaged in performative governance to prevent citizen complaints from amalgamating into large-scale public-opinion crises, as the next chapter will show.

In recent years, the state has taken several major initiatives to improve the effectiveness of environmental governance. In 2016, the MEP started sending "supervisory groups" to all provinces to investigate local environmental practices. These inspections were not announced in advance, to avoid giving local governments time to tip off the enterprises. An MEP official told me that inspection teams hired their own cars so that local governments wouldn't know of their whereabouts.[82]

These inspections have left behind a trail of sacked officials and closed enterprises. In turn, local governments have ramped up enforcement in anticipation of central government visits. Empirical research finds improved air quality following the inspections, though the effect seems short lived.[83] Denise van der Kamp calls such top-down pollution control measures "blunt-force" regulation.[84]

In 2017, the NDRC announced that environmental protection would carry more weight than economic development in the performance evaluation of local officials—an unprecedented move coming just a decade after the notion of green GDP was rejected by local officials. Also starting in 2017, the authority to nominate municipal EPB directors was transferred from the municipal party committee to provincial EPBs. Although approval from municipal leadership is still needed to confirm the nominations, this transfer of authority can potentially give the EPBs greater autonomy from local economic interests. The 2018 "super ministries" reform (*dabuzhi gaige*) further introduced changes designed to solve the structural problems produced by "fragmented authoritarianism." For example, the State Council streamlined many environmental governance functions that had been spread across different agencies and assigned them to the new, strengthened MEE.

All these recent changes have resulted in more stringent environmental enforcement. A conservationist in Beijing told me that the forestry police in the capital now responds immediately to reports of regulatory violations, whereas a few years ago they ignored most complaints.[85]

Green Mountain and Gold Mountain

These recent reforms have followed Xi Jinping's ascent to power. Xi's ideology, known as the "Chinese Dream" (*Zhongguo meng*), includes not only economic prosperity and national strength, but also "a beautiful environment."[86] On various occasions in his political career, Xi reiterated what became known as the Two Mountains Theory (*liangshan lilun*) of sustainable development: "clear water and green mountains are as valuable as mountains of gold and silver [*lüshui qingshan jiushi jinshan yinshan*]."[87] Xi's penchant for "ecological civilization" (*shengtai wenming*) is consistently expressed at home and abroad.

There was a time when Chinese delegates laid low and avoided leading discussions in international climate negotiations. A former member of the UK government said that a Chinese climate negotiator once told him that "the West talks about leadership as if everyone wants it."[88] China had no ambition for environmental leadership: the Chinese wanted to be neither the vanguard nor the laggard, but somewhere in the middle.

Yet this passive stance began to shift when Xi came into office. In his Letter to the Eco Forum Annual Global Conference in 2013, Xi wrote that "ushering in a new era of ecological progress and building a beautiful China is an important element of the Chinese Dream. . . . Protecting the environment, addressing climate change and securing energy and resources is a common challenge for the whole world. China will continue to assume its due international obligations."[89] During Xi's visit to the White House in September 2015, he and President Barack Obama issued a joint statement on climate change, including China's pledge to roll out a national carbon emissions trading market and contribute $3.1 billion to help developing countries with climate adaptation.[90]

When President Trump initiated the US withdrawal from the Paris Agreement in 2017, some feared China would be the next to abandon ship. But so far there has been no sign of this. Foreign Minister Wang Yi pledged at the UN Climate Action Summit in September 2019 that the exit of the United States from the Paris Agreement would not impede the "collective will of the international community."[91] Ma Jun, a prominent Chinese environmentalist and policy advocate, affirmed China's intention to "truly lead the fight against climate change" in the September 2019 issue of *Time* magazine, writing alongside environmentalist icons like Jane Goodall and Al Gore.[92] In a surprise announcement at the UN

General Assembly meeting in September 2020, Xi declared that China would become carbon-neutral by 2060.[93]

Beneath any smooth rhetoric always lies a choppy reality. The plain boring fact is that environmental governance, even at the height of recent reforms, is still a mixed bag of positives and negatives, and ups and downs. The discrepancy between rhetoric and practice, where it exists, can be explained by three inter-related trade-offs that China still faces: (1) the institutional trade-off between national and subnational interests; (2) the political trade-off between governance priorities and societal demands, including those between the demands of differ-ent societal groups; and (3) the ultimate, existential trade-off between environ-mental protection and economic needs.

During the early years of reform, localities were given wide latitude to experi-ment and improvise. This way of decentralizing decision making—both by default and by design—is partly why China managed to grow so rapidly and adapt so effectively. But decentralization has not helped minimize local pollution problems; indeed, it may have exacerbated them. It remains to be seen whether the recent institutional reforms and central inspections will bring about long-lasting improvements.

As China ramps up pollution control, it must still solve the problem of com-plex and contradictory public demands. On one hand, there is a growing mid-dle class that is demanding cleaner air; on the other hand, there is still a large population in urgent need of improved livelihoods. On top of these conflicting demands is the ongoing conversion of population and land from rural to urban, which in turn changes the structure of demand while putting further stress on the environment.

Nothing captures the trade-off between governance priorities and societal demands more vividly and painfully than the country's coal-to-gas policy. In October 2017, in an effort to curb coal consumption and improve winter air quality, the central government ordered coal-fired boilers to be replaced with natural gas in twenty-eight northern Chinese cities, covering 300 million house-holds and myriad enterprises.[94] Given the new terms of performance evaluation emphasizing environmental protection, local officials responded fervidly, even overshooting the designated targets of coal abatement in some areas.

What looked like a success story of pollution control and carbon reduction quickly went awry. In November, as winter descended, gas prices skyrocketed and became unaffordable for the common folk. Increased demand also led to a nationwide gas shortage. (China imports most of its oil and almost half of its nat-ural gas.) In some villages, the demolition of coal boilers was not followed up with the timely installation of gas infrastructure. Stories of freezing schoolchildren generated a frenzy on social media. In December 2017, a great policy reversal lifted the ban on coal burning and ordered the implementation of the coal-to-gas policy to cease. In less than two months, the pendulum had swung back, as the dream of clean air was defeated by the harsh reality of human survival.[95]

Ultimately, China has arrived at the precipice of a brutal existential trade-off between environmental sustainability and economic needs. The coal-to-gas story shows that this trade-off is not some utility function maximized at the individual level. Rather, what's more excruciating is the societal-level trade-off between the preferences of different groups. When GDP growth drops from 6.2 percent to 6 percent, some breathe cleaner air but others lose their entire livelihoods.

This trade-off is acute not only for China, but also for much of the world's population. That is true despite the high hope, and the legitimate hope, placed in "green growth," or fast economic growth at significantly reduced emissions. China is now a leader in the development and deployment of low-carbon energy technologies (LCET) such as solar power, wind power, and electric vehicles.[96] But the current speed of development and adoption of LCETs and renewables has been far outpaced by the speed of global warming caused by human activities. For now and the foreseeable future, growth itself—whether it's green or not—converts into emissions. As one observer put it bluntly, "About four out of five people on earth have never taken a flight. Many of them cannot wait."[97]

BELEAGUERED BUREAUCRATS

A prince, therefore, need not actually have all the qualities I have
enumerated, but it is absolutely necessary that he seems to have
them.

—*The Prince*, Niccolò Machiavelli

Max is in his late twenties.[1] Sporting a pair of white Converse, black-framed glasses, and with a penchant for basketball and video games, he is a typical college-educated Chinese man of his age. In 2011, Max graduated from a top Chinese university with a master's degree in Environmental Science and Engineering. As graduation approached, he faced a dilemma that torments millions of highly educated Chinese youths every year: should he seek his fortune in the private sector, or enter the *tizhi* ("the system") for the *wending* (stability) it offers?

Like many young people, Max dreams of success. He told me it doesn't matter what kind of success: it could be money or it could be status (*diwei*). But if he had to choose, he'd pick money—when I first met him in 2013, many of his classmates from his top "985" university were already making good money.[2] But Max's mother had a different view. For her, a job in the tizhi meant a handsome salary, generous benefits, social honor, and, most important, wending. For many of her generation, who "ate bitterness" during their swaddling years in the 1950s, came of age in the tumultuous 1960s and 1970s, witnessed the roiling uncertainties of the 1980s, and traversed the sea changes of the 1990s, stability carries a lot of weight.

After much introspection, Max honored his mother's wish and joined millions of other Chinese graduates to study for the Civil Service Examination (*gong-wuyuan kaoshi*)—China's system for selecting new civil servants every year. The Civil Service Exam is the modern offspring of the imperial examination system (*keju*) that gave the Chinese state its lifeblood for millennia. When the moribund Qing court abolished the exam in 1905, as a part of modernizing reforms to salvage the dynasty, it achieved the opposite of its goals. Young men who would otherwise have been studying for the exam in hopes of joining the bureaucratic state found better prospects as agents of the revolution.[3] It would take almost a century for the revolutionary party to bring back the exam to recruit the nation's best and brightest—this time as agents of the regime.[4]

It would hardly be a stretch to say that the Civil Service Exam is one of the most competitive exams in the world. In 2019, the exam for national-level positions (*guokao*) boasted an admission rate of only 1.05 percent, about one-fifth the admission rate for Harvard College's class of 2022.[5] Exams for provincial positions can be just as competitive, especially in the poorest provinces, where attractive private-sector alternatives are few and far between. Competition is also fierce in rich provinces like Jiangsu and Zhejiang, where civil servant salaries sometimes exceed those in Beijing.[6]

This formidable challenge didn't deter Max. Thanks to months of study, he excelled in the written exam, then shined again in the face-to-face interview. He was eventually awarded a position in the tizhi—at the municipal Environmental Protection Bureau of Lakeville. Although this job will never make him as rich as some of his former classmates braving the capitalist storms in the world of business, and his inner turmoil never truly ceased, he treats his work with the utmost diligence, hoping to ascend the political ranks and attain the other kind of success—status.

Max's struggles and aspirations resemble those of many civil servants who make up the seven-million-strong machinery of the Chinese state. Most of these state agents have never touched a gun, much less pointed one at a dissident; never shaken hands with a mayor, much less a member of the Politburo; and never spent time in Beijing outside of visiting the Great Wall. Like most people, their primary concerns in life are the food on their table and the roof over their head. And therefore, like most people, they care a great deal about holding onto their jobs, earning raises, and pursuing promotions.

So let us delve into the world of Chinese bureaucrats and watch them in action. For what gets them up in the morning and keeps them awake at night is, at base, the very same thing as the "institutions" or "incentives" that we social scientists see shaping "state behavior."

Lakeville

Lakeville is a bustling big city in the coastal Yangtze River Delta, a tri-provincial region embracing metropolitan Shanghai. The city is densely populated and fairly well-off, with a per capita GDP about twice that of the nation's average.

The Yangtze Delta suffers from severe air pollution. While its smog problem is not as infamous as that of the Jing-Jin-Ji Metropolitan Region of Beijing, Tianjin, and Hebei, it is still easily discernible and plenty perturbing. In 2013, most cities in the Yangtze Delta had average *PM2.5* levels more than twice the Ministry of Environmental Protection's baseline standard (35 $\mu g/m^3$).[7] Smog smothered Lakeville for two-thirds of the year. In January 2014, air quality on all but two days of the month was "very unhealthy," according to the MEP's classification scheme, meaning that "every person in the population may experience serious health effects." Even this grave assessment might have understated the problem, as the MEP's standards were criticized for being too lenient and "misleading."[8]

Lakeville is one of China's "urban champions," where the Rostowian "stages of growth" that proceed seamlessly along an extended, teleological route are compressed into flat spacetime.[9] Bedecked with skyscrapers and blanketed in smog, with the most incandescent of neon lights flickering around the most unflinching of socialist slogans, these cities represent the vivacity and gallimaufry of contemporary Chinese life. Beyond Beijing's seeming omnipresence, they are home to China's growing middle class, and the loci of their social, economic, and political lives.

It was early summer 2013 when I arrived in Lakeville to conduct fieldwork, carrying with me an interest in "the variation in the stringency of local environmental enforcement in China" and a stack of twelve hypotheses.[10] My baseline expectation was that the more economically developed regions would have stronger state capacity, a more outspoken citizenry holding such "postmaterial values" as environmentalism, and therefore stricter enforcement of environmental regulations—in short, substantive governance.[11] Given Lakeville's relative economic modernity, I expected to find "high stringency in environmental enforcement" there.[12]

There is nothing an elegant hypothesis should be more afraid of than the harsh test of reality. Soon after I entered the field, my stack of hypotheses fell apart like Sartori's "cat-dog"—concepts and hypotheses that can be conjured in theoretical abstraction but cannot be identified or verified in real life.[13] In a nutshell, I was surprised by the Lakeville EPB's abject inability to enforce environmental regulations. As I explained at some length in chapters 1 and 2, China's environmental bureaucracy was hampered by a serious capacity deficit. Lakeville was no exception.

This observation belied Lakeville's impressive placement in any ranking of governance quality among Chinese cities. By all measures of what we might mean by a region's "modernity"—be it level of development, education of its citizenry, or connectivity with the world—Lakeville, and the Yangtze Delta at large, outstrips other parts of China, eclipsed only perhaps by the Pearl River Delta megalopolis in Guangdong Province. But as I quickly learned when researching Lakeville's environmental governance, better governance isn't quite the same as "good governance," and high state capacity in the aggregate doesn't mean high capacity in every domain.

What was even more puzzling than this lack of substantive environmental governance in a relatively developed region was *how hard* bureaucrats at the Lakeville EPB worked nonetheless. Since they could do so little to enforce environmental regulations, and they had no delusions to the contrary, why weren't their efforts as limited as their efficacy? Why didn't they just go through the basic motions and spend most of their office time drinking tea, browsing the news, "chatting online and monitoring the stock market," as inertly as state bureaucrats in a "clear water yamen" (*qingshui yamen*) are so often expected to behave?[14]

Instead, a job at the EPB turned out to be grueling. Bureaucrats often worked ungodly hours and met with onerous physical demands. This surprised not only me but also Max, soon after he joined the Lakeville EPB. Most significantly, if the EPB wasn't enforcing environmental regulations all that rigorously, what were the bureaucrats doing with their time?

The Lakeville EPB

The Lakeville EPB is the governmental organization responsible for enforcing environmental laws, policies, and regulations in the city. Before taking a closer look at this agency and seeing how well it either conforms to or departs from conventional theories of bureaucratic behavior, let's briefly revisit Weber's influential anatomy of "modern officialdom":[15]

- [Official] jurisdictional areas . . . are generally ordered by rules, that is, by laws or administration regulations.
- The regular activities . . . are assigned as official duties.
- The authority to give the commands . . . is distributed in a stable way.
- [Only] persons who qualify under general rules are employed.
- [There] is supervision of the lower offices by higher ones.
- The management . . . is based on written documents.
- Public monies and equipment are divorced from the private property of the official.
- Official activity [is segregated] from the sphere of private life.
- Office management . . . presupposes thorough training in a field of specialization.

- [Office management] . . . follows general rules, which are more or less stable, more or less exhaustive, and which can be learned. Knowledge of these rules represents a special technical expertise which the officials possess.
- The possession of educational certificates . . . is usually linked with qualification for office.

Weber describes such "rules, means-ends calculus, and matter-of-factness" as "rational."[16] Nowadays, "Weberian bureaucracy" is often invoked in praise of an organization's "rationality," even though "rationality" was entirely value-neutral to Weber, and often a subject of his critique.[17]

A significant body of literature on the Chinese bureaucracy, whether in its imperial, Maoist, or reform-era guises, stresses its departure from Weberian rationality.[18] But this verdict is by no means conclusive, for two important reasons. First, if we stop seeing "rationality" as praise (or often as code for "the rule of law"), and if we stop seeing pure types (such as patrimonialism, prebendalism, and rationalism) as mutually exclusive, then there is plentiful evidence for bureaucratic rationalization in China, as I will demonstrate momentarily.[19] Second, as the previous two chapters have discussed and as this chapter will continue to document, the Chinese state is internally complex and constantly evolving.[20] Any characterization of Chinese bureaucracy at a specific moment in time should be subject to reappraisal.

So how has the Chinese state evolved? In the past few decades, rationalization has been steadily unfolding within the state along the lines of Weberian "modern officialdom" mentioned earlier. First, authority relations within state agencies, at least at the street level, have seen a clear departure from the kind of patrimonialism or traditionalism endemic under Mao. In a deep dive into Mao-era factory life, Andrew Walder described the relationship between superiors and subordinates as "neo-traditionalism . . . a clientelist system in which public loyalty to the party and its ideology is mingled with personal loyalties between party branch officials and their clients."[21] Walder revealed that superiors in the workplace controlled the distribution of vital yet scarce resources such as housing, loans, medical care, childcare, and opportunities for promotion and party membership, leaving workers highly dependent on their superiors. Workers, in turn, earned scarce economic and political resources by displaying personal loyalty to their superiors. In one extreme example, a retired senior bureaucrat told me that when he worked in a factory before Reform, he hand-washed his supervisor's underwear to curry favor.[22]

In comparison, individuals' dependence on their workplace significantly declined under Reform with the introduction of the private market and modern management methods.[23] Most people now acquire housing—although often with major strain—in a private market.[24] One no longer needs the approval of a workplace supervisor to marry or divorce. Officeholding in the public sector has become a professional "vocation"—beginning with the strenuous Civil Service Exam that was gradually rolled out in the past three decades.[25] Work and private life are separated (to the extent that private life isn't entirely subsumed by work under the notorious "996" system).[26] The means of governance—money and equipment—are divorced from the private property of civil servants (barring grand or petty theft by corrupt officials, of course). A few years ago, the state banned officials from using government vehicles for personal purposes such as grocery shopping or picking up one's children from school.

Despite the persistence of hierarchical authority through the "one level down" system, whereby every office supervises the offices immediately below it in the nomenklatura system, bureaucrats are no longer virtual personal servants to their supervisors. This isn't to say that patronage no longer matters. Empirical research finds that personal networks matter more for promotion at higher-level positions within the regime, whereas lower-level officials may rely on substantive performance to get promoted.[27] Based on my observations in 2013 and 2014, very few street-level bureaucrats at the Lakeville EPB had a "background" (*beijing*). Most were like Max, who comes from an obscure town in a distant province and who obtained a civil service job by studying hard.

Second, the state has moved away from the sort of laissez-faire prebendalism that prevailed in the early reform era. Back then, local governments and bureaucracies were allowed to retain a substantial part of their revenues, often stashed in so-called "little gold chests" (*xiao jinku*), outside the radar and reach of upper authorities. Yuen Yuen Ang contends that such quasi-prebendalism, and even the corruption that came with it, was beneficial for China's economic growth.[28] Fiscal decentralization in general has been credited as the magic potion of China's successful takeoff.[29]

Beijing eventually decided that the costs of fiscal decentralization outweighed the benefits, however. The sweeping 1994 fiscal reform recentralized financial administration, in part to alleviate regional fiscal inequality, in part to lessen the leverage wielded against the center by several rich provinces. The ensuing "two lines of income and expenditure" (*shouzhi liangtiao xian*) reforms since the early 2000s further prohibited local governments from levying arbitrary charges (*luan shoufei*) and hoarding revenue.[30] Now, payments to state agencies from individuals and firms are deposited directly into the treasury, while agencies' budgets come from a separate line of centralized revenue. Some local EPBs in the 1990s and early 2000s relied on pollution levies to keep themselves afloat.[31] This practice is no longer viable since the "two lines" reform.[32]

Against this larger backdrop of bureaucratic modernization, and other institutional developments mentioned in the previous chapter, the Lakeville EPB appears to have rationalized, as can be seen by its increasing size, improving technology, formalization of rules, division of labor, and the professionalization of its workforce. In 2013, the EPB had nine internal divisions (*chu*) and twelve subsidiaries, each with a different responsibility, including personnel, finance, administrative approval, regulatory enforcement, environmental monitoring, ecological preservation, automobile exhaust management, and public education.[33] The bureaucracy's structure continues to be updated as old functions become obsolete and new governance needs emerge.[34]

As of 2013, the Lakeville EPB employed about 450 civil servants, who served a population of several million. By all accounts, the Lakeville EPB's workforce was professional and specialized. The salary and benefits package offered by government positions wouldn't appeal to well-educated graduates like Max if these jobs weren't considered stable (the Yangtze Delta is a dreamland of private-sector careers). In 2013, the EPB hired only a handful out of hundreds of applicants. Most employees under thirty-five held at least a master's degree in a relevant academic field, such as chemistry, materials science, environmental sciences and engineering, or law. New hires undergo months of training and must pass additional tests to become certified environmental inspectors. In my daily conversations with the bureaucrats, their knowledge of the environmental sciences often put me to shame.

The EPB's Weberian evolution was also apparent in the formalization of internal rules and administrative procedures. At the beginning of the year, the director of each bureaucracy signs a "target responsibility letter" (*mubiao zeren shu*) with the municipal leadership. The document, which reads like a contract, outlines the concrete targets the bureaucracy promises to meet by the end of the year. Every internal division or subsidiary also signs its own target responsibility letter with the office that supervises it. In painstaking detail, these "contracts" specify not only the targets but also the departments and individuals responsible for meeting each target. For example, one district EPB's target responsibility letter in 2012 consisted of fifteen abstract goals, including "Evaluate firms' environmental ratings," "Ensure the timely collection of pollution levy," and "Enforce the 'Three Simultaneities' regulation and the Environmental Impact Assessment System," as well as forty-two specific tasks, among them "Provide certification training for one radiation safety inspector" and "Publish more than five articles in the *Lakeville Environment* magazine."

EPB offices communicate with each other through the electronic delivery of "work assignment notices" (*gongzuo lianxidan*), which document the date and details of the assignment and the offices responsible for completing it. Target responsibility letters and work assignment notices are the epitome of a bureaucracy's "formal rationality." Importantly, however, these tasks and assignments are not always fulfilled in meaningful ways, leading to a glaring gap between "formal rationality" and "substantive rationality"—an inherent pathology of bureaucracy, according to Weber.

At the end of each year, every bureaucrat and office—from the lowest section (*ke*) level to the bureau (*ju*) level—undergoes a performance evaluation. Each bureaucrat and office first submits a self-evaluation report to their superior. The supervisor then evaluates their subordinates based on these reports and sometimes on their independent investigations.[35]

Authority relations within the EPB are hierarchical but much less "traditional" than what we read in Walder's study of Mao-era organizations. At work, I saw bureaucrats display professional subordination toward their superiors, but they generally offered input freely in discussions. During lunch breaks and after work, superiors and subordinates often mingled in a friendly manner—with much less awkwardness than I had expected—although rank differential in friend circles was seldom more than one level, partly due to age differences. At least on the surface, superiors' decision-making power was only exercised in work-related matters. Superiors are forbidden from requesting personal favors from their subordinates, and I didn't witness any such requests being made in the workplace.

None of these observations precludes the possibility that illicit clientelist practices might go on in the dark. It also doesn't imply in any way that corruption has been eliminated in China. The trajectory I highlight here is an unmistakable transformation of state bureaucracies from patrimonialism and prebendalism *in the direction of* legal-rationalism over the past four decades.

Double Trouble

Though the Lakeville EPB is now duly decked out in Weberian attire, much of what occurred beneath the surface defies substantive rationality. Two troubles plagued the agency and its bureaucrats: limited capacity and intense public scrutiny.

First, despite significant expansion and apparent rationalization, environmental governance in Lakeville still faced many of the same well-documented hardships that handicap local EPBs across China—namely, a paucity of administrative capacity and political clout to enforce laws and regulations.

The Lakeville EPB is not self-evidently weak. Every inspector at the agency carried a "law enforcement iPad" with applications allowing them to access each enterprise's complete environmental record. They use this device to upload new inspection data, which when synced with the EPB's central database can then be accessed from all EPB computers and iPads. The air bags the inspectors use to collect air samples are imported from Australia and cost twenty yuan (about three US dollars) apiece. The Lakeville EPB also has two subsidiary research centers with cutting-edge technology and seasoned environmental experts. Inland EPBs did not enjoy such material and human resources. From what I could gather during my visits to municipal EPBs in Sichuan and Guizhou in 2014, they had no "law enforcement iPads" and kept most of their inspection records on paper.

But as I showed in chapter 2, capacity is relative. Whether the Lakeville EPB is "strong" or "weak" depends not just on its own personnel, vehicles, equipment, and expertise, but also (and more importantly) on its authority to exert itself by enforcing laws and regulations over businesses. In other words, it doesn't matter if the Lakeville EPB has fancy technology if the object of its enforcement and its allies in the state are more influential in the local "political ecology."[36] At the time of my research, local EPBs were deprived of superstructural power, across the board.

As of 2013, the Lakeville EPB oversaw nearly nine thousand "key-point" (*zhongdian*) polluting enterprises (*wuran qiye*). Only a handful would receive even a modest fine each season (and that small number surely wasn't because all the others abided by environmental regulations). To order factories to close, the EPB needed authorization from the municipal leadership—something it rarely bothered to request, knowing that municipal authorities were reluctant to absorb the outsize economic and social costs of pollution control.

To be sure, Lakeville officials were well aware of the city's pollution problems and the urgency of "industrial upgrading" (*chanye shengji*)—a term now ubiquitous in Chinese policy documents. The city's developmental plans are unequivocal in their promotion of greener industries such as tourism, finance, electronic commerce, and renewable energy. However, industrial upgrading is easier said than done. Even an economy as modern and well-connected as Lakeville's still depends heavily on high-polluting manufacturing enterprises. In 2013, manufacturing accounted for almost half of the city's GDP. In my conversations with Lakeville officials and bureaucrats, it became clear that environmental protection, despite its salience in the public discourse, was perceived as a lower priority than economic development: especially infrastructural development, housing development, and support for the city's flagship businesses.

In backstage office conversations, EPB bureaucrats lamented the impossibilities of their jobs on a daily basis: districts and counties evading their requests to punish enterprises that violated regulations; upper-level authorities ignorant of

local conditions; bad apples from a neighboring province dumping solid industrial waste across the provincial border; and highfalutin environmental scientists
at local universities and research institutions hectoring the EPB at interagency
meetings, showing no appreciation or sympathy for the agency's meager
status.

Again and again, the same description emerged in my conversations with
bureaucrats in Lakeville and elsewhere: "The EPB is a weak bureaucracy [*Huanbao shi ruoshi bumen*]."[37] This isn't some "cheap talk" excuse used by the agency
to justify avoiding strenuous efforts. Interviewees often referred to the EPB's
weakness as "common sense" (*changshi*). This observation about EPB incapac-
ity also appears frequently in academic research.[38] In contrast, the Development
and Reform Councils (Fagaiwei) are often unreservedly referred to as "strong
bureaucracies" (*qiangshi bumen*) or "agencies with real power" (*shiquan bumen*).
Even electricity and water companies are far more influential than the EPB in
any given place.

Another term often invoked to describe the EPB's weakness is a "clear water
yamen" as opposed to a "fat water yamen," as mentioned in the previous chapter. Clear water agencies either generate less revenue or are on the periphery of
governance concerns. They wield little authority and command few economic
resources. Positions in fat water yamens draw aspiring bureaucrats and officials
because of their higher salaries, bonuses, and informal incomes. They also offer a
better chance of promotion to more prominent positions within the party-state.[39]
Sometimes, a lateral move to the EPB from a position at the same bureaucratic
rank in a different agency would mean the end to one's upward political mobility.[40] The gap between clear water and fat water yamen has narrowed in recent
years under intense anticorruption measures, but the ceiling of political advancement is still much higher for employees of stronger bureaucracies.

I arrived at the Lakeville EPB at the height of China's latest ongoing anticorruption campaign. Investigations surrounding the soon-to-be-sacked Zhou
Yongkang (China's former police chief) had commenced, and the campaign's
investigations were a source of daily gossip in the office. In a clear water yamen like
the Lakeville EPB, corruption was indiscernible. Yet the agency—consisting as it
did of tiny "flies" and not mighty "tigers"—still felt the full impact of the campaign.
By the end of 2013, the agency had stopped reimbursing bureaucrats for business
meals and transportation for fear of anticorruption investigations. Bureaucrats
paid a significant part of the logistical costs of environmental inspections, such
as meals, gasoline, and lodging, out of their own pocket. These observations are
supported by recent research showing that the anticorruption campaign has had
debilitating impacts on local bureaucracies—the kind of prebendal practices

once believed to have contributed to rapid economic growth are now the object of punishment.⁴¹ In this situation, the EPB had even more reason to lay low and refrain from action. Yet the agency remained puzzlingly energetic, if not necessarily effective.

"The Common Folk Nowadays"

Such bureaucratic energy is fueled by Lakeville's residents—the second dimension of "double trouble" for the EPB, and an even bigger headache. The many environmental problems that afflict Lakeville—especially air pollution—have provoked much discontent. Crucially, citizen complaints can threaten the career stability that drew bureaucrats like Max to this "clear water yamen" in the first place.

Citizens had many channels to voice their dissatisfaction directly to the state, including the Provincial Governor's Mailbox (*shengzhang xinxiang*), the Mayor's Hotline (*shizhang rexian*), the Mayor's Mailbox (*shizhang xinxiang*), the EPB Director's Mailbox (*juzhang xinxiang*), the Environmental Protection Hotline (*huanbao rexian*), and the EPB's Online Petition (*wangshang xinfang*). They can also write letters, make phone calls, and pay personal visits to the EPB office. Both the provincial government and the municipal government have information centers (*xinxi zhongxin*) that process and redirect citizen complaints. Complaints redirected from the provincial government to Lakeville are labeled "provincial-redirected" (*shengzhuan*); otherwise they're labeled as "municipal-level" (*shiji*). Basically, all complaints about environmental pollution in Lakeville eventually arrive at its EPB, where they are individually processed and addressed.⁴²

In 2013, the Lakeville EPB responded to more than ten thousand environmental complaints (about three hundred per day), of which 52 percent concerned air pollution, 19 percent noise pollution, and 17 percent water pollution. Within the category of air pollution, industrial waste air and dust at construction sites were the main sources of citizen complaint. Vehicle exhaust gases generate relatively few complaints (with the exception of diesel emissions from trucks and concrete mixers), although those account for a significant amount of urban air pollution—about 30 to 40 percent.

The fewest complaints were lodged in February—usually the month of the Spring Festival, when citizens are busy celebrating or traveling—even though it is typically one of the worst months for air pollution. After the festival, the level of environmental complaints rises exponentially, especially around the "Two

Sessions" (*lianghui*), the People's Congress and People's Political Consultative Conference (usually taking place in spring), when citizen attention to politics is heightened. For the rest of the year, the number of complaints gradually decreases, until a slight rebound in November, when air quality significantly deteriorates for the first time after pollution lets up in the spring.

Lakeville citizens are anything but quiescent. A candid remark often heard in the EPB's office was that "the common folk nowadays are powerful" (*xianzai de laobaixing hen lihai de*) or "the common folks nowadays are hard to deal with" (*xianzai de laobaixing hen nan duifu de*). A favorite story circulating among these beleaguered bureaucrats involved several farmers who protested against a neighboring county's EPB by moving into its office with their rice cookers and camping out for five straight days, playing poker to pass the time. On another occasion, the Lakeville EPB was compelled to launch a major investigation into waste-water pollution at a paper plant because the complainant, who eventually turned out to be an employee of a rival factory, managed to obtain the EPB director's cell phone number and filed a petition via personal text message. The director had no legal responsibility to address complaints that arrived by text message, but he immediately ordered inspections anyway.

Worse yet, an "environmental problem" (*huanjing wenti*) is not a well-defined term; it can include anything loosely related to the living environment. Many complaints that fell outside the EPB's purview still found their way to its desks: noise from construction sites, smoke from food stalls, flies in restaurant food, and occasionally even traffic jams. Much time was spent redirecting these complaints to the proper agency, usually the Urban Management Bureau (Chengguan). Even legitimate complaints are not always motivated by sincere environmentalism. For example, factories near residential areas hurt property values, prompting some citizens to use environmental complaints to pressure factories to relocate.

Some of the most interesting conversations I have had with state bureaucrats have been about the differences among government agencies. These agencies all have different organizational cultures, different levels of physical and intellectual demands, and different material and emotional rewards for employees. (There are few things people enjoy talking about more than their jobs: the perquisites, hassles, bosses, colleagues, milestones, and setbacks.) Tellingly, no one I've ever talked to has aspired to work for the Petitions Bureau (Xinfangban), or for the petition offices within other agencies. Lower salary and benefits are downsides, but the demands of managing public relations are another. A former state bureaucrat who now works in the private sector told me euphemistically: "The Petitions Bureau is for those with patience and a tender heart . . . who wish to help the people resolve their problems, even though most of their problems cannot be resolved by you."[43] Such was life at the Lakeville EPB in 2013.

Citizen complaints are taken seriously because they exert a tangible impact on the agency's public image and the bureaucrats' career security. Although civil servants are ultimately disciplined by internal rules, public opinion often plays a decisive—and sometimes capricious—role in their fate. It was not uncommon for social media storms to fall unexpectedly on the EPB. For example, an EPB official in a nearby county was demoted when her lavish housewarming party became public knowledge, and another bureaucrat was disciplined for wearing "flamboyant" jeans to a public event.

Whenever they were out in public, environmental inspectors meticulously maintained their image and were constantly on the lookout for suspicious citizens. If they stopped for lunch between inspections, even at a modest restaurant, they would take off their uniforms before leaving the car. The fear was that citizens would post pictures of them eating out on Weibo, and add vivid embellishment that turned the pictures into evidence of state corruption. A lunch order for four inspectors was restricted to three dishes and a soup; a larger meal would look bad if a picture of it were to appear on social media. As a bureaucrat confided to me, "Public opinion is irrational" (*minyi shi bu lixing de*). Irrational or not, the power of public scrutiny was keenly felt.

Weak bureaucracies like the EPB were usually saddled with blame in public opinion crises. It's historically common for Chinese citizens to contact lower-level bureaucratic offices when grievances first arise, then take them up the political hierarchy if they remain unresolved. Today, using the official petitioning system is not necessarily the most effective option. Social media draws attention far more quickly. A post on Weibo can immediately reach both higher-ups (by simply tagging them) and the masses. It's not rare for posts that strike a nerve with the public to gather millions of views nationwide. I will offer some examples in the next two chapters.

To avoid fallout from upper-level authorities who wield de jure power to discipline and fire their subordinates, lower-level bureaucrats try to neutralize public grievances before they escalate. It's important to emphasize that the de jure power of dismissal by upper-level authorities would be exercised much less often if citizens didn't have de facto influence over the state. Superiors may wield the sword, but it's often citizen scrutiny that generates the guilty verdict.

This kind of accountability—punishment of state officials for defying public opinion—is different from electoral accountability in democracies, at least in principle. First, it is less formalized: it does not happen at a regular time and in a fixed manner that follows legal procedures. Second, it does not just affect politicians who seek elected office, while leaving the "independent civil service" alone. Instead, both senior officials and street-level bureaucrats are vulnerable to public scrutiny in China.

Performative Governance in Action

Out of concern for its public image, which is tangibly tied to the bureaucrats' career security, the Lakeville EPB was highly sensitive to public opinion. Despite the agency's multiple formal functions, bureaucrats spent most working hours—about 75 percent, during the five months of my participant observation—addressing citizen complaints. When complaints intensified, the EPB's apparent Weberianness would disintegrate: planned operations were cast aside, the division of labor broke down, and the agency would divert most of its resources and manpower to the single task of responding to the avalanche of citizen complaints.

This level of sensitivity to public opinion had not always been evident. For instance, a deputy director's schedule in the first week of 2005 included seven tasks for ten half-days: six meetings with the municipal government and one livestock farm inspection. Three half-days were left blank and marked as "flexible." By 2013, "flexible" half-days were unheard of: the number of meetings had remained the same but the number of field trips had increased. In the first week of that year, the schedule for the same deputy director position included five field trips to "investigate and research" (*diaoyan*) local environmental complaints. This urgency to appease restive citizens, however, takes the EPB back to its original problem—a lack of capacity to actually solve most citizen complaints.

Given the double trouble of low capacity and high scrutiny, bureaucrats engaged in performative governance—the symbolic display of good governance for their public audience. The performative governance I refer to is quite different from so-called "performance projects" (*zhengji gongcheng*): those grandiose and extravagant infrastructural endeavors, such as airports, bridges, parks, and city lighting, that local officials use to call attention to their developmental accomplishments. Performance projects, especially in underdeveloped regions, have drawn a fair amount of central government criticism for being wasteful and useless. The following excerpt comes from a 2019 central government decree entitled "Notice on Rectifying the Excessiveness of 'Performance Projects' or 'Face Projects' such as 'Landscape Lighting Projects'": "[Some] local leaders refuse to proceed from their local realities, and to develop the local economy and people's livelihood with both feet on the ground. Instead, they are keen on superficial work and airbrushing reality. They engage in relentless borrowing to prop up their face, and hope to change the appearance of backwardness overnight with artificial prosperity."[44]

The performative governance I observe is a far cry from these white elephants. Instead of grandiosity and pomposity, it focuses on "the little things": attitudes, gestures, intentions. One day, a bureaucrat called this "face work" when reflecting on the inspections they conducted. Readers might recognize that "face work" was also Goffman's term to describe impression management in interpersonal behavior; it just happened to be the bureaucrat's own expression for performative governance.[45]

As my introductory chapter explained, the repertoire of performative governance lies in the notion of "service-oriented governance." This type of governance is directed toward providing citizens with a satisfying "user experience" when they interact with government agencies. Here I focus on three key attributes of performative governance: first, appearing *responsive* to public opinion; second, demonstrating the *benevolence* of the state's intentions; and third, making these efforts *visible* to the public.

Symbolic Responsiveness

In the last two decades, the notion of "responsive government" (*huiyingxing zhengfu*) has gained traction in Chinese public administration. This development is noteworthy. Government responsiveness to citizen preferences is the very essence of democracy—according to Robert Dahl, it is what defines democracy.[46] The prominent Chinese academic and policy advisor Yu Keping explains responsiveness this way: "Public administrative organizations must respond to citizens' demands in a timely and responsible fashion. . . . [They] must regularly and proactively consult citizens' opinions, explain policies, and answer questions."[47] Responsiveness is conceived as an important aspect of good governance and a core aspiration of the CCP's political reforms.[48] These institutional reforms have been picked up by academic research, giving rise to a sizable literature on "authoritarian responsiveness," predicated on the important insight that officials in authoritarian regimes are not deaf to citizen demands.[49] Some scholars believe that institutions of responsiveness are a key ingredient in the resilience of authoritarian regimes.[50]

To be sure, substantive responsiveness—the conformity of public policy outcomes to societal preferences—is far from absent in China. Reform-era politics is rife with policy changes driven by bottom-up pressures, such as the abolishment of agricultural taxes and fees in 2006 after mounting peasant protests,[51] and the legalization of private businesses after their widespread de facto emergence within society.[52] Even in the domain of environmental protection, substantive responsiveness is sometimes evident. Recent studies have found nationwide declines in major air and water pollutants since Premier Li Keqiang's declaration of a "War on Pollution" in 2014.[53]

Substantive responsiveness is not limited to high-level policymaking; it can also be found in quotidian governance. The following text box shows an example of a Lakeville citizen's complaint about bus fares in 2018, which brought a response from the DRC that included substantial changes in bus ticket pricing, as well as minor policy changes that benefit the citizenry at large.

"Complaint about Lakeville Development and Reform Commission's Lack of Supervision of Bus Fares"

Complaint Excerpt

To whom it may concern: I write to complain about the DRC's lack of supervision of the municipal bus company. After Line X switched its route on April 8, the length of the new route became 4 kilometers shorter than the original. However, the bus fare is the same as before. This is a violation of the Regulation on Pricing Standards of Public Buses. In addition, Line X has overcharged for years, even before the route switch. It can be seen that your respected commission has shown serious negligence in the implementation of your relevant regulatory functions. . . . I sincerely hope your respected commission will seriously and diligently deal with this issue concerning people's livelihood, effectively perform your relevant functions, and protect the legitimate rights and interests of citizens.

Response Excerpt

Based on the situation reported by the complainant, our commission immediately contacted the municipal bus company and verified the bus fare for Line X, and found the complainant's reported situation to be accurate. First, we immediately asked the municipal bus company to reform and rectify [*zhenggai*], and in the same afternoon to adjust its bus fares according to the lengths of the routes. Second, we urged the municipal bus company to speedily apply for an adjustment of bus fares, including Line X. The application was received on April 14 and approved. Third, we have asked the municipal bus company to provide a complete list of bus lines, including fares and lengths of each route. Our next step is to fully investigate the list. Fourth, to avoid similar situations from occurring in the future, we will establish a long-term mechanism requesting that the municipal bus company regularly submit an updated list of routes and fares, and we will regularly inspect the pricing of bus fares.

But not all responsiveness is substantive. The essence of substantive responsiveness is the resolution of, and not just attention to, citizens' problems. By contrast, symbolic responsiveness differs in its lack of actual—or even attempted—resolution of the underlying problem. The needs satisfied by symbolic responsiveness are not the same as the bread-and-butter kind met by substantive policy changes, as in the bus fare example above. Symbolic responsiveness aims to give citizens the perception that their voices are being heard, and to give them a sense of empowerment vis-à-vis the state.[54]

The Lakeville EPB's petition office is open seven days a week, including holidays. An internal rule held that every citizen complaint should be answered within two to three weeks; in practice, most were answered within three days. EPBs in some districts affected by environmental problems proactively collected citizen complaints by holding regular "open hearings" (*tingzheng hui*). I attended two of these in Lakeville and one in Shenzhen, during which citizens, business representatives, and EPB bureaucrats sat around a table to discuss local pollution problems and potential solutions. Usually, the citizens would vehemently air their grievances, the business representatives would state that their emissions were safe and met regulatory standards, and the EPB bureaucrats would play what they called a "mediating" role.

Three times during my time at the Lakeville EPB, citizen complaints spiked to critical levels that utterly derailed the agency's regular functions. At these moments, bureaucrats in nonenforcement offices, such as the Propaganda and Education Division and the Planning and Finances Division, would be called in to participate in various "law enforcement operations" (*zhifa xingdong*) with environmental inspectors. But most of those speedy responses did not promise any policy changes, issue any fines, or close any polluting enterprises.

My interviews with EPB bureaucrats in other parts of China uncovered similar sensitivity to public opinion. "In the middle of my siesta one day, I was awakened by a continuous knocking on my window," a bureaucrat at the Shenzhen EPB reported. "I opened the curtain and jumped to my feet when I saw a citizen right outside the window, ready to lodge a complaint."[55] The bureaucrat joked that the knocking had caused her a "near heart attack."[56] In Chengdu, an EPB bureaucrat answered my question about citizen complaints by eagerly enlightening me about the "folk ferocity" (*minfeng biaohan*) of the Sichuan people.[57]

Symbolic responsiveness is not unique to Lakeville. Based on data collected by Tianguang Meng at Qinghua University, of all the formal environmental petitions received by China's municipal governments in 2013, only 29 percent led to any government response whatsoever; and of all those responses delivered, 87 percent were merely symbolic.[58]

Benevolence

It is not enough just to respond. A second element of performative governance is demonstrating benevolent intentions to citizens. Indeed, the Chinese translation of "good governance" is "benevolent governance" (*shanzheng* or *shanzhi*): *shan* is not only an objective evaluation but also a normative construct. This means that the moral intentions of political authorities matter as much as policy outcomes in defining good governance.

EPB bureaucrats pulled out all the stops to demonstrate just how benevolent and service-oriented they were. Typical acts of benevolence include gestures of care and submission to the people. When petitioners arrived at the agency with their complaints, they were offered a cup of warm tea and a comfortable couch to rest on. In fact, the EPB's only leather couch sat in its petition office, which is one of the EPB's biggest and brightest rooms, decorated with potted palms. In contrast, office space for cadres was downsized in recent years.

The size and style of government buildings are considered an important representation of the state's image. They used to be regulated by the 1999 "Construction Standard for Office Space of Party and State Organizations" (Dangzheng jiguan bangong yongfang jianshe biaozhun). Even though the 1999 standard called for "strict thrift," it was only loosely enforced.[59] One well-known example of architectural extravagance was in Wangjiang County—a poverty-stricken county in Hunan—where in 2010 the government erected office buildings that were eight times the size of the US White House, causing much public outcry. In the early 2000s, a district government in Anhui literally modeled their government building after the White House; the party secretary who built the "Fuyang White House" on expropriated land was eventually sentenced to death on corruption charges.

While government buildings and offices once embodied symbols of luxury, they are now being replaced with symbols of humility. The "Construction Standard" was revised in 2014 during the anticorruption campaign.[60] The new standard restricts the size of government offices and requires their design to be "solemn, simple, economic, and resource-conserving," while prohibiting "luxury," such as "sunrooms, indoor gardens, scenic corridors, stage lighting and sound equipment, bronze gates, and luxurious revolving doors," among other accoutrements.[61] While the main government building (*zhengfu dalou*) used to be every city's architectural icon, it is now outshone by the flashier citizen centers (*shimin zhongxin*).

As part of their training, bureaucrats learned the proper manners of public relations management. When fielding calls from citizens, for example, they should never be the first to hang up, regardless of the call's content or the caller's tone. Occasionally, a caller's grievance would turn out to be irrelevant to environmental pollution. When a citizen called one evening to complain about the "air pollution" caused by his neighbor's pungent cooking, he was given free rein to vent all his longstanding grudges against said neighbor. Another time, an angry citizen called to complain about environmental problems in his neighborhood, but the conversation was soon sidelined by his weepy confession that his wife had just left him—and the bureaucrat handling the call promptly turned into a therapist. These stories became raw material for gossip on the back stage as bureaucrats bemoaned the impossible responsibility they had to bear for local pollution under withering public scrutiny.

One time, a bureaucrat who usually worked as an inspector, but had been "borrowed" by the petition office to help manage escalating complaints, told his co-workers that while answering calls the previous night he was yelled at by a citizen for forty minutes straight. When I asked why he had not just cut the conversation short, he answered with a question of his own: "Do I let him curse at me or do I want to lose my rice bowl?" (*Burang ta ma wo, wo de fanwan hai yaobuyao le?*).[62]

Visibility

Just as important as symbolic responsiveness and benevolence were efforts to make sure performative governance goes public—so that it's visible on the front stage of public communication. Each online complaint was immediately published and quickly answered, with details of the investigation. The EPB website also publishes photo-illustrated stories of its inspections. While the stories are mostly accurate, they are sometimes embellished or dramatized to move the audience: inspectors braving the snow to collect water samples from a river; working all night for several consecutive nights to catch polluters; tirelessly pursuing polluters and sternly admonishing them; and outsmarting evasive polluters during inspections (even if the enterprise eventually went unpunished).

Every year the municipal government holds multiple televised town hall events. Directors of functional bureaucracies give presentations on stage, followed by Q&As with citizen representatives. During one town hall, a citizen showed pictures of polluted rivers in the city and asked the directors if they were ashamed to see them: "Do your faces turn red or not?" Another citizen joked about inviting calligraphers to try using the black water from local rivers as ink, which brought a round of audience applause. A third citizen handed each director a cup of dark-colored water from a local river, and demanded that the directors examine the malodorous fruits of their lackluster performance. Although local pollution was mostly beyond the EPB's control, the director nonetheless observed the water sample carefully, took a deep sniff, and sincerely apologized for their insufficient efforts. Local newspapers covered these exchanges the next day, describing citizen feedback as "hot and spicy" (*huola*).

But visibility isn't always desired. The agency has a love-hate relationship with the media (to be detailed in the next chapter). On the one hand, the more local environmental problems appear in the news, the more citizen complaints flood the agency, and the more hours must be worked to address them. On the other hand, the agency needs the news media to publicize their efforts, even when they cannot resolve the problem. As a weak bureaucracy struggling to fulfill its mandates, the EPB's preference was to lay low and stay out of the media spotlight. But when public opinion crises loom, as they often did, positive representation of the agency's efforts in the news can help it weather the storm. Public records of performative governance also provide a potential force field when cascades of blame start showering from above.

A similar love-hate dynamic could be seen in the agency's relationship with civil society organizations, many of which are staffed by former journalists.[63] On the one hand, the environmental bureaucracy at both central and local levels has historically worked closely with environmental NGOs on issues ranging from policy advocacy to public education about environmentalism.[64] The MEP enjoyed a reputation for friendliness toward domestic activists and international actors (including foreign government agencies like the USEPA and the State of California). Forging alliances with societal actors helped advance the agency's influence.[65] Ironically, such camaraderie worked better in the 1990s and 2000s, when environmental problems were less salient. In recent years the relationship has been complicated by the rising political sensitivity of environmental issues and the regime's decreased tolerance toward social movements. As a result, the EPB has distanced itself from NGOs and activists.[66]

Foul Air Law Enforcement Operation

Nothing captures the dynamics of performative governance better than the Foul Air Law Enforcement Operation. In October 2013, the Lakeville EPB noticed a spike in citizen complaints about air pollution. There was also an increase in "repeated petitions" (*chongfu xinfang*), which the EPB treated with extra caution. Many of the complaints came from residential areas in the vicinity of an industrial development zone—District S.

District S was one of the nation's earliest Economic and Technological Development Zones (ETDZ). Similar to the better-known Special Economic Zones, which jumpstarted China's urban economic reforms in the late 1970s and early 1980s, ETDZs—many concentrated in the Yangtze Delta—had preferential policies such as lower tax rates that attracted international and domestic capital investment. Between 2008 and 2013, industrial output in District S grew by an average of 30 percent per year. This growth rate has since slowed, but it still hovers over 8 percent. In 2013, District S produced about 15 percent of Lakeville's total industrial output.

Most enterprises in the district were manufacturing plants, primarily concentrated in the machinery, food, and medical industries. Some were multinational firms that put familiar products on store shelves around the world—snacks, spices, perfumes, glassware, tires, phone parts. These firms contributed substantial revenue to the local government, but also caused enormous air pollution that troubled local residents.

The problem was exacerbated by the highly mixed use of land. In the 2000s, cheaper land prices in District S attracted real estate developers who built two dozen residential compounds around the development zone, occupying about a quarter of the district's land. A dozen colleges and universities opened campuses there as well. By 2013, about half a million Lakeville citizens lived in District S. Not surprisingly, the proximity of industrial enterprises to residential areas turned District S into a hotbed of environmental complaints.

That October, a heavy smog descended on Lakeville, caused by a combination of factors: coal burning in north China that travels southward, car emissions, local industrial activities, and meteorological conditions. Middle-class citizens would eventually come to don N95 masks on days like this, but in 2013 masks were sparingly spotted, even as complaints about pollution were rising. In the mornings I would see pictures on social media of Lakeville's cityscape obscured by a thick film of grey smog. It wasn't just Lakeville: friends in Beijing and Shanghai had similar complaints. Though air pollution may seem localized, often it is not.

There are complaints we share with friends and family in small talk, and then there are *complaints* that we take the time and effort to compose and send to our government. The second type, which arrived at the Lakeville EPB in October 2013, came mostly from residents around industrial zones like District S. These citizens were perennially bothered by industrial waste air, but their mood was made much worse by the onset of heavy smog. The complaints were candid. In one fierce online petition (*wangshang xinfang*), a District S resident fumed: "Has everyone at the EPB dropped dead [*huangbaoju de ren si guang le*]? Why is no one taking care of this strong rubber smell [*xiangjiao wei zheme nong meiren guan*]? Taxpayers are raising a bunch of lazy animals [*nashuiren yangle nimen zhequn buzuowei de chusheng*]. Are you in bed with the businesses you regulate [*nimen shibushi guanshanggoujie langbeiweijian*]?"

Another petitioner opened a five-hundred-word complaint with quotes from Xi Jinping's speeches and writings: "The General Party Secretary said that clear water and green mountains are as valuable as mountains of gold and silver." After detailing their neighborhood's waste air problems and referencing an exhaustive list of government regulations and academic research, the citizen ended with a stern warning: "[I] hope the government will respond to public outcry in order to preserve its public trust [*gongxinli*]."

Other common phrases in these complaints include the following:

"Smelly air stinks up the heavens" (*chouqi xuntian*).
"Smelly air disturbs the residents" (*chouqi raomin*).
"Odor stings the nose" (*qiwei cibi*).
"[I] dare not keep the windows open" (*bugan kaichuang*).
"[Company name] stealthily discharges waste air" (*toupai feiqi*).
"[Air pollution] affects residents' physical and psychological health" (*yingxiang jumin shenxin jiankang*).
"The EPB does nothing" (*huanbaoju buzuowei*).
"EPB supervision is lacking" (*huanbaoju jianguan buli*).
"Return the residents' rights to breathe fresh air" (*huan jumin huxi xinxiankongqi de quanli*).

Two things are clear in these complaints. First, citizens are upset about air pollution and are not holding back in expressing their discontent to the state. "Preference falsification" is absent, and "rights consciousness" is abundant.[67] Second, citizens hold the environmental bureaucracy responsible for taking care of the problem.

The EPB is quite trepidatious about citizen petitions, especially when many citizens complain at once. Scholars have found that such events with "collective action potential" are more likely to invite government censorship than are individual criticisms.[68] But large-scale complaints are also more likely to trigger a positive government response—be they symbolic or substantive. The state often simultaneously represses protests (such as with censorship and arrests) and redresses the underlying problems (such as with compensations and policy changes).[69]

In our case, the Lakeville EPB could neither make arrests nor close factories. But it wasn't entirely at the end of its rope. After a few agency meetings to discuss citizen complaints, the EPB launched a "law enforcement operation" that involved intensive inspections targeting specific areas and industries. In one meeting, bureaucrats discussed whether the operation should be called the Waste Air (*feiqi*) Law Enforcement Operation, the Air Pollution (*daqi wuran*) Law Enforcement Operation, or the Foul Air (*chouqi*) Law Enforcement

Operation. "Foul Air" was eventually chosen, and the operation's objective would be to address complaints related to the *smell* of the air. The logic was that the terms "waste air" or "air pollution" might call attention to the agency's inability to solve the underlying problem. (In the end, even the foulness of the air remained unresolved.)

The entire operation lasted four weeks and consisted of three stages: investigation, inspection, and analysis and response. First, bureaucrats compiled a data set of some two hundred citizen complaints, either received directly by the agency or redirected from other agencies. They pinned the geographic origin of every complaint on a map, identified three problem areas where the complaints were heavily clustered, including District S and two other locations, and decided to target the operation in these areas. They also compiled a list of the thirty firms most often mentioned in citizen complaints, including rubber factories, plastic factories, printing and dyeing factories, food producers, wastewater treatment plants, fertilizer plants, and livestock farms.

Inspectors then spent three days in District S and other targeted areas to verify the complaints, driving around in a white SUV emblazoned with blue characters that read "environmental inspection" (*huanjing jiancha*). They called this investigative process "touching base" (*modi*). Their SUV traveled down the main streets of District S with the windows rolled down, and the inspectors in the passenger seats would poke their heads out and sniff scrupulously for noticeable signs of foul air, taking notes of where the odors were strongest. Even from the street, the industrial smells in District S were abhorrent.

Bureaucrats also reached out to some petitioners asking for details about their complaints, such as which hour of the day the odor was strongest, which day of the week was the worst, and which side of the factory the odor came from. By the end of the week, the agency had devised a plan of action.

The second stage of the operation lasted two weeks and consisted of daily surprise visits to two or three enterprises on the EPB's list of suspected polluters. Upon arrival, inspectors would ask a representative of the firm, either the owner or a manager, to be an eyewitness to the inspection (at least two inspectors must also be present for the inspection to have legal effect). The look of genuine surprise on the faces of the factory guards as the inspectors approached the gate was all it took to know that these enterprises weren't notified of the inspections in advance. The bureaucrats did tell me that some county EPBs in the same province had "informants" (*xianren*) who tipped off enterprises about upcoming inspections—some informants even owned stocks in local businesses—but I never saw this at the Lakeville EPB.

A guard would usually try to stall the inspectors at the gate while calling his boss on the phone, or one guard would try to stall the inspectors while another ran inside to alert their boss of the inspectors' arrival. After a few minutes, a manager would walk out to greet the inspectors. Sometimes the manager would invite the inspectors to their office to rest and have tea, another stalling tactic to give the factory time to turn on any pollution treatment facilities that weren't operating that day. Of course, seasoned inspectors knew exactly what was going on. Politely turning down the invitation, they would proceed with their inspection.

The first step of the inspection is to check the enterprise's Pollution Permit, its latest Environmental Impact Assessment Report, and the status of its pollution abatement facilities—whether they were up-to-date and running when the inspectors arrived. At the time of my research, Lakeville was rolling out a plan to "online monitor" (*zaixian jiankong*) enterprise emissions, but few enterprises had installed online monitoring systems, and those that had done so could easily manipulate their data at the source points before the data was transmitted to the EPB. The EPB still collected all their emissions data the traditional way, through physical inspections. But even the few minutes between the inspectors' arrival at the factory gate and their entry into the production facility could give the enterprise a chance to quickly prepare for the inspection. Hence inspectors insisted on seeing the pollution treatment facilities immediately upon arrival.

Next, inspectors would select three "monitoring spots" (*jiancedian*) for collecting air samples. These spots were carefully chosen based on regulatory requirements: they must be close to the production facility and at the edge of the factory property. Inspectors marked the locations on a factory map and then used an automatic air sampler, which weighed less than five pounds, to put three samples from each monitoring spot into reusable Australian-made airbags. It was my job to help hold the airbags and carry the air sampler during these inspections.

Every inspection was meticulously recorded with photographic, video, and written evidence. Inspectors took pictures of the factory interiors, the pollution abatement facilities, the factory representatives who accompanied the inspections, the inspectors going about their work, and any evidence of regulatory violations. They also took pictures at the exact moment when every air sample was collected to show the location of the monitoring spot, the identities of the two or more inspectors present, and the presence of factory representatives.

These pictures serve two purposes. First, should the enterprise challenge the findings—for example, claiming that nobody watched the inspectors collect their samples, making the samples invalid—the EPB had a record of the entire inspection. But since most enterprises went unpunished, the burden of demonstrating procedural fairness was rarely a problem. The main purpose of these pictures was to be posted on the EPB's website or included in their work reports to showcase their investigatory efforts.

At the end of each visit, inspectors wrote up a detailed report on paper and entered it into the EPB's Law Enforcement iPad using a special application designed for EPB use. (These iPads are state property and can only be used for inspections.) The inspectors then asked enterprise representatives to read and verify the entire inspection record, and to sign it and fingerprint it if they agreed with it. Inspection records entered into the application were synced with the EPB's central database, which can be accessed from other EPB devices.

Most representatives cooperated with the inspectors patiently and politely, but not all. The cunning owner of one fertilizer plant insisted that he was illiterate and wouldn't sign the inspection report because he couldn't make out what the characters meant. An inspector proceeded to read the entire inspection record out loud to him, but the owner still refused to sign, claiming that he couldn't understand what he was hearing. At their wits' end, the inspectors decided to record a video showing the owner's refusal to cooperate. Since the plant owner was reluctant to be filmed, one inspector tried distracting him with idle conversation as another approached from the side to capture the video. Only after they had the owner on camera saying "I won't sign" did they leave the plant.

The entire process of each inspection couldn't seem more "formal rational." Instead of just muddling through—as one might expect, given the agency's inefficacy—inspectors followed administrative laws and regulations with utmost scrupulousness. For example, regulations dictate that half the air samples must be collected from specific locations right outside the factory border. When the factory wall was too high for the inspector to extend the snorkel of the air sampler "right outside the factory border," inspectors would climb a ladder to the top of the wall so they could do so.

Had I simply watched the inspections, I might have concluded that the EPB is an exemplary Weberian bureaucracy that enjoyed high capacity. I admit this was my initial impression. Only after I made further observations from the agency's back stage and eventually learned the outcomes of the inspections was I forced to reconsider.

A few days into the operation, inspectors encountered a peculiar event: at all the enterprises they visited, the pollution abatement facilities were operating perfectly upon their arrival. Inspectors noticed this anomaly immediately, since most of the enterprises visited on previous days had reported some kind of problem with their pollution treatment facility—for example, it had unaccountably broken down the day before the inspection and was awaiting repair. But on that day, all the factories were practicing perfect "corporate social responsibility."

This responsible practice turned out to be illusory. Conversations with locals revealed that word of the inspections had spread among polluters, who had changed most of their production to take place under cover of night, between midnight and 6:00 a.m., when residents and EPB bureaucrats were believed to be asleep. "You have to go there after midnight and smell for yourself," a citizen suggested.

That advice was promptly followed. Surreptitious and sleep-deprived "night inspections" (*yecha*) were added to the operation, launching at 2:00 or 3:00 a.m. Bureaucrats alternated the night shift so that the grueling duty wouldn't fall on the same two or three individuals; section heads worked more nights than their subordinates. I was allowed on only one night inspection and was adamantly dissuaded from joining more for my own good.

During these nighttime inspections, even experienced inspectors were appalled by the foul air in District S. After staying in a fertilizer plant for an hour one night, their uniforms and SUV were tainted by a rank odor of livestock manure that lingered for an entire week, even after repeated cleaning. Just as the odor was fading, a visit to a livestock farm brought it back, stronger and more rancid. The odor on the inspectors' clothes also wafted into the EPB's offices, inviting chatter and laughter for days; every morning someone would ask, "Can you still smell it on me?" One said that his wife told him to sleep in the office; another joked that there had to be a foul air law enforcement operation on the bureaucrats themselves because their own bodies had become a walking "source point" (*wuranyuan*).

Daytime inspections weren't much easier on the nose—or on the brain. One brutal tour of several chemical and plastic plants left me without any memory of the morning for a few hours afterward. Bureaucrats told me it was a normal effect of inhaling the chemical substances. At several points during the Foul Air Operation, as I held my breath while following the inspectors around a factory, my mind would wander: I regretted my choice of dissertation topic and pondered how many years of my life I'd sacrificed for this scholarly endeavor. These thoughts were probably irrational, but at the time there were no words to describe the varieties of industrial odor other than that they were simply unbearable. Eventually I learned to favor the organic stench of livestock farms over the chemical malodor of plastic factories and the smoky fetor of rubber plants, deciding that my brain was more important to me than my nose.

One day, as inspectors drove from one enterprise to another, they speculated on the health impact of industrial waste air. They believed that everyone working at these factories, from owners to workers, would have shortened lives. They also said that pregnant female inspectors had a higher-than-normal rate of miscarriage from breathing industrial waste air; thus, pregnant bureaucrats were relieved of inspection duties to protect both mother and child. At the time, inspectors didn't wear facial masks during inspections—in retrospect, perhaps they should have.

During the inspections I saw a genuine ethos of hard work. I never interrupted to ask the inspectors for their assessment of the enterprise's environmental practices, nor did I venture my own—my method was observation, not engagement, and I was careful not to introduce observer effect. But as the operation unfolded, I became convinced that most inspected factories would have to be found guilty. To me, no technical analysis was needed to determine the egregious violations we encountered; and judging from the inspectors' expressions as they approached the factories, they seemingly would have agreed with me that punishments were richly deserved.

The only factory that seemed to pass the inspectors' own smell test was a Japanese-funded rubber plant. A Chinese manager in a green uniform, who appeared very knowledgeable about environmental regulations, gave us a tour. He showed off the plant's newly installed pollution treatment facility, which turns on automatically as production starts, thus preventing the enterprise from slipping through the loopholes of regulatory enforcement, as he put it. When the inspectors told the manager about citizen complaints of foul air, he explained that they had to keep the factory windows open to protect their workers' health, and waste air might be escaping through the windows. As the inspectors returned to their car, one commented, "The Japanese are politically suspect, but they do well on environmental protection."

After each inspection, air samples were delivered to the Environmental Monitoring Station (an EPB subsidiary); there, they would be diluted to one-twentieth of their original concentration. Then six certified "smell testers" (*xiubianyuan*) would perform a "human sensory analysis" on the samples (that is, sniff them) and vote on whether environmental regulations had been violated.[70] According to the Emission Standards for Odorous Pollutants (GB 14554-93, Echou wuranwu paifang biaozhun), industrial waste air should not have odors that cause "unpleasant senses" (*buyukuai ganjue*) to the human body.[71] A related regulation (GB/T14675-93) explains the scientific basis and procedures of the human sensory analysis, which is also practiced in other parts of the world.[72]

The actual chemical substances in the air samples were not tested, despite the availability of chemosensoring technologies.[73] In other words, it didn't matter if the waste air was harmful but odorless; nor did it matter if the waste air was smelly but harmless. Despite the agency's formal mandate to assess and mitigate pollution, its investigation was limited to the stench of waste air that triggered citizen complaints. The goal of the operation was to placate the residents and prevent further complaints, not to solve the underlying problem of harmful air quality—because they lacked the authority to do so.

Mercifully my time with the Foul Air Operation came to an end. Having endured the backbreaking labor of inspections, climbed smokestacks, descended into sewage ditches, and having both lost my memory (briefly) and ruined my favorite sweatshirt (permanently), I felt a little like a soldier at the end of the Long March—ready to see the enterprises punished and the people saved. But that triumph never came. The Environmental Monitoring Station eventually concluded that only four enterprises had violated the Emission Standards for Odor Pollutants: two rubber factories, a food manufacturer, and a fertilizer plant. This was a surprisingly small number given the widespread environmental violations we had seen during the inspections. Ironically, the Japanese rubber plant that had impressed the inspectors with its environmental practices made it onto the list of four.

Even though I had intentionally refrained from commenting on the EPB's work throughout my time there, I couldn't hide my surprise upon hearing the results of the analysis. "Only four? Not possible!" I blurted out. Having been there myself, I thought it had to be more than four. "That is just the result of the analysis," an inspector responded with a calmness that perplexed me, given how diligently I'd seen him work during these inspections. Perhaps he was hiding his disappointment, but he surely didn't seem surprised by the outcome. (Although I tried to secure as many vantage points as possible from within the agency, I wasn't able to see the actual air sample analysis or learn how the verdict was reached.)

After the results came out, the EPB summoned the owners or managers of the four enterprises to its office to complete a "written deposition" (*bilu*). There they were interviewed again about their enterprises and pollution control measures. The representatives cooperated in the deposition, except for the owner of the fertilizer plant—the very person who had claimed to be illiterate during the inspection. Upon being told that his plant was found to have broken environmental regulations, he threatened to jump out of the EPB's fourth-floor window. Word of his ploy traveled fast and far in the office, but it didn't generate much concern among the bureaucrats. They were already familiar with his performative tactics: according to the bureaucrats, his father, the late owner of the plant, also had a reputation for *threatening* self-defenestration, without ever bringing himself to do so.

Then it dawned on me: if the disposition of a fertilizer plant's late owner was common knowledge among the bureaucrats, that meant they must have interacted with him repeatedly over the years, along with other polluting enterprises in their jurisdiction. It also suggested that the frequent inspections of businesses and periodic fines might not have had much downstream impact on their behavior. When I did the math for some large enterprises, I realized that the cost of electricity to operate pollution treatment facilities during production can be higher than the fine they'd likely receive for not operating them. The firms' "rational choice," therefore, was to keep paying the periodic fines and to put off purchasing, updating, or operating pollution treatment equipment for as long as possible. I later learned through interviews with manufacturers in Lakeville that some knew they wouldn't be profitable in the long run, given rising labor costs in the Yangtze Delta and their exclusion from the government's list of supported industries. So they might as well "smash the pot that is already cracking" (*po guanzi po shuai*)—recklessly produce and pollute to maximize short-term profit, since closure loomed on the horizon.[74]

After conducting the depositions, the EPB wrote up reports based on the deposition transcripts, combining them with inspection records, photographic and video evidence, and environmental analysis reports to establish administrative cases against the four enterprises. The Laws and Regulations Division calculated fines based on the extent of their violation: between 20,000 and 50,000 yuan (about US$3,137 to US$7,844 in 2013). Though these fines were modest—the firms' annual industrial output could exceed US$1 billion—they were among the largest the EPB had ever meted out to enterprises in the city.

Last, the Petitions Office issued formal responses to every citizen complaint. The responses underscored the EPB's serious concern about the complaint and the efforts made to address it. Each response contained a detailed list of the measures taken to investigate the complaint, such as the timing and length of inspections, names of the firms investigated, details from the inspections, whether regulatory violations were discovered (usually a no), and other efforts made by the local government to tackle pollution problems. They also included language expressing the EPB's heartfelt dedication to resolving pollution problems for citizens and promised a list of concrete improvements in the future. Each response ended by thanking the petitioner for their "support for the work of environmental governance." The following text box shows the EPB response to a citizen complaint mentioned earlier.[75]

Citizen Complaint and EPB Response

Citizen Complaint

Has everyone at the EPB dropped dead? Why is no one taking care of this strong rubber smell? Taxpayers are raising a bunch of lazy animals. Are you in bed with the businesses you regulate?

State Response

Greetings! Your petition was received. Our Bureau's historical tracing of pollution sources in the district and our inspectors' investigation of citizen complaints found that the pungent odor affecting [District S] originates from the I. Spices Company and the C. Tires Company. [Our Bureau] treats industrial air pollution as a very serious issue and is actively enforcing air pollution regulations. . . . Air pollution enforcement emphasizes resolving issues with human senses. As a result, I. Spices and C. Tires have been included as key-point enterprises in the "Three Year Plan for Air Pollution Control." . . . In addition to expediting air quality enforcement, [we] will increase the frequency of on-site inspections. We will seriously punish enterprises whose waste air violates regulations and those that do not operate waste air treatment facilities regularly. Thank you for your concern and support for our environmental governance!

A reader skeptical of my theory might claim that what I have just described was not performative governance, but substantive governance. Since citizens mentioned odors in their complaints, perhaps they only wanted the odor problem resolved, and cared less about the substance of industrial waste air. The EPB, by this interpretation, sincerely wanted to resolve people's odor complaints and launched an appropriate operation—substantive responsiveness. But citizens' referencing strong odor as evidence of air pollution should not suggest that the odor was all they cared about, unless we believe Chinese citizens had no concerns for their health. Even if citizen complaints had been purely about odorous air, the EPB's efforts still proved futile, given the minimal punishment imposed on the polluters. All four enterprises fined would be found guilty again of environmental violations in the years to come.

A few months after the Foul Air Law Enforcement Operation, the city of Lakeville was ensnared in another environmental crisis, this time about strange tastes in the tap water. Complaints and speculations circulated widely on WeChat and Weibo, until almost every resident could taste strangeness flowing from their faucets. (Bureaucrats believed that many of the complaints were psychosomatic.) The controversy was immediately picked up by local media, and the EPB's phones rang off the hook, leading to a two-month law enforcement operation that resulted in the punishment of two factories. The strange taste returned five months later and triggered yet another law enforcement operation.

After Foul Air

My description of the Lakeville EPB's performative governance is naturally limited to the time period when the study was conducted. The previous two chapters showed that as pollution control gained priority on the government's agenda, and as the environmental bureaucracy's capacity improved over time—especially since the 2018 administrative reform—EPB enforcements have become more substantive. The Lakeville EPB now has the authority to issue fines twice as large as those they issued in 2013, and they are occasionally authorized to shut down factories. The city's industrial upgrading unfolds slowly but steadily, with many polluting firms relocating to inland provinces. What this means for the nation as a whole is an entirely different story, but at least in Lakeville, industrial upgrading is surely making the air cleaner.

While my theory projects that EPB governance will move in a substantive direction given its rising capacity, I'm not suggesting that substantive governance has already been achieved. In my recent interviews with bureaucrats, business owners, academic experts, and NGOs, the common description of the EPB has shifted from "the EPB is a weak bureaucracy," as mentioned earlier, to "the EPB is *now* a strong bureaucracy" (*huanbao xianzai shi qiangshi bumen*).[76] But this new phrase is often uttered with a knowing smirk and a hint of sarcasm—like how someone might refer to a little nephew who's just grown into a gangly teen—suggesting that the speakers acknowledge the EPB's rising status but still ultimately dismiss it as a weak bureaucracy whose strength cannot yet compare to that of its bureaucratic competitors or corporate targets.

When I revisit Lakeville's petition website today, years after completing my fieldwork there, I still see complaints and responses similar to those posted in 2013. One of the two rubber plants found guilty in the Foul Air Operation remains a hot source of citizen complaints. The following text box shows a complaint from 2019 and the EPB's reply.[77] The reply detailed the inspections, analyses, and findings, but concluded that there was no violation of environmental regulations by the rubber plant, despite the petitioner's repeated complaints. And though the reply indicated the factory's plan to relocate, other citizens complaining about the same factory suspected this promised relocation was no more than cheap talk.

"Severe Pollution in District S Caused by a Lack of Supervision by the Environmental Bureaucracy"

Complaint Excerpt

I live near [Enterprise N], and I can smell pungent odors in the air almost every day. Am I going to get cancer from breathing this air all the time? I hope you will seriously investigate polluting enterprises, and tax their pollution to improve air quality! I hope the mayor and governor can pay unannounced visits to our district and experience the bitterness of smelling rubber every day! Return the residents' rights to breathe clean air!

Response Excerpt

Greetings! . . . Even though enterprises' waste air emissions meet regulatory standards, that doesn't mean zero emissions. In poor weather conditions, especially at night, when pollutants cannot effectively diffuse, it is true that strange odors can be detected. Our on-site inspection of waste air treatment facilities and online monitoring data found no abnormalities. Analysis of air samples from the enterprise shows that odor concentration at the factory border was below 10, and the maximum concentration of nonmethane hydrocarbons was 2.6 mg/m. Test results conform to emission standards. In the wake of central and provincial government inspections, we will actively promote capacity relocation of [Name of a different enterprise]. . . . We will work with the electric power department to conduct real-time monitoring of electricity consumption, and use "smart power" [zhihui dianli] to monitor the operational status of waste air treatment facilities at [Name of a different enterprise]. Next, we will follow up with the relocation of enterprises and urge them to do a better job at collecting and treating industrial waste air.

The following text box shows a 2020 complaint in which the citizen blamed the EPB for its "all talk, no action" approach.[78]

"No Action. No Resolution to the Problem"
Complaint Excerpt

Air quality in [District S] is bad. Do you have children and elderly relatives at home? Are you willing to have your family live in this environment? Air quality was great during the pandemic when the factories were off; the air was sweet. I've made repeated complaints to no avail. A lot of talking on the phone, but what's the point if the problem is not solved? District S blames District B; District B blames District S. Well, it is the municipal EPB's problem. No need to call me to explain. If you've solved the problem, I can tell with my nose.

Response Excerpt

Greetings! . . . District S is situated next to District B. According to meteorological data, the wind blows from the southeast. Our bureau conducted inspections of enterprises northeast of the petitioner's residential area; we did not find enterprises that emit waste air. In recent years, the district has been actively pursuing air pollution control. Key point enterprises are requested to install online monitoring. Companies X, L, and H have either ceased production or relocated. In the future, we will step up enforcement of enterprises that attract petitions and work with district EPBs to ensure the environmental quality of residential areas.

Formal and Substantive Rationality

This is perhaps a good time for us to return to the notion of bureaucratic rationality, which is commonly understood as a bureaucracy's clearly defined and delimited functional mandates, formal-legal procedures designed to maximize outputs, division of labor among educated and trained professionals, and internal accountability buttressed by predictable rules of reward and punishment. By these standards, the Lakeville EPB is highly rational, especially compared to the patrimonial and prebendal images of the Chinese state that constitute conventional wisdom.

But the agency is also "irrational" if it ultimately fails at its primary mandate—to protect and improve the local environment. This tension between the "form" of bureaucracy and the outcome it produces, or *between formal and substantive rationality*, was a central concern in Weber's thinking about modern capitalist and administrative organizations. Though he had much admiration for rational bureaucracy—its efficiency, scale, productivity, and so on—Weber also worried about unintended consequences. Does formalism lead to a decoupling of means and ends? Will bureaucracy harden into an iron cage that entraps its personnel, strip all meaning from their work, and disfigure them into "specialists without spirit, hedonists without heart"?[79]

The Lakeville EPB seems to corroborate Weber's concerns. Inspections turned out to have little impact on the outcome—most enterprises were shielded from punishment because of their contribution to the local economy—and thus the meticulous conduct of the inspections, with its rigid adherence to rules and regulations, may be interpreted as mere formalism, divorced from the intended outcome of reducing emissions.

But the agency's pursuit of *performative governance* was much more than formalism: it went above and beyond the bureaucratic motions in its strenuous efforts to avoid appearing as specialists without spirit and hedonists without heart. In this sense, the Lakeville EPB sought to project an image that departs noticeably from "rationality"—personal rather than impersonal, sensitive rather than calculating, warm rather than cold, modest rather than haughty. This doesn't get the agency all the way to substantive governance, given its lack of authority to improve environmental outcomes. But it may well be "rational" in another sense—if, and only if, we redefine the organization's "end" not as protecting the environment, but as appeasing citizen complaints. (Whether it actually succeeds at making citizens happy is the subject of the next chapter.)

Neither Don Quixote nor Machiavelli

Goffman writes about two types of actors: at one extreme is the "sincere" actor who is so taken in by his own act that he cannot admit to the performative nature of his action; at the other extreme is the "cynical" actor who is aware of the performative nature of his acts and who behaves strategically, either out of pure self-interest or "for the good of the community."[80]

Let's call the sincere actor Don Quixote and the cynical actor Machiavelli.[81] These EPB bureaucrats were not Don Quixotes who had a deluded belief in their heroic self-images when they knowingly tilted at windmills. They carried out performative governance with very little idealism, and with the realistic expectation that many of their efforts would be fruitless, knowing the EPB was not a "bureaucracy with real power."

Nor did the bureaucrats engage in performative governance as some kind of Machiavellian master plan—or "autocratic handbook"—to manipulate the citizenry in order to "stay in power," as political science arguments tend to go.[82] Bureaucracies are, after all, composed of *normal people* with ordinary aspirations and fears, and *most people* are neither Don Quixotes nor Machiavellis. Those who enter a bureaucracy quickly adapt to its organizational culture and practices, with few opportunities or incentives to pause and ask themselves why.

Getting a degree in the environmental sciences or applying for a job in the EPB would seem to indicate that some bureaucrats—if not all—began with some level of interest in environmental protection and some measure of duty to the commons. Yet being deprived of a sense of efficacy in their job seems to have changed the bureaucrats' beliefs. As I interviewed bureaucrats in multiple agencies, I discovered that employees in the environmental protection system (*huanbao xitong*), especially those working on the front line at local EPBs, seemed to be no more worried about environmental pollution than were bureaucrats in other agencies. EPB bureaucrats were always quick to explain why raising incomes and providing employment were just as important as environmental protection, if not more so, in China's current stage of development. One of my interviewees even invoked Hegel's well-known (and much-abused) quote, "What is reasonable is real, and what is real is reasonable" (*cunzai ji heli*), to justify why current efforts were sufficient. On the other hand, bureaucrats in other agencies were more than happy to discuss the importance of environmental protection, not least because they were not actually responsible for carrying it out.

In November and December 2013, as the smog intensified, several inspectors developed symptoms of upper respiratory infection, but they dismissed it as a common cold. When I came down with a cough myself, I was told in all serious-ness that my lungs had been "Westernized" by the years I had spent abroad. Such a belief could be genuine: as Anton Chekhov supposedly wrote in a letter to his brother, "The air of one's native country is the healthiest air." But it couldn't be clearer that the bureaucrats possessed the knowledge and expertise to know that air pollution causes respiratory ailments. Their refusal to make this association was more likely a cognitive correction of the dissonance between their latent desire to improve the environment and their blatant inability to do so. Bureau-crats generally avoided making negative remarks about air pollution in Lakev-ille because they felt responsible—but simultaneously not responsible—for the lack of improvement. This is strikingly consistent with Zacka's finding from the United States that "since bureaucrats do not have the capabilities to live up to the demands of the role, they narrow their understanding of these demands to bring them in line with the capabilities they can marshal in practice."[83]

A sense of inefficacy is perhaps a main source of disillusionment in all kinds of careers. Goffman writes that actor exhaustion and cynicism can catalyze "perfor-mance disruption," where actors "come to experience a special kind of alienation from self and a special kind of wariness of others."[84] Butler calls this "performative breakdown"—when actors simply refuse to play their roles. In this situation, some may choose to "exit."[85] A classic example of performative breakdown caused by actor exhaustion and exit is the princess played by Audrey Hepburn in the film *Roman Holiday.* Fed up with the diplomatic performances she had to keep enact-ing, she escaped from her role to experience life unscripted, if only for a day.

This also seems to be the pattern with the youngest and most ambitious agents at local EPBs, who may seek greener pastures in the private sector or in more powerful bureaucracies. By the time I arrived at the Lakeville EPB, Max was already eager to leave the agency to join a more powerful one. He studied and took (internal) tests twice to be transferred, and finally succeeded three years later. When I met with him after his transfer, he remarked that during his EPB years he felt like a frog at the bottom of a well (*jingdizhiwa*): "My vision was narrow when I worked at the EPB.[86] Now I know that environmental protection is only a small piece of the governance puzzle. There are bigger things for the government to worry about."[87]

Appendix: Case and Methods

What kind of case is Lakeville? Is Lakeville representative of China? Is my single-case study of Lakeville theory-building, theory-testing, or hypothesis-generating? Does it enjoy any external validity? In other words, do lessons from Lakeville travel elsewhere?[88] Or does "the case [I] choose affect the answer [I] get?"[89] These are familiar questions confronted by case studies. This final part of the chapter addresses these questions, beginning with a play-by-play account of my ethnographic data collection and analysis. It then explores the general lessons that might be drawn from Lakeville, while cautioning against the deification of generalization as an analytical holy grail.

Data Collection

My inquiry into environmental governance began with a summer of interviews around China, wherever personal connections took me. At the time, it wasn't hard to obtain interviews with state bureaucrats and officials, but the results weren't terribly fruitful. Whenever I met a new interviewee, much of the time was devoted to getting to know one another, with me entertaining the interviewee's curiosity about my own background and my life in the United States. The following text box shows excerpts from one thirty-minute interview with a deputy director at a municipal EPB. By the time it was over, I hadn't even gotten a chance to ask my third question.

After four months of such (admittedly often enjoyable) conversations, I had gained only a superficial impression of the state, with its inner workings remaining a mystery. Intriguing insights would occasionally emerge, but I was left to wonder how systematic these insights were. The snowball kept rolling, but my project did not.

Interview Excerpt with an EPB Official

ME: "Thank you for setting aside time out of your busy schedule to talk to me. I want to learn about [city's name]'s experience in pollution control in the past few years. Here is a consent form . . ."

EPB OFFICIAL: "What is this?" [Looks at consent form suspiciously.] "What is this for?"

ME: "Just so you know that you can end the conversation at any time if you don't wish to answer my questions."

EPB OFFICIAL, putting the consent form aside: "[Name of mutual acquaintance] said you study at Harvard University. Is that true?"

ME: "Yes."

EPB OFFICIAL: "Is Harvard in Boston?"

ME: "Yes. I'm here to work on my doctoral dissertation on environmental governance. And [name of acquaintance] said I should come here to learn from you . . ."

EPB OFFICIAL: "How long have you lived in America?"

ME: "Six years now."

EPB OFFICIAL: "Have you gotten used to it?"

ME: "Yes, although it was difficult at the beginning."

EPB: "Have you gotten used to eating Western food?"

ME: "Yes, I'm not a picky eater."

EPB OFFICIAL: "Girls are better than boys at adjusting to new environments."

ME: "Perhaps."

(The conversation continued for more than twenty minutes in this vein.)

. . .

EPB OFFICIAL: "What questions do you have for me?"

ME: "I want to learn about [city's name]'s experience in pollution control in the past few years. Specifically, what kind of measures have been successful and what kind of challenges have you encountered?"

EPB OFFICIAL: "We have given more importance to environmental protection in recent years. President Xi has said that 'green water and blue mountain are gold mountain and silver mountain' . . . . However, environmental protection cannot be achieved at the expense of having a full stomach [chifan]. If all the factories are closed, how are workers going to eat? That is a problem. So paying attention to environmental protection is right, but we have to take it one step at a time. How long did it take America to improve their environment? If it took America that long, how can China achieve it in only a few years?"

ME: "I agree that there has to be a balance. What do you think are some of the biggest challenges facing the EPB's efforts to implement environmental policies?"

EPB OFFICIAL: "The first is that enterprises do not cooperate with us [qiye bu peihe]. The second is that the common folk do not understand

> [*laobaixing bu lijie*]. What the EPB can do is limited. Ultimately, we must
> rely on policy support [*zhengce zhichi*], and I'm not just talking about
> environmental policy, I'm talking about industrial policy and industrial
> upgrading [*chanye shengji*]. Environmental protection comes down to
> industrial policy. After industries are upgraded, pollution problems will
> be solved. . . . But the common folk do not care; they think it's all the
> EPB's problem."
>
> (The conversation ended here because we ran out of time. I was unable to
> follow up on the EPB official's final point.)

Much ink has been spilled on the limitations of interviews held in authoritarian settings. But the challenges of eliciting full and truthful information through interviews are far more universal than that. Bureaucratic organizations—public or private—subject employees to nondisclosure agreements to prevent them from releasing proprietary or sensitive information.[90] Moreover, employees have few incentives to reveal information that could jeopardize their employers, because their self-interests are intertwined. As Weber puts it: "The individual bureaucrat is . . . forged to the community of all the functionaries who are integrated into the mechanism. They have a common interest in seeing the mechanism continue its functions and the societally exercised authority carry on."[91] Loose lips sink ships, as chapter 6 will show.

But we shouldn't rush to the conclusion of "preference falsification" when interviews are less productive than we had hoped.[92] Social scientific questions (especially survey questions) often get so convoluted, their angles so peculiar, their jargon so vague, that normal people simply can't wrap their heads around them, let alone answer them in a meaningful way. Even people who carry out their jobs immaculately might never pause to "conceptualize" what they do— that's what puts bread on a social scientist's table, not theirs.

Realizing that my surface observations of the state were yielding little, I tried to get behind the front stage and understand state behavior through participant observation. I was able to obtain this valuable opportunity at Lakeville's EPB, and for the next five months I showed up every workday to "marinate" in the agency's organizational life.[93] Freshly devoid of working hypotheses, I had nothing to prove and everything to understand. I reset the research process without clear dependent or independent variables, but with a general question of "How does environmental governance work?" It wasn't until I fully understood the "how" that I was able to begin asking sensible "why" questions.

Gradually, I let concepts and hypotheses emerge through grounded theory—a method of positivist inquiry that begins with the systematic collection and categorization of field data, followed by the abstraction of concepts and theories from such data, which are iteratively tested with new observations.[94] A key difference between grounded theory and the experimental method is that "grounded theory methods explicitly unite the research process with theoretical development. Hence the rigid division of labor between empiricists and theorists breaks down."[95]

My grounded theory proceeded in the following fashion. I recorded ethnographic observations in a journal with as many details and as much objectivity as possible. Hilary Putnam helpfully points out that a clean separation of fact and value (or of subjective and "objective" observations) is impossible.[96] But one can still try not to let personal values affect the data one collects. I strictly avoided reaching conclusions during the initial weeks of my participant observation. And if I interpreted my observations at any time, I always separated those interpretations from my observational data. The following text box shows an entry in my field journal.

I returned from my weekend trip yesterday. My flight was delayed so I got in late, after midnight. I was exhausted and as a result I was ten minutes late for work today. I got to the office when the section was already in a meeting. I sat down at the table and [name of section head] criticized me for being late. It was a bit embarrassing so I don't think I will be late again. A part of me was happy that I was treated like a regular employee, even though I am not.

At the meeting, the section made plans for the EPB's next big move: a law enforcement operation targeting industrial air pollution. Apparently there have been a lot of complaints about air pollution recently. I was asked to help [Bureaucrat A] put together a map that assigns citizen complaints to their geographic areas of origination. Once that is done, inspectors will drive to these areas to look around and "touch base" [*modi*]. Then the section will convene again to discuss which firms to target.

They spent the rest of the morning and most of their afternoon (about four hours) reading citizen complaints and marking them on a map of the city. Citizen complaints clearly cluster around a few locations: District S, District T, and District X.

In late afternoon the party members attended an hour-long "democratic life meeting" [*minzhu shenghuohui*]. The theme of the meeting was to correct the "luxury wind" [*shemizhifeng*]. People engaged in criticism and self-criticism of their luxurious pursuits. . . . [Bureaucrat B] criticized herself for owning a Louis Vuitton purse—a symbol of the luxury wind. [Bureaucrat C] was up next, and criticized herself for owning a *fake* Louis Vuitton, stating that although it was a counterfeit, it still symbolized her desire for luxury products. Some covered their mouths to hide their amusement. When the meeting was over, young colleagues made fun of [C] for her "brilliant" remark, because it was both heartfelt and harmless. The best kind of self-criticism, I heard, is self-praise disguised as self-criticism: for example, "I work too hard." Sometimes people would exchange notes of criticism with each other in advance, just to make sure that no feelings are hurt during the meeting.

After work, the section went to dinner together at [name of local restaurant], where they exchanged flattery and gossip. The section head [who was in his early thirties] retreated into the "second line," and let older bureaucrats, especially Auntie G, take over command as the life of the party. Auntie G boasted about her family. Bureaucrats talked about the stock market. Auntie G and Old Q offered advice on single co-workers' dating lives. Both [Bureaucrat K] and [Bureaucrat W] had their dating life questioned. [Bureaucrat K, a female bureaucrat in her late twenties] was clearly not interested in the conversation. But Auntie G kept pushing the subject . . .

In recording my observations, I aimed for extensiveness and deliberately avoided "cherry-picking." Some observations—such as what Henry Brady and David Collier call "causal process observations"—eventually gain prominence over others.[97] But the researcher could not, and perhaps should not, have any confidence in the prominence of specific data points during the data collection itself. For example, a trivial detail like what the bureaucrats ate for lunch might seem irrelevant initially. Yet the painstaking caution with which they ordered and enjoyed their lunch in public became critical evidence of their sensitivity toward public opinion. I treated all these "little things" as potential clues and recorded as many as possible to the best of my ability, acknowledging that most of them might turn out to be "useless."[98] Only after events started repeating themselves in my notes did I begin to form new hypotheses, which I then tested against new observations and in my future interviews.

My ethnographic participation differed, by both necessity and design, from that of some "rogue sociologists."[99] I didn't shape-shift the way Sudhir Venkatesh did in his marvelous study *Gang Leader for A Day*, when he joined a criminal gang in Chicago—even leading it for a day—to study that city's urban poor.[100] I was less involved than that. I accompanied environmental inspectors on most field trips to inspect polluting enterprises and sometimes helped carry the air sample collectors and airbags during inspections; I sat in on agency meetings, including several at two district EPBs; and I helped process citizen complaints. But I did not present myself on the street as an actual EPB inspector, because I was not one. My primary goal was to understand governance, not to promote good governance.[101]

Any method by which "subjects" become aware of the presence of the researcher—be it ethnographic or experimental—raises the potential for "observer effect" or "Hawthorne Effect."[102] The risk is that subjects may change their behavior once they're aware of being observed and potentially judged. But this risk is premised on the assumption that the subject cares. Since I had nothing to do with the bureaucrats' promotion or discipline, and I was neither an authority figure nor an honored guest, there was simply no reason for the bureaucrats to alter their behavior for my audience.

Moreover, while concerns about observer effect are valid, we would be wise not to exaggerate them. Recent studies in economics and political science have challenged the significance of Hawthorne Effects in field experiments.[103] People might notice a new face in town, but their attention quickly returns to themselves. Bureaucrats may be parallel cogs in an ever-moving mechanism, but every person is first and foremost the protagonist in their own Tolstoyan story.

Still, to ensure that there was no observer effect, I always stayed in the background. I kept quiet during encounters with firms and citizens, never passing verbal judgments on the bureaucracy's operations. I also refrained from behaviors that defied the organizational culture. For example, the job of environmental inspector required them to climb to the top of smokestacks, source points of industrial waste air, to collect air samples. Usually female inspectors stay below as the men boldly do the climbing—an act of chivalry in China that might be seen as gender discrimination in the United States. At first, I insisted on climbing to the top because I didn't want special treatment. (Admittedly, I also wanted to see what was at the top of the smokestack.) But then I realized that my intention not to violate one norm actually violated another. Given my insistence on climbing, female inspectors felt pressured to do the same. I was constantly on the alert for such rare situations; in this case I immediately stepped back and returned to my role as observer.

Beside observer effect, we must avoid observer bias. Prolonged interaction with one's subjects can cloud a researcher's objectivity. A researcher who develops an affinity with the subjects of a study may interpret the data too sympathetically; a researcher who has become frustrated with the subjects may interpret the findings too cynically. This is indeed a problem faced by many social scientists, especially when they are studying topics and places that are politically and morally charged. A conscientious researcher should strive not to let their biases—sympathetic or cynical—creep into the research process.

But sympathy, or empathy, is not just a challenge; it can be an opportunity. The ability to understand another person's condition from their perspective is not only what makes the world go around.[104] It's also an incredibly useful tool in social scientific research. Empathy requires standing back from one's own values and beliefs to understand those of others. It demands that the researcher relates to their subjects on a human level, with no method but the mighty method of common sense. On common sense, Donald Campbell writes "After all, man is, in his ordinary way, a very competent knower, and qualitative common-sense knowing is not replaced by quantitative-knowing. . . . This is not to say that such commonsense naturalistic observation is objective, dependable, or unbiased. But it is all that we have. It is the only route to knowledge—noisy, fallible, and biased though it be."[105]

On the Generality-Specificity Dichotomy

It was Sartori who popularized the notion that "case studies are most valuable—for the comparativist—as *hypothesis-generating* inquiries."[106] Without a comparison of two or more cases, Sartori writes, we don't have a generalization.[107] He adds, "Case studies sacrifice generality to depth and thickness of understanding, indeed to Verstehen: one knows more and better about less . . . Conversely, comparative studies sacrifice understanding-in-context—and of context—to inclusiveness: one knows less about more."[108] A natural extension of this argument holds that any theory generated from case studies should be tested, ideally experimentally, against a larger set of cases, so that we know if it's generalizable or externally valid. And if the theory doesn't work on a wider set of cases, it's probably because the original case study suffered from selection bias.[109]

These allegations turn scholars away from single case studies on two grounds: first, the taste for theories that explain more cases rather than fewer (unless the single case is of world-historical importance, such as the French Revolution);

second, the belief that without comparisons there is no theory. On the first point, one may argue that because Lakeville isn't as world-historically important as, say, the French Revolution, we should be less interested in studying it. I won't dive into a response to this challenge—there are many sociopolitical reasons for why things that attract more interest may not be objectively or normatively more important. I'll simply say: fair enough.

The second challenge—that there can be no theory without comparison or experimentation—is worthy of discussion because it deals with the "scientific" part of inquiry. Contrary to Sartori's insistence, I would argue that general theories *can* emerge without explicit comparisons. The most general theory of all—general relativity—was built without comparison of two or multiple universes. In fact, general relativity was falsified by experiments for years before it was experimentally confirmed. (It turned out that the initial experiments were faulty.)[110] Does that mean that during those years before it could be experimentally verified, general relativity didn't contribute to our knowledge of the universe?

One might then ask: Without experiments, how can we know whether a theory is good or bad? Theoretical physicists "know" by examining the internal elegance of a theory: Is it simple? Is it symmetric? Does the math/logic add up? Some social scientists—especially formal theorists—share this taste. Of course, beauty isn't validity, though many theoretical physicists consider the two inseparable.

Another way of "knowing" the value of a theory is through a full appreciation of its internal validity. An in-depth case study with careful abstraction and attention to detail fulfills this task; it is a necessary and sufficient method for theory generation.[111] And just because a theory coming out of Lakeville doesn't explain Sunnyvale, that doesn't mean the theory about Lakeville is *wrong*.[112] Sometimes the case one chooses *is* the answer one gets, and the answer can stand tall without needing to "travel" elsewhere—especially in disciplines where roving theories banish stationary ones.

More important, internal validity should never be sacrificed for the sake of external validity. This sacrifice is clear in Sartori's admission that one knows less about more through wider comparisons. Here, Sartori sidesteps the point that external validity relies on internal validity, and not vice versa. Knowing less about more may thus mean knowing virtually nothing at all.

On Representativeness

Those who still desire more generality/external validity to appreciate a case study may fairly ask: How representative is Lakeville? Can lessons from Lakeville travel to other parts of China? Other parts of the world? Is Lakeville a "most likely," "least likely," "critical," or "deviant" case?[113] Or none of the above?

Lakeville is obviously not a representative sample of the diversity that is China. According to the World Bank, 40 percent of the Chinese population lived in rural areas in 2019, a proportion that may be larger or smaller depending on what "urban" and "rural" mean.[114] (For example, a substantial part of China is neither clearly rural nor urban, but what geographers call "desakota," which is not necessarily a "transitional" stage of urbanization, but can be a stable ecology.)[115] Political dynamics in tight-knit rural communities can be very different from those in large cities (gemeinschaft versus gesellschaft). For example, state-society interaction is more personal in rural areas, with the state appearing not as street-level civil servants but as "temple-level" social elites.[116] But these urban-rural differences need not be rigid. There is much overlap in the ways policies are implemented.[117] The collective aspect of resistance and the relational aspect of repression are also found in both city and countryside.[118] Finally, with the rise of digital governance and neighborhood-level networks of surveillance, the difference between state-society relations and state-society intimacy in urban and rural areas wanes.[119]

If Lakeville is not representative of China, what kind of lessons can we extrapolate from studying it? For starters, we may problematize the belief that ecological representativeness is the only standard for case selection, because this wisdom is premised on an assumption of sameness rather than diversity.[120] To be sure, ecological representativeness is crucial in demographic, medical, and some economic research, for a variety of scientific and normative reasons. But the point of Lakeville is not that it is an "average" Chinese city, because there is no such thing as an average Chinese city—just as there is no average country, average democracy, or average authoritarian regime. The "representativeness" of Lakeville is that it suffers a common governance conundrum that can be found throughout the world—that is, high public demand for an issue's resolution but low state capacity to resolve it. Since this problem surely travels, any study that addresses it can travel alongside it.

AUDIENCE APPRAISAL

Public opinion is an invisible, mysterious, irresistible power. . . . Nothing is more mobile, nothing more vague, nothing stronger. Capricious though it is, nevertheless it is truthful, reasonable, and right much more often than one might think.

—Napoleon

We must believe that the vast majority of the people have the ability to judge right from wrong.

—Deng Xiaoping

Citizen K wakes up in the morning. Wondering what time it is, he reaches for his cell phone on the nightstand. Phone in hand, he quickly scrolls through emails, news feeds, and social media to check in with the world before getting ready for work. Over breakfast, he keeps scrolling as he waits for his coffee to cool, and writes brief responses to messages that seem urgent. In the car, he listens to the radio, usually to news stories but sometimes a little music to wake up. When he first sits down in his office, he's not yet in the mood for working, so he checks the news again on his computer. An article about a mysterious taste in the tap water catches his eye.

Suddenly, as if someone has knocked at the door, he snaps back to attention. All the day's tasks and meetings surface from the back of his mind. He quickly closes all the websites as if to purge the world—all the violence, the celebrations, the outrage—entirely from his life. For now at least. He opens an unfinished report from yesterday and starts typing, fingers waltzing to their prescribed course of march.

Later in the day, when he runs into colleagues in the hallway, they bring up the news as small talk, and he exchanges agreements and polite disagreements with them. He harbors many grievances against those in power and their policies, but his time is better spent on finishing these reports: there are bills to pay and children to feed. Somewhere around 4:00 p.m. he runs out of steam, starts to scroll through the websites again, and decides to head home. Over dinner, the TV drones while the family chats about their day. There's an important meeting in the capital, armed conflict in the Middle East, a mysterious virus in Africa. But when his daughter tells him about her day at school, the news anchor's symphonious voice fades into a background hum.

Citizen K is a typical consumer of modern media. He and others like him are relatively apolitical, tune in and out of the news at random times, and have more immediate worries than high-order political matters. They have never met a powerful politician, never petitioned the government, and never think about questions like "On a scale of one to five, how legitimate is your political system?" Of course, dormant impressions of the authorities lie deep in their mind and are occasionally updated and periodically activated through glimpses of the news, conversations with friends, and daily life experiences.

Citizen K is the performative state's *pivotal audience*. The state knows that there will always be some, living within and beyond its borders, who derive moral gratification or monetary gains from challenging its mandate. Let's call them O (for opposition). It is nearly impossible to change O's mind, and nothing the state does, short of relinquishing its rule, will satisfy O. The state keeps close tabs on O; but when it comes to tipping the balance of power between the state and its most implacable opponents, it is K's opinion that truly matters.

K's opinion may well be mysterious, mercurial, and even unfathomable. It can change swiftly over the course of days, if not hours.[1] Capricious though it is, K's opinion is what makes or breaks a state at critical times.[2] It was citizens like K who showed up at Nicolae Ceaușescu's rally on Palace Square on December 21, 1989, only to surprise him with a stunning overthrow. It was citizens like K who joined the Tunisian revolution in 2011 after witnessing the state's violent crackdown on protests. It is citizens like K who wear "I hate politics" on their lips; but when the time comes, they can prove surprisingly willing to set aside their reports, throw up their hands, break free of the iron cage, and exclaim "enough is enough." It is K's love and fear that the state seeks.

The state competes with O for K's attention and support. And it does so in the theater of public opinion—in K's daily news feeds, on his smart phone and computer screens, in his newspapers, on his radio, and on the television screen in his dining room.

This chapter examines the citizen audience's appraisal of performative governance—positive, negative, and everything in between. I focus on ordinary citizens like K. The word *ordinary*, according to Nancy Bermeo, "underscores the fact that [these citizens] have no extraordinary powers vis-à-vis the state in which they live. They are neither politicians nor military officers. They spend most of their lives in personal endeavors—earning money, supporting families, and pursuing whatever leisure activities their social status allows. They are the people who compose the vast majority of the citizenry in virtually every country in the world."[3] They even include street-level bureaucrats themselves.

Unlike the activist citizen, whose attention to their cause is enduring and whose beliefs are resolute, the ordinary citizen's attention is sporadic, their beliefs malleable. Unlike the activist citizen who actively seeks political change—from smaller policy adjustments to larger regime change—the ordinary citizen's primary purpose is to lead the best private life possible with the hand they are dealt. Where the activist citizen throws themselves into politics, the ordinary citizen is pulled into politics. The ordinary citizen is a "political man" only insofar as politics is an inescapable part of modern life.[4]

Behind every dramatic protest scene is the plain boring fact that most people rarely protest or petition in ordinary times.[5] The previous chapter mentioned that the Lakeville EPB received more than ten thousand petitions in 2013. While this number seems large, it constitutes less than 1 percent of the city's population. In a nationwide public opinion survey I will introduce momentarily in this chapter, 93 percent of respondents reported that they had never contacted their local governments about pollution problems.[6] Even among those who have filed complaints with the state, only a tiny fraction would qualify as "political activists." This means that most citizens might not regularly and personally encounter the kind of performative governance detailed in the previous chapter.

Yet a lack of direct contact with the EPB doesn't stop citizens from receiving information and forming opinions about government performance. The performative state, therefore, must go the extra mile to reach Citizen K.

That extra mile is paved by the news media. During the Foul Air Law Enforcement Operation, as the Lakeville EPB pulled out all the stops to address citizen complaints, their efforts were reported simultaneously in the local newspapers and television programs. The news media—especially local news—is a conduit through which performative governance reaches a wider audience.

We should begin by stressing an important point that might not be obvious: the media isn't completely devoid of critical agency in contemporary China.[7] Marketization in recent decades has lowered the barriers to entry and spawned a plethora of public and private platforms—television channels, radio stations, newspapers, magazines, news websites, bulletin boards, blogs, vlogs, podcasts, and other social networking applications—all at the citizen's disposal. Even state media must compete with myriad private and public outlets, because it now also relies on advertising revenue, and thus on a willing readership. While sensitive topics, such as central leaders, mass protests, and ethnic tensions remain untouchable, other issues can be reported with relative freedom. In this competitive business, state media must adapt its reporting to the modern audience's taste for authenticity, controversy, entertainment, outrage, scandal, and schadenfreude. Chinese media is often eager to unleash its "supervisory function" (*jiandu zuoyong*) with critical reporting on local government behavior, especially at the street level.[8]

For that reason, the EPB cannot take the news media's favorability for granted. More often than not, it finds itself a target of the media's unwelcome attentions. As an unpublished guide for civil servants cautions: "In emergency situations, reporting by the news media sometimes conflicts with the agency's own knowledge [of the issue]." To counter negative news reporting, the guide instructs civil servants not to "be taciturn in front of the camera" (*zai jingtou qian chenmo guayan*) and not to "proactively give up the right to speak to the media" (*zhudong fangqi xinwen huayu quan*). Instead, civil servants should not shy away from "the battlefield of public opinion" (*yulun zhanchang*). They should "face up directly to the media" (*zhimian meiti*) and "not only do [their jobs], but also speak to the media, because speaking is a part of doing."[9]

This chapter investigates the performative state's victories and defeats on "the battlefield of public opinion." I ask three related questions: First, how does performative governance reach a wider audience? Second, does performative governance work at convincing the citizen audience of the state's virtues? Third, and more broadly, how significant are environmental problems in the public consciousness? How important are they to ordinary citizens like K? How do Chinese citizens think about environmental protection?

To answer these questions, I collected multiple types of quantitative and qualitative data. First, in spring 2015 I ran a public opinion survey (henceforth referred to as the Urban Environmental Attitudes Survey, or UEAS) of 6,164 adult citizens in thirty Chinese cities, using random digit dialing. This survey offers quantitative descriptions of public opinion concerning pollution, environmental protection, and perceptions of government performance. The appendix at the end of this chapter explains the UEAS in greater detail and compares its sample with the China Family Panel Survey (CFPS).

I supplemented the UEAS with a separate survey, conducted in 2016 among six hundred Lakeville residents, on their habits of media consumption and their evaluations of different governance domains (the Urban Media Consumption Survey, or UMCS). This chapter's appendix contains more details of this survey as well.

Additionally, I constructed a measure of performative governance using local newspapers in the same thirty cities covered by the UEAS and used regression analysis to understand whether performative governance translates into public approval of local environmental governance. This "objective" measure of performative governance indeed correlates positively with citizens' perception of government efforts, as well as with citizen satisfaction with local environmental governance in the UEAS.

Further, between 2013 and 2019, I conducted two sets of semistructured interviews. The first set was with EPB bureaucrats in Beijing, Guangdong, Sichuan, and Guizhou provinces, as well as journalists, newspaper editors, and television news producers in Zhejiang, Guangdong, and Sichuan provinces. I wanted to understand how state agencies interact with the media and how the media reports on local environmental news. I triangulated each piece of interview evidence used in this book with at least two additional independent sources.[10]

I conducted the second set of interviews with residents of Lakeville and Beijing—each interview was about two hours long. My goal was not to repeat what the surveys had attempted, which is to ascertain general patterns in public opinion. Rather, I wanted to understand the complex thought processes, emotions, and mixed feelings that are hard to unearth with anonymous, time-limited, clear-cut survey questions. For this reason, the best interview subjects were those who were comfortable devoting their precious time and serious thoughts to a conversation. I used convenience sampling to find my subjects, while striking for a balance on socioeconomic characteristics including age, gender, occupation, and income.

I used the standard of saturation rather than representativeness to determine my sample size.[11] Initially, I didn't set an upper limit on how many interviews I would collect. When the number approached forty in 2016, I noticed certain patterns repeating in the interviewees' answers, so I had reached a point of diminishing returns. I stopped after forty interviews in Lakeville. I then interviewed twenty residents in Beijing to tentatively explore potential north-south variations. I conducted follow-up interviews with six Lakeville residents in summer 2019.

Since the sixty citizens interviewed were most likely not representative of the general population, my analysis of their attitudes in this chapter will interpret their narratives rather than reporting their averages and distributions. Interview evidence should not be directly compared with survey findings. Instead, in-depth interviews offer potential explanations for the correlations found in the quantitative analysis. They also offer informative anomalies that defy survey results. These deviations are often not a result of sample differences, but the ways in which questions are asked and answers are interpreted.[12]

In the last part of this chapter I use interview data to show how people's awareness of an issue's *existence*, their perceived *severity* of the issue, and their *grievances* about the issue can become separated in their thinking. Even when citizens perceive pollution to be severe, they might not feel aggrieved enough to take action or demand policy change.

The Shape of Scrutiny

While pollution, especially air pollution, had become a hot-button issue in China by the 2010s, there was less comprehensive information on how citizens felt about pollution and their assessment of government performance in pollution control. We knew generally that pollution had become a serious problem in China, and that Chinese citizens seemed upset about it, but we knew relatively little about the *depth* and the *substance* of their concern. If nothing else, the UEAS produced valuable information about citizens' environmental beliefs, their perceptions of pollution, and their evaluation of environmental governance. The UMCS offers supplementary data on urban citizens' media consumption habits, their trust in different media sources, their ranking of the urgency of various social issues, as well as their evaluation of different state agencies, including the EPB.

The two surveys generated a few striking insights. First, perceived severity of environmental pollution was very high. A UEAS question asked respondents to evaluate the impact of air pollution on their health. Twenty-two percent believed that air pollution had had a "very substantial" harmful impact on their health; another 35 percent believed the impact was "somewhat substantial."

Table 2 ranks the perceived severity of nine "social problems" (*shehui wenti*) that are common concerns of urban citizens: corruption, pollution, consumer prices, medical care, employment, traffic, stock market, public safety, and education, drawing on a question in the UMCS. Respondents were asked which three of the nine social problems were most severe. Environmental pollution received the second most mentions, after corruption—due in part to the amount of media attention these two issues received around the time the survey was conducted.

The UMCS only covered Lakeville, so the results cannot be extrapolated to the entirety of China. For comparison, table 3 shows results from a question in the 2016 CFPS asking the respondent to score the severity of eight social problems on a scale of 0–10. CFPS respondents rated inequality as the most serious problem, followed by environmental pollution and government corruption. (Inequality was not included in the UMCS as a substantive issue.) This largely confirms the finding that Chinese citizens perceive environmental pollution to be severe.

Second, the UEAS finds that citizens' perception of air quality in their own city of residence correlates quite strongly with reality. One question asked respondents to evaluate their city's air quality in 2014 from very bad (1) to very good (5).

TABLE 2   Perceived severity of social problems (2016 UMCS)

	PERCENTAGE AGREES
Corruption	55%
Environmental pollution	51%
Consumer prices	39%
Medical care	37%
Employment	32%
Traffic	31%
Stock market	23%
Public safety	22%
Primary and secondary education	11%

TABLE 3   Perceived severity of social problems (2016 CFPS)

	PERCEIVED SEVERITY (0=LEAST SEVERE . . . 10=MOST SEVERE)
Inequality	6.67
Environmental pollution	6.32
Corruption	6.30
Employment	6.15
Medical care	5.93
Education	5.80
Housing	5.73
Social security	5.59

Figure 4 shows a strong correlation between citizens' negative perceptions of air quality and average levels of airborne *PM2.5* in the thirty cities in 2014 ($r(28)= -0.66, p<0.001$).

Third, most respondents saw air pollution as a local problem. One UEAS question asked respondents to identify the main source of air pollution in their city. Forty percent believed it was industrial waste air; 39 percent vehicle emissions; 13 percent dust from construction sites. Only 6 percent believed that local air pollution came from other cities and provinces. This contrasts with a government-sponsored study which found that 26 percent to 42 percent of PM 2.5 pollution in Beijing came from other regions in 2018, while 45 percent came from local vehicle emissions.[13]

When asked about the political causes of air pollution, 43 percent of respondents in the UEAS said they believed air pollution was mainly caused by the government's lack of stringent law enforcement (*zhengfu zhifa buyan*); an equivalent

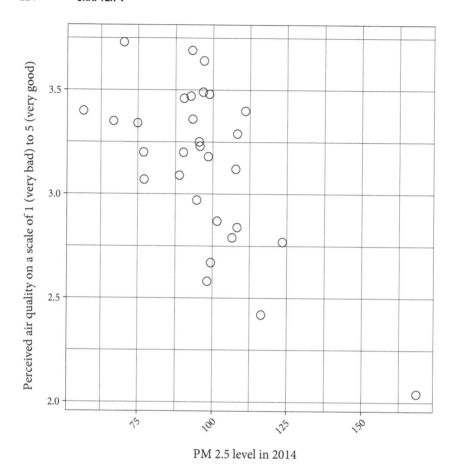

FIGURE 4. Strong negative correlation between objective air pollution and perceived air quality in 2014

43 percent blamed the illegal behavior of individuals and enterprises (*qiye huo geren bushoufa*); and 14 percent attributed pollution to underdeveloped legal institutions (*falü fagui bujianquan*). Crucially, when asked whether pollution control was within the power (*lisuonengji*) of their municipal government agencies, 86 percent agreed with the statement. This suggests yet again that public scrutiny falls heavily on the local bureaucracy.

These results are supported by citizens' low confidence in the EPB compared to some other agencies. Table 4 compares citizens' reported confidence in the courts, the police, the EPB, and the Urban Management Bureau (Chengguan), based on an UMCS question. Urban Management is one of the least popular agencies—if not *the* least popular agency—in China. It sunk into infamy during

TABLE 4   Trust in state institutions

	CONFIDENCE (1=LEAST CONFIDENT . . . 5=MOST CONFIDENT)
Courts	2.72
Police	2.67
EPB	2.23
Urban management	1.97

rapid urbanization, when its agents were deployed to city corners to disperse street hawkers, demolish buildings, and dislodge "nail houses." Their abrasive attitudes before the age of service-oriented governance left a deep negative impression in people's minds. In a featured story on People.cn (Renminwang), a bureaucrat who had worked in urban management in Beijing for twenty-seven years recounted that in the 1990s "[our] law enforcement model at the time, compared to now, can in fact be called reckless law enforcement [*huluan zhifa*]." Despite recent reforms aiming at more professionalism, the bureaucrat admitted that the largest challenge to his work was "the lack of understanding and support by the people."[14] This was corroborated by the 2016 UMCS. Urban Management ranked the lowest in citizen trust. The EPB enjoys a better public image than that, but its score is still lower than that of the courts and the police.

To understand citizens' policy preferences, a UEAS question asked, "When environmental protection comes in conflict with economic development, is environmental protection or economic development more important?" A surprising 79 percent of respondents chose environmental protection over economic development—a large proportion even considering the potential effect of survey demand. Out of curiosity, I took an informal poll in a classroom of master's students in public policy at the Harvard Kennedy School in 2015, and the results were in stark contrast: 80 percent of students in the class chose economic development over environmental protection, if the two were to come in conflict. It goes without saying that these results can't be compared in a scientific sense, given the differences in the two populations and their priors. But the contrast does help demonstrate the intensity of environmental concerns in China.

Taken together, these findings indicate that: (1) Chinese citizens see environmental pollution as a serious problem that tangibly affects their livelihood; (2) their perceptions of air pollution match quite well with objective reality; and (3) they believe that pollution control is within the wherewithal of local governments. My claim in previous chapters about high public scrutiny thus finds substantial support.

The Battlefield of Public Opinion

High scrutiny drags otherwise introverted bureaucrats onto the "battlefield of public opinion." Again, with little power to substantively improve the environment, the EPB would prefer to lay low and not invite attention. "One thing less is better than one thing more" (*duo yishi buru shao yishi*) was a prevailing attitude among the EPB bureaucrats in Lakeville. Bureaucrats in Shenzhen and Chengdu also recounted to me their trepidation toward the media. A bureaucrat at the Chengdu EPB grumbled that "whenever air pollution is bad, I worry that we will make it to the news."[15] (He further attributed high public scrutiny to the myriad environmental NGOs operating in the lush and mountainous province of Sichuan, where the giant panda sanctuaries are located.)

But bureaucrats have also learned that while they can try to avoid individual journalists, they can't entirely avoid the news. Severe air pollution is not something that can be hidden from public view, and laying low won't prevent grievances from arising. When a local concern catches the attention of journalists, they often reach out to relevant agencies for comments. If bureaucrats do not actively participate in the news process to ensure favorable reporting, the agency's image may be damaged.

For example, when an especially thick smog descended on Nanjing (capital of Jiangsu Province) one Saturday in November 2013, a journalist contacted Nanjing's municipal EPB for comment. In response, the EPB told the journalist that their experts were "off duty" on weekends and therefore couldn't answer any questions. The following morning, that response was critically covered by China National Radio's popular "News Exchange" (*xinwen zongheng*) program. The following text box shows excerpts of the news reporting and commentary.[16]

"Nanjing EPB Responds to Smog-Locked City: Experts Are Off on Weekends and Cannot Answer Questions"

Yesterday, Nanjing city was locked in smog again. The air all around was grey. Cars traveling on the Nanjing Yangtze River Bridge seemed to be shuttling through a mist. Masks reappeared on pedestrians' faces. At two in the afternoon, Nanjing's real-time air quality index (AQI) reached 175, meaning moderate pollution. On this smoggy weekend, a journalist contacted the Nanjing EPB about Nanjing's air pollution. But they were met with the following response: experts are off-duty during the weekend and cannot answer questions about smog.

When the smog hits, people's utmost concern is when such conditions will pass and when they can engage in outdoor activities with peace of mind again. Ordinary people's concerns are precisely the responsibilities of relevant bureaucracies. Yet the phrase "off-duty on weekends" [*zhoumo xiuxi*] seems to suggest that [smog] has nothing to do with them. How can you rest when the people are restless? Perhaps experts at the Nanjing EPB live in a vacuum?

The next day, the national radio's coverage of the Nanjing EPB's lackadaisical response was reprinted by news outlets all over China. For example, the following text box shows excerpts from an opinion piece in *Guangzhou Daily* entitled "Both Smog and Bureaucratic Attitude Need Treatment."[17]

"Both Smog and Bureaucratic Attitude Need Treatment"

One may be biased to completely repudiate the Nanjing EPB's efforts at smog control based on their words that "experts are on a break." However, the EPB's cold response has indeed damaged its public credibility [*gongxinli*]. Admittedly, experts are also ordinary people and their taking a break on weekends seems reasonable. However, people were so outraged by these words not because experts were on a break, but because of the haughty attitude displayed by the EPB.

In the face of sudden onset of smog, shouldn't the EPB enter "battle mode" immediately? In a situation like this, using "on a break" as an excuse shows [the EPB's] bureaucratism [*guanliaozhuyi*]. . . . If this kind of attitude does not change, even the best foreign equipment cannot cure the smog problem.

The EPB, like other functional bureaucracies [*zhineng bumen*], should fulfill its function of "serving the people." . . . In the face of public questions and concerns, the EPB is obliged to satisfy people's right to information. Functional bureaucracies must take the people seriously, and must not be evasive and insensitive [*mamuburen*]. At this moment, it is imperative not only to treat smog, but also to treat the attitudes of bureaucracies.

That same day, BBC China published a letter from a Chinese netizen (italics added):

> *Sometimes it is not the emergency incidents themselves that discredit the image of governments and officials, but the government's attitude in the*

process of responding to these incidents. This is a manifestation of the lack of media awareness and experience among some functional bureaucracies. . . . The Nanjing EPB's response reminds us that government agents must improve their *manners* [*suzhi*], and learn how to deal with the media. . . . At the same time, the key to improving one's media manners is to correct one's awareness. . . . If [bureaucrats] understand what their job is, they will not repeat such a stupid mistake again.[18]

To prevent such "emergency incidents" (*tufa shijian*) from erupting in the first place, local EPBs try to take preemptive measures, analyzing citizen complaints and past public-relations mishaps. But they've also learned an important social-scientific lesson: prediction is difficult, if not impossible. As one bureaucrat at the Shenzhen EPB told me, "It's very hard to predict the timing, duration, scale, and eventual consequences of emergency incidents."[19] He believed that such unpredictability is caused not only by the volatile nature of pollution, but also by the amplifying effect of the news media: "Sometimes the initial scope of the incident is not necessarily large. But when the news media intervenes and spreads the story widely, turning it into a hot social issue, it may cause public psychological panic and social disorder."[20]

Therefore, some EPBs have encouraged their bureaucrats to be more proactive (*zhudong*) with their media outreach. The guide to emergency response cited earlier makes three recommendations on how bureaucrats can better engage with the news media:

- First, improve one's professional knowledge and skills. Thoroughly learn the relevant laws, regulations, and bureaucratic functions, so that one can answer journalists' questions accurately.
- Second, change one's attitude and accrue experiences. Proactively reach out to the media and be adept in guiding the media. Increase regular contacts with journalists, and accept more interviews, so that in the situation of an emergency they can respond calmly.
- Third, be objective and rational. When facing journalists, speak the truth, objectively explain the process, *but avoid speaking about results* [emphasis added].

The last point in particular captures the essence of performative governance, which focuses on good governance as professional conduct, benevolent gestures, and sincere efforts when substantive outcomes are not flattering for the agency's image. "Avoid speaking about results" suggests that the EPB is cognizant of its inability to substantively resolve citizen complaints.

Interestingly, no street-level bureaucrat I interviewed expressed any interest whatsoever in "proactively reaching out to the media," despite what the training guide encourages. To them, media attention was mostly unwanted attention, although they recognized the importance for the agency to insert itself into the news cycle once crises appear on the horizon. Senior bureaucrats were more likely to believe in proactive impression management and active contacts with local journalists. The Lakeville EPB assigned a bureaucrat to take charge of dealing with various local media outlets.

Performative Governance in the News

To see if performative governance makes it into the news and to gauge its impact on public opinion, I analyzed the daily newspaper in each of the thirty cities covered in the UEAS.

Daily newspapers are trusted sources for local news in China. A UMCS question asked respondents to select their most trusted outlets for local news out of Xinhuanet (run by the central government's news agency), *Southern Weekly* (a historically more liberal newspaper based in Guangzhou that has nationwide readership), the provincial government-run daily newspaper in the respondent's province, the municipal government-run daily newspaper in the respondent's city, Weibo, WeChat, and the *New York Times*. Table 5 shows that besides the Xinhua News Agency, the daily newspaper in the respondent's city is their most trusted source of local news. Even though respondents often use Weibo and WeChat, they don't consider social media a credible news source, nor do they rely on international reporting, such as the *New York Times*, for local stories. By way of comparison, table 6 ranks the respondents' choices for trusted sources of international news in the UMCS: Xinhua still ranks at the top, followed by the *New York Times*. Weibo and WeChat remain the least trusted outlets for international

TABLE 5 Trust as source of local news

Xinhuanet	68%
Municipal daily newspaper	59%
Southern Weekend	45%
Provincial newspaper	40%
WeChat	35%
Weibo	28%
New York Times	25%

TABLE 6   Trust as source of international news

Xinhuanet	78%
New York Times	62%
Southern Weekend	46%
Municipal daily newspaper	38%
Provincial newspaper	26%
WeChat	25%
Weibo	25%

stories. I use local newspapers because Xinhuanet does not have comprehensive coverage of subnational happenings.

To understand how the media covers environmental news, I interviewed journalists, editors, and TV news producers. A television news program director in Zhejiang Province told me state media outlets generally engaged in three types of reporting on public policy issues such as environmental protection.[21] The first is "policy interpretation" (*zhengce jiedu*), which publicizes new environmental policies, laws, and regulations. This type of reporting is rare and only occurs when there are major policy changes. The second type is what the journalists call "propaganda reporting" (*xuanchuan baodao*), periodically done at the request of government officials (for example, on important occasions) to boast about the local government's achievements. The third type is "supervisory reporting" (*jiandu baodao*), which is the journalists' terminology for news reports that fall outside the territory of propaganda. Their ostensible function is to scrutinize the state with "public opinion supervision" (*yulun jiandu*).

Unlike dry and dull propaganda, supervisory reporting is more investigative and interactive. It focuses on specific local happenings, usually triggered by public attention, offering vivid details of journalistic investigation, citizen interviews, and government agencies' efforts to resolve the issue. To be sure, even supervisory reporting wouldn't go so far as to criticize individual officials (such as the party secretary, governor, or mayor) in their locality. But they can still engage in critical reporting of the issues in question and the bureaucracies in charge.

EPB bureaucrats have little control over policy interpretation or propaganda reporting, but they must insert themselves into supervisory reporting. When an environmental issue grips public attention—for example, a day of heavy smog, tap water suddenly tasting strange, or rivers changing color—journalists would reach out to the EPB for information and comments as they conduct their investigation. Then comes the opportunity for the agency to showcase its sincere concern and active efforts. (The cost of not doing so is evident in the earlier example of Nanjing EPB's "off-duty" response to the journalist's inquiry about smog.) When local EPBs appear in the news media, they usually appear in supervisory reporting.

Working with three Chinese-speaking research assistants, we first extracted all reporting that covered the local EPBs in the thirty cities over the twelve-month period prior to the UEAS survey. We then went through each article to code whether it covered the EPB's *efforts* at solving local environmental problems. To qualify, a news article had to be longer than one-eighth of a page and consist of details of the EPB's efforts to address local environmental concerns. I counted the total number of such articles for each city, and used this measure as a proxy for the intensity of performative governance in the news.

One should naturally question to what extent these articles capture performative governance instead of substantive governance. It is indeed extremely hard to identify performative governance based on frontstage observations alone, because a primary purpose of performative governance is to foster the image of substantive governance. For example, news coverage of the Foul Air Law Enforcement Operation detailed in chapter 3 could easily be misread as substantive governance, unless the reader had the time and interest to investigate and follow up on the outcomes of the operation. And since the punishment of the four firms was also covered in the news, it could easily give the impression that there was severe and sufficient punishment on polluting enterprises, especially to citizens living outside of District S. I called the operation performative because I had experience from the backstage to know that the punishments were only slaps on the wrist, as the bureaucrats themselves fully recognized.

If we wanted a "real" measure of performative governance, we would gather such data from every state agency's backstage, or through a survey of bureaucrats. Even if such data collection were possible, the performative efforts thus uncovered would have no impact on public opinion unless they entered the public consciousness. And we now know that the passage to public consciousness runs through the news. Therefore, to study public perception, what we want is not a "real" measure of performative governance on the bureaucratic backstage, but its representation in the news. My careful reading of the news thus serves as my "best estimate" quantitative measure for the intensity of performative governance as it is experienced by the Chinese public.

On average, each daily newspaper published twenty-one articles that my research assistants and I coded as performative governance over the twelve-month period (s.d.=9.4). The following text box shows a prime example of performative governance making it into the news.[22]

"An Open Letter that Rewards Petitions"

"Whatever a citizen's concern may be, they will receive a response from me [*minyousuohu, woyousuoying*]," . . . says Xi Xingping [a deputy EPB director], who devotes most of his time and energy to environmental petitions work. . . .

He and his co-workers take turns receiving citizen complaints in the office; they often stay up all night to deal with just one telephone complaint. . . .

"The way we handle petitions needs to keep pace with the times [*yushijujin*]." Xi Xingping and his co-workers often exchange ideas about their work, create innovative ways of addressing environmental complaints; . . . [they] often go back to look at past investigations of citizen complaints, and focus on cases that cause the strongest citizen reaction.

[The rest of the article lists multiple examples of citizen complaints and how the EPB responded to them.]

The next text box shows an example of the Nanjing EPB's performative governance in the news four years after learning the hard lesson of nonresponsiveness.[23]

"Nanjing Covered in Smog on New Year's Eve, the EPB Issues Tickets"

On the morning of January 2, [air] pollution in downtown Nanjing deteriorated . . . visibility was consistently low. . . . Although it is a holiday, the Nanjing EPB is still taking "blue warning" emergency measures. A reporter from *Modern Express* learned that the EPB dispatched six inspection teams yesterday. . . . One team inspected construction sites, one team inspected enterprises in Jiangnan district, two teams inspected chemical plants in Jiangbei district, and the other two teams inspected the streets and government infrastructural projects. On January 2, [our] reporter followed the inspectors to the sites. Representatives on multiple construction sites reported that they had received notices from the EPB to mitigate construction dust and take relevant measures. . . . Yet there were individual construction sites that were perfunctory in their dust control measures. [The rest of this article lists two construction sites that received tickets and one that received a warning. It also explains that the seven enterprises inspected had all "implemented emission reduction measures in strict accordance with regulatory requirements."]

To check whether these news reports corresponded with citizen perceptions, I examined the correlation between my objective measure and a UEAS question. The question asked respondents how often they had read about government efforts to address local pollution problems in the past twelve months (from never=1 to often=4). There is indeed a positive correlation between citizens' average perception of government efforts in the thirty cities and my objective measure extracted from the daily newspapers, although this correlation is not statistically significant, possibly due to the limited number of cities covered in the survey ($r(28)=0.25$, $p=0.18$).

Citizen Approval

In this section, I use regression analysis to study the relationship between the prevalence of performative governance in the news and level of citizen approval for local environmental governance. To measure citizen approval, the UEAS asked respondents to evaluate their municipal government's performance (*biaoxian*) in environmental governance over the past year (from very bad=1 to very good=5).[24] The average approval score was 3.3 (s.d.=0.25), with 89 percent of respondents answering unambiguously. Another question asked citizens to evaluate government performance on a scale of 0–10. Ninety-seven percent of respondents offered a clear answer; the average score was 6.5. Answers to these two questions show high correlation ($r=0.67$, $p<0.001$).[25]

I use linear mixed effects models with city-level random effects to examine the relationship between performative governance in the news and citizens' approval of environmental governance in their city.

$$Approval\ of\ local\ environmental\ governance_{ij}$$
$$= \alpha_{0j} + \beta_0\ Performative\ Governance_j + \delta X'_j + \gamma Z'_{ij} + \epsilon_{ij}$$

The dependent variable is citizen i's approval of environmental governance in city j, where the citizen resides. The main independent variable is the amount of news reporting on performative governance appearing in the city's daily newspaper in the twelve months prior to the survey. The model also contains a number of city-level control variables (X'_j), including average PM 2.5 levels in the twelve months prior to the survey as a measure of air pollution (and a proxy for substantive performance) and GDP per capita, as well as individual control variables (Z'_{ij}), including gender, age, income, education, perception of air quality, and levels of environmentalism, measured by whether they would choose

TABLE 7 Descriptive statistics

	MEAN	S.D.	N
Approval of environmental governance (1=least approve . . . 5=most approve)	3.30	1.15	5516
Performative governance in the news (12 months prior to the survey)	21	9.4	6164
Average PM 2.5 level	96.65	19.56	6164
Perceived air quality (1=very bad . . . 5=very good)	3.15	1.13	6065
Environmentalist (3=choose environment, 2=neutral, 1=choose economy)	2.72	0.6	6043
GDP per capita	70,440	39,247	6164
Female	43%	–	6164
Age	37	12	6164
Income	19,557	26,774	4854
Education (1=primary school, 2=middle school, 3=high school, 4=vocational school, 5=college, 6=MA, 7=PhD)	3.4	1.27	6116

Note: Performative governance in the news, PM 2.5 level, and GDP per capita are measured at the city level.

environmental protection over economic development should the two come into conflict. Table 7 presents descriptive statistics.

I fit two linear mixed-effects models to individual-level data, using multiple imputation to account for missing data.[26] The first model includes PM 2.5 level as a control; the second substitutes PM 2.5 level with perception of air quality. Table 8 reports the findings, showing a positive correlation between performative governance and citizen approval, holding all else constant. This is statistically significant in both models. Every additional news article on performative governance is associated with an average 0.008-point increase in citizen approval on a five-point scale. Regression results also unsurprisingly show a negative correlation between a city's average air pollution level (both objective and perceived) and an individual's approval of local environmental governance: as pollution rises, approval falls. This is significant in both models. In addition, approval is higher among respondents who are older, poorer, and less educated. I repeat the analysis using approval on a scale of 0–10 as an alternative measure of the outcome variable, and the results remain similar.

Quantitative results in this section offer suggestive evidence that performative governance may improve citizen approval, all else being equal. They also suggest,

TABLE 8 Linear mixed effects regression estimates on citizen approval of environmental governance

	APPROVAL	APPROVAL
Performative governance	0.008*	0.008**
in news	(0.004)	(0.002)
PM 2.5 level	−0.005**	−
	(0.002)	
Perceived air quality	−	0.476***
		(0.012)
Log (GDP pc)	−0.161*	0.001
	(0.075)	(0.047)
Environmentalist	−0.037	−0.020
	(0.024)	(0.022)
Female	0.003	0.003
	(0.030)	(0.027)
Age	0.007***	0.003**
	(0.001)	(0.001)
Log (income)	−0.055**	−0.032*
	(0.016)	(0.015)
Education	−0.074***	−0.054***
	(0.012)	(0.011)
Observations	6,164	6,164
Conditional R^2	0.05	0.24

Note: $p \leq 0.1$; * $p \leq 0.05$; ** $p \leq 0.01$; *** $p \leq 0.001$. Standard errors in parentheses.

not surprisingly, that Chinese citizens still long for substantive governance, since air pollution is significantly associated with citizen disapproval. The lack of longitudinal data doesn't allow me to estimate how stable and long-lasting these effects are. However, it should be reiterated that from the bureaucrats' perspective, performative governance is intended to diffuse short-term crises that fall on the agency, not to generate long-term support for the regime.[27]

Petition or Protest

Readers may nevertheless wonder what citizens' approval of local environmental governance means for how they relate to the political system as a whole. The UEAS did not have any questions about "regime support" specifically; but two survey questions provide a window into this matter by gauging the respondents' propensity to use petition and protest as two distinct ways of making their voices heard by the state.

The first question proposed the following scenario: "Suppose your neighborhood is afflicted by industrial waste air. After calling the environmental hotline to complain, you are simply told that the surrounding enterprises have not violated regulations in their emissions. Are you more likely to: (1) accept this result, (2) not accept this result but keep quiet, or (3) not accept this result and keep seeking accountability [*zhuize*]?" Eighty-seven percent of respondents provided a clear answer. Among them, 11 percent said they would accept the result, 38 percent said they would not accept the result but would keep quiet, while 52 percent said they would keep seeking accountability. I use this question to approximate the respondent's proclivity to use the petition system: those who said they would accept the result have the lowest petition propensity (coded as 1); those who said they would not accept but keep quiet have medium petition propensity (coded as 2); those who said they would keep seeking accountability have the highest petition propensity (coded as 3).

In the second question, the respondent is reminded about a protest against the Ningbo government for green-lighting the construction of a para-xylene (PX) factory: "In 2012, Ningbo citizens, out of concern for certain chemical plants' impact on public health, collectively took to the streets and marched on the municipal government to express their opposition."[28] It then asked: "If a similar situation happened in your city, would you participate in the protest?" Ninety-seven percent of respondents provided a clear answer. Among them, 65 percent said they would participate in such a protest (coded as 3), 7 percent said they might (coded as 2), and 28 percent said they would not (coded as 1).

I use ordinal logistic regressions to examine whether citizens' approval of local environmental governance affects their likelihood of using either petitions or protests to express their dissatisfaction.[29] The dependent variable is individuals' propensity to engage in either petition or protest. The main independent variable is their approval of local environmental governance. The model also includes PM 2.5 levels and GDP per capita as city-level control variables, as well as gender, age, income, education, and environmentalism as individual controls.

Table 9 presents results from the logit analysis, using multiple imputation to account for missing data.[30] Specifically, the numbers in table 9 describe how individuals' odds to petition or protest change with each unit increase on the independent variables. Strikingly, citizens who are more satisfied with local government performance are more likely to keep petitioning the government (i.e., work within the system) whenever it fails to resolve their problem. Each unit increase of approval increases an individual's odds to use petition by 11 percent.

But citizens who are more satisfied with local environmental governance are less likely to participate in protests against the government. Each unit increase of approval reduces an individual's odds to use protest by 5 percent.

TABLE 9 How approval changes odds to petition and protest

	CHANGE OF *PETITION* ODDS WITH EACH UNIT INCREASE OF APPROVAL	CHANGE OF *PROTEST* ODDS WITH EACH UNIT INCREASE OF APPROVAL
Approval of local environmental governance	+11%***	–5%*
PM 2.5 level	–	–
Log (GDP_pc)	–	–
Environmentalist	+35%***	+45%***
Female	–19%***	–12%*
Age	–0.5%*	–
log (income)	–	–5%*
Education	+20%***	–8%**
Observations	6,164	6,164
McFadden's Pseudo R^2	0.02	0.01

Note: $p \leq 0.1$; * $p \leq 0.05$; ** $p \leq 0.01$; *** $p \leq 0.001$. Only statistically significant results are reported.

In addition, more environmentalist citizens are more likely to both petition and protest. Females are less likely to both petition and protest. Interestingly, more educated citizens are more likely to petition but less likely to protest.

Overall, analysis in this section offers suggestive evidence that from an ordinary citizen's perspective, complaints may be a healthy part of state-society interaction. It also indirectly confirms the logic for performative governance, from the street-level bureaucrat's perspective: assuaging citizen complaints that flow into the petition system may help prevent full-blown crises of public opinion.[31]

Issue, Knowledge, and Grievance

We learned in an earlier section that citizens report greater disapproval of government performance in cities where air pollution is measurably worse. But this is not the entire story about public opinion—which is, after all, marked by complex psychological foundations and day-to-day instability.

In 2014–16, I conducted sixty semistructured interviews with urban citizens (forty in Lakeville, twenty in Beijing) about their perception of government performance in pollution control and environmental protection. The main lesson I drew from these citizen interviews was that the objective existence of a problem ("issue"), public perception of its severity ("knowledge"), and felt dissatisfaction over the issue ("grievance") are distinct phenomena that do not always correspond.

First, most people—at least those living in a Humean world—would agree that objective facts about public issues can be established, or at least approximated, independent from individual perceptions, values, and emotions. For example, manmade climate change, like gravity, is a real *issue*, regardless of whether people believe it.[32]

Second, individuals may possess diverse kinds of *knowledge* regarding the same issue—in terms of both awareness of its substance and perception of its severity. For example, the statement "climate change is severe" is ultimately based on the speaker's perception or normative judgment of the issue.

Third, individuals may harbor different levels of grievances over the issue, which may or may not correlate with their knowledge of the issue. For example, someone may believe that climate change is real and severe, and yet still feel indifferent to it. Perhaps the individual pays little attention to the issue, or believes that there are other issues even more urgent or important than climate change, or that the problem is too big to be solved. Perhaps the individual owns or works in a coal mine. To be sure, grievances can also emerge from perceived knowledge over what is in fact a nonissue, as seen most clearly in conspiracy theories.

Existing research on public opinion has paid attention to both the issue-knowledge gap and the issue-grievance gap. For example, in a study of the American public's delayed attention to air pollution in the 1950s and 1960s, Matthew Crenson wrote: "The issues we ignore sometimes seem to be more important than the ones that receive attention. The decisions that we fail to make often seem to be more critical for the life of the nation than the ones that we do make."[33] Fast forwarding to today, there is still a large gap between the objective threat of climate change and both popular belief in its severity and the grievances resulting from that knowledge.

The issue-awareness or issue-grievance gap can also exist between "nonissues" and the acute public attention paid to them. For example, scholars find that the low probability of terrorist attacks on any given day doesn't correspond with the high popular fear that they might occur. The gap between the low importance of a nonissue and the extensive attention and acute grievance it arouses can also be seen in popular conspiracy theories.

The knowledge-grievance gap is less recognized in public opinion research. One example of such a gap is public perceptions of inequality. Martin Whyte's research found that people in some countries with severe income inequality (such as the United States, China, and Japan) are more accepting of inequality than people in more equal places (such as Western Europe).[34] This may be explained by cultural mores in highly unequal places that emphasize the individual work ethic and downplay the structural reasons for wealth differentials. The notion of "false consciousness" is one important explanation for the knowledge-grievance gap.

Gaps between issue, knowledge, and grievance emerged frequently in my interviews. Of particular interest is evidence of the knowledge-grievance gap. Most interviewees believed that pollution was severe, but not everyone was emotionally perturbed by it, or thought that dramatic changes had to be made. This finding suggests, first and foremost, that we should be careful when interpreting survey results: perception of the severity of a problem is not equivalent to active concern about the issue, which is not equivalent to political disapproval, which is not equivalent, in turn, to antiregime attitudes or a loss of legitimacy.

A number of my interviewees in Lakeville recognized that environmental problems were severe yet still considered existing government measures acceptable. In 2014 air pollution data had become widely available through cellphone apps, on government websites, and in weather reports. When I asked for comments on the city's air quality, only one person described it as good. Many offered vivid descriptions of memorable experiences with extreme air pollution. "Sometimes smog is so heavy in the morning, it feels like the end of the world," a twenty-nine-year-old retail manager told me.[35] Yet, far fewer interviewees vocalized strong demand for swift and decisive policy changes.

Status quo acceptance may have different causes. For some, it could stem from a lack of efficacy similar to what Mary Gallagher calls "informed disenchantment."[36] One thirty-four-year-old freelancer from District S told me she felt "despair" (*juewang*) from years of suffering the pungent waste air. After repeatedly complaining and never seeing the issue resolved, she had decided to move as soon as she had saved enough for a down payment on a new place in a different district, far away from factories.[37]

Most of those who live farther from the sources of industrial pollution rationalized their status quo acceptance with economic arguments. Many interviewees freely acknowledged the importance of environmental protection. But few believed that environmental protection should jeopardize people's economic livelihood—a caveat to the survey question that forced the respondent to choose between the two, which yielded a significantly different finding than my qualitative interviews.

The perceived importance of the economy was especially pronounced among interviewees in the north, despite the north's worse air quality. Mr. Zhang, a forty-seven-year-old government employee in Beijing, said, "You cannot choke to death on air pollution. But you can freeze to death without heating."[38] As I contended in chapter 2, this perceived trade-off is by no means unfounded, especially for people whose income is tied to high-polluting sectors and for those who cannot afford higher energy costs.

Interviewees often made references to how long the United States and Europe took to clean up their environments. Ms. Chen, a twenty-nine-year-old bank clerk, said, "America and Europe both took a long time to resolve their pollution problems. It will be the same in China. . . . Only after the economy has successfully transformed [*zhuanxing*] can pollution completely disappear."[39] Ms. Xia, a thirty-two-year-old business owner, recounted: "I remember reading about the London smog. . . . If in a developed Western country [*xifang fada guojia*], with an open and transparent government, it took . . . how many years? . . . I don't think [a speedy resolution] is possible in China."[40]

My most memorable interview was with Mr. Du, a twenty-six-year-old barista at a Starbucks in Lakeville. Mr. Du is skeptical of environmental protection. He believed that the popular documentary *Under the Dome* was funded by American foundations to sow domestic discord in China. His skepticism was heightened after reading Cixin Liu's Hugo Award–winning science fiction novel, *The Three-Body Problem*. One of the book's villains is an American eco-terrorist who helped an alien civilization in their plot to colonize earth. Much like a certain American president, who once claimed that "the concept of global warming was created by and for the Chinese in order to make US manufacturing noncompetitive," Mr. Du believed that the notion of environmental protection was introduced to China as an American conspiracy to stymie Chinese development.[41] But even Mr. Du acknowledged that air pollution was bad. Du's attitudes demonstrate an especially glaring chasm between knowledge of an issue (pollution) on one hand and a lack of grievance (support for stricter environmental protection measures) on the other.

The knowledge-grievance gap has also been identified in other studies. In the years since my ethnographic fieldwork, I supervised two senior theses on air pollution in China at Harvard University and the University of Pittsburgh. Both students, after spending a summer in China conducting in-depth semi-structured interviews, independently reached the conclusion that there was generally a lack of public interest in taking individual or collective action about air pollution—something neither of them had expected to find before departing for fieldwork in China, based on all the reporting of "airpocalypse" in the news. Alexandra Foote's interviews in Beijing found that inaction stemmed from a sense of inefficacy expressed through an overarching sentiment of "*meibanfa*"—"there is nothing one can do."[42] Alyssa Martinec uses system justification theory to explain the "rationalization" of air pollution among the urban middle class in Shanghai, with a significant number of her interviewees invoking economic concerns and lauding government efforts.[43]

Given the poor air quality in Lakeville in 2013–14, it is especially interesting to consider the opinions of those who saw government performance in a positive light. Two distinct narratives emerged in the positive affirmations of environmental governance in Lakeville. First, some interviewees mentioned the "good attitude/manners" (*taidu*) of state agents, suggesting that demonstrating benevolent intentions—a core element of performative governance—may have indeed gained sympathy for the state, even when its substantive performance was visibly subpar. Ms. Xia remembered the time her neighbor called the environmental hotline: "They called her back a few days later to tell her they'd discovered no violation of regulations. . . . They insisted there was no violation, but their attitude was not bad [*taidu bucuo*]."[44]

An improvement in "attitude" was often mentioned by interviewees when describing government agents. An environmental NGO worker in Beijing, who was in regular contact with local EPB offices, spoke of a dramatic improvement in the government's responsiveness: "A few years ago nobody would give a damn about your complaints. Now as soon as you make the call they show up immediately."[45] As the previous chapter shows, by lowering itself in front of citizens—sometimes acting as their virtual punching bag—the state gives citizens a sense of power and efficacy, even when it cannot resolve their problems.

This insight finds support in the American context as well, as Bernardo Zacka relates:

> [Bureaucrats'] demeanor . . . contributes to shaping how the encounter with the state will be experienced—whether it will "feel" welcoming or transactional, considerate or inquisitive, respectful or demeaning. . . . It is, in part, through our encounters with street-level bureaucrats that our perception of the legitimacy and trustworthiness of our political institutions is shaped. Some studies have even shown that *how* policies are implemented can have greater impact on people's perception of legitimacy than *what* those policies are.[46]

In addition to the benevolence it displays, the promissory nature of performative governance is a second rationale leading a significant number of citizens, especially those living far from the sources of pollution, to expect environmental quality to improve in the future. For example, Ms. Zhou, a sixty-year-old retiree in Lakeville, said, "I see in the news that our government has done some things lately. . . . The government is treating [environmental protection] with increasing importance in recent years."[47] But when asked what the government had done, she had a hard time recalling specific examples. This suggests merely showing up could help gain the agency more visibility and approval. A thirty-eight-year-old college lecturer in Lakeville saw the government's increasing transparency with air pollution data as a signal that substantive measures would follow.[48]

This expectation that air quality would improve was supported in the UEAS: one question asked respondents if they believed air quality would improve in the future. Fifty percent said they believed air quality would "likely improve" in the next three years, and 21 percent believed it would "definitely improve" in the next three years. This expectation of future improvements recalls Hirschman's distinction among "exit, voice, and loyalty" as responses to poor organizational performance.[49] For Hirschman, "loyalty" isn't an uncritical acceptance of bad results, but rather a willingness to stand by the system in the expectation that its performance will eventually improve.

In sum, my interviews offer several potential explanations for the knowledge-grievance gap—performative governance being one of them.

In fall 2019, I followed up with six interviewees who had expressed especially strong opinions about environmental protection (positive or negative) in our 2014 meetings. All of them noted significant improvement in air quality in Lakeville.

Ms. Xia, who was pessimistic about the prospects of pollution control in 2014, had become more hopeful: "My daughter is learning about environmental protection in her primary school science classes. For example, last week she had to take a test on waste sorting [*laji fenlei*] at school. And even we adults have to learn what is 'dry garbage' and what is 'wet garbage.'"[50] That year, forty-six major cities were mobilized to implement a new policy of garbage sorting and recycling. According to the Ministry of Housing and Urban-Rural Development, the policy had already covered over seventy-seven million households by December 2019.[51]

Starbucks barista Mr. Du's interest had moved on to the unfolding US-China trade war. With many friends working in the service industry—some of them migrants—he divulged personal stories of the economic slowdown: high-end restaurants closing, friends moving back to their inland hometowns (*hui laojia*), a few thinking about taking the exam to enter a master's program (*kaoyan*). When I asked him about air pollution, he paused for a second and simply responded "it's not important," and said nothing further.[52]

Meanwhile, retiree Ms. Zhou thought pollution was no longer a major problem at all. When I asked why, she replied, "Because I haven't seen them [environmental bureaucrats] in the news in a while."[53]

Appendix: Survey Methods

The UEAS was commissioned to the Horizon Group, a reputable survey agency based in Beijing. It was administered using random digit dialing, or computer assisted telephone interviews (CATI), whereby a computer randomly generates numerical combinations to create a telephone number: the first three digits were randomly selected from a set of numbers used by the three biggest service providers in China (China Mobile, China Unicom, and China Telecom); the next four digits were usually the city area code; and the last four digits were randomly generated. Those who answered the phone must have lived in the city for at least a year to qualify as a resident and respondent.

The UEAS covered thirty cities: Changchun, Changzhi, Changzhou, Chongqing, Deyang, Guilin, Guiyang, Hangzhou, Hefei, Hohhot, Jinzhou, Lanzhou, Luoyang, Nanchang, Nanning, Rizhao, Shenzhen, Shijiazhuang, Tai'an, Taiyuan, Xianyang, Xining, Yan'an, Yichang, Yinchuan, Wenzhou, Wuhan, Wuxi, Zhongshan, and Zhuzhou. These cities were selected to allow for geographic diversity and variation in air quality.

In the UEAS, a total of 673,987 dialing attempts were made; of those, 216,214 people answered the phone. Of those, 153,047 refused to participate in the survey, 20,729 did not qualify for the interview, 30,536 dropped out, and 6,796 completed the survey (the rest did not complete the survey or were dropped for other reasons). The effective sample size is 6,164. This success rate is normal for telephone interviews in China. Main reasons for dropout included language barrier (e.g., low success rate in Guangdong because many locals only speak Cantonese); the survey taking longer than respondents had expected; and people thinking it was a telephone scam. Political sensitivity was not a big concern because discussing and complaining about environmental pollution was widespread around the time of this research, and would fit with the government's own narrative on the need for environmental protection.

Table 10 compares sample characteristics of the UEAS, including gender, age, income, and education, with the 2016 sample from the China Family Panel Survey.

TABLE 10 Comparison of 2015 UEAS and 2016 CFPS

CHARACTERISTIC	UEAS (N = 6,164)	CFPS (N = 16,230)	DIFFERENCE	95% CONFIDENCE INTERVAL	P-VALUE
% Female	43%	51%	−8.0%	−9.5%, −6.5%	<0.001
Mean age	37	46	−9.0	−9.4, −8.6	<0.001
Mean Education Level	3.41	2.44	1.0	0.87, 1.1	<0.001
Mean Household size	4.29	3.97	0.32	0.28, 0.37	<0.001
Mean income	75,243	72,320	2,923	−737, 6,584	0.12

Note: Welch two-sample t-test for equality of proportions

The UMCS was also administered using random digit dialing. The success rate (number of completed survey divided by number of people who picked up the phone) was 3 percent. The sample size was 600; 51.3 percent of the respondents were female. The median age of the respondents was between thirty and thirty-nine; the median education level was college; and the median household income was between 100,000 and 120,000 yuan (about US$15,923 to US$19,108 in 2015).

PERFORMATIVE BREAKDOWN

A basic problem for many performances . . . is that of information control; the audience must not acquire destructive information about the situation that is being defined for them.

—Erving Goffman

Performative governance surely doesn't work all the time, nor does it work on everyone. For "between action and consequence lies a chasm that no one can bridge, let alone control."[1] While the motivation behind performative governance is to give the citizenry an impression of good governance, this doesn't mean it's always effective. If it were, there would be no need for repression or redistribution, or for petitions and protests. Thus it's worth examining when performative governance ceases to occur or fails to work—performative breakdown.[2]

In fact, the smoking gun of performative breakdown has already appeared in previous chapters. Explanations for breakdown can be sorted into three broad categories. First, performative governance may subside when there is a change in underlying conditions, that is, low capacity and high scrutiny. Chapters 1, 2, and 3 called attention to the increasing capacity of the Chinese EPB, and the growing evidence of its substantive governance in recent years.

Second, performative breakdown may result from performer cynicism. Goffman writes that the pressure to perform can exasperate or exhaust some actors, who "come to experience a special kind of alienation from self and a special kind of wariness of others."[3] Dissatisfied bureaucrats might choose to exit their organization. But unless cynical actors speak up, or the entire cast of actors changes their behavior en masse, performative governance may continue without significant interruption.

Third, performative governance may fail to impress its targets, resulting in a communication breakdown between the actors and their audience. Although in chapter 4 I find a positive correlation between performative governance and public approval, I don't assume this to be a stable equilibrium. In chapters 3 and 4 I also began to address audience cynicism—when citizens, for whatever reason, refuse to give credence to the images projected by performative governance. Performative governance can convince some citizens of the state's virtue, but it can't convince them all.

This penultimate chapter further explores the sources of audience cynicism. Specifically, I focus on the importance of destructive information, defined as "facts which, if attention is drawn to them during the performance, would discredit, disrupt, or make useless the impression that the performance fosters."[4] Goffman, who is keenly interested in such "performance disruptions," writes that "a basic problem for many performances . . . is that of information control; the audience must not acquire destructive information about the situation that is being defined for them."[5] In our case, when the state fails at information control, it increases the likelihood of destructive information coming to light.

The rest of this chapter offers four case studies of performative governance, including three examples of performative breakdown. While so far this book has primarily dealt with air pollution, here I venture into other issue areas. I first trace two well-known public health crises—the Flint water crisis in the United States and the Covid-19 outbreak in Wuhan—to demonstrate the power of destructive information to cause performative breakdown. I then compare two water-pollution crises, in Vietnam and China, to further substantiate how state failure at information control increases the odds of performative breakdown.

Flint

The archway over South Saginaw Street still stands, proudly proclaiming Flint, Michigan, to be "Vehicle City." The sign, and the identity it claims, are but sorry remnants of the city's former industrial glory, first heralded by the birth of General Motors in 1905. Flint is now one of the poorest cities in America: one in every five houses downtown is vacant; 40 percent of its residents live below the poverty line. Its crime rate is among the highest in the country.

By the 2010s, Flint had sunk into financial jeopardy. In April 2014, to save money, the city switched its source of tap water from the Detroit River to the Flint River. Soon residents were complaining that their tap water had strange colors, a peculiar taste, and a smell like rotten eggs. Reports of health problems followed, including skin rashes, autoimmune disorders, lead poisoning, and an outbreak of Legionnaires' disease.

City officials summarily dismissed the barrage of complaints. In April 2015, an entire year after health problems first emerged, Mayor Dayne Walling defiantly tweeted that "My family and I drink and use the Flint water every day, at home, work, and schools."

Two months later, fourteen months after Flint residents first began falling ill, a "rogue agent" from the US Environmental Protection Agency (USEPA) named Miguel Del Toral blew the whistle in an internal memo. The memo revealed that lead levels in the water of Flint homes were several times higher than the EPA's allowable limit. The memo was soon leaked to the American Civil Liberties Union (ACLU), which forwarded it to Michigan Radio, effectively publicizing the case.[6]

Heightening scrutiny forced city and state officials into the spotlight. In a July 2015 television interview, Mayor Walling performed an act used by officials around the world during water-contamination crises—he downed a cup of what was purported to be Flint's tap water. When Michigan Radio interviewed the state's Department of Environmental Quality, its spokesperson said, live on air: "Anyone who is concerned about lead in the drinking water in Flint can relax."[7]

But lead there was. A team of Virginia Tech researchers found elevated lead levels in 40 percent of Flint homes. Another study showed high lead levels in the blood of Flint children. Belatedly, as Christmas approached, newly elected mayor Karen Weaver declared a state of emergency. The City of Flint was found in violation of the 1974 federal Safe Drinking Water Act for having discontinued its corrosion control treatment in the city's aged service pipes, jeopardizing the health of 100,000 residents.[8]

In January 2016, almost two years after the problem first emerged, Michigan governor Rick Snyder dispatched the National Guard to hand out bottled water door to door.[9] During a US congressional hearing in March, Snyder portrayed himself as a victim of the crisis: "Sipping a bottle of water held with trembling hands," *The Guardian* reported, he told lawmakers "I kick myself every day over what happened in Flint."[10] Snyder said he blamed himself for having been deceived by "career bureaucrats" in his administration.[11]

Snyder's theatrics were rejected by the whistleblower, who curtly averred: "The State is complicit."[12] And they were similarly challenged by a University of Michigan study, which stated that Snyder "bears significant legal responsibility" for his lack of substantive measures earlier: "[The complaints] were not hidden from the governor . . . he had a responsibility to listen and respond."[13]

By the end of 2016, a dozen employees in the Michigan Department of Environmental Quality (MDEQ) and Michigan Department of Health and Human Services (MDHHS) faced criminal charges, including misconduct, conspiracy to tamper with evidence, and neglect of duty. In 2017, several MDHHS officials were charged with involuntary manslaughter for the year-long coverup, as well as their obstruction of the investigation process. But for the people of Flint, it was "too little, too late."[14] Shocked by the state's extended delay in acknowledging and addressing the problem, a schoolteacher asked: "How can this be happening in the United States of America?"[15]

How indeed? Rewind to the height of the Flint water crisis in January 2016. When evidence emerged that the City of Flint and the State of Michigan had ignored warnings from the USEPA about possible lead in the water, Governor Snyder was put under the spotlight to explain the state's prolonged inaction. He said that he had waited months to declare a state of emergency because he needed "a formal request from the county to act." He highlighted other efforts made by the state to salvage the situation, proclaiming: "We've worked hard but we need to get more connection to the citizens of Flint."[16] When *The Washington Post* asked Michigan Senate minority leader Jim Ananich of the Democratic Party to comment on Snyder's claims, Ananich said, "The administration is acting like this is a *public relations problem* for the governor and not acting like this is a *public health crisis*, and that is the problem."[17]

Rivalry between Democrats and Republicans notwithstanding, Ananich was making a valid point: when the problems first emerged, Flint and Michigan authorities had ignored citizen complaints and warnings from the EPA.[18] After the EPA whistleblower leaked the internal memo to the ACLU and the issue was picked up by media, officials first turned to the performative, as seen in Mayor Walling's water-drinking theatrics and Governor Snyder's trembling hands. But performative governance wasn't enough to contain the public opinion crisis. Substantive measures came, albeit belatedly, after the scandal was brought to the attention of the entire nation through the Virginia Tech study and President Obama's authorization of federal aid to alleviate the emergency.[19]

Wuhan

Five years later, in Wuhan, the provincial capital of China's inland Hubei Province, what would become a much larger public health crisis was beginning to unravel. Though very different, in some ways it would prove eerily similar to the Flint water crisis.

On January 3, 2020, Dr. Li Wenliang, an ophthalmologist at Wuhan Central Hospital, was summoned by the district police department. There Li received an "admonition" (*xunjie*)—the "lightest punishment for minor crime" (*fanzui qingjie qingwei*) in the form of criticism and education—for posting "inaccurate" (*bushushi*) information online.[20] Specifically, the information that Li had posted in a WeChat group of his former medical school classmates had created the impression that the formidable SARS virus, which had stricken China in 2003, had returned. Dr. Li later released the Admonition Letter (*xunjieshu*) given to him, which read as follows:

> On December 30, 2019, in WeChat Group '. . . [name redacted]; [you] made untrue comments about seven confirmed SARS cases from Huanan Fruits and Seafood Market. . . . Your behavior has seriously disturbed social order, and stepped beyond the boundary of what the law allows, . . . [it is] an illegal behavior! The police bureau hopes you will actively cooperate, listen to the persuasion of the civil police [*minjin*], and cease illegal activities. Can you do it?

Li's handwriting under the stamp of his fingerprint says: "Yes." The Admonition Letter then reads:

> We hope you will calm down and reflect on this, and we sternly warn you that if you do not correct your behavior, and continue to break the law, you will be punished by law! Do you understand?

Li's handwriting under another stamp of his fingerprint says: "Understood."[21]

Dr. Li would later become known as one of the eight whistleblowers of the 2019 novel coronavirus (Covid-19) outbreak, first identified in Wuhan. These eight citizens, all doctors, were admonished for spreading rumors about the virus online, and news about their infractions was widely broadcast on state media in early January.[22] Unlike Del Toral, Dr. Li only meant to warn his former classmates, fellow doctors all, to take precautions against the new virus; he even asked members of the chat group not to distribute his messages, but one of them ignored his request. Yet by the time the world learned Li's name, Wuhan officials were already at the center of public outrage over their mishandling of the outbreak, assailed for their lack of transparency during the month after the virus was discovered in the city. In December 2019 there were already signs that the virus could be spread from person to person, but Wuhan authorities kept this information from the public and failed to contain the virus in the busy month before the lunar new year.[23]

Dr. Li returned to work the day after receiving the admonition. Only a week later he fell ill after contracting the virus from a patient. A month after that, he passed away in Wuhan Central Hospital, where he worked. He was only thirty-four.

By the time Li was admitted into the ICU in early February, he had already been rehabilitated by the court of public opinion, as well as an opinion from the Supreme People's Court, which stated that "although the new pneumonia [*xinxing feiyan*] is not SARS, the content of [Li's post] was not completely fabricated.[24] If the public had listened to [Li's] 'rumor' at the time, and, out of panic and fear of SARS, took measures such as wearing masks, strict disinfection, and avoiding visiting wild animal markets, this could have been a blessing that would help us better control the virus today."[25]

On February 6, 2020, the night Dr. Li died, an information tsunami inundated the Chinese Internet.[26] It started around 9:30 p.m., when the news of Li's death flooded social media and was later confirmed by *People's Daily* and the World Health Organization (WHO) on their social media accounts, among other sources. The public's deep sadness over the heroic whistleblower's death and the sobering realization that the virus could kill someone so young and healthy fused with righteous anger over Li's earlier mistreatment by state security.

An accidental hero, Li was crowned *the* whistleblower of Covid-2019, and the celebration of his bravery became an act of tacit resistance against a system that lacked transparency. Li's admonition letter was widely reposted on social media, as was his memorable statement that "a healthy society should not have only one kind of voice."[27] His acquiescent utterance at the end of the admonishment letter—"Understood" (*mingbai*)—became a symbol of performative submission to repressive authorities. Public outrage even spilled over into criticism of the entire political system, and references to "freedom of speech"—words that would surely have been censored in ordinary times—gained traction on social media.

The public furor swelled for hours. But around midnight a strange new wave of reports emerged, claiming that Li had not yet passed away. Wuhan Central Hospital reported that he was still fighting for his life with the help of an artificial lung. This caused much confusion among Li's admirers, but it also turned their crushing despair into a glimmer of hope, and their scathing condemnation of authorities into prayers for a miracle that the beloved doctor would survive.

Yet public opinion quickly shifted course again. Another wave of posts doubting the nature of the rescue effort soon eclipsed the prayers on social media for Li's recovery. Suspicious netizens questioned the authorities' motive in using extracorporeal life support after the patient's heart had stopped beating. A few unsourced but widely shared posts claimed that Li was only put on life support after his heart had stopped beating, so as to divert the public's wrath over political mismanagement toward hope for a medical miracle—and the eventual disappointment at the lack of a miracle. Others claimed that authorities wanted to wait till people were asleep to announce the bad news.[28] When Wuhan Central Hospital finally announced on Weibo at 3:48 a.m. that Li had passed away despite "an all-out rescue effort" (*quanli qiangjiu*), one of the most upvoted comments accused authorities of "performative rescue" (*biaoyanshi qiangjiu*) by allegedly putting a dead person on life support to manage public opinion.

It's still not clear whether the emergency treatment Dr. Li received between 10:00 p.m. on February 6 and 3:00 a.m. on February 7 was simply performative. But it would be a likely scenario—a case where an extreme lack of state capacity (to revive a dead person) coincided with an extreme abundance of public scrutiny (over the quality of medical treatment Dr. Li received). It's also unclear whether hospital authorities, local officials, or higher-level officials made the decision to put Li on extracorporeal life support. But needless to say, whoever was responsible felt cornered by public opinion and decided they had to display a genuine "all-out rescue effort" to quell the flames of popular fury.

However, the "all-out rescue effort" could not even temporarily diffuse the mounting discontent. Popular references on social media to "[theatrical] performance" (*biaoyan*) and "performative rescue" suggest that the public was not convinced by the state's purportedly benevolent intentions.

Destructive Information

These two cases from Wuhan and Flint help shed light on the power of destructive information—information that is incompatible with the impression a performance is intended to foster.

Tracing how the Flint scandal unfolded, it's evident that America's democratic institutions played a minimal role in preventing a serious public health crisis over the basic need for clean water—a crisis that festered for an entire year before receiving attention, and to this day still awaits full resolution.[29] Competition between political parties was neither the culprit nor the cure. Instead, it was the publicization of the problem and the dissemination of information among the wider public, through the media and the Internet, that triggered a somewhat substantive response from the State of Michigan and the White House. Wuhan similarly demonstrated the power of destructive information to bring state malpractice to light, and to render performative governance ineffective at calming public anger.

Destructive information is often released by critical actors whose interest is the greater good.[30] This occurred in both Flint and Wuhan. In an interview, Del Toral, the Flint whistleblower, expressed his bitterness about the "cesspool" of the USEPA: "It's all of this 'don't find anything bad' crap at the EPA that is [the] reason I desperately want to leave. I am not happy to find bad things. . . . It is completely stressful because it means children are being damaged and I have to put up with all of the political crap. . . . I truly, truly hate working here."[31]

Whistleblowing is an extreme example of performer cynicism, when an actor goes off-script not only to "be true to oneself" but also to knowingly betray their team. Such betrayal will likely bring retaliation from the system—firing, arrest, exile, lawsuits, and blacklisting are a few common fates of whistleblowers. This makes whistleblowing an act that is heroic in legend but often frowned on in real life.

The fact that Del Toral was called a "rogue agent" is not only indicative of the secretive ways in which bureaucracies operate. It's also a telling sign that most people in most systems where they have a vested interest—political, economic, or social—participate in perpetuating the scripts of these systems for various conscious, unconscious, or falsely conscious reasons, even in the face of systemic negligence or malpractice.

As Goffman puts it, "A team must be able to keep its secrets and have its secrets kept."[32] There may well be other Flints that the general public has no knowledge of because potentially destructive leaks were plugged before they had a chance to come to light. The #MeToo Movement in late 2017 was a prime example of how systematic malpractice can remain invisible for a long time before entering public consciousness.

If whistleblowers were the only safeguard against governance failures, the world would be a much bleaker place. The rest of this chapter shifts attention from individual whistleblowers to the larger information environment: from actors to structures. Specifically, I focus on the conditions under which the state fails at information control, which increases the amount of destructive information and thus the likelihood of audience cynicism. Notably, the social media storm on the night of Dr. Li's death shows that when the information environment is relaxed—censorship loosened for a few hours on the night of February 6–7, 2020, allowing for terms like "freedom of speech" to pick up steam— audience cynicism can develop rapidly.[33]

A controlled information environment shouldn't be equated with low audience scrutiny. Scrutiny can be high in a controlled information environment, such as during a theatrical play; scrutiny can also be low in a laissez-faire information market when the audience isn't paying attention to the issue in question. What information control limits is *destructive* information. In both Flint and Wuhan, destructive information made scrutinizing citizens rethink the "definition of the situation," that is, the competence, responsiveness, and benevolence of the state in its efforts to keep them safe.[34]

Information Control

If Flint and Wuhan belong to two national political systems that are "most different," we now turn to two regimes conventionally considered "most similar"—China and Vietnam.[35] Both are Communist Party–ruled single-party regimes with partially liberalized economies—"socialism with Chinese characteristics" in China and a "socialist-oriented market economy" in Vietnam. Both regimes maintain a tight grip on the political sphere; Freedom House has consistently given both the worst-possible score (7) on political rights.

Although China and Vietnam are often treated as "most similar" in the literature, there are important differences between them. First, country size may be an uninteresting variable, but it surely matters. Scholars since Rousseau have argued that democratic institutions are more likely to emerge and be sustained in smaller countries; and Vietnam is about 3.5 percent the size of China. Second, Vietnam and China are at different developmental levels: Vietnam's GDP per capita was US$2,185 in 2016, whereas China's was nearly four times as high, at US$8,123. Third, Vietnam and China have very different relationships with the West, which can affect the kinds of political institutions they adopt and oppositional activity they abide. China is the main rival of the United States. Vietnam, although ruled by a single-party communist regime, is increasingly embraced by the United States as a strategic partner. Fourth, Vietnam's political sphere is slightly more competitive than China's. Some observers consider the party, state, and legislature in Vietnam to be quasi-independent power centers.[36] While it's debatable how much decision making in China is actually centralized, and what political competitiveness in Vietnam actually means when the dominant party doesn't permit competitors, there are unquestionably institutional differences between the two. That said, the two regimes have abundant similarities according to most typologies, especially when compared to most other conceivable pairs of regimes.

Parallel water pollution crises occurred in China and Vietnam, but with divergent trajectories. In both crises, water sources were polluted by industrial waste, resulting in major public outcry. In response, officials in both countries piously engaged in performative governance—they went swimming in the water to showcase the state's responsiveness. But performative governance didn't impress Vietnamese citizens as much as it did in China.

I argue that this difference in citizens' appraisal of performative governance can be partly explained by the structural variation in the two countries' information environment. Even though both regimes seek to restrict civil liberties such as freedom of expression and freedom of association, there is a glaring difference in their ability to control the Internet. The Internet penetration rate is similar in China and Vietnam: based on World Bank data from 2015, 53 percent of the population were Internet users in both countries. However, the level of content filtering is much higher in China than it is in Vietnam.[37] While China maintains "one of the most pervasive and sophisticated regimes of Internet filtering and information control in the world," the Vietnamese Internet is more like the Wild

West.[38] Consider the simple fact that Vietnam is one of Google and Facebook's largest markets, whereas both are blocked in China.

The variation in content filtering stems not from a difference in the two regimes' intention to control the Internet, but from their very different capacities. This is partly explained in turn by the different starting points of their economic reforms. Both China and Vietnam liberalized their economies with the help of foreign direct investment—China's economic reform officially started in 1978, and Vietnam's started in 1986. This eight-year difference has been critical to the shape of their information environments. By the time the Internet and social media had become an unavoidable part of business and life, the Chinese government already had the necessary financial and human capital for adapting to emerging information challenges, whereas the Vietnamese government did not.

In the first decade of the twenty-first century, China successfully developed its powerful homegrown search engine, Baidu, and social media alternatives like Weibo and WeChat, whereas Vietnam still lacks the capacity to do so. Vietnam's native search engine, Coc Coc, attempts to challenge Google, but has yet to succeed. (Google has captured about 60 percent of the browser market, compared to Coc Coc's 25 percent.) Coc Coc's initial success came from offering "something both unique and highly valued: easy and consistent access to Facebook."[39] At the time of this study, the Vietnamese economy is still in a deeper condition of dependence on foreign direct investment, and foreign firms often demand full Internet access as a prerequisite for entry. China, on the other hand, has embarked on a full-blown promotion of homegrown industries.

Lacking the capacity to filter Internet content, the Vietnamese government has resorted to arresting violators. But when it comes to information control, the physical arrest of individual journalists is a less sophisticated and effective tool than content filtering. Despite the high number of arrests, the Vietnamese Internet has become "a contested space": dissidents use social networking and blogging platforms to spread disruptive information about the government, while the government attempts to counter them by flooding the Internet with progovernment information, even setting up its own Facebook pages.[40] Although recent reporting shows the Vietnamese government's increasing willingness to censor—with companies like Facebook purportedly working with the Ministry of Information and Communication to "prevent offensive content," and Google partially obliging the government's request in 2017 to remove YouTube clips that defamed Vietnamese leaders—as of 2016 there was little evidence of content restriction on Facebook.[41] Again, Facebook and Google are both blocked in China.

In the rest of this chapter, I trace the development of two unconnected water pollution crises in China and Vietnam. In doing so, I show how the information environment shapes citizens' exposure to disruptive information, as well as their susceptibility to cynicism when encountering performative governance. In China, performative governance after a water crisis effectively mollified public criticism because knowledge of the discrepancy between performative governance and substantive results didn't become widespread. In Vietnam, performative governance turned into performative breakdown because the public had access to destructive information about the state from the very beginning of the crisis, thanks to Vietnam's less-controlled information environment.

Swimming Gate

Rui'an is a county-level city in the coastal province of Zhejiang, under the jurisdiction of Wenzhou city, a municipality renowned for its entrepreneurial culture. During economic reform, Rui'an was one of the first coastal Economic Development Zones, and it prospered by cornering the market on the manufacturing of three products: vehicle parts, machinery, and synthetic polymers. Its strong export sector earned Rui'an such nicknames as "the shoe capital of China" and "the car parts capital of China," and it gained a spot on a list of China's "one hundred strong" counties.[42]

Wenzhou and its surrounding areas are the birthplace of many successful private entrepreneurs, such as Jin Zengmin, the board chairman of Mao Yuanchang Eyeglasses Company. The fabled eyeglasses manufacturer and reseller was founded in 1862 in the provincial capital of Hangzhou, a three-hour drive from Rui'an.

During the Spring Festival in February 2013, Jin went home to visit family and attend an international forum of Wenzhou businessmen. After the forum, he brought a few business friends with him on a visit to his home village in Rui'an. Jin was particularly nostalgic about a river in his neighborhood, called Immortals' Landing (Xianjiang), where he swam as a child, his mother washed rice, and locals rowed dragon boats during the sweltering days of summer.[43]

But when his car approached the neighborhood, Jin and his friends were greeted by a stench that immediately counseled retreat. It was one of the most repulsive scenes he'd witnessed in his life: every inch of the river's surface was covered with kitchen waste, plastic bottles, used lanterns, and other refuse. It looked like a landfill.[44]

Jin was piqued by his home village's marked decline, and humiliated in front of his friends and potential business partners. Though he usually kept a low profile, he turned to the best weapon he could think of—social media. On February 26, he unleashed a storm of fury on Weibo. In a post that included pictures of

Immortals' Landing, Jin wrote: "This is the neighborhood that produces the largest number of leather shoes in the country. Wastewater from shoe factories is discharged directly into this river. . . . Cancer rates among residents are ridiculously high. If the director of the [Rui'an] EPB dares to swim in this river for 20 minutes, I will pay [them] 200,000 yuan [US$32,076 in 2013]." Jin ended the post by tagging the public Weibo accounts of regional media and government offices.

Because of the post's sardonic tone and shock value, as well as Jin's reputation as the chairman of a well-respected company, his challenge to the EPB quickly picked up steam online. Within a day, it had received more than seven thousand mentions on Sina Weibo and Tencent Weibo, two of the largest microblog platforms in China.[45] Interviewed by the *Metropolitan News*, Hangzhou's daily newspaper, Jin lamented his mother and sister's cancer diagnoses, attributing them to the pollution in Rui'an, as well as his children's refusal to visit their home because of the foul-smelling river: "No one wants to live here."[46]

When the *Qianjiang Evening News*, a provincial newspaper, managed to reach the director of the Rui'an EPB, its director gave a perfunctory response, saying that Jin's critique had been dealt with seriously and claiming that the pollution in Immortals' Landing was mainly caused by residents' discharging garbage into the river (despite the hundreds of rubber factories bestriding its banks).[47] This reporting was immediately reprinted by other outlets. Xinhuanet, the website of China's official press agency, gave its story the headline "Businessman Offers 200,000 Yuan to Watch EPB Director Swim in River; EPB Director Laughs It Off."[48]

The brouhaha fermented in the days that followed. Netizens leaped at Jin's dark humor and started a bidding war, daring their local EPB directors to swim in the polluted rivers of their own neighborhoods. Within three days, the bid was raised to 300,000 yuan (US$48,115 in 2013) by a resident of Cangnan. "EPB directors invited to swim in the river" (*huanbao juzhang xiahe youyong*) became one of the most often-repeated items in the microblog-sphere. Hundreds of thousands of people piled on in the online discussions.[49]

It was only when the fracas had escalated into "Swimming Gate" (*youyong men*)—a reference to Nixon's Watergate scandal—that officials in Zhejiang finally issued public pledges to restore the local rivers. During the annual Two Sessions in March, the mayor of Wenzhou announced a five-year plan to clean up the rivers and make them swimmable.[50] The governor of Zhejiang declared that he wanted to see local EPB directors swim in every river in the province.[51] The provincial party secretary insisted that "whatever is on the common folk's minds is what we do" (*baixing xiang shenme, women jiuyao gan shenme*).[52] For the rest of the year, Zhejiang EPBs ostensibly went to war on water pollution. A procession of law enforcement operations was launched to catch those who were illegally discharging industrial wastewater.

A few months after Jin's post, citizens in Zhejiang were amazed to read in their morning papers that EPB directors had gone river-swimming as promised.[53] In a public event called "Protect the Mother River," fifteen county and municipal EPB directors as well as a deputy mayor and a municipal party secretary swam three hundred meters across the Lan River, along with hundreds of citizens. An image depicting bare-chested, broad-waisted officials jumping into the river in the rain—gawked at by citizens gathering on the banks with their cameras—grabbed headlines. Another image that captured a few bobbing heads as officials puffed and paddled their way across the river was reminiscent of Mao's historic swim across the Yangtze River in 1966. In a third photo, the party secretary of Lanxi, cozily wrapped in a beach towel, smiled at the crowd as he left the river on the opposite side. "They really went swimming!" was reported on Weibo by media outlets all over China, including *People's Daily* and the *Global Times*, with cheers that "EPB officials finally responded with real action."[54]

It appeared as though the rivers in Zhejiang Province had been restored after people dared their local EPB directors to swim in them. But careful observers would notice that the Lan River—where EPB directors swam—was one of the cleanest rivers in Zhejiang to begin with. The Lan's main tributary, the Qiantang, is an active river that runs from the inland provinces of Anhui and Jiangxi through Zhejiang and out to the East China Sea. As the main source of tap water for urban citizens in Zhejiang, it's less polluted than regional rivers like the one in Rui'an, which lies three hundred kilometers southeast of the Lan. More intensive industrial activities along the Qiantang River take place around downstream towns such as Jiande, Tonglu, and Fuyang, which leaves the upstream Lan far cleaner. Thus the EPB's response to Jin's Weibo complaints about river pollution in Rui'an amounted to a performative non sequitur.

Although the Rui'an EPB did organize a trash cleanup of the river after Swimming Gate, no other attempts at regulating industrial activities in the area were found. In the same year, water pollution in Zhejiang showed no overall signs of improvement. In the winter, citizens complained periodically about strange tastes in their tap water.[55] In May, the culprit was found to be glyphosate, an active ingredient in most herbicides.[56] In December it was 2-tert-butylphenol, a kind of phenol used to produce resin and pesticides. Ironically, the strange tastes were eventually traced to factories along the Lan, the very river where EPA directors had swum back in September.[57]

The rivers might still run polluted, but the power of the swim quickly became apparent. A splashy spectacle noted in thousands of media outlets all over China sent a strong signal that public concern had triggered a dramatic response from officials. The almost comical images of officials stripped down to their swimwear and jumping into the river for the enjoyment of citizens fostered the impression that citizens had exercised control over the actions of officials. The state had lowered itself—even stripped itself down—in front of its citizens, giving them a sense of power. After all, who wouldn't relish the idea of chastened political officials reduced to swimming before a laughing public? How evil could a government possibly be if it strips down to its trunks and goes swimming at its citizens' behest?

Despite sporadic media reports that questioned whether the officials were merely "putting on a show" (*zuoxiu*), public reaction to the swim was overwhelmingly positive. *Southern Metropolitan News*, a newspaper in Guangdong known for its critical journalism, published an opinion piece entitled "Directors Went into River to Seal the Mouths of Doubters." The article comments: "The meaning of officials going swimming was not to test water quality, but a response to public sentiments. The latter is much more important. A polluted river harms only a region, yet tainted public sentiments harm the whole nation."[58] Many other newspapers echoed this view. An opinion piece in *Legal Evening News* read, "EPA directors went swimming for real . . . meaning that they were carefully listening to public sentiments instead of putting themselves high above the people and not responding to their concerns."[59]

Four years later, a mayor in Henan replicated those swimming theatrics, and the act was applauded by an opinion piece in *China Environmental News*, a newspaper managed by the MEP. The title: "A Mayor Goes Swimming in the River, So What If He Was Putting on a Show?"[60]

"We Choose Fish"

Ha Tinh, meaning "peaceful river," is a coastal province in north-central Vietnam. On its western border with Laos sits the High Slope (Pu Mat) reserves, home to several near-extinct wildlife species such as the Indochinese tiger, the Indian elephant, the Annamite striped rabbit, the Ussuri dhole (a wild dog with catlike ears—a cat-dog), and the saola (also known as the Asian unicorn—one of the world's rarest large mammals). On the province's eastern border stretches a 137-mile open coastline with large estuaries and hundreds of species of fish living harmoniously in what the Vietnamese call the Eastern Sea and the Chinese call the South Sea. Ha Tinh is poor and rural, with a GDP that accounts for only 1.1 percent of the national GDP among Vietnam's sixty-three provinces.[61] Eighty percent of its population lives in rural areas, sustained by farming and fishing—agriculture, forestry, and fishery account for 35 percent of the province's GDP.

Ha Tinh's coastline has always been blue: cosmic blue at dusk and dawn, sapphire blue at noon. But on the morning of April 6, 2016, its coast turned gray when the tide washed ashore millions of dead sea creatures.[62] Almost instantaneously, images of beaches and coastal waters covered with massive swaths of fish carcasses started trending on Facebook. Similar scenes appeared along the shores of the neighboring coastal provinces of Quang Binh, Quang Tri, and Thua Thien-Hue, as well as in Da Nang, a popular beach town some 600 miles south of Ha Tinh. In the month that followed, more than 100 tons of dead fish were picked up, including several deep-sea species and a young whale.[63] Hundreds of people were believed to have fallen ill from consuming poisoned fish.[64]

As soon as the incident came to light, word spread on Facebook that the fish die-off was caused by toxic wastewater discharged into the ocean by Formosa Ha Tinh Steel—a $10 billion steel plant in Ha Tinh's Vung Ang Economic Zone. The plant was built and operated by Taiwan's Formosa Plastics—notorious for environmental violations around the globe—through a local joint venture.

As mentioned, since 1986 Vietnam's economic reforms had relied heavily on foreign direct investment. In 2006, the Vietnamese government established the Vung Ang Economic Zone to take advantage of its geographic proximity to two deep-water ports, National Highway 1A (which cuts north-south across Vietnam), and National Road 12A (which runs west into Laos and Thailand). Like the special economic zones that jumpstarted China's growth, Vung Ang attempts to attract foreign capital with business-friendly policies such as low land taxes. A dozen foreign firms, mainly heavy industries, soon moved in, including Formosa.

Formosa immediately denied allegations that it was responsible for the massive fish die-off in Ha Tinh. A plant director interviewed by local television said dismissively, "Many times in life, people have to make a choice: either to catch and sell fish and shrimp, or to build a modern steel industry. You cannot choose both."[65] Although Formosa quickly apologized for the director's "careless speech," it couldn't stop the statement "I Choose Fish" (*Toi Chon Ca*) from rapidly trending on Facebook.

On April 26, after three weeks of grievances seething both online and off, Vietnamese authorities inspected the Formosa plant and gathered samples from affected areas. The following day, Vietnam's Ministry of National Resources and Environment (MNRE) held a press conference at its Hanoi headquarters. In a room packed with domestic and foreign reporters, Deputy Minister Vo Tuan Nhan claimed that initial testing of seawater in the affected areas had shown no breach of regulatory standards that would point to Formosa's wrongdoing. Instead, he stated that the fish die-off was caused by either wastewater from "human activities" or a phenomenon called red tide, attributed to abnormal algae bloom.[66] Nhan concluded that "this is a complicated issue that has happened in many places around the world, requiring time to identify causes. . . . It is necessary to research the cause systematically, fundamentally, and in a fact-based way."[67]

That weekend, various central and local officials showed up in the affected areas—and in front of TV cameras—to swim in the ocean and eat fish. Ha Tinh's provincial officials were the first to entertain themselves with a morning dip. As he came out of the water, an MNRE official greeted the reporters on the beach with a contented smile and said that the water was safe and met national standards. That evening, the minister of Information and Communications bought two tuna fish from a port in Quang Binh, the province south of Ha Tinh. Local fishermen prepared a tuna meal and he devoured it for the camera. The chairman of the Da Nang People's Committee bought 100 kilograms of tuna from a local port, after the camera "accidentally" caught a fisherman telling him that the fish was safe to eat. The following morning, Da Nang officials took a photogenic swim at the famous My Khe beach, splashing water and waving to the camera. After the swim, they "witnessed" the process of fresh fish caught offshore being certified as safe for consumption.[68]

But the Vietnamese officials' scrupulously orchestrated and publicized gestures didn't seem to appease the citizens. During the national holiday in the first week of May, citizens held rallies across Vietnam—first on Facebook, and then in real life—to press authorities to take substantive action.[69] They asked for a verdict on the culprit of the disaster.[70] In Hanoi, hundreds of protesters rallied near the Opera House holding signs that read "Fish need clean water, people need transparency" (*Ca can nuoc sach, dan can minh bach*).[71] In Ho Chi Minh City, protests drew thousands.[72] Despite a one-day blackout of Facebook in mid-May, protests continued throughout the month, leading some to claim that it was the largest protest since the Vietnamese Communist Party took power.[73] In response to the May protests, Prime Minister Nguyen Xuan Phuc convened a meeting to implement emergency responses, acknowledging that it was the most serious environmental crisis Vietnam had faced.[74]

On June 30, a verdict was finally reached. Appearing at a press conference, Minister Tran Hong Ha lamented that he had just "experienced 84 days of heavy stress," and announced that citizens had been correct from the beginning—Formosa was indeed responsible for discharging toxic industrial wastewater into the ocean.[75] The chairman of Formosa Ha Tinh Steel and several managers joined the press conference to offer their deep apologies and perform their humble bows. The company pledged to pay 11.5 trillion Vietnamese dong (US$500 million) in damages.[76] Two months later, Minister Tran and provincial leaders in Quang Tri took another swim in the ocean at Cua Viet beach and enjoyed seafood afterwards. "Don't you find the sea beautiful? Don't you think it's great for swimming?" Tran asked reporters at the scene.[77]

Vietnamese officials' performative swim in the Ha Tinh crisis failed miserably in its attempt to impress the public. From the very beginning, citizens were exposed to an enormous volume of destructive information about government performance. Facebook in particular provided a fertile ground for information (and misinformation) to blossom and compete in a relatively laissez-faire marketplace of content.

This information environment allowed an ecological crisis to mutate over the course of several months into a crisis of national sovereignty. Because Formosa is Taiwanese-owned and employed Chinese workers, environmental grievances eventually blended with anti-Chinese sentiments. A popular Facebook post by a prominent Hanoi University professor declared that "poisoning of the sea was a major crime against the Vietnamese people and humanity. Those who attempt to conceal the truth are traitors to the nation."[78] But nationalism wasn't the only factor that rendered performative governance ineffective. Considering how readily Vietnamese citizens protest against homegrown environmental outrages, it's questionable whether public reaction would have been significantly different if the polluter had been a well-connected Vietnamese company.

Vietnam leads the world in its per capita number of Facebook users. Facebook enjoys not only skyrocketing advertising revenue in the country, but also clear advantages over government sources in the competition for audience attention. Minister of Propaganda Vo Van Thuong compared Facebook's first-mover advantage to the early bird that catches the worm: "Nowadays, it is the early-bird newspaper, not the major one, that will triumph."[79] Former prime minister Nguyen Tan Dung admitted in a cabinet meeting that banning Facebook was impossible for both economic and social reasons.[80] Recognizing the political headaches that Facebook, Google, and YouTube can cause, the regime has long had plans to develop domestic alternatives, but the endeavor has made little progress.[81]

On the unfettered rise of social media in Vietnam and the threat it poses to the state, Jonathan London writes, "[The VCP] is trying to do something that no leaders have had to do in the past . . . which is essentially address public outrage that is being freely expressed on a daily basis."[82] Thu Huong Le observes that "it's nearly impossible to contain the flow of information on social media. Simmering conflicts are brought to the surface. In this case, incompetent governance was revealed."[83] The Vietnamese government eventually caved and set up its own Facebook page, competing with dissidents in the sea of information through livestreaming press conferences and deploying "public opinion shapers" to "counteract hostile online forces."[84] While these reactive tactics are more useful than nothing when it comes to airbrushing the state's image, they are far less effective at preventing the emergence and spread of destructive information than preemptive content filtering would be, as it operates in China.

The Infinite Information Game

As Goffman relates, impression management is an iterative "information game—a potentially infinite cycle of concealment, discovery, false revelation, and rediscovery."[85] In this game no player—actor or audience, state or society—is naïve. If anything, Goffman states, "the witness is likely to have the advantage over the actor."[86] The state wields a monopoly over the legitimate use of physical force, but it often loses its pronounced advantage on the battleground of public opinion.

This chapter contends that to the extent that performative governance can be effective at appeasing its citizen audience, it may be conditioned on a lack of *destructive information* shedding unwelcome light on the incongruency between substantive performance and performativity. I further argue that destructive information is more likely to emerge in less-controlled information environments, rendering performative governance less effective. Although information freedom is highly correlated with regime type, the Flint case shows that even in democracies there are informational black holes.

When performative governance breaks down, the state must either live with a loss of reputation or respond with substantive efforts. Thus it is not surprising that substantive governance sometimes follows performative governance, moving the political process forward as an ever-shifting punctuated equilibrium.

More often than not, however, what comes after the breakdown of performative governance is not substantive governance, but *nothing*. As public attention fades over time—as always—scrutiny subsides, the curtain falls, and the lights dim. The performative state takes a bow. The three cases of performative breakdown described in this chapter (Flint, Wuhan, and Vietnam) all had ambiguous endings. Formosa continues to operate in Ha Tinh; residents affected by the 2016 spill are still appealing for compensation.[87] The coronavirus first discovered in Wuhan grew into a full-blown global pandemic and continues to afflict the world. Six years after Flint residents found strange colors and tastes in their tap water, the city has yet to restore clean water to all of its residents. Because of the lack of clean water, Flint became one of the areas in the United States to be worst affected by the Covid-19 pandemic.[88] An eighty-two-year-old Flint resident who lost her daughter to the pandemic told a reporter: "The two main sources of our existence in this world are air and water. And they are messing with both of them."[89]

Conclusion

PERFORMANCE AND PERFORMANCE

In the English language, words like *performance, role, actor, audience*, and *setting* are laced with double meanings—one theatrical, the other substantive.[1] But when these words are used in political contexts today, their theatrical connotations disappear or are assumed to be epiphenomenal. A government's "performance" means the quality of its public service delivery, measured by some objective standards: GDP growth obtained, dollar amounts distributed, number of individuals insured, exactness of regulations enforced, volume of emissions reduced, quantity of jobs created, number of deaths prevented, and so on. A "role" means a function, a "setting" means a situation, and a political "actor" simply means someone in politics.

Even the word *person*, when traced back to its Latin origin of *persona*, means a theatrical mask: "A recognition of the fact that everyone is always and everywhere, more or less consciously, playing a role. . . . It is in these roles that we know each other; it is in these roles that we know ourselves."[2] Nowadays, the "person" has been taken out of "persona." While "persona" refers to "an individual's social façade or front," or "the personality that person projects in public," "person" means the breathing flesh and bones underneath the mask—the substance of homo sapiens, and not its appearance.[3]

This separation of appearance and substance follows a long tradition among Enlightenment thinkers. Kant says the substance of the world—the "thing-in-itself" (*Ding an sich*)—is unknowable because it exists independently of our senses. Schopenhauer further developed Kant's idea in his magnum opus distinguishing between the world as thing-in-itself and as "representation" (*vorstellung*) that is experienced, perceived, or imagined by its beholders. Kant believes we can only know something by its appearance, but it is the modern sciences' mission to get us closer to an understanding of the thing-in-itself.

The same process of separation has unfolded in the social sciences. Any standardization by way of concepts, metrics, and methods attempts to strip the world of its theatrical representations to reveal the "underlying phenomenon."[4] For better and for worse, this book has made an attempt to intellectually separate what is commonly called "government performance" from the government's *theatrical representation* of its performance. This is then further separated from citizens' perception of the government's performance. Specifically, it has been concerned with uncovering what happens when substantive performance and theatrical performance—accomplishments and appearances—collide and blend in the critical domain of China's contemporary environmental governance.

I use "performative governance" to describe the theatrical representation of good governance, especially when substantive performance is wanting. I've shown that when the environmental bureaucracy lacked the ability to fulfill its function of improving environmental outcomes, it engaged in performative governance to appease its scrutinizing citizen audience. But performative governance is not always effective at achieving its purpose—I further examine when it is and when it is not.

My book has sought to make sense of the performative dimension of governance. In so doing, I have drawn inspiration from a wealth of literature that reveals the ubiquity of theatrical performance in politics and explores its intimate connection to political power. I opened with a story from Ancient Rome, where oratory performance was key to political success, and effective politicians were often compared to great actors: "How the orator stood, how he dressed and held himself, letting his toga fall in just the right way, his expressions, the power and tone of his voice were all vital aspects of an advocate's job."[5] Even skeptics who believed that oratory had no place in science and philosophy—"the Greek view"—agreed that "[its] proper sphere [is in] the law-courts and political debates."[6]

Politics today is no less theatrical than it was in ancient Rome. Barack Obama's victory in the 2008 American presidential election has been explained by his "performative success" at using symbolic, cultural representations to forge an emotional connection with voters.[7] This idea that politics is performative is familiar to scholars of democracy—where politicians' electoral success largely depends on their mass popularity.[8]

Theatrical performance isn't unique to democratic politics. In ancient China, a touchstone of a ruler's virtue was their proper performance of rites and sacrifices.[9] Han and non-Han rulers alike used rites to build state power and legitimize state authority.[10] Similarly, rituals in Tokugawa Japan held the social fabric together—even the scrupulous performance of deathbed adoption ceremonies had profound meanings for the integrity of the political order.[11] John Dewey described rituals as a "great positive agent" for social cohesion.[12]

There are, of course, important differences between the performance of Caesarian charisma and the performance of social rituals. Charisma is uninhibited; ritual is rigid. Charisma is instinctive; ritual is methodical. Charismatic performance takes the audience by surprise, whereas ritual moves an audience with the familiar. The effect of charismatic performance is ecclesiastical enchantment; it casts a spell. The effect of ritual is more disciplinary; it lays down rules. As different as they may be, both types of performance have been wellsprings of political power.

Others see the relationship flowing in the reverse direction, or in both directions. Clifford Geertz adamantly insists that the state's spectacles were not "means to political ends" but ends in themselves—"power serves pomp, not pomp power."[13] Lisa Wedeen's study of Syria under Hafiz al-Assad posits a recursive relationship: on one hand, coerced participation in Assad's cult of personality enforced citizens' obedience to the regime; at the same time, "acting as if" may plant the seeds for rebellion.[14]

Not only are peace and order theatrically enacted; so are violence and chaos. Lee Ann Fujii reveals that political violence takes on a performative dimension when "actors stage violence for graphic effect."[15] Isaac Reed's study of the early American Republic shows that the state "performed [itself] into being" by acting out and publicizing the "legitimate use of violence."[16] Julia Strauss and Jeffrey Javed's studies of CCP land reform find that the theatrical public display of struggle sessions was essential to the new regime's consolidation.[17]

Though immersed in vastly different academic traditions and attending to widely disparate geographic terrains, these scholars share a parallel observation: the theatrics of the state are an essential part of what upholds the state.[18]

Theatrical performance is used not only to prop up power, but also to subvert it. What is the "power of the powerless" if not to use their symbolic compliance with authorities to evade punishment for their substantive noncompliance, to regurgitate familiar narratives of the powerful so as to legitimize new demands from below, and to act in accordance with symbols of the past and the indigenous so as to usher in elements of the future and the foreign?[19]

Turning to Bureaucracy

While theatrical performance by charismatic authorities and crafty subalterns has been thoroughly demonstrated, the bureaucratic apparatus of the state itself remains underexamined as a theatrical actor. The stereotypical image of a modern bureaucracy is the opposite of performative. Weber writes: "Bureaucracy develops the more perfectly, the more it is *'dehumanized,'* the more completely it succeeds in eliminating from official business love, hatred, and all purely personal, irrational, and emotional elements which escape calculation."[20] Such dehumanization embodies the "rationality" of bureaucracy. While charismatic performance is spontaneous, bureaucratic performance is regimented. While charisma is passionate, bureaucracy is detached. Charisma enchants; bureaucracy disenchants.

As ever, ideal types are only ideal types; they are never meant to be "picture copies of reality."[21] The vast literature on bureaucracy around the world has convincingly shown how its actual practice differs from the Weberian ideal type.

Perhaps the most interesting problematization of bureaucratic rationality comes from Weber himself. Weber expounded at great length about the tension between "formal" and "substantive" rationality—a tension that revealed itself in chapter 3. "Formal rationality" represents the impersonality, objectivity, calculability, and matter-of-factness of bureaucratic rules and procedures permeating the modern world, whereas "substantive rationality" sees "from the point of view of some particular substantive end, value, or belief."[22] In this sense, a behavior is "substantively rational" if it fulfills its stated ends, values, or beliefs, regardless of what they are.[23]

Formal rules and procedures are often designed for the optimal achievement of specific substantive ends or values.[24] For example, formal legal procedures are drafted to uphold the substantive end of justice. Formal institutions of democracy are created for the substantive end of the common good. Formal organizations of bureaucracy are structured to support the substantive end of effective governance.

But "form" and "substance" often decouple in real life. Legal decisions rendered by the letter of the law might run into conflict with popular norms and values.[25] Democratic institutions do not always prevent the election of bad leaders and the making of poor decisions.[26] Bureaucratic rules and procedures might prove indifferent to the impact that governance actually has on society.

This decoupling of formal and substantive rationality, of means and ends, was of great concern to Weber. He explored how a rational, impersonal, ascetic spirit could bring about efficiency and productivity, while also lamenting its engendering of a new species of "*homo politicus* . . . [and] *homo oeconomicus*" who "performs his duty best when he acts without regard to the person in question . . . without hate and without love, without personal predilection and therefore without grace."[27] They are the fabled "specialists without spirit, hedonists without heart."[28]

The CCP is all too familiar with this critique. I have yet to find evidence that any of its founders read Weber, but they surely read Marx. Well-known differences notwithstanding, Marx and Weber showed many parallels in their thinking.[29] Marx said, "Proletarians have nothing to lose but their chains"; Weber similarly described the bureaucrat as a small cog "chained to his activity."[30] At a deeper level, Weber and Marx shared a normative interest in the substantive— Weber in substantive rationality and Marx in substantive democracy. Unlike Marx, Weber scarcely let his own values appear on paper.[31] Perhaps that's one reason why Weber was of little use to China's communist revolutionaries, who were looking for practical solutions to China's problems in the first half of the twentieth century.

It was originally not the persuasiveness of Marxist doctrines but the successful power seizure by Lenin's October Revolution that convinced Chinese nationalists of the value of Marxism-Leninism. For they wanted something that would free China from the trappings of an ancient "despotic bureaucracy."[32] Many adjectives have been used to describe China's ancient regime, its imperial bureaucracy. Weber called it "patrimonial," and argued for its inferiority to Western legal-rationalism. The CCP called it "feudal," and strived to create an entirely new form of organization that would help China transcend not just feudalism but also "rational" capitalism.

To reach the substantive end of socialism, this new organization kept an "anti-bureaucratic ghost" alive in a "bureaucratic machine."[33] Unlike capitalist societies that surrender substantive economic ends to formal means of production, and surrender substantive democracy to formal institutions like multi-party elections, the CCP would let its values and ends drive its bureaucratic forms and means. In recruitment and promotion the party stressed "red over expert." In policy implementation the party relied on mass mobilization rather than bureaucratic routinization. It was all to keep the revolutionary spirit alive and prevent the party from descending into the very kind of sclerotic structure it had just overthrown. What materialized under Mao was a "politicized bureaucracy," where revolutionary purity trumped bureaucratic rationality.[34] For this reason, Chinese bureaucracy under Mao never formalized in the way Weber said socialism required.[35]

Mao's successors sought to shed some of Maoism's irrational tendencies. They wanted to inject the bureaucratic state with a dose of the modernity and rationality that had been sorely missing. While the system still suffers from patrimonialism (in the form of patron-client relationships) and prebendalism (in the case of corruption), a simultaneous process of bureaucratic rationalization is not to be overlooked. This rationalization proceeds in a strictly Weberian sense: formalization of rules and procedures, adulation of technology and technical expertise, and even, very recently, replacing human decision-making with artificial intelligence.[36]

But bureaucratic rationalization brought the CCP straight back to its original problem: the chasm between the formal and the substantive. While regulations have mushroomed, they can be poorly implemented. Laws have strengthened, but they often fail to conform to popular expectations of justice. While bureaucratic procedures have multiplied, they are often carried out with little thought or concern for their effects. As Weber puts it: "Formal rationality itself does not tell us anything about real want satisfaction."[37]

As a party that, from its very first days, has based its legitimacy on popular acclaim, the CCP attends constantly to "real want satisfaction." Its founders believed that what distinguished their political party from China's previous rulers, including those who came to power through revolution, was its humble roots, which grew deeply in the soil of the people. As early as 1939, Liu Shaoqi warned that all successful revolutionaries in the prior century had lost their popular mandate upon assuming power; the party must consciously avoid repeating their failure.[38]

Many have thus used "performance legitimacy" to describe the CCP's power in the reform era.[39] The idea is that modern authoritarian regimes by definition lack electoral institutions for "procedural legitimacy," so their popularity must rely on substantive "performance." Dingxin Zhao goes so far as to write that "government performance stands alone as the sole source of legitimacy in China."[40] Scholars differ on what performance encapsulates: from economic development, reducing income inequality, and anticorruption to national defense, social stability, environmental protection, and any kind of "good governance."[41] But in one way or another, a government's "performance" is portrayed as its ability to "bring measurable benefits to the people."[42] In the case of China, all roads eventually lead back to the extraordinary statistics of double-digit GDP growth, and of hundreds of millions of Chinese citizens being lifted out of poverty.

No careful or neutral observer would deny the CCP's reform-era performance in "real want satisfaction." But neither would anyone—including the party itself—claim that the party always manages to deliver what citizens demand and deserve. For one, governments always face resource constraints; it's impossible to satisfy all societal demands. For another, the many substantive "ends" might come into conflict with one another, such as in the case of economic development and environmental protection. Although the Chinese government is seeking to overcome this conflict by promoting renewable energy, there is still a long way to go before "green growth" becomes reality.

When substantive governance is hard to come by but public demands are pronounced, what does the government do? This book has argued that it engages in performative governance.

Formalism and Performativity

Performative governance is a bastard child of formal and substantive rationality, of bureaucratic rule and "real want satisfaction," of "performance" and "legitimacy." There is a side to performative governance that is highly formalistic—it follows procedures, keeps records, leaves behind a trail of forms, pictures, and numbers, and doesn't deviate too far from its prescribed route of march. At the same time, there is another side to performative governance that is spontaneous and improvised—it relaxes routines, adapts its script to the public mood, and sympathetically engages its audience. Performative governance thus has both a formal side and a theatrical side.

The formal side of performative governance has attracted the party's critical attention in recent years. There have been gathering complaints about formalism (*xingshizhuyi*) in both official discourse and popular commentary.[43] Weber referred to formalism rather flatteringly as the "'spirit' of rational bureaucracy."[44] But formalism is a patent pejorative in the CCP's terminology. An epithet originally borrowed from the Soviets, formalism refers to the prioritization of "form" (*xingshi*) over "content" (*neirong*) or "substance" (*shizhi*).[45] Mentions of formalism have skyrocketed in recent years in the *People's Daily*, often appearing alongside the expressions "empty talk" (*konghua*), "word games" (*wenzi youxi*), "mountains of documents and oceans of meetings" (*wenshanhuihai*), "complicated procedures" (*chengxu fuza*), and "pursuing forms and not effects" (*zhuiqiu xingshi, buzhong shixiao*).[46]

Xi Jinping's ongoing campaign against formalism, launched in 2018, has targeted policy implementation that "uses flamboyant forms to replace concrete implementation" (*yong honghonglielie de xingshi daiti le zhazhashishi de luoshi*) or "uses a glamorous appearance to cover up contradictions and problems" (*yong guangxianliangli de waibiao yangai le maodun he wenti*).[47] These "flamboyant forms" include not only the kind of white elephants and Potemkin villages the party has been consistently critiquing ("performance projects"), but also other mundane bureaucratic actions that are divorced from substantive results. The Party's abundant critiques of "formalism" suggest that the kind of performative governance identified in this study is likely not limited to a single bureaucracy in a single locality.

Chinese scholars have attributed "formalism" to the excessive burdens shouldered by street-level bureaucrats. Fang Ning, a prominent Chinese academic and policy advisor who leads the Institute of Political Science at the Chinese Academy of Social Sciences, contends that formalism results from the higher-ups' unreasonable expectations and failure to appreciate the lack of resources and funds at the street level: "Without the necessary conditions [for policy implementation], how can there not be formalism?"[48]

"Grassroots fatigue" (*jiceng pibei*) became a new catchphrase around 2018.[49] Observers found "passiveness . . . fatigue . . . poor mood . . . complaints" to be widespread among street-level bureaucrats, who, without the capacity to implement policies, can only resort to busywork that merely "leaves traces" of their efforts.[50] This eventually led the central government to declare 2019 a "Grassroots Burden Reduction Year" (*jiceng jianfu nian*), mandating a 30–50 percent reduction in the amount of documents and meetings, and limiting policy documents to ten pages.[51] Again, this suggests that the strains experienced by the Lakeville EPB's beleaguered bureaucrats are by no means unrepresentative.

But the performative governance documented in this book has traits that depart decisively from formalism as it is typically understood. While formalism captures bureaucratic performativity for the audience of upper-level authorities, performative governance sees citizens as its main audience. While formalism is a byproduct of a bureaucracy's internal organization (e.g., classic principal-agent problems), performative governance results from a bureaucracy's external orientation.

Consider the following example of pure "formalism" that caught much attention during Xi Jinping's ongoing poverty alleviation campaign: "When higher-ups demanded photographic proof of their home visits [to poverty-stricken households], some aid workers made up for missing winter photos by posing in cold-weather clothing during summer house calls."[52] This kind of theatrical performance is orchestrated singularly for the audience of higher-ups, assuming villagers had no power or channels to bring this kind of duplicity to wider attention.

But as we have seen throughout this book, performative governance is public spirited, if not always public serving. As the introductory chapter explains, performative governance emerged through the state's turn from "management-oriented governance" toward "service-oriented governance." Like a modern economic enterprise, the state increasingly sees citizens as its customers. And like customer service representatives, state bureaucrats answer citizens' calls, listen to their stories, and sympathize with their laments. They display an outward devotion to addressing citizens' complaints even when their demands cannot be met. Occasionally performative governance breaks free of its bureaucratic routines entirely, as when officials go swimming in rivers to prove themselves just because citizens challenged them to. The role state bureaucrats play in today's China is shifting evermore from "cadre" to "civil servant."

Civil Servants in the Information Age

On a late night in March 2019, a young man was stopped by traffic police for riding his bicycle the wrong way on a one-way street in Hangzhou. Such an encounter is usually a nonstory: the police issues a ticket, and the cyclist reluctantly accepts the fine.

However, in this instance, the young man suddenly broke down, howling and bawling inconsolably. As he wailed, he explained that he had taken a shortcut because his girlfriend was locked out of their apartment; he had to deliver keys to her quickly before returning to work, where his team awaited him, and where he had been working overtime every night. The double pressure at work and home had been mounting. Being stopped by the police while frantically rushing between his two duties was the last drop that forced open the floodgate of tears.

Upon hearing the young man's plight, the police officer on duty sat down next to him as he wept, telling him that "it is fine to vent by crying, we will be here to guard you." He consoled the cyclist, and gave him advice on work-life balance. The young man eventually calmed down and apologized for losing his composure, while the officer again reassured him: "Crying is not a face loss. Life is a struggle. After letting the pressure out, wipe off your tears and face life anew. All you did was violate the traffic law, it is not a big deal." The cyclist did not receive a ticket.

This interaction was caught on the police officer's body camera and the video quickly went viral. Many of China's millennial generation said they could identify with the young man's despair, as they themselves faced tremendous pressure both at work and at home. Netizens also applauded the policeman's compassionate handling of the situation, saying that it made them feel "warm."[53] The young man himself later joined an online discussion to thank the police officer for being so helpful and "gentle" (wenrou).

When the local news asked the officer in question to comment on the event, he said: "When I saw [the young man] breaking down I thought of myself when I was younger. Every young person will face setbacks in life, but everything will eventually be okay."[54] When asked what he thought about Netizens' praise that he was "tender like water" (rouqingsishui), the officer explained: "[What I did] was normal. Facing criminals is different from facing ordinary people. After the event [I] reflected on whether my law enforcement in the past had been humane [*renxinghua*] enough."

This unstaged interaction between a policeman and a citizen shows that performative governance is not always strategic. It also shows performative governance is not always mutually exclusive with other types of state behavior—even the coercive hand of the state can affect gentle touches at times. An overlapping theme between this story and environmental governance, however, is the power of public scrutiny. When civil servants can be evaluated, rewarded, and punished by public opinion, their outward behavior deviates from the bureaucratic archetype: slow, sluggish, mechanical, arrogant, spiritless, heartless. They start to resemble politicians desirous of the people's love.

Bureaucracy was once defined by its secrecy and its blindness to public opinion. As Marx writes: "The general spirit of bureaucracy is secret, mysterious, safeguarded inside itself by hierarchy and outside by its nature as a closed corporation. Thus public political spirit . . . [appears] to bureaucracy as betrayal of its secret."[55] The CCP was never devoid of public spirit, as its rise to power through a social revolution in the first place relied on mass support. Nevertheless, the party's operations through the functional, bureaucratic state apparatus have long been described as "secretive."[56] This is, of course, not unique to China. The very purpose of an "independent civil service" in a democracy is to protect the independent operations of government bureaucracies from the interventions of political parties and politicians, and thus from the whipping winds of public whim.

But that too has started to change. Public scrutiny, supercharged by the rise of social media, forces the inward-looking bureaucracy and its introverted bureaucrats into the limelight—for better and for worse. For better, it can expose bureaucratic dysfunction. For worse, it may obstruct the efficacy of experts. In a world where every interaction between bureaucrats and citizens may potentially be put on public display, and where the security of bureaucratic careers is vulnerable to public scrutiny, bureaucratic behavior can no longer be so secretive, aloof, and impersonal. The classic distinction between politicians and bureaucrats thus collapses. Outward-facing bureaucracy is a defining feature of governance in the information age.

Glossary

accountability	责任性	zerenxing
administrative approval	审批	shenpi
Administrative Approval Division	行政审批处	Xingzheng shenpi chu
admonition	训诫	xunjie
affairs bureau	事务部门	shiwu bumen
agency/bureaucracy with real/actual power	实权部门	shiquan bumen
Air Quality Management Division	大气环境管理处	Daqi huanjing guanli chu
amnesty gold medal	免死金牌	miansi jinpai
arbitrary charge	乱收费	luan shoufei
attitude	态度	taidu
background	背景	beijing
battlefield of public opinion	舆论战场	yulun zhanchang
be sent to the cold palace	打入冷宫	daru lenggong
benevolence	善	shan
benevolent governance	善治	shanzhi
big taxpayer	纳税大户	nashui dahu
bureau	局	ju
bureaucratism	官僚主义	guanliaozhuyi
business bureau	业务部门	yewu bumen
Center for Environmental Protection Propaganda and Education	环保宣教中心	Huanbao xuanjiao zhongxin
Center for the Management of Solid Wastes	固废管理中心	Gufei guanli zhongxin
Central Organization Department	中组部	Zhongzubu
China Machine Industry Association	中国机械工业协会	Zhongguo jixie gongye xiehui
Chinese Dream / China Dream	中国梦	Zhongguo meng
citizen center	市民中心	shimin zhongxin
civil police	民警	minjing
Civil Service Examination	公务员考试	gongwuyuan kaoshi
Clear waters and green mountains are as valuable as mountains of gold and silver	绿水青山就是金山银山	lüshui qingshan jiushi jinshan yinshan
cleanliness and honesty	廉洁	lianjie
clear water yamen	清水衙门	qingshui yamen

cold palace	冷宫	lenggong
college entrance exam	高考	gaokao
Commission of Economy and Information	经济和信息化委员会 / 经信委	Jingji he xinxihua weiyuan-hui / Jingxinwei
common folk	老百姓	laobaixing
common sense	常识	changshi
complicated procedures	程序复杂	chengxu fuza
comprehensive management of public safety	社会治安综合治理	shehui zhi'an zonghe zhili
Construction Standard for Office Space of Party and State Organizations	党政机关办公用房建设标准	Dangzheng jiguan ban-gong yongfang jianshe biaozhun
content	内容	neirong
core bureaucracies	核心部门	hexin bumen
dark pipe	暗管	anguan
decentralization, management, and service	放管服	fangguanfu
Detachment of Environmental Supervision	环境监察支队	Huanjing jiancha zhidui
Development and Reform Commission	发改委	Fagaiwei
directly administered	直属	zhishu
Director's Mailbox	局长信箱	juzhang xinxiang
division	处	chu
Division for the Control of the Total Amount of Pollutants	总量控制处	Zongliang kongzhi chu
Division for the Management of Automobile Exhausts	机动车尾气管理处	Jidongche weiqi guanli chu
does nothing	不作为	buzuowei
ecological civilization	生态文明	shengtai wenming
Economic and Technological Development Zone	经济技术开发区	jingji jishu kaifa qu
effectiveness	有效	youxiao
emergency incident	突发事件	tufa shijian
emission reduction / energy saving and emission reduction	节能减排	jieneng jianpai
Emission Standards for Odorous Pollutants	恶臭污染排放标准	Echou wuranwu paifang biaozhun
empty talk	空话	konghua
end to one's political career	仕途终结	shitu zhongjie
enforcement agency	执法部门	zhifa bumen
Environmental Impact Assessment	环境影响评价	huanjing yingxiang pingjia
Environmental Impact Assessment Report	环评报告	huanping baogao
environmental inspection	环境监察	huanjing jiancha
environmental problem	环境问题	huanjing wenti
environmental protection	环保	huanbao

Environmental Protection Hotline	环保热线	huanbao rexian
Environmental Protection Leading Group	环境保护领导小组	Huanjing baohu lingdao xiaozu
environmental protection system	环保系统	huanbao xitong
Exterminate the Four Pests	除四害	Chusihai
face project	面子工程	mianzi gongcheng
fat water yamen	肥水衙门	feishui yamen
Finance Bureau	财政局	caizheng ju
Flatbread Bureau	烧饼办	Shaobingban
folk ferocity	民风彪悍	minfeng biaohan
form	形式	xingshi
formalism	形式主义	xingshizhuyi
foul air	臭气	chouqi
frog at the bottom of a well	井底之蛙	jingdizhiwa
functional bureaucracy	职能部门	zhineng bumen
General Learning Questions	大学问	Daxuewen
General Office	办公厅	Bangongting
General Office of the State Council	国务院办公厅	Guowuyuan bangongting
good governance	善治 / 善政	Shanzhi / shanzheng
government building	政府大楼	zhengfu dalou
gradual democracy	渐进民主	jianjin minzhu
Grassroots Burden Reduction Year	基层减负年	Jiceng jianfu nian
grassroots fatigue	基层疲惫	jiceng pibei
hot and spicy	火辣	huola
hot social issue	社会热点问题	shehui redian wenti
humane	人性化	renxinghua
immediate response to complaints	接诉即办	jie su ji ban
imperial examination system	科举	keju
implementation bureau	执行部门	zhixing bumen
In Agriculture Learn from Dazhai	农业学大寨	Nongye xue Dazhai
incremental democracy	增量民主	zengliang minzhu
industrial upgrading	产业升级	chanye shengji
industrial waste air	工业废气	gongye feiqi
informant	线人	xianren
information center	信息中心	xinxi zhongxin
investigate and research	调研	diaoyan
justice	公正	gongzheng
key point	重点	zhongdian
land and resources	国土资源	guotu ziyuan
law enforcement operation	执法行动	zhifa xingdong
legitimacy	合法性	hefaxing
little gold chest	小金库	xiao jinku

little state council	小国务院	xiao guowuyuan
Lost Book of Zhou	逸周书	Yi Zhou Shu
luxury wind	奢靡之风	shemizhifeng
machine industry	机械工业	jixie gongye
major criminal case	重大刑事案件	zhongda xingshi anjian
major environmental crisis	重大突发环境事件	zhongda tufa huanjing shijian
management-oriented government	管理型政府	guanlixing zhengfu
manners	素质	suzhi
mass incidents	群体性事件	quntixing shijian
Mayor's Hotline	市长热线	shizhang rexian
Mayor's Mailbox	市长信箱	shizhang xinxiang
Men will conquer nature	人定胜天	rendingshengtian
Ministry of Commerce	商务部	Shangwubu
Ministry of Construction	建设部	Jianshebu
Ministry of Ecology and Environment	生态环境部	Shengtai huanjing bu
Ministry of Electronics Industry	电子工业部	Dianzi gongye bu
Ministry of Environmental Protection	环境保护部	Huanjing baohu bu
Ministry of Fuel and Chemical Industries	燃料化学工业部	Ranliao huaxue gongye bu
Ministry of Health	卫生部	Weishengbu
Ministry of Machine Industry	机械工业部	Jixie gongye bu
Ministry of Machinery and Electronics	机械电子工业部	Jixie dianzi gongye bu
Ministry of Ordinance Industry	兵器工业部	Bingqi gongye bu
Ministry of State Security	国家安全部	Guojia anquan bu
monitoring spot	监测点	jiance dian
mountains of documents and oceans of meetings	文山会海	wenshanhuihai
municipal-level	市级	shiji
My country is destroyed, but the mountains and rivers are still here	国破山河在	Guo po shan he zai
National Civil Service Examination	国家公务员考试 / 国考	Guojia gongwuyuan kaoshi / guokao
National Conference on Environmental Protection	全国环境保护会议/大会	Quanguo huanjing baohu huiyi/dahui
National Development and Reform Commission	国家发展和改革委员会 / 国家发改委	Guojia fazhan he gaige weiyuanhui / Guojia fagaiwei
National Health and Family Planning Commission	国家卫生和计划生育委员会	Guojia weisheng he jihua shengyu weiyuanhui
Natural Ecology Division	自然生态处	Ziran shengtai chu
new pneumonia	新型肺炎	xinxing feiyan

News Exchange	新闻纵横	Xinwen zongheng
night inspection	夜查	yecha
noise pollution	噪音污染	zaoyin wuran
Office for the Control and Management of Three Wastes	三废控制管理办公室	Sanfei kongzhi guanli bangongshi
oil yamen	油水衙门	youshui yamen
One thing less is better than one thing more	多一事不如少一事	duoyishi buru shaoyishi
one-stop shop	最多跑一次	zuiduo paoyici
one item veto rule	一票否决	yipiao foujue
online monitoring	在线监控	zaixian jiankong
open hearing	听证会	tingzhenghui
Online Petition	网上信访	wangshang xinfang
Organization Department	组织部	Zuzhibu
Organization and Personnel Division	组织人事处	Zuzhi renshi chu
patriotic hygiene campaign	爱国主义卫生运动	aiguozhuyi weisheng yundong
performance	表现	biaoxian
performance	绩效	jixiao
performance / performativity	表演	biaoyan
performance evaluation	绩效考核	jixiao kaohe
performance projects	政绩工程	zhengji gongcheng
performative rescue	表演式抢救	biaoyanshi qiangjiu
personnel	人事	renshi
Petition Bureau	信访办	Xinfangban
Planning and Finances Division	规划财务处	Guihua caiwu chu
Policies and Regulations Division	政策法规处	Zhengce fagui chu
policy interpretation	政策解读	zhengce jiedu
policy support	政策支持	zhengce zhichi
political engineering	政治工程	zhengzhi gongcheng
Political and Legal Affairs Commission	政法委	Zhengfawei
pollute first, clean up later	先污染, 后治理	xian wuran, hou zhili
polluting enterprises	污染企业	wuran qiye
pollution abatement facility	排污设备	paiwu shebei
Pollution Permit	排污许可证	paiwu xukezheng
Pollution Prevention and Control Division	污染防治处	Wuran fangzhi chu
primacy of citizens	民本位	minbenwei
primacy of officials	官本位	guanbenwei
Propaganda and Education Division	宣传教育处	Xuanchuan jiaoyu chu
propaganda reporting	宣传报导	xuanchuan baodao
Provincial Governor's Mailbox	省长信箱	shengzhang xinxiang
provincial-redirected	省转	shengzhuan

public finance	财政	caizheng
public finance mouth	财政口子	caizheng kouzi
Public Security Bureau	公安局	Gonganju
public opinion supervision	舆论监督	yulun jiandu
public participation	公众参与	gongzhong canyu
public security incidents	公共安全事件	gonggong anquan shijian
public trust/credibility	公信力	gongxinli
pursuing forms and not effects	追求形式, 不重实效	zhuiqiu xingshi, buzhong shixiao
putting on a show	作秀	zuoxiu
reform and rectify	整改	zhenggai
relevant agencies	相关部门	xiangguan bumen
repeated petitions	重复信访	chongfu xinfang
responsive government	回应型政府	huiyingxing zhengfu
responsiveness	回应	huiying
rule of law	法治	fazhi
Scientific Monitoring Division	科学监测处	Kexue jiance chu
section	科	ke
seek accountability	追责	zhuize
service-oriented government	服务型政府	fuwuxing zhengfu
smart power	智慧电力	zhihui dianli
smash the cracking pot	破罐子破摔	po guanzi po shuai
smearing socialism	给社会主义抹黑	gei shehuizhuyi mohei
smell tester	嗅辨员	xiubianyuan
Smelly air stinks up the heavens	臭气熏天	chouqi xuntian
smog	**雾霾**	wumai
social problem	社会问题	shehui wenti
social status	社会地位	shehui diwei
Some Decisions on the Protection and Improvement of the Environment	关于保护环境的若干决定	Guanyu baohu he gaishan huanjing de ruogan jueding
source point	污染源	wuranyuan
Special Economic Zone	经济特区	jingji tequ
stability	稳定	wending
staff bureaus	幕僚部门	muliao bumen
State Bureau of Machine Industry	国家机械工业部	Guojia jixie gongyeju
State Economic and Trade Commission	国家经济贸易委员会	Guojia jingji maoyi weiyuanhui
State Environmental Protection Agency	国家环境保护局	Guojia huanjing baohu ju
State Family Planning Commission	国家计划生育委员会	Guojia jihuashengyu weiyuanhui
State Oceanic Administration	海洋局	Haiyangju
State-Owned Assets Supervision and Administration Commission	国有资产监督管理委员	Guoyou zichan jiandu guanli weiyuanhui

status	地位	diwei
stealthily discharge waste air	偷排废气	toupai feiqi
strict thrifty	厉行节约	lixing jieyue
strong bureaucracy	强势部门	qiangshi bumen
substance	实质	shizhi
super ministries reform	大部制改革	dabuzhi gaige
supervision is lacking	监管不力	jianguanbuli
supervisory group	督查组	duchazu
supervisory function	监督作用	jiandu zuoyong
supervisory reporting	监督报导	jiandu baodao
Swimming Gate	游泳门	youyong men
the system	体制	tizhi
target responsibility letter	目标责任书	mubiao zeren shu
tender like water	柔情似水	rouqingsishui
three wastes	三废	sanfei
touch base	摸底	modi
transparency	透明	touming
two lines of income and expenditure	收支两条线	Shouzhi liangtiaoxian
Two Sessions	两会	Lianghui
Two Mountains Theory	两山理论	liangshan lilun
Urban Management Bureau	城管	Chengguan
Use only one hook to fish, and only shoot birds that are flying	钓而不纲, 弋不射宿	Diaoerbugang, gebushesu
waste air	废气	feiqi
waste/garbage sorting	垃圾分类	lajifenlei
Water Management Division	水环境管理处	Shui huanjing guanli chu
weak bureaucracy	弱势部门	ruoshi bumen
What is reasonable is real, and what is real is reasonable	存在即合理	cunzai ji heli
Whoever generates pollution manages it	谁污染谁治理	Shei wuran shei zhili
whistleblowing on the streets, rapid check-in from relevant bureaucracies	街巷吹哨, 部门报道	jiexiang chuishao, bumen baodao
word games	文字游戏	wenzi youxi
work assignment notice	工作联系单	gongzuo lianxidan
workplace / work unit	单位	danwei
work team	工作组	gongzuozu
written deposition	笔录	bilu

Notes

INTRODUCTION

1. For details of the Dolabella trial, see Adrian Goldsworthy, *Caesar: Life of a Colossus* (New Haven: Yale University Press, 2006), 71–73; Henriette Van der Blom, *Oratory and Political Career in the Late Roman Republic* (New York: Cambridge University Press, 2016): 165–80.

2. Goldsworthy, *Caesar*, 72.

3. Van der Blom notes that "Caesar may have wished for exactly this outcome of the trial because he had avoided creating influential enemies while obtaining oratorical fame." Van der Blom, *Oratory and Political Career*, 154.

4. Goldsworthy documents that "the odds [were] stacked against [Caesar]," but "Caesar was not seeking to attack the Sullan regime, but was simply choosing a prominent man to prosecute." Goldsworthy, *Caesar*, 71–72.

5. To be sure, *The Prince*, and the phrase "better to be feared than loved" in particular, is an anomaly amid Machiavelli's republican beliefs, in the same way "Caesarism" might occlude the dictator's republicanism. See Mary G. Dietz, "Trapping the Prince: Machiavelli and the Politics of Deception," *American Political Science Review* 80, no. 3 (1986): 777–99; Peter Baehr, *Caesar and the Fading of the Roman World: A Study in Republicanism and Caesarism* (Routledge, 2017).

6. Observers note that after Caesar came to power he relied less on oratory performance. Van der Blom, *Oratory and Political Career*, 151.

7. Van der Blom, *Oratory and Political Career*, 154–55.

8. Goldsworthy, *Caesar*, 79. Also see Van der Blom, *Oratory and Political Career*, 154–57.

9. Van der Blom, *Oratory and Political Career*, 147 and 167.

10. Goldsworthy, *Caesar*, 73.

11. Max Weber, *Economy and Society: An Outline of Interpretive Sociology*, trans. Guenther Roth and Claus Wittich (Berkeley: University of California Press 1978), 241–54.

12. Max Weber, "Politics as a Vocation," in *From Max Weber: Essays in Sociology*, trans. and ed. H. H. Gerth and C. Wright Mills (New York: Oxford University Press, 1946), 116. Italics added.

13. Weber, *Economy and Society*, 1111.

14. Weber, "Politics as a Vocation," 79.

15. On the many meanings of "rationality" in Weber's writing, see Rogers Brubaker, *The Limits of Rationality: An Essay on the Social and Moral Thought of Max Weber* (Abingdon-on-Thames, UK: Routledge, 2013).

16. Weber talks in depth about the tension between the "formal" and "substantive" rationality of bureaucracy, arguing that although bureaucracy is *geared toward* substantive rationality, it sometimes fails to produce it. I will return to this crucial tension in subsequent chapters and the conclusion.

17. Weber, *Economy and Society*, 960.

18. Weber, *Economy and Society*, 988. Karl Marx and Friedrich Engels, "The Communist Manifesto," in *Karl Marx: Selected Writings*, ed. David McLellan (Oxford: Oxford University Press, 2000), 251. Max Weber, "The Protestant Ethic and the Spirit

of Capitalism," in *The Protestant Ethic and the Spirit of Capitalism and Other Writings*, trans. and ed. Peter Baehr and Gordon C. Wells (New York: Penguin Books 2002), xxiv. "Shell as hard as steel" is more commonly rendered as the "iron cage" in Talcott Parsons's translation of the 1919 version of *The Protestant Ethic*. See Peter Baehr, "The 'Iron Cage' and the 'Shell as Hard as Steel': Parsons, Weber, and the Stahlhartes Gehäuse Metaphor in the Protestant Ethic and the Spirit of Capitalism," *History and Theory* 40, no. 2 (2001): 153–69.

19. Bureaucracy also "inevitably accompanies *mass democracy*," although this coexistence is a constant source of tension. Weber, "Bureaucracy," in Gerth and Mills, *From Max Weber*, 224. A similar argument appears as Robert Michels' "iron law of oligarchy." Robert Michels, *Political Parties: A Sociological Study of the Oligarchial Tendencies of Modern Democracy*, trans. Eden Paul (Eastford, CT: Martino Fine Books, 2016).

20. Some insist that the Chinese bureaucracy is meritocratic, others describe it as patrimonial. These perspectives are of course not mutually exclusive. But both interpretations have been associated with the perpetuation of bureaucratic authoritarianism in China. For patrimonialism, see, e.g., Andrew G. Walder, *Communist Neo-Traditionalism: Work and Authority in Chinese Industry* (Berkeley: University of California Press, 1988). For meritocracy, see, e.g., Daniel Bell, *The China Model: Political Meritocracy and the Limits of Democracy* (Princeton, NJ: Princeton University Press, 2015). While the duel to settle on *one ideal type* for Chinese bureaucracy is prolific, it is not always productive. For example, although Weber is known to have described Chinese bureaucracy as patrimonial, he simultaneously recognized that meritocracy, enshrined in China's imperial examination system, helped uphold patrimonialism. See Max Weber, "The Chinese Literati," in Gerth and Mills, *From Max Weber*, 416–41.

21. See Chun Lin, *The Transformation of Chinese Socialism* (Durham, NC: Duke University Press, 2006); Elizabeth J. Perry, "The Populist Dream of Chinese Democracy," *Journal of Asian Studies* 74, no. 4 (2015): 903–15; Ethan Leib and Baogang He, eds., *The Search for Deliberative Democracy in China* (New York: Springer, 2006); Iza Ding and Michael Thompson-Brusstar, "The Anti-Bureaucratic Ghost in China's Bureaucratic Machine," *China Quarterly* 248, no. S1 (2021): 116–40.

22. See e.g., Perry, "Populist Dream"; Wenfang Tang, *Populist Authoritarianism: Chinese Political Culture and Regime Sustainability* (New York: Oxford University Press, 2016).

23. The literature on public opinion and political participation in China is too massive for me to be all-inclusive. For some examples, see Elizabeth J. Perry, "Challenging the Mandate of Heaven: Popular Protest in Modern China," *Critical Asian Studies* 33, no. 2 (2001): 163–80; James Reilly, *Strong Society, Smart State: The Rise of Public Opinion in China's Japan Policy* (New York: Columbia University Press, 2011); Jessica Chen Weiss, *Powerful Patriots: Nationalist Protest in China's Foreign Relations* (New York: Oxford University Press, 2014); Rory Truex, *Making Autocracy Work: Representation and Responsiveness in Modern China* (New York: Cambridge University Press, 2016); Bruce Dickson, *The Dictator's Dilemma: The Chinese Communist Party's Strategy for Survival* (Oxford: Oxford University Press, 2016).

24. See Anna L. Ahlers, Mette Halskov Hansen, and Rune Svarverud, *The Great Smog of China: A Short History of Air Pollution* (Ann Arbor: Association for Asian Studies, 2020).

25. Alastair Jamieson, "Beijing Olympics Were the Most Polluted Games Ever, Researchers Say," *Telegraph*, June 22, 2009, https://www.telegraph.co.uk/sport/olympics/london-2012/5597277/Beijing-Olympics-were-the-most-polluted-games-ever-researchers-say.html, accessed June 29, 2020.

26. *PM*2.5 are airborne fine particles that are 2.5 microns or less in diameter. The small size of *PM*2.5 allows them to penetrate human lungs and enter the blood stream, causing respiratory and cardiovascular problems.

27. Beijing's initial response was to accuse the US Embassy of meddling in China's domestic affairs. It eventually moved to require all local governments to disclose hourly air pollution levels to their citizens.

28. E.g., Louisa Lim, "Beijing's 'Airpocalypse' Spurs Pollution Controls, Public Pressure," *National Public Radio*, January 14, 2013, https://www.npr.org/2013/01/14/169305324/beijings-air-quality-reaches-hazardous-levels, accessed June 29, 2020.

29. Nicola Davison, "Rivers of Blood: The Dead Pigs Rotting in China's Water Supply," *The Guardian*, March 29, 2013, https://www.theguardian.com/world/2013/mar/29/deadpigs-china-water-supply, accessed June 29, 2020.

30. "China's 100 Cancer Villages [Zhongguo Baichu Zhiai Weidi]," *Phoenix Weekly* [*Fenghuang Zhoukan*], April 2009; China Central Television, "Toxic Running Tracks are Made with Industrial Waste [Dupaodao Jingshi Gongye Feiliao]," June 21, 2016, http://news.xinhuanet.com/fortune/2016-06/21/c_129080075.htm, accessed June 29, 2020; Javier C. Hernandez, "Chinese Parents Outraged after Illnesses at School Are Tied to Pollution," *New York Times*, April 18, 2016, https://www.nytimes.com/2016/04/19/world/asia/chinapollution-cancer-changzhou.html?_r=0, accessed June 29, 2020; Chen Jing, "Cadmium Rice Reappears: Why Can't 'Poisonous Rice' be Eradicated? [Gedami Chongxian: 'Dudami' Weihe Lüjinbujue?]," *Xinjingbao*, April 25, 2020, http://www.bjnews.com.cn/opinion/2020/04/25/721079.html, accessed June 29, 2020.

31. Rafael Lozano et al., "Global and Regional Mortality from 235 Causes of Death for 20 Age Groups in 1990 and 2010: A Systematic Analysis for the Global Burden of Disease Study 2010," *The Lancet* 380 (2012): 2095–128. For future projections, see Qing Wang et al., "Estimation of *PM*2.5-Associated Disease Burden in China in 2020 and 2030 using Population and Air Quality Scenarios: A Modelling Study," *Lancet Planetary Health* 3.2 (2019): e71–e80, https://doi.org/10.1016/S2542-5196(18)30277-8.

32. Te-Ping Chen, "Living in China Takes 3½ Years Off Your Life," *Wall Street Journal*, September 12, 2017, https://www.wsj.com/articles/living-in-china-takes-3-years-offyour-life-1505209673, accessed June 29, 2020.

33. Rachel Stern, *Environmental Litigation in China: A Study in Political Ambivalence* (Cambridge: Cambridge University Press, 2013), 9.

34. Daniel Gardner, "China's 'Silent Spring' Moment?" *New York Times*, March 29, 2015, https://www.nytimes.com/2015/03/19/opinion/why-under-the-dome-found-a-readyaudience-in-china.html, accessed June 29, 2020.

35. "Main Responsibilities of the Ministry of Ecology and Environment [Shengtai Huanjingbu Zhize]," Ministry of Ecology and Environment of the People's Republic of China, http://www.mee.gov.cn/zjhb/zyzz/201810/t20181011_660310.shtml, accessed June 29, 2020.

36. A pseudonym I use to anonymize the identities of research subjects.

37. Denise S. van der Kamp, "Blunt Force Regulation and Bureaucratic Control: Understanding China's War on Pollution," *Governance* 34, no.1 (2021): 191–209. John Helveston and Jonas Nahm, "China's Key Role in Scaling Low-Carbon Energy Technologies," *Science* 366, no. 6467 (2019): 794–96. Jingjing Jiang et al., "Research on China's Capand-Trade Carbon Emission Trading Scheme: Overview and outlook," *Applied Energy* 178 (2016): 902–17.

38. Yifei Li and Judith Shapiro, *China Goes Green: Coercive Environmentalism for A Troubled Planet* (Hoboken, NJ: John Wiley & Sons, 2020).

39. Andrew Mertha, "'Fragmented Authoritarianism 2.0'": Political Pluralization in the Chinese Policy Process," *China Quarterly* 200 (2009): 995–1012.

40. See John P. Burns and Xiaoqi Wang, "Civil Service Reform in China: Impacts on Civil Servants' Behaviour," *China Quarterly* 201 (2010), 58–78; Xueguang Zhou, Hong Lian, Leonard Ortolano, and Yinyu Ye, "A Behavioral Model of 'Muddling Through' in the Chinese Bureaucracy: The Case of Environmental Protection," *China Journal* 70 (2013): 120–47.

41. Weber, *Economy and Society,* 216–17.

42. Weber, *Economy and Society*, 6; 19–20.

43. https://www.merriam-webster.com/dictionary/performative, accessed June 29, 2020. The dictionary definition for *performative* has changed several times over the years of this book's making, showing just how fast a term's meaning can evolve, especially when it gets picked up by public discourse. It seems the more time passes, the more intentionality and negative connotation are imputed to the word. The term's skyrocketing popularity over the past few decades can be seen through a Google Ngram search.

44. J. L. Austin, "Performative Utterances," in *The Semantics-Pragmatics Boundary in Philosophy*, ed. Maite Ezcurdia and Robert J. Stainton (Peterborough, Ontario: Broadview Press, 2013), 22. Also see J. L. Austin, *How to Do Things with Words* (London: Oxford University Press, 1962), originally given as the 1955 William James Lecture.

45. Austin, "Performative Utterances," 28.

46. *Merriam-Webster* demonstrates this definition through the following example: "When expressing outrage is as easy as posting a hashtag, a meme, or an empty black square, there's a question of whether that outrage is genuine or *performative*." See Alia E. Dastagir, "George Floyd, Lea Michele, and the Problem with Performative Outrage," *USA Today*, June 4, 2020, https://www.usatoday.com/story/news/nation/2020/06/04/george-floyd-lea-michele-and-problem-performative-outrage/3137994001/, accessed June 30, 2020.

47. See Michel Callon, ed., *The Laws of the Markets* (Oxford: Blackwell, 1998); Donald MacKenzie, Fabian Muniesa, and Lucia Siu, eds., *Do Economists Make Markets?: On the Performativity of Economics* (Princeton, NJ: Princeton University Press, 2008).

48. Albert O. Hirschman, *The Passions and the Interests: Political Arguments for Capitalism before its Triumph* (Westport, CT: Greenwood, 1997).

49. See Victor Turner, *The Anthropology of Performance* (Cambridge, MA: PAJ Publications: 1988); Clifford Geertz, *Negara: The Theater State in Nineteenth-Century Bali* (Princeton, NJ: Princeton University Press, 1980).

50. See Pierre Bourdieu, trans. Richard Nice, *Distinction: A Social Critique of the Judgment of Taste* (Cambridge, MA: Harvard University Press 1984); Pierre Bourdieu, trans. Richard Nice, *The Logic of Practice* (Stanford, CA: Stanford University Press, 1992).

51. Judith Butler, "Performative Acts and Gender Constitution: An Essay in Phenomenology and Feminist Theory," *Theatre Journal* 40, no. 4 (1988): 519–31; Judith Butler, *Gender Trouble: Feminism and the Subversion of Identity* (New York: Routledge, 1990). Butler argues that both gender and sex are socially constructed—an argument that has been subjected to criticisms.

52. Butler, "Performative Acts," 270.

53. See Erving Goffman, *The Presentation of Self in Everyday Life* (New York: Anchor Books, 1959).

54. Goffman, *Presentation of Self,* 7.

55. Goffman, *Presentation of Self*, chapter 3.

56. See Judith Butler, "Performative Agency," *Journal of Cultural Economy* 3, no. 2 (2010): 147–61.

57. Butler's normative, agentic theory also sets her apart from Bourdieu, whose structural approach has been critiqued for being too passive, if not overdetermined. See

Terry Lovell, "Thinking Feminism with and against Bourdieu," *Feminist Theory* 1, no. 1 (2000): 11–32; Lisa Adkins and Beverley Skeggs, eds., *Feminism after Bourdieu* (Oxford: Blackwell, 2004).

58. See Robert Futrell, "Performative Governance: Impression Management, Teamwork, and Conflict Containment in City Commission Proceedings," *Journal of Contemporary Ethnography* 27, no. 4 (1999): 494–529; Jeffrey Edward Green, *The Eyes of the People: Democracy in an Age of Spectatorship* (Oxford: Oxford University Press, 2010); Elzbieta Matynia, *Performative Democracy* (Abingdon-on-Thames, UK: Routledge, 2015). For performative democracy in hybrid regimes see Andrew Wilson, *Virtual Politics: Faking Democracy in the Post-Soviet World* (New Haven, CT: Yale University Press, 2005).

59. Jie Yang, *Unknotting the Heart: Unemployment and Therapeutic Governance in China* (Ithaca, NY: Cornell University Press, 2015); Yongshun Cai, "Irresponsible State: Local Cadres and Image-Building in China," *Journal of Communist Studies and Transition Politics* 20, no. 4 (2004: 20–41); Alex L. Wang, "Symbolic Legitimacy and Chinese Environmental Reform," *Environmental Law* 48, no. 4 (2018): 699–760.

60. Pushkala Prasad, "Symbolic Processes in the Implementation of Technological Change: A Symbolic Interactionist Study of Work Computerization," *Academy of Management Journal* 36, no. 6 (1993): 1400–29. For symbolic implementation of environmental policies in China, see Ran Ran, *China's Local Environmental Politics* [*Zhongguo difang huanjing zhengzhi: zhengce yu zhixing zhijian de juli*] (Beijing: Central Compilation and Translation Press, 2015). Patricia Bromley and Walter W. Powell, "From Smoke and Mirrors to Walking the Talk: Decoupling in the Contemporary world," *Academy of Management Annals* 6, no. 1 (2012): 483–530.

61. Goffman, *Presentation of Self*, 72.

62. Kimberly J. Morgan and Ann Shola Orloff, eds., *The Many Hands of the State: Theorizing Political Authority and Social Control* (New York: Cambridge University Press, 2017).

63. Peter Hall, "Aligning Ontology and Methodology in Comparative Research," in *Comparative Historical Analysis in the Social Sciences*, ed. James Mahoney and Dietrich Rueschemeyer (New York: Cambridge University Press, 2003), 373–404.

64. Austin, "Performative Utterances."

65. Victor Turner, *From Ritual to Theater: The Human Seriousness of Play* (Cambridge, MA: PAJ Publications, 1982), 91.

66. Giovanni Sartori famously took political science to task for its obsession with "degreeism," or "the abuse (uncritical use) of the maxim that differences in kind are best conceived as differences of degree." Giovanni Sartori, "Comparing and Miscomparing," *Journal of Theoretical Politics* 3, no. 3 (1991): 248.

67. On the notion of common sense, see Antonio Gramsci, *Prison Notebooks* (New York: Columbia University Press, 2007).

68. Vivien Schmidt calls some of these attributes "throughput," which she distinguishes from "input" institutions of participation and representativeness. Schmidt, "Democracy and Legitimacy in the European Union Revisited: Input, Output and 'Throughput,'" *Political Studies* 61, no. 1 (2013): 2–22. On "input institutions" in authoritarian regimes, see Andrew J. Nathan, "Authoritarian Resilience," *Journal of Democracy* 14, no.1 (2003): 6–17.

69. See James L. Gibson, "Understandings of Justice: Institutional Legitimacy, Procedural Justice, and Political Tolerance," *Law & Society Review* 23, no. 3 (1989): 469–96; Jason Sunshine and Tom R. Tyler, "The Role of Procedural Justice and Legitimacy in Shaping Public Support for Policing," *Law & Society Review* 37, no. 3 (2003): 513–48.

70. It's important to note that "democracy" can mean different things in different societies. See Andrew J. Nathan, *Chinese Democracy* (Berkeley: University of California Press,

1986); Tianjian Shi and Jie Lu, "The Meaning of Democracy: The Shadow of Confucianism," *Journal of Democracy* 21, no. 4 (2010): 123–30.

71. See Dingxin Zhao, "The Mandate of Heaven and Performance Legitimation in Historical and Contemporary China," *American Behavioral Scientist* 53, no. 3 (2009): 416–33; Yuchao Zhu, "'Performance Legitimacy' and China's Political Adaptation Strategy," *Journal of Chinese Political Science* 16, no. 2 (2011): 123–40; Hongxing Yang and Dingxin Zhao, "Performance Legitimacy, State Autonomy and China's Economic Miracle," *Journal of Contemporary China* 24, no. 91 (2015): 64–82.

72. See Stephen M. Weatherford, "How Does Government Performance Influence Political Support?" *Political Behavior* 9, no.1 (1987): 5–28; Jose Antonio Cheibub, "Political Regimes and the Extractive Capacity of Governments: Taxation in Democracies and Dictatorships," *World Politics* 50 (1998): 349–76; Bruce Bueno De Mesquita and George W. Downs, "Development and Democracy," *Foreign Affairs* 84, no. 5 (2005): 77–86.

73. See Seymour Martin Lipset, "Some Social Requisites of Democracy: Economic Development and Political Legitimacy," *American Political Science Review* 53, no. 1 (1959): 69–105. For the ideological foundations of Supreme Court legitimacy, see Brandon L. Bartels and Christopher D. Johnston, "On the Ideological Foundations of Supreme Court Legitimacy in the American Public," *American Journal of Political Science* 57, no. 1 (2013): 184–99. For a challenge to the Bartels and Johnston thesis that Supreme Court legitimacy is rooted in the public's ideology and "performance satisfaction," see James L. Gibson and Michael J. Nelson, "Is the U.S. Supreme Court's Legitimacy Grounded in Performance Satisfaction and Ideology?" *American Journal of Political Science* 59, no.1 (2015): 162–74.

74. Yuhua Wang, *Tying the Autocrat's Hands: The Rise of the Rule of Law in China* (Cambridge: Cambridge University Press, 2015). Iza Ding and Jeffrey Javed, "The Autocrat's Moral-Legal Dilemma: Popular Morality and Legal Institutions in China," *Comparative Political Studies* 54, no. 6 (2021): 989–1022.

75. "Report by Hu Jintao at the Seventeenth National Congress (Excerpts) [Hu Jintao Zai Dang de Shiqici Quanguo Daibiao Dahui Shang Zuo Baogao (Zhaiyao)]," Central Government of the People's Republic of China, October 15, 2007, http://www.gov.cn/ldhd/2007-10/15/content_776431.htm, accessed June 29, 2020.

76. "Report by Hu Jintao at the 18th National Congress [Hu Jintao Zai Zhongguo Gongchandang Di Shibaci Quanguo Daibiao Dahui Shang de Baogao]," Central Government of the People's Republic of China, November 17, 2012, http://www.gov.cn/ldhd/2012-11/17/content_2268826.htm, accessed June 29, 2020. Italics added.

77. In 2015, the State Council established a working group to coordinate the "transformation of government functions." Three years later, this administrative reform adopted the name of "decentralization, management, and service" (*fangguanfu*), and the working group expanded to include ministers from every functional bureaucracy under the State Council. See General Office of the State Council, "Notice on the Establishment of a Coordination Group to Promote the Transformation of Government Functions [Guowuyuan bangongting guanyu chengli tuijin zhineng zhuanbian xietiao xiaozu de tongzhi]," April 21, 2015, http://www.gov.cn/zhengce/content/2015-04/21/content_9648.htm; General Office of the State Council. "Notice on the Establishment of a Coordination Group to Promote the Transformation of Government Functions as well as 'Fangguanfu' Reforms [Guowuyuan bangongting guanyu chengli guowuyuan tuijin zhengfu zhineng zhuanbian he 'fangguanfu' gaige xietiao xiaozu de tongzhi]," July 25, 2018, http://www.gov.cn/zhengce/content/2018-07/25/content_5309035.htm.

78. See Elizabeth J. Perry, "Chinese Conceptions of 'Rights': From Mencius to Mao-and now," *Perspectives on Politics* 6, no. 1 (2008): 37–50.

79. "Premier Li Urges Responding to People's Concerns in Time," State Council of The People's Republic of China, February 18, 2016, http://english.www.gov.cn/premier/news/2016/02/18/content_281475291965095.htm, accessed June 29, 2020.

80. Jirong Yan, "Build a Service-Oriented Government Based on Public Satisfaction [Jianshe Renmin Manyi de Fuwuxing Zhengfu]," *Guangming Daily*, January 21, 2020, https://epaper.gmw.cn/gmrb/html/2020-01/21/nw.D110000gmrb_20200121_2-16.htm, accessed June 29, 2020.

81. See Jidong Chen, Jennifer Pan, and Yiqing Xu, "Sources of Authoritarian Responsiveness: A Field Experiment in China," *American Journal of Political Science* 60, no. 2 (2016): 383–400; Christopher Heurlin, *Responsive Authoritarianism in China* (Cambridge: Cambridge University Press, 2016); Zheng Su and Tianguang Meng, "Selective Responsiveness: Online Public Demands and Government Responsiveness in Authoritarian China," *Social Science Research* 59 (2016): 52–67; Rory Truex, *Making Autocracy Work*; Greg Distelhorst and Yue Hou, "Constituency Service under Nondemocratic Rule: Evidence from China," *Journal of Politics* 79, no. 3 (2017): 1024–40. For "authoritarian responsiveness" outside China, see Edmund Malesky and Paul Schuler, "Nodding or Needling: Analyzing Delegate Responsiveness in an Authoritarian Parliament," *American Political Science Review* 104, no. 3 (2010): 482–502.

82. Guangsheng Chen, *Toward Good Governance* [*Zouxiang shanzhi*] (Hangzhou: Zhejiang University Press, 2007).

83. Perry, "Populist Dream."

84. See Keping Yu, "Incremental Democracy and Political Reform [Zengliang Minzhu yu Zhengzhi Gaige]," in *Reform Consensus and China's Future* [*Gaige Gongshi yu Zhongguo Weilai*], ed. Central Compilation and Translation Bureau (Beijing: Central Compilation and Translation Press, 2013), 33–51. Yu differentiates "incremental democracy" (*zengliang minzhu*) from "gradual democracy" (*jianjin minzhu*); the latter is primarily concerned with the speed of democratization. Instead of democratization through multiparty elections or separation of powers, incremental democracy means the expansion of citizens' political rights to a "pareto optimality" without necessarily relinquishing the party's leadership. In this sense, incremental democracy is closer to the notion of "subnational democracy" in the comparative politics literature.

85. For China's projection of its international image, see Xiaoyu Pu, *Rebranding China: Contested Status Signaling in the Changing Global Order* (Stanford, CA: Stanford University Press, 2019).

86. J. Macgowan, *Sidelights on Chinese Life* (Philadelphia: Lippincott, 1908), 187; cited in Goffman, *Presentation of Self*, 25.

87. See Dimitar D. Gueorguiev and Paul J. Schuler, "Collective Charisma: Elite-Mass Relations in China and Vietnam," *Problems of Post-Communism* 68, no. 3 (2021): 1–12.

88. See table 5 in Anthony Saich, "The Quality of Governance in China: The Citizen's View," HKS Faculty Research Working Paper Series RWP 12–051, John F. Kennedy School of Government, Harvard University, http://nrs.harvard.edu/urn-3:HUL.InstRepos:9924084, accessed June 29, 2020.

89. See Vivienne Shue, "Legitimacy Crisis in China?" in *State and Society in 21st Century China: Crisis, Contention, and Legitimation*, ed. Peter Hays Gries and Stanley Rosen (New York: Routledge, 2004), 37–62; Yang, *Unknotting the Heart*; Christian P. Sorace, *Shaken Authority: China's Communist Party and the 2008 Sichuan Earthquake* (Ithaca, NY: Cornell University Press, 2017); Bin Xu, *The Politics of Compassion: The Sichuan Earthquake and Civic Engagement in China* (Stanford, CA: Stanford University Press, 2017); Jennifer Pan, "How Chinese Officials Use the Internet to Construct Their Public Image," *Political Science Research and Methods* 7, no. 2 (2019): 197–213.

90. Even if performative interactions with citizens are ultimately to impress senior authorities, we should still be interested in the drivers of this behavior. Nor should we exaggerate how much control senior authorities have over street-level bureaucrats, as discretion is a consistent theme in the literature on street-level bureaucracy. See, e.g., Michael Lipsky, *Street-Level Bureaucracy: Dilemmas of the Individual in Public Service*

(New York: Russell Sage Foundation, 2010); Bernardo Zacka, *When the State Meets the Street: Public Service and Moral Agency* (Cambridge, MA: Harvard University Press, 2018); Kevin J. O'Brien and Lianjiang Li, "Selective Policy Implementation in Rural China," *Comparative Politics* 31, no. 2 (1999): 167–86.

91. For performative politics in the Soviet bloc, see, e.g., Jeffrey Kopstein, *The Politics of Economic Decline in East Germany, 1945–1989* (Chapel Hill: University of North Carolina Press, 2000); Alexei Yurchak, *Everything Was Forever, Until It Was No More: The Last Soviet Generation* (Princeton, NJ: Princeton University Press, 2013).

92. Andrew J. Nathan, "Authoritarian Resilience," *Journal of Democracy* 14, no. 1 (2003): 6–17.

93. See Stephen White, "Economic Performance and Communist Legitimacy," *World Politics* 38, no. 3 (1986): 462–82; Martin K. Dimitrov, "What the Party Wanted to Know: Citizen Complaints as a "Barometer of Public Opinion" in Communist Bulgaria," *East European Politics and Societies* 28, no. 2 (2014): 271–95.

94. See Xi Chen, *Social Protest and Contentious Authoritarianism in China* (Cambridge: Cambridge University Press, 2012); Jing Chen, *Useful Complaints: How Petitions Assist Decentralized Authoritarianism in China* (Lanham, MD: Rowman & Littlefield, 2016); Kevin J. O'Brien, ed., *Popular Protest in China* (Cambridge, MA: Harvard University Press, 2009); Martin K. Dimitrov, "Internal Government Assessments of the Quality of Governance in China," *Studies in Comparative International Development* 50, no.1 (2015): 50–72.

95. Jamie Gangel and Shelby Lin Erdman, "Former Presidents Obama, Bush and Clinton Volunteer to Get Coronavirus Vaccine Publicly to Prove It's Safe," CNN, December 3, 2020, https://edition.cnn.com/2020/12/02/politics/obama-vaccine/index.html.

96. For the potential benefits of concept stretching, see David Collier and James E. Mahon Jr., "Conceptual 'Stretching' revisited: Adapting Categories in Comparative Analysis," *American Political Science Review* 87, no. 4 (1993): 845–55.

97. Zacka, *When the State Meets the Street*, 11. Zacka's study was conducted in the United States, and he limits his insights to democracies. This study will show that similar predicaments and similar moral ambiguities exist in nondemocracies.

98. Zacka, *When the State Meets the Street*, 9.

99. Niccòlo Machiavelli, *Discourses on Livy, Book III Chapter 40,* trans. Harvey C. Mansfield and Nathan Tarcov (Chicago: University of Chicago Press, 1996), 299.

100. Dietz, "Trapping the Prince."

101. Glen Newey, "Political Lying: A Defense," *Public Affairs Quarterly* 11, no. 2 (1997): 93–116. Also see John J. Mearsheimer, *Why Leaders Lie: The Truth about Lying in International Politics* (Oxford: Oxford University Press, 2013).

102. Goffman, *Presentation of Self*, chapters IV–VI; Butler, "Performative Agency."

103. Albert O. Hirschman, *Exit, Voice, and Loyalty: Responses to Decline in Firms, Organizations, and States* (Cambridge, MA: Harvard University Press, 1970).

104. Goffman, *Presentation of Self,* 141.

105. Richard Bonney, "Some Preliminary Remarks on Possibilities of Research," cited in Bourdieu, "Rethinking the State: Genesis and Structure of the Bureaucratic Field." *Sociological Theory* 12, no. 1 (1994): 4.

1. ANATOMY OF THE STATE

1. See Charles Tilly, "War Making and State Making as Organized Crime," in *Bringing the State Back In*, ed. Peter B. Evans, Dietrich Rueschemeyer, and Theda Skocpol (New York: Cambridge University Press, 1985), 172. For how violent conflicts shape state-building outside of Europe, see, e.g., Miguel Centeno, *Blood and Debt: War and*

the Nation-State in Latin America (University Park: Pennsylvania State University Press, 2002); Dan Slater, *Ordering Power: Contentious Politics and Authoritarian Leviathans in Southeast Asia* (New York: Cambridge University Press, 2010); and Mark Dincecco and Yuhua Wang, "Violent Conflict and Political Development Over the Long Run: China versus Europe," *Annual Review of Political Science* 21 (2018): 341–58.

2. See Chalmers A. Johnson, *Peasant Nationalism and Communist Power: The Emergence of Revolutionary China, 1937–1945* (Stanford, CA: Stanford University Press, 1962); Mark Selden, *The Yenan Way in Revolutionary China* (Cambridge, MA: Harvard University Press, 1971); Suzanne Pepper, *Civil War in China: The Political Struggle, 1945–1949* (Lanham, MD: Rowman & Littlefield Publishers, 1999); and Elizabeth J. Perry, *Anyuan: Mining China's Revolutionary Tradition* (Berkeley: University of California Press, 2012).

3. Emil Ludwig, *Napoleon*, trans. Eden Paul and Cedar Paul (New York: Modern Library, 1915), 168.

4. Although Mao was eventually credited for the CCP's successful mobilization and military strategies, these were in fact collective inventions. See Roy Hofheinz, *The Broken Wave: The Chinese Communist Peasant Movement, 1922–1928* (Cambridge, MA: Harvard University Press, 1977) for an account of Peng Pai's role in peasant mobilization in the 1920s. See Perry, *Anyuan*, for a discussion of Li Lisan's role in crafting the CCP's urban mobilization strategies. On how wartime mobilization strategies falter at everyday governance, consider the use of moral incentives in political mobilization, which helps boost national cohesion and military morale, but fails to deliver economic productivity. See Elizabeth Perry, "Moving the Masses: Emotion Work in the Chinese Revolution," *Mobilization: An International Quarterly* 7, no. 2 (2002): 111–28; and Jeffrey Javed, *Righteous Revolutionaries: Morality and Violence in the Forging of State Authority after the Chinese Communist Revolution* (Ann Arbor: University of Michigan Press, 2022).

5. Weber, "Politics as Vocation," 78. Weber defines "legitimate" as "considered to be legitimate."

6. Weber, "Politics as Vocation," 78.

7. Online at https://www.marxists.org/archive/trotsky/1907/1905/ch31.htm, accessed April 26, 2021.

8. For the popularity of Weber's definition, also see discussion in Morgan and Orloff, "Many Hands," 4.

9. Weber's lecture was delivered two years after the October Revolution in Russia, an event that drew his strong interest.

10. For a summary of the waxing and waning of intellectual interest in the notion of state autonomy in the twentieth century, see Michael Mann, "The Autonomous Power of the State: Its Origins, Mechanisms and Results," *European Journal of Sociology* 25 (1985): 185–213. Also see Theda Skocpol, "Bringing the State Back In: Strategies of Analysis in Current Research," in *Bringing the State Back In*, ed. Peter B. Evans, Dietrich Rueschemeyer, and Theda Skocpol (New York: Cambridge University Press, 1985), 3–43.

11. See Peter Evans and James E. Rauch, "Bureaucracy and Growth: A Cross-National Analysis of the Effects of 'Weberian' State Structures on Economic Growth," *American Sociological Review* 64, no. 5 (1999): 748–65.

12. For a notable exception, see Amartya Sen's introduction to Adam Smith, *The Theory of Moral Sentiments* (New York: Penguin 2010). Another term falsely attributed to Smith was the "night-watchman state." This term of derision was directed at Smith's theory of the state by the nineteenth-century German jurist and prominent social-democratic thinker Ferdinand Lassalle. See Gavin Kennedy, *Adam Smith's Lost Legacy* (London: Palgrave 2005), 215–16.

13. See Andrei Shleifer and Robert W. Vishny, *The Grabbing Hand: Government Pathologies and Their Cures* (Cambridge, MA: Harvard University Press, 1998). John Lewis Gaddis, *The Cold War: A New History* (New York: Penguin, 2006), 1–2, 263–64; Tony Shaw, "'Some Writers are More Equal than Others': George Orwell, the State and Cold War Privilege," *Cold War History* 4, no. 1 (2003): 143–70.

14. V. I. Lenin, trans. Robert Service, *The State and Revolution* (New York: Penguin 1992), 86.

15. Five years after the October Revolution, Lenin expressed his concern that the state had been "overthrown [but] has not yet been overcome." Vladimir Lenin, "Better Fewer, but Better," https://www.marxists.org/archive/lenin/works/1923/mar/02.htm, accessed May 9, 2021. On "high modernism" see James C. Scott, *Seeing Like a State: How Certain Schemes to Improve the Human Condition Have Failed* (New Haven, CT: Yale University Press, 2008).

16. Bourdieu, "Rethinking the State," 1.

17. See, e.g., Tania Murray Li, "Beyond 'the State' and Failed Schemes," *American Anthropologist* 107, no. 3 (2005): 383–94; Morgan and Orloff, "Many Hands."

18. The small size and limited reach of states in premodern times meant that they might not have been able to claim anything like a legitimate monopoly of the use of violence, and whatever monopoly they enjoyed might have been more transient than what states enjoy today.

19. Tilly, "War Making," 180.

20. Weber, *Economy and Society*, 956.

21. Weber, *Economy and Society*, 956.

22. Weber, *Economy and Society*, 956.

23. This is a different sort of blurring than the one that plagues "patrimonial" and other premodern systems, in which the state is treated as the personal property of the ruler.

24. Weber, "Politics as a Vocation," 80.

25. "A Revelation of the Total Number of Chinese Civil Servants: 'Too Many Officials and Too Few Agents' at About 7,167,000 Persons [Zhongguo Gongwuyuan Zongshu Pilu: Guan Duo Bin Shao Yue 716.7 Wan Ren]," *China Economic Weekly* [*Zhongguo Jingji Zhoukan*], June 21, 2016, http://www.chinanews.com/gn/2016/06-21/7911130.shtml, accessed June 30, 2020.

26. Shakespeare, *Henry IV*.

27. Michael Mann, "The Autonomous Power," 113.

28. Michael Mann, *The Sources of Social Power*, vol. 3, *Global Empires and Revolution, 1890–1945* (Cambridge: Cambridge University Press, 2012), 7–9. Mann did not use the term *superstructural*, which I adopt, metaphorically, from Marx's famous distinction between a society's material "base," i.e., its division of the means of production along class lines, which he sees shaping its "superstructure" of culture, ideologies, and institutions.

29. Peter Evans, *Embedded Autonomy: States and Industrial Transformation* (Princeton, NJ: Princeton, 1995); Francis Fukuyama, *State Building: Governance and World Order in the 21st Century* (London: Profile Books, 2014); Juan Linz and Alfred Stepan, *Problems of Democratic Transition and Consolidation: Southern Europe, South America, and Post-Communist Europe* (Baltimore: Johns Hopkins, 1996); Dan Slater, Benjamin Smith, and Gautam Nair, "Economic Origins of Democratic Breakdown? The Redistributive Model and the Postcolonial State," *Perspectives on Politics* 12, no. 2 (2014): 353–74; Slater, *Ordering Power*; Steven Levitsky and Lucan Way, "The Durability of Revolutionary Regimes," *Journal of Democracy* 24, no. 3 (2013): 5–17.

30. James Fearon and David Laitin, "Ethnicity, Insurgency, and Civil War," *American Political Science Review* 97, no. 1 (2003): 75–90.

31. Fukuyama, *State Building*, 20.

32. Michael Mann, "Infrastructural Power Revisited," *Studies in Comparative International Development* 43, no. 3–4 (2008), 355. Weber, *Economy and Society,* 968.

33. José Antonio Cheibub, "Political Regimes and the Extractive Capacity of Governments: Taxation in Democracies and Dictatorships," *World Politics* 50, no. 3 (1998): 349–76. Slater, Smith, and Nair, "Economic Origins." Some states' revenues rely more on taxation than others do. For instance, the so-called "rentier states," such as Saudi Arabia, Nigeria, and Russia, can generate revenue by selling natural resources like oil, natural gas, and minerals on international markets, thereby reducing their reliance on income taxes from ordinary citizens. Hazem Beblawi, "The Rentier State in the Arab World," *Arab Studies Quarterly* 9, no. 4 (1987): 383–98; Michael Ross, "Does Oil Hinder Democracy?," *World Politics* 53, no. 3 (2001): 325–61.

34. Fukuyama, *State Building*, 5.

35. Evans and Rauch, "Bureaucracy and Growth."

36. See Yuen Yuen Ang, *How China Escaped the Poverty Trap* (Ithaca, NY: Cornell University Press, 2016); Junyan Jiang, "Making Bureaucracy Work: Patronage Networks, Performance Incentives, and Economic Development in China," *American Journal of Political Science* 62, no. 4 (2018): 982–99; Agnes Cornell, Carl Henrik Knutsen, and Jan Teorell, "Bureaucracy and Growth," *Comparative Political Studies* 53, no. 14 (2020): 2246–82.

37. See, e.g., Alice H. Amsden, *Asia's Next Giant: South Korea and Late Industrialization* (Oxford: Oxford University Press, 1989); Evans and Rauch, "Bureaucracy and Growth"; Chalmers Johnson, *MITI and the Japanese Miracle: The Growth of Industrial Policy: 1925–1975* (Stanford, CA: Stanford University Press, 1982).

38. Daniel P. Carpenter, *Reputation and Power: Organizational Image and Pharmaceutical Regulation at the FDA* (Princeton, NJ: Princeton University Press, 2010).

39. Kenneth Lieberthal and Michel Oksenberg, *Policy Making in China: Leaders, Structures, and Processes* (Princeton, NJ: Princeton University Press, 2020), 17. Also see Kenneth Lieberthal, "The Fragmented Authoritarianism Model and Its Limitations," in *Bureaucracy, Politics, and Decision Making in Post-Mao China*, ed. Kenneth Lieberthal and David M. Lampton (Berkeley: University of California Press, 1992), 1–30.

40. Lieberthal, "Fragmented Authoritarianism," 3–4. It goes without saying that the story behind the making of each policy is different. Lieberthal and Oksenberg illustrate their framework through energy policy, but they do not claim that "fragmented authoritarianism" is behind every single policy. See Lieberthal and Oksenberg, *Policy Making in China*, 20–21.

41. See chapter 4 of Lieberthal and Oksenberg, *Policy Making in China*; Kevin O'Brien and Lianjiang Li, "Selective Policy Implementation in Rural China," *Comparative Politics* 31, no. 2 (1999): 167–86; Iza Ding and Denise van der Kamp, "High Maintenance or Low Maintenance? Uneven Environmental Policy Implementation in China," Working Paper.

42. See Johnson, *MITI*; Evans and Rauch, "Bureaucracy and Growth"; Peter B. Evans, *Embedded Autonomy: States and Industrial Transformation* (Princeton, NJ: Princeton University Press, 1995).

43. This statement may be controversial given the high hopes rightfully placed in "green growth." I will address this contention in the next chapter. For a specific example of how growth and the environment come into conflict, see Mark Wang, Michael Webber, Brian Finlayson, and Jon Barnett, "Rural Industries and Water Pollution in China," *Journal of Environmental Management* 86, no. 4 (2008): 648–59.

44. See, e.g., Eva Bellin, "The Robustness of Authoritarianism in the Middle East: Exceptionalism in Comparative Perspective," *Comparative Politics* 36, no. 2 (2004): 139–57. Scholars of the rentier state often argue that these states may develop strong coercive capacity without offering society "representation." For a challenge to this thesis, see Steffen

Hertog, "The 'Rentier Mentality', 30 Years On: Evidence from Survey Data," *British Journal of Middle Eastern Studies* 47, no. 1 (2020): 6–23.

45. See, e.g., Daniel Carpenter, *The Forging of Bureaucratic Autonomy: Reputations, Networks, and Policy Innovation in Executive Agencies, 1862–1928* (Princeton, NJ: Princeton University Press, 2001).

46. The metaphor of the autocratic state as "stationary bandits" is from Mancur Olson, "Dictatorship, Democracy, and Development," *American Political Science Review* 87, no. 3 (1993): 567–76.

47. Gerth and Mills, *From Max Weber*, 197.

48. Gerth and Mills, *From Max Weber*, 197.

49. Elizabeth J. Perry, "Making Communism Work: Sinicizing a Soviet Governance Practice," *Comparative Studies in Society and History* 61, no. 3 (2019): 535–62.

50. Valerie J. Karplus and Mengying Wu, "Crackdowns in Hierarchies: Evidence from China's Environmental Inspections," MIT Sloan Research Paper no. 5700–19, doi: 10.2139/ssrn.3449177; Denise van der Kamp, "Can Police Patrols Prevent Pollution? The Limits of Authoritarian Environmental Governance in China," *Comparative Politics* 53, no. 3 (2020): 403–33.

51. Gerth and Mills, *From Max Weber*, 261.

52. Tung-Tsu Chu, *Local Government in China Under the Ch'ing* (Cambridge, MA: Harvard University Asia Center, 1962).

53. Jean C. Oi, "The Role of the Local State in China's Transitional Economy," *China Quarterly* 144 (1995): 1132–49; Li'an Zhou, "Governing China's Local Officials: An Analysis of Promotion Tournament Model [Zhongguo Difang Guanyuan de Jinsheng Jinbiaosai Moshi Yanjiu]," *Economic Research Journal [Jingji Yanjiu]* 7 (2007): 36–50; Hongbin Li and Li-An Zhou, "Political Turnover and Economic Performance: The Incentive Role of Personnel Control in China," *Journal of Public Economics* 89, no. 9–10 (2005): 1743–62. For challenges to this thesis, see, e.g., Victor Shih, Christopher Adolph, and Mingxing Liu, "Getting Ahead in the Communist Party: Explaining the Advancement of Central Committee Members in China," *American Political Science Review* 106, no. 1 (2012): 166–87.

54. Central Organization Department [Zhongzubu], "Notice on Improving the Performance Evaluation of Local Party-State Leadership and Cadres [Guanyu Gaijin Difang Dangzheng Lingdao Banzi he Lingdao Ganbu Zhengji Kaohe Gongzuo de Tongzhi]," December 10, 2013, http://renshi.people.com.cn/n/2013/1210/c139617-237 93409.html.

55. Lipsky, *Street-Level Bureaucracy*.

56. See Bo Rothstein, "Creating Political Legitimacy: Electoral Democracy versus Quality of Government," *American Behavioral Scientist* 53, no.3 (2009): 311–30.

57. For a critique of the role of social media in the Iranian protests of 2009, see Golnaz Esfandiari, "The Twitter Devolution," *Foreign Policy*, June 8, 2010.

58. Lipsky, *Street-Level Bureaucracy*, 10.

59. Chen Xi, *Social Protest*; Peter L. Lorentzen, "Regularizing Rioting: Permitting Public Protest in an Authoritarian Regime," *Quarterly Journal of Political Science* 8, no. 2 (2013): 127–58; Ching Kwan Lee and Yonghong Zhang, "The Power of Instability: Unraveling the Microfoundations of Bargained Authoritarianism in China," *American Journal of Sociology* 118, no. 6 (2013): 1475–1508; Martin K. Dimitrov, "Internal Government Assessments."

60. This decree was issued after several public safety accidents, such as the 2015 chemical explosion and fire in the Port of Tianjin, which caused more than a thousand deaths and injuries, environmental pollution, and strong public outrage. General Office of the

Communist Party of China, General Office of the State Council [Zhonggong Zhongyang Bangongting and Guowuyuan Bangongting], "Strengthen the Implementation of Cadre Responsibility System Concerning the Comprehensive Management of Public Security [Jianquan Luoshi Shehui Zhi'an Zonghe Zhili Lingdao Zerenzhi Guiding]," March 24, 2016, http://politics.people.com.cn/n1/2016/0324/c1001-28222211.html.

61. Ma Liang, "The Effects of Public Participation on Government Performance Evaluation: A Multi-Level Analysis of Chinese Cities [Gongzhong Canyu de Zhengfu Jixiao Pinggu Zouxiao le ma?—Jiyu Zhongguo Chengshi de Duocen Fenxi]," *Comparative Economic and Social Systems* [*Jingji Shehui Tizhi Bijiao*] 197, no. 3 (2018): 113–24.

62. People.cn, "A Revolutionary Party is Most Afraid of Not Hearing People's Voices [Yige Geming Zhengdang, Jiupa Tingbudao Renmin de Shengyin]," October 25, 2016, http://cpc.people.com.cn/n1/2016/1025/c69113-28805875.html.

63. Catherine Boone, *Political Topographies of the African State: Territorial Authority and Institutional Choice* (New York: Cambridge University Press, 2003).

64. Jennifer Murtazashvili, "Pathologies of Centralized State-Building," *PRISM* 8, no. 2 (2019): 54–67.

65. Anna Grzymala-Busse, *Rebuilding Leviathan: Party Competition and State Exploitation in Postcommunist Democracies* (Cambridge: Cambridge University Press, 2007).

66. O'Brien and Li, "Selective Policy Implementation."

67. Bellin, "Robustness of Authoritarianism."

68. Evans, *Embedded Autonomy*; Chalmers Johnson, *MITI*; Ezra F. Vogel, *The Four Little Dragons: The Spread of Industrialization in East Asia* (Cambridge, MA: Harvard University Press, 1991).

69. Lily L. Tsai, *Accountability without Democracy: Solidary Groups and Public Goods Provision in Rural China* (Cambridge: Cambridge University Press, 2007).

70. Melanie Manion, "Policy Implementation in the People's Republic of China: Authoritative Decisions versus Individual Interests," *Journal of Asian Studies* 50, no. 2 (1991): 253–79; Iza Ding and Denise van der Kamp, "High Maintenance or Low Maintenance?"; Dorothy J. Solinger and Yiyang Hu, "Welfare, Wealth and Poverty in Urban China: The *Dibao* and its Differential Disbursement," *China Quarterly* 211 (2012): 741–64.

71. Sorace, *Shaken Authority*.

72. Mann, "Autonomous Power," 188.

73. See Pu, *Rebranding China*, for a discussion of China's mixed strategy of status signaling on the international stage.

74. People.cn, "6 Billion People Earning 1000 Yuan a Month? The National Statistics Bureau Responds," June 15, 2020, http://politics.people.com.cn/n1/2020/0615/c1001-31747507.html.

75. Xiaojun Li, "Access, Institutions, and Policy Influence: The Changing Political Economy of Trade Protection in Post-reform China" (PhD diss., Stanford University, 2013).

76. Sheena Chestnut Greitens, "Rethinking China's Coercive Capacity: An Examination of PRC Domestic Security Spending, 1992–2012," *China Quarterly* 232 (2017): 1002–25, 8, 11.

77. Greitens, "Rethinking China's Coercive Capacity," 8.

78. Phone interview with Chinese academic expert on cadres, June 21, 2020.

79. Thanks to Stan Hok-Wui Wong and Yu Zeng for their data.

80. Stan Hok-Wui Wong and Yu Zeng, "Getting Ahead by Getting on the Right Track: Horizontal Mobility in China's Political Selection Process," *Journal of Contemporary China* 27, no. 109 (2018): 61–84.

81. Wong and Zeng, "Getting Ahead."

82. *Xinjingbao*, "Multiple Environmental Protection Directors Are Reposted to Become Local First-Hands [duowei huanbao tingzhang zhuangang difang yibashou]," April 30, 2019, http://www.xinhuanet.com/politics/2019-04/30/c_1124435572.htm.

83. Interview with retired organization department official, November 2013.

84. Yuen Yuen Ang, "Counting Cadres: A Comparative View of the Size of China's Public Employment," *China Quarterly* 211 (2012): 676–96.

85. For "predatory" see Nathaniel Taplin, "How China's SOEs Squeeze Private Firms," *Wall Street Journal*, February 7, 2019, https://www.wsj.com/articles/how-chinas-soes-squeeze-private-firms-11549530183. For "developmental" see Victor Nee, Sonja Opper, and Sonia Wong, "Developmental State and Corporate Governance in China," *Management and Organization Review* 3, no. 1 (2007): 19–53; Geoffrey C. Chen and Charles Lees, "Growing China's Renewables Sector: A Developmental State Approach," *New Political Economy* 21, no. 6 (2016): 574–86.

86. David Blumenthal and William Hsiao, "Privatization and its Discontents: The Evolving Chinese Health Care System," *New England Journal of Medicine* 353, no. 11 (2005): 1165–70.

87. Mit Ramesh, Xun Wu, and Alex Jingwei He, "Health Governance and Healthcare Reforms in China," *Health Policy and Planning* 29, no. 6 (2013): 663–72; Wang Shaoguang, "State Policy Orientation, Extractive Capacity and the Equality of Healthcare in Urban China," *Social Sciences in China* 6 (2005): 101–20.

88. The boundary between state and society is again blurred here. Technically, most public hospitals are subsidiaries of the NHC, but doctors tend not to see themselves as a part of the state.

2. OLD WOES AND NEW PAINS

1. Lingyun Zhao, Lianhui Zhang, Xinghua Yi, and Jianzhong Zhu, *The Construction of Ecological Civilization with Chinese Characteristics [Zhongguo tese shengtai wenming jianshe daolu]* (Beijing: China Financial and Economic Publishing House, 2014).

2. United Nations, "Report of the United Nations Conference on the Human Environment," June 1972, https://www.un.org/ga/search/view_doc.asp?symbol=A/CONF.48/14/REV.1.

3. One account of Chinese attitudes at the Stockholm Conference records that "China's position is naturally largely unknown, but to judge from Chinese internal press and radio the dangers of environmental degradation . . . are at least as well understood there as they are in the West." Wayland Kennet, "The Stockholm Conference on the Human Environment," *International Affairs* 48, no. 1 (1972): 33–45.

4. *People's Daily*, "'Tang Ke Spoke on Behalf of Chinese Delegate about China's Stance on the Protection and Improvement of Human Environment at the United Nations Conference on the Environment [Woguo Daibiaotuan Tuanzhang Tang Ke zai Lianheguo Renlei Huanjing Huiyi Shang Fayan Chanshu Woguo dui Weihu he Gaishan Renlei Huanjing Wenti de Zhuzhang]," June 11, 1972.

5. Government of the PRC, "Situation of Environmental Protection [Huanjing Baohu Zhuangkuang]," July 27, 2005, http://www.gov.cn/test/2005-07/27/content_17757.htm.

6. Government of the PRC, "Footprints of the Republic—1973: The Beginning of Environmental Protection [Gongheguo de Zuji—1973 Nian: Huanjing Baohu Kaishi Qibu]," August 31, 2009, http://www.gov.cn/test/2009-08/31/content_1405410.htm.

7. I use "environmental state" to refer to China's official environmental protection system (*huanbao xitong*), which consists of the environmental bureaucracies and institutions of environmental protection. It doesn't suggest that the entire state is environmentalist. Mary Alice Haddad and Stevan Harrell use "eco-developmental state" to refer to

the current status of state-led environmentalism in East Asia: the primary goal is still economic growth, and the state welcomes environmentalism only as far as it assists economic growth. Mary Alice Haddad and Stevan Harrell, "The Evolution of the East Asian Eco-Developmental State," in *Greening East Asia: The Rise of the Eco-Developmental State*, ed. Ashley Esarey, Mary Alice Haddad, Joanna Lewis, and Stevan Harrell (Seattle: University of Washington Press, 2020), 5–31.

8. Sean Fleming, "Climate Change Helped Destroy These Four Ancient Civilizations," *World Economic Forum*, March 29, 2019, https://www.weforum.org/agenda/2019/03/our-turn-next-a-brief-history-of-civilizations-that-fell-because-of-climate-change/.

9. Xiuqi Fang et al., "Transmission of Climate Change Impacts from Temperature Change to Grain Harvests, Famines, and Peasant Uprisings in Historical China [Lengnuan, Fengqian, Jihuang, Nongmin Qiyi: Jiyu Liangshi Anquan de Lishi Qihou Bianhua Yingxiang Zai Zhongguo Shehui Xitong Zhong de Chuandi]," *Science China Earth Sciences* 58 (2015): 1427–39.

10. Mark Elvin, "The Environmental Legacy of Imperial China," *China Quarterly* 156 (1998): 733–36.

11. Elvin, "Environmental Legacy"; Frederic Wakeman, *The Great Enterprise: The Manchu Reconstruction of Imperial Order in Seventeenth-Century China* (Berkeley: University of California Press, 1985): 48–58; Jianxin Cui, Hong Chang, George S. Burr, Xiaolong Zhao, and Baoming Jiang, "Climatic Change and the Rise of the Manchu from Northeast China during AD 1600–1650," *Climatic Change* 156, no. 3 (2019): 405–23.

12. John Luke Gallup, Jeffrey D. Sachs, and Andrew D. Mellinger, "Geography and Economic Development," *International Regional Science Review* 22, no. 2 (1999): 179–232, nber.org/papers/w6849.pdf.

13. Kenneth Pomeranz, *The Great Divergence: China, Europe, and the Making of the Modern Economy* (Princeton, NJ: Princeton University Press, 2009).

14. Elizabeth J. Perry, *Rebels and Revolutionaries in North China, 1845–1945* (Stanford, CA: Stanford University Press, 1980).

15. Mark Elvin, *The Retreat of the Elephants: An Environmental History of China* (New Haven, CT: Yale University Press, 2008): 9.

16. Shanhong Zhang, Yujun Yi, Yan Liu, and Xinghui Wang, "Hydraulic Principles of the 2,268-Year-Old Dujiangyan Project in China," *Journal of Hydraulic Engineering* 139, no. 5 (2013): 538–46.

17. For an earlier episode of hydraulic engineering causing environmental degradation during the Song dynasty, see Ling Zhang, *The River, the Plain, and the State: An Environmental Drama in Northern Song China, 1048–1128* (Cambridge: Cambridge University Press, 2016).

18. Elvin, "Environmental Legacy."

19. Elvin, "Environmental Legacy," 735–36.

20. Robert Marks, *The Origins of the Modern World: A Global and Ecological Narrative from the Fifteenth to the Twenty-first Century* (Lanham, MD: Rowman & Littlefield Publishers, 2006).

21. Elizabeth Kolbert, *The Sixth Extinction: An Unnatural History* (London: A&C Black, 2014). The "big five" extinction events are the end-Ordovician extinction, late Devonian extinction, end Permian extinction, late-Triassic extinction, and end-Cretaceous extinction.

22. Meera Subramanian, "Anthropocene Now: Influential Panel Votes to Recognize Earth's New Epoch," *Nature*, May 21, 2019, https://www.nature.com/articles/d41586-019-01641-5. So far, there's no scientific consensus as to the starting date of the Anthropocene. Candidates include the conquest of the "new world," the rise of mercantile capitalism, the Industrial Revolution, and the dropping of the first atomic bomb.

23. To be sure, Chinese industrialization started well before 1949. For records of environmental pollution during the late Qing and the Republican period, see Ahlers, Hansen, and Svarverud, *Great Smog.*

24. Julia Strauss, "Morality, Coercion and State Building by Campaign in the Early PRC: Regime Consolidation and After, 1949–1956," *China Quarterly* 188 (2006): 901.

25. Jisheng Yang, *Tombstone: The Great Chinese Famine, 1958–1962* (New York: Farrar, Straus and Giroux, 2013).

26. Roderick MacFarquhar and Michael Schoenhals, *Mao's Last Revolution* (Cambridge, MA: Belknap Press, 2006), 262. Andrew Walder and Yang Su, "The Cultural Revolution in the Countryside: Scope, Timing and Human Impact," *China Quarterly* 173 (2003): 74–99.

27. Stevan Harrell coined the term *high socialism.* For academic studies of pollution and environmental protection under Mao, see Judith Shapiro, *Mao's War against Nature: Politics and the Environment in Revolutionary China* (Cambridge: Cambridge University Press, 2001); Ahlers, Hansen, and Svarverud, *The Great Smog.*

28. Robert B. Marks, *China: Its Environment and History* (Lanham, MD: Rowman & Littlefield, 2012), 285.

29. Marks, *China.* The original quote is in Qu Geping, *Population and the Environment in China,* trans. Kiang Batching and Go Ran (Boulder, CO: Lynne Rienner, 1994), 61.

30. Marks, *China,* 285. Also see Barry Naughton, "The Third Front: Defense Industrialization in the Chinese Interior," *China Quarterly* 115 (1988): 351–86.

31. Marks, *China,* 286. Recent historical research finds that Dazhai had actually received central government subsidies, at least later on.

32. Author's translation. "People's Capital Does Not Allow Living Sparrows, 3 Million People Mobilized, 83,000 Sparrows Annihilated in a Day [Renmin Shoudu Burong Maque Shengcun, Sanbaiwanren Zongdongyuan Diyitian Jianmie Bawansan]," *People's Daily,* April 20, 1958.

33. Shapiro, *Mao's War against Nature,* 88.

34. Friedrich Nietzsche, *Human, All Too Human* (1878; reprint Cambridge: Cambridge University Press, 1986). Despite his disagreements with Darwinists, Nietzsche was influenced by the theory of evolution. For example, in *On the Genealogy of Morals,* Nietzsche argues that moral institutions are products of power struggles between the strong and the weak, as opposed to the innate benevolence of any group. This is a Darwinist account of morality. Friedrich Nietzsche, *On the Genealogy of Morals* (Oxford: Oxford University Press, 1996).

35. Nietzsche's "will to power" means more than the desire to conquer and obtain. He claims that the will to power may be channeled in different ways, from the crude domination of one's environment to the more benign endeavors of the arts and sciences ("sublimation" of the will). Friedrich Nietzsche, *The Joyous Science,* trans. R. Kevin Hill (New York: Penguin Classics, 2019).

36. Social Darwinism was popularized after the publication of *On the Origin of Species* in 1859. Notable social Darwinists include Herbert Spencer, Francis Galton, and, some would argue, Darwin himself.

37. This isn't to say there was no scramble for power before the Enlightenment.

38. Carolyn Merchant, *The Death of Nature: Women, Ecology, and the Scientific Revolution* (New York: Harper & Row, 1980).

39. E.g., Elizabeth Economy, *The River Runs Black: The Environmental Challenges to China's Future* (Ithaca, NY: Cornell University Press), 36.

40. Fung Yu-lan, *A Short History of Chinese Philosophy* (New York: Simon and Schuster, 1997). For a comprehensive, demystified analysis of Daoism's disposition toward nature, see N. J. Girardot, James Miller, and Liu Xiaogan, eds., *Daoism and Ecology: Ways within a Cosmic Landscape* (Cambridge, MA: Harvard University Press, 2001).

41. Marks, *Origins of the Modern World*.

42. Analects Book VII; author's translation.

43. Wang Yangming, *Wang Yangming Quan Ji* [*Complete Works of Wang Yangming*] (Beijing: Hong Qi Chu Ban She, 1996); author's translation.

44. See, e.g., Keguo Tu, "Confucian Ecological Ethics and Human Environmental Development [Rujia Shengtai Lunli Yu Ren de Huanjing Fazhan]," http://www.china kongzi.org/gxdt/200707/t20070725_2364374.htm.

45. Olivia Boyd, "A Rise in Confucianism Will Make China's Leaders More Eco-Conscious," China Dialogue, November 8, 2021, https://chinadialogue.net/en/nature/ 5312-a-rise-in-confucianism-will-make-china-s-leaders-more-eco-conscious/.

46. Elvin, *Elephants*, 93.

47. Pan Yue and Zhou Jigang, "The Rich Consume and the Poor Suffer the Pollution," *China Dialogue*, October 27, 2006, https://chinadialogue.net/en/business/493-the-rich-consume-and-the-poor-suffer-the-pollution/.

48. Stevan Harrell, unpublished chapter.

49. Ahlers, Hansen, and Svarverud, *Great Smog*, 59.

50. Stevan Harrell, unpublished chapter.

51. "1973: First Step of Environmental Protection [1973 Nian: Huanjing Baohu Kaishi Qibu]," *Xinhua News*, August 30, 2009, http://www.gov.cn/jrzg/2009-08/30/con tent_1404821.htm.

52. Jesse Turiel, Iza Ding, John Chung-En Liu, "Environmental Governance in China: State, Society, and Market," *Brill Research Perspectives in Governance and Public Policy in China* 1, no. 2 (2017): 6.

53. One of the first mentions was in *People's Daily*, "Tang Ke Spoke."

54. Fang Xin, "Economic Development and Environmental Protection [Jingji Fazhan he Huanjign Baohu]," *People's Daily*, June 16, 1973.

55. Fang, "Economic Development."

56. Jiaqing Tao and Xueyong Ai, "Must Speed Up Environmental Protection Work [Huanjing Baohu Gongzuo Yao Zhuajin]," *People's Daily*, October 15, 1973.

57. *People's Daily*, "State Council Notice to Vigorously Launch the Patriotic Hygiene Campaign [Guowuyuan guanyu dali kaizhan aiguo weisheng yundong de tongzhi]," April 5, 1977. *People's Daily*, "State Council Sends Notice to Revolution Committees in Various Provinces, Cities and Autonomous Regions, Raises Six Demands to Persistently Launch the Periotic Hygiene Campaign [Guowuyuan tongzhi ge sheng shi zizhiqu gewei-hui he guowuyuan gebuwei, tichu jianchi kaizhan aiguo weisheng yundong liuxiang yaoqiu]," April 8, 1978.

58. "1973: First Step."

59. "Situation of Environmental Protection [huanjing baohu zhuangkuang]."

60. Huan Guo, "Attach Importance to Environmental Protection Work [zhongshi huanjingbaohu gongzuo]," *People's Daily*, September 17, 1974.

61. Zhou, "Governing China's Local Officials"; Yuen Yuen Ang, *China's Gilded Age: The Paradox of Economic Boom and Vast Corruption* (Cambridge: Cambridge University Press, 2020).

62. On local resistance to implementing national policies, see, e.g., Harry Harding, *Organizing China: The Problem of Bureaucracy, 1949–1976* (Stanford, CA: Stanford University Press, 1981); Manion, "Policy Implementation"; O'Brien and Li, "Selective Policy Implementation."

63. Dexter Roberts, "China: Choking on Pollution's Effects," *Bloomberg*, November 29, 2005, https://www.bloomberg.com/news/articles/2005-11-28/china-choking-on-pollutions-effects.

64. Jing Wu, Yongheng Deng, Jun Huang, Randall Morck, and Bernard Yeung, "Incentives and Outcomes: China's Environmental Policy," National Bureau of Economic Research Working Paper no. 18754 (2013), https://www.nber.org/papers/w18754.

65. State Council Leading Group on Environmental Protection, "Key Points on Environmental Protection Work [*huangjing baohu gongzuo huibao yaodian*]," no. 79 (1978), December 31.

66. International learning is especially intensive in environmental and energy policies. See Lieberthal and Oksenberg, *Policy Making in China*; Robert Falkner, "International Sources of Environmental Policy Change in China: The Case of Genetically Modified Food," *Pacific Review* 19, no. 4 (2006): 473–94; Han Shi and Lei Zhang, "China's Environmental Governance of Rapid Industrialisation," *Environmental Politics* 15, no. 2 (2006): 271–92.

67. An alternative explanation for why authoritarian regimes adopt legal, electoral, and other institutions is to achieve a veneer of legitimacy in the eyes of their citizenry or the international community. See, e.g., Tom Ginsburg and Tamir Moustafa, *Rule by Law: The Politics of Courts in Authoritarian Regimes* (Cambridge: Cambridge University Press, 2008); Wang, "Symbolic Legitimacy." This explanation applies to some cases—for example, where international aid and loans come with governance conditionalities—but not others. First, it is an empirical question whether authoritarian regimes intend to hitch their legitimacy to legal procedures as opposed to other things like economic performance and nationalism. More important, building institutions is expensive; regimes wouldn't undertake it unless there are real foreseeable benefits to governance. This has been well-documented by the literature on legal reforms in China. See Stanley B. Lubman, *Bird in a Cage: Legal Reform in China after Mao* (Stanford, CA: Stanford University Press, 1999); Randall Peerenboom, *China's Long March Toward Rule of Law* (Cambridge University Press, 2002); Yuhua Wang, *Tying the Autocrat's Hands*.

68. Genia Kostka, "Command without Control: The Case of China's Environmental Target System," *Regulation & Governance* 10 (2016): 58–74.

69. Companies specializing in the EIA have not been well regulated, making them susceptible to monetary and political influence. When evaluating EIA reports, local EPBs tend to focus more on the procedure of impact evaluation rather than the accuracy of the facts in the report, which would require significant effort to verify.

70. Arthur P. J. Mol and Neil T. Carter, "China's Environmental Governance in Transition," *Environmental Politics* 15, no. 2 (2006): 149–70. Susan Martens, "Public Participation with Chinese Characteristics: Citizen Consumers in China's Environmental Management," *Environmental Politics* 15 (2006): 211–30. Andrew Mertha, *China's Water Warriors* (Ithaca, NY: Cornell University Press, 2008). Bryan Tilt, "The Political Ecology of Pollution Enforcement in China: A Case from Sichuan's Rural Industrial Sector," *China Quarterly* 192 (2007): 915–32. Andrew Mertha, "'Fragmented Authoritarianism 2.0': Political Pluralization in the Chinese Policy Process," *China Quarterly* 200 (2009): 995–1012. Benjamin van Rooij, Rachel E. Stern and Kathinka Furst, "The Authoritarian Logic of Regulatory Pluralism: Understanding China's New Environmental Actors," *Regulation & Governance* 10 (2016): 3–13. Thomas R. Johnson, "Regulatory Dynamism of Environmental Mobilization in Urban China," *Regulation & Governance* 10 (2016): 14–28.

71. Mertha, "'Fragmented Authoritarianism 2.0.'"

72. Ran Ran, *China's Local Environmental Politics* [*Zhongguo difang huanjing zhengzhi: zhengce yu zhixing zhijian de juli*] (Beijing: Central Compilation and Translation Press, 2015), 63.

73. Qi Ye, *Research on China's Environmental Governance* [*Zhongguo huanjing jianguan tizhi yanjiu*] (Shanghai: Shanghai Sanlian Press, 2008), 158.

74. Ran, *China's Local Environmental Politics*, 64–65.

75. On the role of local leaders in environmental policy implementation, see Sarah Eaton and Genia Kostka, "Authoritarian Environmentalism Undermined? Local Leaders' Time Horizons and Environmental Policy Implementation in China," *China Quarterly* 218 (2014): 359–80.

76. Interview in Zhejiang, June 2014.

77. For more, see Kenneth Lieberthal, "China's Governing System and Its Impact on Environmental Policy Implementation," https://www.wilsoncenter.org/sites/default/files/Lieberthal%20article.pdf; Abigail R. Jahiel, "The Organization of Environmental Protection in China," *China Quarterly* 156 (1998): 757–87; Xiaoying Ma and Leonard Ortolano, *Environmental Regulations in China: Institutions, Enforcement, and Compliance* (Lanham, MD: Rowman and Littlefield, 2000).

78. E.g., Jahiel, "The Organization"; Mol and Carter, "China's Environmental Governance"; Qi, *China's Environmental Management;* Barbara J. Sinkule and Leonard Ortolano, *Implementing Environmental Policy in China* (Westport, CT: Greenwood, 1995); Bruce Gilley, "Authoritarian Environmentalism and China's Response to Climate Change," *Environmental Politics* 21, no. 2 (2012): 287–307.

79. Elizabeth Economy, "Environmental Governance in China: State Control to Crisis Management," *Daedalus by American Academy of Arts & Sciences* 143 (2014): 184–97.

80. See David M. Lampton, ed., *Policy Implementation in Post-Mao China* (University of California Press, 1987); Elizabeth J. Perry, "From Mass Campaigns to Managed Campaigns: 'Constructing a New Socialist Countryside,'" in Sebastian Heilmann and Elizabeth Perry, eds., *Mao's Invisible Hand: The Political Foundations of Adaptive Governance in China* (Cambridge, MA: Harvard University Press, 2011): 30–61.

81. *Yamen* refers to the office or residence of a public official in the Chinese Empire (Oxford Dictionary). In modern Chinese language *yamen* is used as a metaphor for government offices.

82. Interview with MEE official in Beijing, November 2019.

83. Valerie J. Karplus and Mengying Wu, "Crackdowns in Hierarchies: Evidence from China's Environmental Inspections," Working Paper (September 4, 2019), at https://ssrn.com/abstract=3449177. Denise van der Kamp, "Can Police Patrols Prevent Pollution? The Limits of Authoritarian Environmental Governance in China," *Comparative Politics* 53, no. 3 (2021): 403–33.

84. Denise S. van der Kamp, "Clean Air at What Cost? The Rise of Blunt Force Pollution Regulation in China," PhD diss., University of California, Berkeley, 2017.

85. Interview with conservationist in Beijing, December 2019.

86. Xi Jinping, *The Governance of China* (Beijing: Beijing Books, 2018).

87. This theory was first articulated in 2005, when Xi was the party secretary of Zhejiang Province.

88. Interview with former climate negotiator of the UK, December 2019.

89. Xi, *Governance of China.*

90. The White House, "U.S.-China Joint Presidential Statement on Climate Change," September 25, 2015, https://obamawhitehouse.archives.gov/the-press-office/2015/09/25/us-china-joint-presidential-statement-climate-change.

91. Umair Irfan, "The UN Climate Action Summit was a Disappointment," *VOX*, September 24, 2019, https://www.vox.com/2019/9/24/20880416/un-climate-action-summit-2019-greta-thunberg-trump-china-india.

92. Ma Jun, "How China Can Truly Lead the Fight Against Climate Change," *Time*, September 12, 2019, https://time.com/5669061/china-climate-change/.

93. Smriti Mallapaty, "How China Could be Carbon Neutral by Mid-Century," *Nature* 586, no. 7830 (2020): 482–84, https://www.nature.com/articles/d41586-020-02927-9.

94. Some were replaced with coal gas instead of natural gas.

95. Steven Lee Myers, "In China's Coal Country, A Ban Brings Blue Skies and Cold Homes," *New York Times*, February 20, 2018, https://www.nytimes.com/2018/02/10/world/asia/china-coal-smog-pollution.html.

96. Michaël Aklin and Johannes Urpelainen, *Renewables: The Politics of a Global Energy Transition* (Cambridge, MA: MIT Press, 2018). John Helveston and Jonas Nahm, "China's Key Role in Scaling Low-Carbon Energy Technologies," *Science* 366, no. 6467 (2019): 794–96, DOI: 10.1126/science.aaz1014.

97. Simon Kuper, "The Myth of Green Growth," *Financial Times*, October 24, 2019, https://www.ft.com/content/47b0917c-f523-11e9-a79c-bc9acae3b654.

3. BELEAGUERED BUREAUCRATS

1. I use this pseudonym to protect this English name confidentiality.

2. The 985 Project and its "211" precursor are initiatives by the Chinese government to build world-class universities.

3. To be sure, the modern-day Civil Service Exam is quite different from the imperial *keju* in both form and topics. For how the abolition of keju—and other late Qing reforms—fueled the 1911 revolution, see Wolfgang Franke, *The Reform and Abolition of the Traditional Chinese Examination System* (Leiden, Netherlands: Brill, 1960); Mary Backus Rankin, *Elite Activism and Political Transformation in China: Zhejiang Province, 1865–1911* (Stanford, CA: Stanford University Press, 1986); and Ying Bai and Ruixue Jia, "Elite Recruitment and Political Stability: The Impact of the Abolition of China's Civil Service Exam," *Econometrica* 84, no. 2 (2016): 677–733.

4. The civil service exam was resurrected in the 1980s, first as an experiment in several functional bureaucracies, and then widened to cover all entry-level positions with the passing of the 2005 Civil Service Law.

5. *Guokao* is not to be confused with *gaokao*—the college entrance examination. In 2019, 1.4 million people qualified to take the Civil Service Exam, competing for 14,500 positions. The most competitive positions in recent years drew close to 10,000 contenders for a single opening. The competition is made even harsher by the stringent qualification requirements, such as an age limit (eighteen to thirty-five) and a college degree. Some positions require a master's degree and certificates in English or computation. See People. cn, "The 2019 National Exam Opens Today: 1,380,000 Applicants Compete for a 95:1 Chance of Passing [2019 Nian Guokao Jin Kaikao: Jin 138 Wan Ren Baoming Guoshen, Jingzhen bi 95:1]," December 2, 2018, http://politics.people.com.cn/n1/2018/1202/c1024-30436595.html.

6. The difficulty in obtaining a permanent position in a state agency varies considerably across localities. Between 2011 and 2017, the application-to-recruitment ratio for provincial civil service exams was highest in Shanghai and Beijing—about 7 percent of all applicants were recruited. The ratio is lowest in Guizhou, a poor inland province where only 2 percent of applicants secured a job. The difficulty also varies within the same locality, as positions in some bureaucracies are more desirable than others. Overall, the average application-to-recruitment ratio is 3 percent across years (2011–17) and provinces. Thanks to Xiang Gao for sharing her data.

7. "Ranking of Urban *PM2.5* Pollution in 2013 Released; The Country Needs Strong Measures," Greenpeace, January 10, 2014, http://www.greenpeace.org.cn/PM25-ranking/. The national guideline for *PM2.5* is in the MEE's Ambient Air Quality Standards (GB3095—2012), accessed April 27, 2021, https://www.mee.gov.cn/ywgz/fgbz/bz/bzwb/dqhjbh/dqhjzlbz/201203/W020120410330232398521.pdf.

8. For example, "Pollution levels that the World Health Organisation considers to be a 'significant concern,' and for which 'immediate actions are recommended' are described as 'good' air quality in China." Steven Q. Andrews, "China's Air Pollution Reporting is Misleading," *China Dialogue*, March 27, 2014, https://chinadialogue.net/en/pollution/6856-china-s-air-pollution-reporting-is-misleading/. Also see He Li, "The New PM2.5 Standard: Can the Deviation of Perception from Index be Changed? [PM2.5 xin biaozhun: nengfou gaibian ganshou yu zhishu de beiligan]," *Science Daily* [*Keji ribao*], December 1, 2011, http://tech.sina.com.cn/d/2011-12-01/11586409712.shtml, accessed April 26, 2020.

9. Kyle A. Jaros, *China's Urban Champions: The Politics of Spatial Development* (Princeton, NJ: Princeton University Press, 2019). Walt Whitman Rostow, *The Stages of Economic Growth: A Non-Communist Manifesto* (1959; reprinted Cambridge: Cambridge University Press, 1990).

10. Quoted from my dissertation prospectus, defended in April 2013.

11. Ronald Inglehart and Christian Welzel, *Modernization, Cultural Change, and Democracy: The Human Development Sequence* (Cambridge: Cambridge University Press, 2005).

12. Quoted from my dissertation prospectus, defended in April 2013.

13. Sartori, "Comparing and Miscomparing," 247.

14. John P. Burns and Xiaoqi Wang, "Civil Service Reform in China: Impacts on Civil Servants' Behaviour," *China Quarterly* 201 (2010), 59.

15. Weber, *Economy and Society*, 956–58.

16. Weber, *Economy and Society*, 1002.

17. See Brubaker, *The Limits of Rationality*.

18. See, for example, Walder, *Communist Neo-Traditionalism*; Yuen Yuen Ang, "Beyond Weber: Conceptualizing an Alternative Ideal Type of Bureaucracy in Developing Contexts," *Regulation & Governance* 11, no. 3 (2017): 282–98; Jiang, "Making Bureaucracy Work"; Bo Rothstein, "The Chinese Paradox of High Growth and Low Quality of Government: The Cadre Organization Meets Max Weber," *Governance* 28, no. 4 (2015): 533–48.

19. After all, it was Weber who referred to China's imperial examination and promotion system, which he believed to have upheld patrimonial rule, as "rational." See Weber, "The Chinese Literati," 416–41. Weber's empirical analyses often point out that his ideal-types are not mutually exclusive. Eisenberg writes that "Weber perceives the Chinese empire to be a highly rationalized form of a patrimonial regime." Andrew Eisenberg, "Weberian Patrimonialism and Imperial Chinese History," *Theory and Society* 27, no. 1 (1998): 83–102.

20. For recent efforts to rationalize governance through digitization, see Gao Xiang and Jie Tan, "From Web to Weber: Understanding the Case of 'One-Go at Most' as ICT-Driven Government Reform in Contemporary China," *China Review* 20, no. 3 (2020): 71–98.

21. Andrew Walder, *Communist Neo-Traditionalism*, 6.

22. Interview with retired senior bureaucrat in Lakeville, June 2016.

23. To be sure, a shadow private market existed under Mao. See, for example, Adam Frost's forthcoming Harvard history dissertation, "Speculating and Profiteering: Entrepreneurship in Socialist China."

24. Private housing has become so unaffordable that it's now a chief complaint of ordinary Chinese people. Some workplaces provide subsidized housing, but this practice is hardly unique to China. Interestingly, recent developments in large private enterprises—such as technology companies like Facebook and Google setting up "campuses" and offering employees such perks as meals and childcare—make them resemble socialist work units.

25. By "vocation" I simply mean occupation, or profession.

26. "996" represents a practice of many Chinese technology companies that demands employees arrive at work at 9:00 a.m. and leave at 9:00 p.m. for six days a week. It recently became a popular term to critically refer to the "culture of working overtime" (*jiaban wenhua*). Working overtime in state bureaucracies is also prevalent, despite the state's vocal critiques of the 996 system.

27. Pierre F. Landry, Xiaobo Lü, and Haiyan Duan, "Does Performance Matter? Evaluating Political Selection along the Chinese Administrative Ladder," *Comparative Political Studies* 51, no. 8 (2018): 1074–105.

28. See Ang, *How China Escaped the Poverty Trap*; Ang, *China's Gilded Age*.

29. Gabriella Montinola, Yingyi Qian, and Barry R. Weingast, "Federalism, Chinese Style: The Political Basis for Economic Success in China," *World Politics* 48, no. 1 (1995): 50–81.

30. http://www.gov.cn/zhengce/content/2016-10/11/content_5117396.htm.

31. Wang et al., "Rural Industries," 654.

32. To be sure, the speed and extent to which central policies are implemented can vary across localities. Coastal provinces are usually the first to implement governance reforms.

33. The Organization and Personnel Division (Zuzhi Renshi Chu) manages the agency's human resources; the Propaganda and Education Division (Xuanchuan Jiaoyu Chu) educates the public about environmental protection; the Planning and Finances Division (Guihua Caiwu Chu) manages the agency's finances; the Policies and Regulations Division (Zhengce Fagui Chu) hires legal professionals who translate laws, policies, and regulations into regulatory decisions concerning individual enterprises; the Administrative Approval Division (Xingzheng Shenpi Chu) issues pollution permits; the Pollution Prevention and Control Division (Wuran Fangzhi Chu) makes regulatory enforcement plans; the Natural Ecology Division (Ziran Shengtai Chu) takes care of mountains, rivers, plants, and animals; the Scientific Monitoring Division (Kexue Jiance Chu) monitors enterprise behavior using cutting-edge technology and methods, such as "online monitoring" of big data; the Division for the Control of the Total Amount of Pollutants (Zongliang Kongzhi Chu) ensures that the city meets its pollution control targets, usually designated at the beginning of the year. In addition to these internal organs, the EPB had 12 subsidiaries: five district EPBs, three research institutes, the Center for Environmental Protection Propaganda and Education (Huanbao Xuanjiao Zhongxin), the Center for the Management of Solid Wastes (Gufei Guanli Zhongxin), the Division for the Management of Automobile Exhausts (Jidongche Weiqi Guanli Chu), and the Detachment of Environmental Supervision (Huanjing Jiancha Zhidui). Some of these offices no longer exist today.

34. For example, in 2017, the Pollution Prevention and Control Division and the Division for the Control of the Total Amount of Pollutants were replaced by the new Air Quality Management Division (Daqi Huanjing Guanli Chu) and Water Management Division (Shui Huanjing Guanli Chu).

35. This performance evaluation procedure isn't altogether different from what I undergo in my own department at the University of Pittsburgh.

36. For how local political ecology affects environmental enforcement, see Tilt, "Political Ecology of Pollution Enforcement.".

37. *Huanbao* is short for "environmental protection" or "environmental protection bureau."

38. See, for example, Ran, *China's Local Environmental Politics*; Qi, *Research on China's Environmental Management System*; Shui-Yang Tang, Carlos Wing-Hung Lo, and Gerald E. Fryxell, "Enforcement Styles, Organizational Commitment, and Enforcement Effectiveness: An Empirical Study of Local Environmental Protection Officials in Urban China," *Environment and Planning* 35 (2003); Pan Jiahua, *China's Environmental Governance and Ecological Civilization [Zhongguo De Huanjing Zhili Yu Shengtai Jianshe]* (Beijing: China Social Science Press, 2015).

39. Wong and Zeng, "Getting Ahead."

40. Interview with retired organization department official, November 2013.

41. See, for example, Erik Wang, "Frightened Mandarins: The Adverse Effects of Fighting Corruption on Local Bureaucracy" (January 7, 2021), https://ssrn.com/abstract= 3314508, accessed June 18, 2021.

42. Channels for petitioning have been streamlined since then. Some provinces now use a single portal to accept all online petitions.

43. Interview with former state bureaucrat in Lakeville, June 2016.

44. *People's Daily*, "Central 'Remain True to Our Original Aspiration and Keep Our Mission Firmly in Mind' Education Work Team Issues 'Notice on Rectifying the Excessiveness of 'Performance Projects' and 'Face Projects' such as 'Landscape Lighting Projects' [Zhongyang buwangchuxin laojishiming zhuti jiaoyu xiaozu yinfa tongzhi zhengzhi jingguan lianghua gongcheng guoduhua deng zhengji gongcheng mianzi gongcheng wenti]," December 3, 2019, http://www.gov.cn/xinwen/2019-12/02/content_5457679. htm, accessed June 30, 2020.

45. Erving Goffman, "On Face-Work," in *Interaction Ritual: Essays in Face-to-Face Behavior*, ed. Erving Goffman (Chicago: Aldine Transaction, 1967), 5–45.

46. Robert Dahl, *Polyarchy: Participation and Opposition* (New Haven, CT: Yale University Press, 1971), 1–2.

47. Keping Yu, "Incremental Democracy [zengliang minzhu]," in *Understanding Chinese Politics [Lijie zhongguo zhengzhi]*, ed. Jing Yuejin, Zhang Xiaojin, Yu Xunda (Beijing: Chinese Academy of Social Science Press, 2011), 74–82.

48. Yu, "Incremental Democracy."

49. For example, Chen et al., "Sources of Authoritarian Responsiveness"; Truex, *Making Autocracy Work*; Distelhorst and Hou, "Constituency Service"; Jonathan Stromseth, Edmund Malesky, and Dimitar D. Gueorguiev, *China's Governance Puzzle: Enabling Transparency and Participation in a Single-Party State* (New York: Cambridge University Press, 2017).

50. See, for example, Nathan, "Authoritarian Resilience."

51. See Bernstein and Lü, *Taxation without Representation*, for an account of how agricultural taxes and fees were a major source of discontent in the Chinese countryside after reform started.

52. Kellee S. Tsai, "Adaptive Informal Institutions and Endogenous Institutional Change in China," *World Politics* 59, no. 1 (2006): 116–41. In the early years of economic reform, private businesses with more than eight employees were still illegal. Many larger businesses registered as collective enterprises (that is, "wearing a red hat") but operated as private ones. This led to the eventual legalization of private enterprises and the party's welcoming of entrepreneurs to join the party, with Jiang Zemin's "Three Represents" ideology.

53. For a summary of changes in most air and water pollutants, see Michael Greenstone, Guojun He, Shanjun Li, and Eric Zou, "China's War on Pollution: Evidence from the First Five Years," National Bureau of Economic Research Working Paper no. 28467, https://www.nber.org/papers/w28467, accessed June 30, 2021. One caveat to these findings is that the emissions reduction was partly due to an economic slowdown, especially since Trump's trade war in 2018. The same study also notes a lack of improvement in the Yangtze Delta's water quality between 2008 and 2018.

54. A parallel example is the White House's "We the People" petitions portal.

55. Siestas are common in China. Some employees keep a folding bed in the office or block off their cubicle with blinds for half-hour naps after lunch.

56. Interview with EPB bureaucrat in Shenzhen, July 2015.

57. Interview with EPB bureaucrat in Chengdu, June 2016.

58. Thanks to Tianguang Meng for sharing his data. Since this dataset captures large-scale petitions, the number of environmental petitions in most cities is only in the single digits. The dataset doesn't include the thousands of individual complaints received every year in cities like Lakeville. I cite this statistic to give readers a sense of the sizable amount of symbolic responsiveness in government response to environmental petitions.

59. NDRC, "Construction Standard for Office Space of Party and State Organizations [Dangzheng jiguan bangong yongfang jianshe biaozhun]," December 21, 1999.

60. State Council, "Regulations on Rigorous Enforcement of Economy and Anti-Waste for the Party and Government Organ [Dangzheng jiguan lixing jieyue fandui langfei tiaoli]," November 26, 2013, http://www.gov.cn/jrzg/2013-11/26/content_2534611.htm, accessed June 30, 2020.

61. NDRC [2014] 2674, "Construction Standard for Office Space of Party and State Organizations [Dangzheng jiguan bangong yongfang jianshe biaozhun]," November 27, 2014, https://www.ndrc.gov.cn/fggz/gdzctz/tzfg/201411/t20141127_1197595.html.

62. "Rice bowl" is a Chinese metaphor for job.

63. Mertha, "Fragmented Authoritarianism 2.0," 997–98.

64. Mertha, *China's Water Warriors*.

65. Yang Zhang, "Allies in Action: Institutional Actors and Grassroots Environmental Activism in China," *Research in Social Movements, Conflicts and Change* 42 (2018): 9–38.

66. Interview with MEP bureaucrat in Beijing, July 2019.

67. Timur Kuran, "Now Out of Never: The Element of Surprise in the East European Revolution of 1989," *World Politics* 44, no. 1 (1991): 7–48. For the rise of "rights consciousness" in China, see for example, Mary E. Gallagher, "Mobilizing the Law in China: 'Informed Disenchantment' and the Development of Legal Consciousness," *Law & Society Review* 40, no. 4 (2006): 783–816; Lianjiang Li, "Rights Consciousness and Rules Consciousness in Contemporary China," *China Journal* 64 (2010): 47–68; and Peter Lorentzen and Suzanne Scoggins, "Understanding China's Rising Rights Consciousness," *China Quarterly* 223 (2015): 638–57.

68. Gary King, Jennifer Pan, and Margaret E. Roberts, "How Censorship in China Allows Government Criticism but Silences Collective Expression," *American Political Science Review* 107, no. 2 (2013): 326–43.

69. For evidence of this in labor relations, see Manfred Elstrom, *Workers and Change in China: Resistance, Repression, Responsiveness* (Cambridge: Cambridge University Press, 2021).

70. Smell testers are also called "panelists" or "human sensors" in the English-language literature. Their sense of smell must be neither acute nor dull. To receive certification, candidates must pass a difficult test that requires them to discern the scents of flowers, caramel, sweat, rotten fruit, feces, and so on; the test must be retaken every three years.

Professional smell testers are forbidden from smoking, drinking, or wearing perfume, and advised to avoid spicy food.

71. Ministry of Ecology and Environment, Emission Standards for Odorous Pollutants, http://english.mee.gov.cn/Resources/standards/Air_Environment/Emission_standard1/200710/t20071024_111822.shtml, accessed June 30, 2020.

72. Ministry of Ecology and Environment, "Environmental Air, Waste Air, and Odorous Air Measurement: Three-Point Comparative Method of Odor Bags (Consultation Draft) (Huanjing feiqi he kongqi, chouqi de ceding: sandianshi bijiao choudaifa)," March 2019, 13–15, http://www.mee.gov.cn/xxgk2018/xxgk/xxgk06/201906/W020190621485478072697.pdf, accessed June 30, 2020. Some researchers have advocated for the use of electronic noses because they're more accurate than human noses. But electronic noses are a novel technology that isn't yet widely used in environmental analysis. And if resolving human complaints is the goal, using technology that's capable of detecting what the human nose cannot delivers minimal political benefit. See A. Brattoli et al., "Odour Detection Methods: Olfactometry and Chemical Sensors," *Sensors* (Basel) 11, no. 5 (2011): 5290–322, https://www.ncbi.nlm.nih.gov/pmc/articles/PMC3231359/, accessed June 30, 2020.

73. Ministry of Ecology and Environment, "On-Site Fast Measurement of Environmental Air: The Chemosensor Method (Consultation Draft)," May 2011, http://www.mee.gov.cn/gkml/hbb/bgth/201105/W020110511535029519957.pdf, accessed June 30, 2020.

74. Interview with owner of a printing and dyeing plant in Lakeville, June 2019.

75. Lakeville EPB's Online Petitions System.

76. Interview with the owner of a polluting enterprise in Lakeville, June 2018; interview with academic expert in Beijing, July 2019; interview with environmental NGO in Beijing, July 2019; interview with government bureaucrat in Lakeville, August 2019.

77. Lakeville EPB's Online Petitions System.

78. Lakeville EPB's Online Petitions System.

79. See Max Weber, *The Protestant Ethic and the "Spirit" of Capitalism and Other Writings* (1905: reprint Penguin, 2002), 171.

80. Goffman, *The Presentation of Self*, 17–21.

81. These are two common, albeit competing, images of authoritarian "state agents."

82. Bruce Bueno De Mesquita and Alastair Smith, *The Dictator's Handbook: Why Bad Behavior Is Almost Always Good Politics* (New York: Public Affairs, 2011).

83. Zacka, *When the State Meets the Street*, 12.

84. Goffman, *The Presentation of Self*, 236.

85. Hirschman, *Exit, Voice, and Loyalty*.

86. A Chinese idiom symbolizing limited outlook or experience: a frog at the bottom of a well can see only a portion of the sky.

87. When I asked him what these "bigger things" are, he said industries, the economy, and urban development (*chengjian*).

88. The "traveling" problem of concepts is discussed in detail in Giovanni Sartori's "Concept Misformation in Comparative Politics," *American Political Science Review* 64, no. 4 (1970): 1033–53.

89. Barbara Geddes, "How the Cases You Choose Affect the Answers You Get: Selection Bias in Comparative Politics," *Political Analysis* (1990): 131–50.

90. See Elizabeth Anderson, *Private Government: How Employers Rule Our Lives (and Why We Don't Talk about It)* (Princeton, NJ: Princeton University Press, 2017) on the parallels between authoritarian and employer restrictions on free speech.

91. Gerth and Mills, *From Max Weber*, 228–29.

92. Timur Kuran, "Now Out of Never: The Element of Surprise in the East European Revolution of 1989," *World Politics* 44, no. 1 (1991): 7–48.

93. Robert Putnam, *Making Democracy Work* (Princeton, NJ: Princeton University Press, 1993), 12.

94. The most comprehensive overview of grounded theory methods and their historical development is in Kathy Charmaz, *Constructing Grounded Theory* (Thousand Oaks, CA: Sage, 2014).

95. Kathy Charmaz, "Grounded Theory," in *Rethinking Methods in Psychology*, ed. Jonathan Smith, Rom Harre, and Luk Van Langenhove (Thousand Oaks, CA: Sage, 1995), 28.

96. Hilary Putnam, *The Collapse of the Fact/Value Dichotomy and Other Essays* (Cambridge, MA: Harvard University Press, 2004). This view challenges the conventional emphasis on objectivity and value-neutrality à la Hume and Weber.

97. Brady and Collier define a causal process observation as an "insight or piece of data that provides information about context, process or mechanism, and that contributes distinctive leverage in causal inference." Henry E. Brady and David Collier, eds., *Rethinking Social Inquiry: Diverse Tools, Shared Standards* (Lanham, MD: Rowman & Littlefield, 2010), 24.

98. Bent Flyvbjerg, *Making Social Science Matter* (Cambridge: Cambridge University Press, 2001), 133.

99. Sudhir Venkatesh, *Gang Leader for a Day: A Rogue Sociologist Takes to the Streets* (New York: Penguin, 2008).

100. Venkatesh, *Gang Leader*.

101. For an account of how governance may be improved in adverse institutional environments, see Zacka, *When the State Meets the Street*.

102. The Hawthorne Effect is named after a study of workers in an electricity factory outside Chicago. During the Hawthorne study, researchers found that worker productivity increased when the workers were aware of being watched, and declined when the study was over.

103. See Jonathan De Quidt, Johannes Haushofer, and Christopher Roth, "Measuring and Bounding Experimenter Demand," *American Economic Review* 108, no. 11 (2018): 3266–302; Jonathan Mummolo and Erik Peterson, "Demand Effects in Survey Experiments: An Empirical Assessment," *American Political Science Review* 113, no. 2 (2019): 517–29.

104. Smith, *Moral Sentiments*.

105. Cited in Bent Flyvbjerg, "Five Misunderstandings about Case-Study Research," *Qualitative Inquiry* 12, no. 2 (2006): 219–45.

106. Sartori, "Comparing and Miscomparing," 252. Italics added.

107. Sartori, "Comparing and Miscomparing," 253–54.

108. Sartori, "Comparing and Miscomparing," 253.

109. Geddes, "Cases You Choose."

110. Steven Weinberg, *Dreams of a Final Theory* (New York: Vintage, 1994).

111. Flyvbjerg, "Five Misunderstandings."

112. We should be careful not to equate a theory's traveling ability with its intrinsic validity. For example, just because a theory of Japanese economic development doesn't explain development in Latin America doesn't make the theory about Japan wrong. It is common for the same phenomenon (e.g., economic development, democratization) to be caused by different factors in different cases and at different times.

113. Harry Eckstein, "Case Studies and Theory in Political Science," in *Handbook of Political Science*, ed. Fred Greenstein and Nelson Polsby (Reading, MA: Addison Wesley, 1975), 79–138.

114. https://data.worldbank.org/indicator/SP.URB.TOTL.IN.ZS?locations=CN.

115. Yichun Xie, Mei Yu, Yongfei Bai, Xuerong Xing, "Ecological Analysis of an Emerging Urban Landscape Pattern—Desakota: A Case Study in Suzhou, China," *Landscape Ecology* 21, no. 8 (2006): 1297–309.

116. Lily L. Tsai, *Accountability without Democracy*; Daniel C. Mattingly, *The Art of Political Control in China* (Cambridge: Cambridge University Press, 2019).

117. For example, campaign-style policy implementation can be found in urban and rural areas alike in China. See, e.g., Kristen E. Looney, *Mobilizing for Development: The Modernization of Rural East Asia* (Ithaca, NY: Cornell University Press, 2020).

118. Yanhua Deng and Kevin J. O'Brien, "Relational Repression in China: Using Social Ties to Demobilize Protesters," *China Quarterly* 215 (2013): 533–52; Mattingly, *Art of Political Control.*

119. Xiang Gao, "State-Led Digital Governance in Contemporary China," in *State Capacity Building in Contemporary China*, ed. Hiroko Naito and Vida Macikenaite (New York: Springer, 2020), 29–45; Jennifer Pan, *Welfare for Autocrats: How Social Assistance in China Cares for its Rulers* (Oxford: Oxford University Press, 2020).

120. For an alternative argument that qualitative case selection should be attentive to questions of representativeness, and ideally even attain at least "typological representativeness," see Dan Slater and Daniel Ziblatt, "The Enduring Indispensability of the Controlled Comparison," *Comparative Political Studies* 46, no. 10 (2013): 1301–27.

4. AUDIENCE APPRAISAL

1. On the instability and unfathomability of public opinion, see e.g., John R. Zaller, *The Nature and Origins of Mass Opinion* (Cambridge: Cambridge University Press, 1992).

2. Kuran's "preference falsification" demonstrates not only the falsification of preferences but also how fast preference can change in a revolution.

3. Nancy G. Bermeo, *Ordinary People in Extraordinary Times* (Princeton, NJ: Princeton University Press, 2003), 3.

4. Seymour Martin Lipset, *Political Man* (New York: Doubleday 1963).

5. Bermeo, in *Ordinary People*, writes that "the vast majority of ordinary people never mobilize in public space," even during extraordinary times of regime crisis and transition (6).

6. This number may potentially be larger given survey demand—for example, some respondents might have wanted to appear as responsible citizens by answering that they had complained to the state about environmental pollutions.

7. On the watchdog role Chinese media can play, see Yuezhi Zhao, *Communication in China: Political Economy, Power, and Conflict* (Lanham, MD: Rowman & Littlefield, 2008); Daniela Stockmann, *Media Commercialization and Authoritarian Rule in China* (Cambridge: Cambridge University Press, 2013); Ya-Wen Lei, *The Contentious Public Sphere: Law, Media, and Authoritarian Rule in China* (Princeton, NJ: Princeton University Press, 2017); Maria Repnikova, *Media Politics in China: Improvising Power under Authoritarianism* (Cambridge: Cambridge University Press, 2017).

8. For more details about the media's supervisory function, see Repnikova, *Media Politics*, chapter 3. Local media are also eager to highlight problems in other regions. See Ting Chen, and Ji Yeon Hong, "Rivals Within: Political Factions, Loyalty, and Elite Competition under Authoritarianism," *Political Science Research and Methods* 9, no. 3 (2020): 599–614.

9. "Introduction to Environmental Emergency Management [Huanjing Yingji Guanli Gailun]," 2013, author's collection.

10. Fact-gathering interviews differ from opinion-soliciting interviews in that information from the second type are used and presented in the analysis as the interviewee's opinion, whereas information from the first type is sometimes presented as "facts," and thus must be triangulated.

11. Mario Luis Small, "How Many Cases Do I Need? On Science and the Logic of Case Selection in Field-based Research," *Ethnography* 10, no. 1 (2009): 5–38.

12. See Zaller, *Nature and Origins*, for the unreliability of survey questions at measuring public opinion.

13. Xinhuanet, "Beijing Releases Latest Analysis of PM 2.5 Sources, Main Source Is Vehicles [Beijing fabu zuixin yilun PM2.5 yuan jiexi, zhuyao laizi jidongche]," May 15, 2018. http://www.xinhuanet.com/politics/2018-05/15/c_1122832062.htm.

14. Xingchun Tian and Rong Liu, "The Past and Present of Urban Management: Where Did Urban Management Institutions Come From? [Chengguan de qianshijinsheng, chengshi guanli zhidu conghe erlai?]," People.cn, October 19, 2011, http://legal.people.com.cn/GB/15940234.html.

15. Interview with EPB bureaucrat in Chengdu, June 2016.

16. "Nanjing EPB Responds to Smog-Locked City: Experts are Off on Weekends and Cannot Answer Questions [Nanjing huanbaoju huiying wumai suocheng: zhoumo zhuanjia xiuxi, wufa zuoda]," China National Radio, November 3, 2013, http://www.chinanews.com/gn/2013/11-03/5456773.shtml.

17. Ya Wan, "Both Smog and Bureaucratic Attitudes Need Treatment [Wumai Yu Guanfang de Taidu Dou Jixu Zhili]," *Guangzhou Daily*, November 4, 2013.

18. Dashou Lin, "Smog Is Inhumane, but the Government Cannot Be Inhumane," BBC China, November 4, 2013, https://www.bbc.com/zhongwen/simp/comments_on_china/2013/11/131104_coc_nanjingsmog.

19. Interview with EPB bureaucrat in Shenzhen, June 2016.

20. Interview with EPB bureaucrat in Shenzhen, June 2016.

21. Interview with television news program director in Zhejiang, July 2015.

22. *Wenzhou Daily*, "An Open Letter that Rewards Petitions [Yifeng xuanshang xinfang de gongkaixin]," May 27, 2013, http://wzrb.66wz.com/html/2015-03/25/content_1793159.htm, accessed June 30, 2016.

23. "Nanjing Covered in Smog on New Year's Eve, the EPB Issues Tickets [Nanjing Xinnian Zao 'Maifu', Huanbaoju Lian Kai Tinggong Da Fadan]," *Xiandai Kuaibao*, January 4, 2017, https://m.nbd.com.cn/articles/2017-01-04/1067057.html.

24. Similar to the English word *performance*, its Chinese translation, *biaoxian*, has both a substantive dimension and a theatrical dimension. It can mean either objectively accomplishing a task, or theatrical performance.

25. Since such questions about local governments are frequently asked in social surveys, I expect self-censorship to be low.

26. Results using listwise deletion remain similar in terms of both significance levels and sizes of the effect.

27. For the relationship between air pollution and regime support, see Meir Alkon and Erik H. Wang, "Pollution Lowers Support for China's Regime: Quasi-experimental Evidence from Beijing," *Journal of Politics* 80, no. 1 (2018): 327–31.

28. Andreas Fulda, "Protests in Ningbo Mark the Birth of a Nation-Wide Environmental Health Movement," *Asia Dialogue*, October 29, 2012, https://theasiadialogue.com/2012/10/29/px-protests-in-ningbo/.

29. A key assumption for using ordinal logistic regression is the proportional odds assumption: the coefficients of explanatory variables are consistent between different thresholds. The two questions were designed in a way to best uphold proportional odds assumption.

30. Results using listwise deletion remain similar in terms of both significance levels and sizes of the effect.

31. This is consistent with findings in the existing literature: e.g., Nathan, "Authoritarian Resilience"; Kevin J. O'Brien and Lianjiang Li, *Rightful Resistance in Rural China* (Cambridge: Cambridge University Press, 2006).

32. There may also be issues that cannot be separated from human perceptions (e.g., financial markets), which this book will not delve into.

33. Matthew A. Crenson, *The Un-Politics of Air Pollution: A Study of Non-Decision-Making in the Cities* (Baltimore: Johns Hopkins Press, 1971).

34. Martin Whyte, *Myth of the Social Volcano: Perceptions of Inequality and Distributive Injustice in Contemporary China* (Stanford, CA: Stanford University Press, 2010). Ya-Wen Lei's analysis of recent survey data offers the important update that Chinese citizens are increasingly upset by income inequality. "Revisiting China's Social Volcano: Attitudes toward Inequality and Political Trust in China," *Socius* 6 (2020): 1–21.

35. Interview in Lakeville, June 2014.

36. Mary E. Gallagher, "Mobilizing the Law in China: 'Informed Disenchantment' and the Development of Legal Consciousness," *Law & Society Review* 40, no. 4 (2006): 783–816.

37. Interview in Lakeville, June 2014.

38. Interview in Beijing, December 2014.

39. Interview in Lakeville, June 2014.

40. Interview in Lakeville, June 2014.

41. Interview in Lakeville, June 2014.

42. Alexandra Foote, "Airpathy: Citizen Apathy and Inaction towards Pollution in Beijing," East Asian Studies Thesis, Harvard University, 2015.

43. Alyssa Matinec, "An Exploration of System Justification in China: Public Opinion on Environmental Policy," BPhil Thesis, University of Pittsburgh, 2019.

44. Interview in Lakeville, June 2014.

45. Interview in Beijing, December 2014.

46. Zacka, *When the State Meets the Street*, 9.

47. Interview in Lakeville, June 2014.

48. Interview in Lakeville, June 2014.

49. Hirschman, *Exit, Voice, and Loyalty*.

50. Interview in Lakeville, November 2019.

51. http://www.gov.cn/xinwen/2020-12/04/content_5567074.htm.

52. Interview in Lakeville, November 2019.

53. Interview in Lakeville, November 2019.

5. PERFORMATIVE BREAKDOWN

1. Baehr, Peter and Gordon C. Wells, "Editors' Introduction," in Max Weber, *The Protestant Ethic and the "Spirit" of Capitalism and Other Writings*, ed. Peter Baehr and Gordon C. Wells (New York: Penguin Books, 2003).

2. Since Butler interprets gender performativity as a practice of cultural hegemony, she argues for its subversion (that is, its breakdown). Butler, "Performative Agency," 150.

3. Goffman, *The Presentation of Self*, 236.

4. Goffman, *The Presentation of Self*, 141.

5. Goffman, *The Presentation of Self*, 22, 141.

6. Lindsey Smith, "After Blowing the Whistle on Flint's Water, EPA 'Rogue Employee' Has Been Silent. Until Now," *Michigan Radio*, Jan. 21, 2016, https://www.michiganradio.org/post/after-blowing-whistle-flints-water-epa-rogue-employee-has-been-silent-until-now.

7. Lindsey Smith, "Leaked Internal Memo Shows Federal Regulator's Concerns about Lead in Flint's Water," *Michigan Radio*, July 13, 2015, http://michiganradio.org/post/leaked-internal-memo-shows-federal-regulator-s-concerns-about-lead-flint-s-water.

8. Del Toral also revealed that the City of Flint had instructed residents to "pre-flush" their taps prior to collecting water samples, so that lead levels in compliance samples would be lower.

9. Mark Guarino, "National Guard Called In to Hand Out Water in Flint, Mich.," *Washington Post*, January 13, 2016, https://www.washingtonpost.com/national/national-guard-called-in-to-hand-out-water-in-flint-mich/2016/01/13/81a0fd88-b961–11e5–829c-26ffb874a18d_story.html?utm_term=.92a268aff6ba.

10. "Flint Activists Still Waiting as Governor Escapes Fallout of Water Crisis," *The Guardian*, April 23, 2018, https://www.theguardian.com/us-news/2018/apr/23/flint-water-crisis-governor-rick-snyder-criminal-trials.

11. "Flint Activists Still Waiting."

12. Jim Lynch, "Whistle-Blower Del Toral Grew Tired of EPA 'Cesspool,'" *Detroit News*, March 28, 2016, https://www.detroitnews.com/story/news/michigan/flint-water-crisis/2016/03/28/whistle-blower-del-toral-grew-tired-epa-cesspool/82365470/.

13. Leonard N. Fleming and Karen Bouffard, "Snyder Partly to Blame for Flint Crisis, UM Report Says," *Detroit News*, February 15, 2018, https://www.detroitnews.com/story/news/michigan/flint-water-crisis/2018/02/15/governor-rick-snyder-flint-water-crisis/110463996/.

14. Guarino, "National Guard."

15. Guarino, "National Guard." For a detailed timeline of the Flint water crisis, see CNN Library, "Flint Water Crisis Fast Facts" (2016); and flintwaterstudy.org, a website created by the Virginia Tech Research Team. https://www.cnn.com/2016/03/04/us/flint-water-crisis-fast-facts/index.html.

16. NPR, "Who's to Blame for Flint's Water Problem?" https://www.npr.org/2016/01/17/463405757/whos-to-blame-for-flints-water-problem#:~:text=For%20many%20people%2C%20the%20blame%20for%20the%20tap%20water%20contamination,his%20resignation%20have%20been%20growing.

17. Guarino, "National Guard." Italics added.

18. Republican governor Rick Snyder was elected in 2010. Republicans gained a majority in the Michigan House and increased the Republican majority held in the Senate.

19. The White House, "President Obama Signs Michigan Emergency Declaration," January 16, 2016, https://obamawhitehouse.archives.gov/the-press-office/2016/01/16/president-obama-signs-michigan-emergency-declaration.

20. PRC Civil Procedure.

21. Translated by the author from the original image of the admonition letter later posted by Li online. The letter serves to record that a formal conversation had taken place between Li and the police. In an interview with *Caixin Media*, Li recalled: "I was worried if I didn't sign it, I couldn't get out of it; so I went there, went through the motions, and left." See *Caixin*, "New Coronavirus 'Whistleblower' Li Wenliang: Truth is More Important than Rehabilitation (Xinguanfeiyan "chuishaoren" Li Wenliang: zhenxiang bi pingfan geng zhongyao)," January 31, 2020. http://china.caixin.com/2020-01-31/101509761.html. This interview was later removed from the Internet.

22. On January 29, the Wuhan Police Bureau released a statement on its Weibo Account, stating that "because the eight people [who were punished for spreading rumors online] had committed very minor offenses [*qingjie tebie qingwei*], the police at the time used education [*jiaoyu*] and criticism [*piping*], but not warning [*jinggao*], fines, or detainment." It is unclear whether Li was one of the eight people.

23. Dali Yang, "China's Early Warning System Didn't Work on Covid-19. Here's the Story," *Washington Post*, February 24, 2020, https://www.washingtonpost.com/politics/2020/02/24/china-early-warning-system-didnt-work-covid-19-heres-story/.

24. Authorities called the virus "new pneumonia" when it was first discovered.

25. *Huaxi Metropolitan News*, "From 'Rumormonger' to 'a Respectable Person,' Dr. Li Wenliang's Beginning of Year 2020 [Cong 'zaoyaozhe' bian 'kejin de ren' yisheng Li Wenliang de 2020 kainian]," February 3, 2020. https://m.chinanews.com/wap/detail/zw/sh/2020/02-03/9076631.shtml.

26. The remainder of this section draws on the author's observation of WeChat and Weibo between the evening of February 6 and the morning of February 7 (China Standard Time), and on Weibo posts and comments extracted during this brief window in time.

27. *Caixin*, "Whistleblower Li Wenliang." Li made this comment in response to a reporter's question about an opinion posted by the Supreme People's Court on its public Weibo account, questioning the appropriateness of the punishment received by the whistleblowers.

28. Ben Westcott, "How Chinese Doctor Li Wenliang Died Twice in China's State Median," *CNN*, February 7, 2020, https://www/cnn.com/2020/02/06/asia/china-li-wen liang-whistleblower-death-timeline-intl-hnk/index.html.

29. "Michigan Congressman Says Flint's Water Still Not Safe to Drink," *The Hill*, January 9, 2019, https://thehill.com/hilltv/rising/424536-flints-congressman-says-water-is-still-not-safe-to-drink.

30. Goffman, *The Presentation of Self*, 144.

31. Lynch, "Whistle-blower." Del Toral later apologized for calling the EPA a cesspool.

32. Goffman, *The Presentation of Self*, 141.

33. Between 1:00 a.m. and 3:00 a.m., the number of posts mentioning "freedom of speech" went from almost zero to more than three thousand, gaining almost two million views, before they were abruptly removed around 4:00 a.m.

34. Goffman, *The Presentation of Self*, 4.

35. For another example of the power of information in deriving similar outcomes in "most different" cases, see Andrew C. Mertha and William R. Lowry, "Unbuilt Dams: Seminal Events and Policy Change in China, Australia, and the United States," *Comparative Politics* 39, no. 1 (2006): 1–20.

36. See Regina M. Abrami, Edmund Malesky, and Yu Zheng, "Vietnam Through Chinese Eyes: Divergent Accountability in Single-Party Regimes," in *Why Communism Did Not Collapse: Understanding Authoritarian Regime Resilience in Asia and Europe*, ed. Martin K. Dimitrov (Cambridge: Cambridge University Press, 2013), 237–75.

37. OpenNet Initiative, "Country Report: Vietnam," https://opennet.net/research/pro files/vietnam; OpenNet Initiative, "Country Report: China," https://opennet.net/research/profiles/china-including-hong-kong, accessed March 30, 2019. For content filtering in China, see Margaret E. Roberts, *Censored: Distraction and Diversion inside China's Great Firewall* (Princeton, NJ: Princeton University Press, 2018).

38. OpenNet Initiative, "Country Report: Vietnam."

39. Jonathan Moed, "This Vietnamese Browser and Search Engine is Daring Google to Step-Up Its Game," *Forbes*, June 6, 2018, https://www.forbes.com/sites/jonathanmoed/2018/06/06/this-vietnamese-browser-search-engine-is-daring-google-to-step-up-its-game/?sh=77822aae48cb.

40. OpenNet Initiative, "Country Report: Vietnam."

41. Dien Luong, "Why Vietnam Can't Hold Back Facebook," *Vnexpress International*, September 10, 2017, https://e.vnexpress.net/news/news/why-vietnam-can-t-hold-back-facebook-3639186.html#:~:text=The%20reason%20is%20not%20hard,put%20them%20under%20its%20control.; My Pham, "Vietnam Says Facebook Commits to Preventing Offensive Content," *Reuters*, April 26, 2017, https://www.reuters.com/article/facebook-vietnam-idINKBN17T0BN.

42. China Net, "China's One Hundred Strong Counties with Investment Potentials in 2013 [2013 zhongguo zui ju touzi qianli zhong xiao chengshi baiqiang xianshi gongbu]," October 21, 2013, http://news.china.com.cn/2013-10/21/content_30357850.htm.

43. *Metropolitan Express* [*Dushi Kuaibao*], "CEO of Mao Yuanchang Glasses Pays 200,000 and Invites EPA Director to Go Swimming in a River [Maoyuenchang dong-shizhang chu 20wan qing huanbaojuzhang xiahe youyon]," February 18, 2013.

44. *Metropolitan Express*, "CEO of Mao Yuanchang Glasses."

45. Xinhuanet, "Businessman Offers 200,000 Yuan to Watch EPA Director to Swim in a River, EPA Director Laughs it Off [Shangren chu 20wanyuan yaoqing huanbao juzhang xiahe youyong, juzhang yixiaoliaozhi]," February 18, 2013, http://news.xinhuanet.com/local/2013-02/18/c_124357770.htm.

46. *Metropolitan Express*, "CEO of Mao Yuanchang Glasses."

47. "15 EPA Directors in Zhejiang Went Swimming in a River, Vice Mayor and Municipal Party Secretary Were the First to Go [Zhejiang 15 ge huanbaoju juzhang xiahe youyong, fushizhang shiweishuji daitou]," *Qianjiang Evening News* [*Qianjiang wanbao*], September 8, 2013, http://news.xinhuanet.com/2013-09/08/c_117273400.htm.

48. Xinhuanet, "Businessman."

49. People's Net [renminwang], "EPA Directors in Zhejiang Swam in Rivers and Earned Trust from People [Zhejiang huanbao juzhang xiahe youyong quxinyumin]," September 10, 2013, http://yuqing.people.com.cn/n/2013/0911/c212785-22880928.html.

50. China National Radio Net [Zhongguo Guangbo wang], "Wenzhou Mayor Responds to Invitation to Swim in the River: It Will Be Realized in Five Years [Wenzhou shizhang huiying guanyuan beiyao xiahe: 5 nian hou shixian shuili youyong]," March 13, 2013, http://china.cnr.cn/yaowen/201303/t20130313_512138016.shtml.

51. China News Net [Zhongguo xinwen wang], "Governor of Zhejiang Responds to 'EPA Officials Swim in River': A Lack of Law Enforcement and Supervision [Zhejiang shengzhang huiying 'huanbao juzhang xiahe': zhifa jiandu budaowei]," March 7, 2013, http://www.chinanews.com/gn/2013/03-07/4625246.shtml.

52. China Environment Net [Zhongguo huanjing wang], "Whatever the Hundred Names Want, We Do [Baixing xiangshenme, women jiuyao ganshenme]," July 4, 2013, accessed June 30, 2016, http://www.cenews.com.cn/sylm/talk/201307/t20130703_744189.htm.

53. *Zhejiang Daily* [*Zhejiang Ribao*], "Fifteen EPA Directors in Zhejiang Went Swimming in a River in Response to the Invitation [Zhejiang 15ge huanbao juzhang yingyao xiahe youyong]," September 9, 2013.

54. *Xinhua Daily News*, September 9, 2013, "Responding to Invitations, Fifteen EPA Directors in Zhejiang Went Swimming in a River [Huiying yaoyue, zhejiang 15 wei huanbao juzhang xiahe youyong]," http://news.xinhuanet.com/mrdx/2013-09/09/c_132703577.htm.

55. When I tried it the strange taste was subtle.

56. *Hangzhou Daily*, "Environmental Protection Under Pressure as the Price of Glyphosate Climbs [Huanbao chengya kaigong shouxian caoganlin jiage jielian pansheng]," April 4, 2013, http://hzdaily.hangzhou.com.cn/dskb/html/2013-04/04/content_1468870.htm.

57. Zhejiang Online [Zhejiang Zaixian], "The Culprit of Strange-tasting Tap Water Uncovered—2-tert-butylphenol [Hangzhou zilaishui yiwei yuanxiong chaming linshudingjibenfen]," January 18, 2014, accessed June 30, 2016, http://zjnews.zjol.com.cn/system/2014/01/17/019816103.shtml.

58. *Southern Metropolitan News* [*Nanfang Dushi Bao*], "Directors Went into River to Seal the Mouths of Doubters [Juzhang xiashui duzhu zhiyizhe de zui]," September 10, 2013.

59. *Legal Evening News*, September 9, 2013.

60. Lu Jinping, "A Mayor Goes Swimming in the River, So What If He Was Putting On a Show? [Shizhang xiahe youyong, zongran zuoxiu you hefang?]," *China Environmental News* [*Zhongguo huanjingbao*], August 9, 2017, https://cenews.com.cn/opinion/plxl/201708/t20170809_845892.html.

61. Based on 2012 figures.

62. Tuấn Ngô, "Thị Xã Kỳ Anh: Cá Chết Hàng Loạt, Thiệt Hại Tiền Tỷ [Kỳ Anh Commune: Mass Dead of Fish, Damage of Billions]," *Báo Hà Tĩnh*, April 7, 2016, http://baohatinh.vn/nong-nghiep/thi-xa-ky-anh-ca-chet-hang-loat-thiet-hai-tien-ty/111853.htm.

63. Linh Tong, "Vietnam Fish Deaths Cast Suspicion on Formosa Steel Plant," *The Diplomat*, April 30, 2016, https://thediplomat.com/2016/04/vietnam-fish-deaths-cast-suspicion-on-formosa-steel-plant/; Chau Mai Ngoc and Yu-Huay Sun, "Fish Death Crisis Prompts Vietnam Waste Water Probe," *Bloomberg*, May 4, 2016, https://www.bloomberg.com/news/articles/2016-05-04/fish-death-crisis-prompts-vietnam-to-probe-waste-water-pipes.

64. Richard Paddock, "Toxic Fish in Vietnam Idle a Local Industry and Challenge the State," *New York Times*, June 9, 2016, https://www.nytimes.com/2016/06/09/world/asia/vietnam-fish-kill.html.

65. Tong, "Vietnam Fish Deaths."

66. Tong, "Vietnam Fish Deaths."

67. Ho Binh Minh and Mai Nguyen, "Vietnam Says No Proof Formosa Steel Plant Linked to Mass Fish Deaths," Reuters, April 27, 2016, https://www.reuters.com/article/us-vietnam-formosa-plastics-environment/vietnam-says-no-proof-formosa-steel-plant-linked-to-mass-fish-deaths-idUSKCN0XO18L.

68. VnExpress, "Vietnam's Top Officials Eat Fish to Calm the Public on Toxic Waters Phobia," May 1, 2016, https://e.vnexpress.net/photo/news/vietnams-top-officials-eat-fish-to-calm-the-public-on-toxic-waters-phobia-3396174.html.

69. Interview with environmental activist and protest organizer in Hanoi, July 2017.

70. Thu Huong Le, "Amid Fish Deaths, Social Media Comes Alive in Vietnam," *The Diplomat*, May 4, 2016, https://thediplomat.com/2016/05/amid-fish-deaths-social-media-comes-alive-in-vietnam/.

71. Le, "Amid Fish Deaths."

72. Gary Sands, "Vietnam's Growing Environmental Activism," *The Diplomat*, October 29, 2016.

73. John Ngo, "Choosing Fish over Steel: Ample Protests and the Large-Scale Death of Fish in Central Vietnam." University of London School of Oriental and African Studies Dissertation, September 2017.

74. Shannon Tiezzi, "It's Official: Formosa Subsidiary Caused Mass Fish Deaths in Vietnam," *The Diplomat*, July 1, 2016, https://thediplomat.com/2016/07/its-official-formosa-subsidiary-caused-mass-fish-deaths-in-vietnam/.

75. VnExpress. "Minister Trần Hồng Hà: 'I Just Experienced 84 Days of Heavy Stress' [Bộ trưởng Trần Hồng Hà: 'Tôi vừa trải qua 84 ngày căng thẳng nặng trĩu']," June 6, 2016, https://vnexpress.net/tin-tuc/thoi-su/bo-truong-tran-hong-ha-toi-vua-trai-qua-84-ngay-cang-thang-nang-triu-3428300.html. Many suspected that phenol, cyanide, and iron hydroxides were just a small fraction of the chemicals leaked; the government did not release information on heavy metals such as lead, mercury, cadmium, and arsenic, because their damages are greater and much more long-lasting. See Mike Ives, "Outrage Over Fish Kill in Vietnam Simmers 6 Months Later," *New York Times*, October 3, 2016, https://www.nytimes.com/2016/10/04/world/asia/formosa-vietnam-fish.html.

76. Ives, "Outrage Over Fish Kill."

77. VnExpress, "Minister Trần Hồng Hà."

78. Ngo, "Choosing Fish," 18.

79. Luong, "Why Vietnam Can't Hold Back Facebook."

80. Le, "Amid Fish Deaths."

81. Interview with retired Vietnamese government official, July 2017.

82. Luong, "Why Vietnam Can't Hold Back Facebook."

83. Le, "Amid Fish Deaths."

84. Le, "Amid Fish Deaths." The government's Facebook page, https://www.facebook.com/thongtinchinhphu/.

85. Goffman, *The Presentation of Self*, 8.

86. Goffman, *The Presentation of Self*, 9.

87. *Focus Taiwan*, "Groups Again Appeal for Compensation in Vietnam Pollution Case," April 17, 2020, https://focustaiwan.tw/society/202004170020.

88. PBS, "Coronavirus Pandemic Threatens Flint, Michigan, with 2nd Major Health Crisis," May 12, 2020, https://www.pbs.org/newshour/show/coronavirus-pandemic-threatens-flint-michigan-with-2nd-major-health-crisis.

89. Leonard N. Fleming, "Covid-19 Compounds Flint's Woes after Contaminated Water Crisis," *The Detroit News*, June 2, 2020, https://www.detroitnews.com/story/news/local/michigan/2020/06/02/covid-19-compounds-flints-woes-after-contaminated-water-crisis/5221851002/.

CONCLUSION

1. See also Iza Ding, "Performative Governance," *World Politics* 72, no.4 (2020): 525–56.

2. This quote by Robert Ezra Park is cited in Goffman, *The Presentation of Self*, 19–20.

3. See https://www.merriam-webster.com/dictionary/persona.

4. A Google Ngram search shows a steady and dramatic increase in the frequency of the term "underlying phenomenon" in books over the twentieth century.

5. Goldsworthy, *Caesar*, 73.

6. Cicero, *On the Orator, Books 1–2*, trans. E. W. Sutton and H. Rackham (Cambridge, MA: Harvard University Press, 1948), xvi.

7. Jeffrey C. Alexander, *The Performance of Politics: Obama's Victory and the Democratic Struggle for Power* (New York: Oxford University Press, 2010).

8. See Green, *Eyes of the People*; Matynia, *Performative Democracy*.

9. Benjamin I. Schwartz, *The World of Thought in Ancient China* (Cambridge: Harvard University Press, 1985), 48.

10. See Macabe Keliher, *The Board of Rites and the Making of Qing China* (Berkeley: University of California Press, 2019).

11. Luke Roberts, *Performing the Great Peace: Political Space and Open Secrets in Tokugawa Japan* (Honolulu: University of Hawaii Press, 2012).

12. John Dewey, "Ethics," in *The Middle Works of John Dewey, 1899–1924*, ed. Jo Ann Boydston (Carbondale: Southern Illinois University Press), 58.

13. Clifford Geertz, *Negara: The Theater State in Nineteenth Century Bali* (Princeton, NJ: Princeton University Press, 1980), 13.

14. Lisa Wedeen, *Ambiguities of Domination: Politics, Rhetoric, and Symbols in Contemporary Syria* (Chicago: University of Chicago Press, 2015).

15. Lee Ann Fujii, "The Puzzle of Extra-Lethal Violence," *Perspectives on Politics* 11, no. 2 (2013): 410–26.

16. Isaac Ariail Reed, "Performative State-Formation in the Early American Republic," *American Sociological Review* 84, no. 2 (2019): 334–67.

17. Julia C. Strauss, *State Formation in China and Taiwan: Bureaucracy, Campaign, and Performance* (Cambridge: Cambridge University Press, 2019). Javed, *Righteous Revolutionaries*.

18. Also see Mara Loveman, "The Modern State and the Primitive Accumulation of Symbolic Power," *American Journal of Sociology* 110, no. 6 (2005): 1651–83. Lisa Wedeen, *Peripheral Visions: Publics, Power, and Performance in Yemen* (Chicago: University of Chicago Press, 2009).

19. On performativity by the powerless see Vaclav Havel, *The Power of the Powerless: Citizens against the State in Central-Eastern Europe* (Armonk, NY: M. E. Sharpe, 1985); James C. Scott, *Weapons of the Weak: Everyday Forms of Peasant Resistance* (New Haven, CT: Yale University Press, 1987); O'Brien and Li, *Rightful Resistance*; Greg Distelhorst and Diana Fu, "Performing Authoritarian Citizenship: Public Transcripts in China," *Perspectives on Politics* 17, no.1 (2019): 106-121; Diana Fu, *Mobilizing without the Masses: Control and Contention in China* (Cambridge University Press, 2018). On the use of cultural symbols to legitimize protest demands see Elizabeth Perry, "Casting a Chinese 'Democracy' Movement: The Role of Students, Workers, and Entrepreneurs," in *Popular Protest and Political Culture in Modern China*, ed. Elizabeth Perry and Jeffrey N. Wasserstrom (Boulder, CO: Westview Press, 1989), 74–92; Joseph W. Esherick and Jeffrey N. Wasserstrom, "Acting Out Democracy: Political Theater in Modern China," *Journal of Asian Studies* 49, no. 4 (1990): 835–65; Jeffrey C. Alexander, "Seizing the Stage: Social Performances from Mao Zedong to Martin Luther King Jr., and Black Lives Matter Today," *Drama Review* 61, no. 1 (2017): 14–42.

20. Weber, *Economy and Society*, 975. Italics added.

21. Baehr and Wells, "Editors' Introduction," xvii.

22. Brubaker, *The Limits of Rationality*, 3.

23. Ends, values, and beliefs can also contradict themselves. For example, in the case of environmental protection, the goal to improve air quality and the goal to satisfy citizen complaints may not always go hand in hand.

24. See Weber, *Economy and Society*, 226.

25. See Ding and Javed, "The Autocrat's Moral-Legal Dilemma."

26. See Iza Ding and Dan Slater, "Democratic Decoupling," *Democratization* 28, no. 1 (2021): 1–18.

27. Weber, *Economy and Society*, 600.

28. Weber, *The Protestant Ethic*, 121.

29. In terms of their differences, Marx saw the state as the vehicle of bourgeois domination, Weber saw it as a distinct status group. Marx argued that individuals' values come from their economic class, whereas Weber believed that values can exist independent of economic class. Marx believed in economic democracy; Weber believed in parliamentary democracy. Yet Marx and Weber expressed similar worries about an "extreme inhospitality of the modern formally rational social and economic order to the values of equality, fraternity and *caritas*." Brubaker, *The Limits of Rationality*, 44.

30. Weber, *Economy and Society*, 988.

31. For similarities and differences between Marx and Weber's analyses, see Karl Lowith, *Max Weber and Karl Marx* (Abingdon-on-Thames, UK: Routledge, 2002).

32. Benjamin I. Schwartz, *Chinese Communism and the Rise of Mao* (Cambridge, MA: Harvard University Press, 2014), 20.

33. To be sure, "substantive rationality" is Weber's term, not the CCP's. In Marxism it would be something akin to "substantive democracy." Ding and Thompson-Brusstar, "The Anti-Bureaucratic Ghost."

34. Ezra Vogel, "Politicized Bureaucracy: Communist China," in *Frontiers of Development Administration*, ed. A. Doak Barnett and Fred W. Riggs (Durham, NC: Duke University Press, 1970): 556–68.

35. Weber, *Economy and Society*, 225.

36. Weber considers technical knowledge "the primary source of the superiority of bureaucratic administration." Weber, *Economy and Society*, 223. China is currently pioneering the use of artificial intelligence in governance, especially in policing.

37. Weber, *Economy and Society*, 109.

38. See Liu Shaoqi, "How to Be a Good Communist," at https://www.marxists.org/reference/archive/liu-shaoqi/1939/how-to-be/ch01.htm.

39. For performance legitimacy in China, see Zhao, "Mandate of Heaven"; Zhu, "Performance Legitimacy"; Yang and Zhao, "Performance Legitimacy." For performance legitimacy in Eastern European communist regimes, see Stephen White, "Economic Performance and Communist Legitimacy," *World Politics* 38, no. 3 (1986): 462–82. Performance legitimacy is assumed to exist primarily in authoritarian regimes. However, whether democratic legitimacy relies on institutions or "performance" remains an empirical question. The recent trend of democratic erosion especially calls into question the extent of institutional legitimacy in democracies.

40. Zhao, "Mandate of Heaven," 428.

41. Such broad operationalization of "performance" begs the question of what cannot be counted as performance. If "performance legitimacy" includes almost everything, then it explains almost nothing.

42. Zhao, "Mandate of Heaven," 427.

43. See Ding and Thompson-Brusstar, "The Anti-Bureaucratic Ghost."

44. Weber, *Economy and Society*, 226.

45. See Roy Chan, "Formalism," in *Afterlives of Chinese Communism: Political Concepts from Mao to Xi*, ed. Christian Sorace, Ivan Franceschini, and Nicholas Loubere (Canberra, Australia: ANU Press), 77–80; Ding and Thompson-Brusstar, "The Anti-Bureaucratic Ghost."

46. Ding and Thompson-Brusstar, "Anti-Bureaucratic Ghost."

47. "What is Formalism and Bureaucratism? Do You Really Understand? [Shenme shi xingshizhuyi, guanliaozhuyi? ni zhende liaojie ma?]," May 7, 2020, http://fanfu.people.com.cn/n1/2020/0507/c64371-31700033.html, accessed August 1, 2021.

48. "Without the Conditions for Implementation, How Can There Not Be Formalism?" *Guancha*, April 3, 2019, https://www.guancha.cn/FangNing/2019_04_03_496159.shtml, accessed August 1, 2021.

49. Xu'en Wang, "Grassroots Fatigue: An Urgent Problem after the 19th Party Congress [Jicen pipei: shijiuda hou jixu zhongshi de wenti]," December 8, 2021, *Financial Times* (Chinese), https://www.ftchinese.com/story/001075391?archive, accessed August 1, 2021.

50. Wang, "Grassroots Fatigue."

51. General Office of the Central Committee of the Communist Party of China, "Notice on Solving the Outstanding Problems of Formalism and Reducing Burdens at the Grassroots Level [Guanyu jiejue xingshizhuyi tuchuwenti wei jiceng jianfu de tongzhi]," March 11, 20219, http://www.gov.cn/zhengce/2019-03/11/content_5372964.htm.

52. Chun Han Wong, "Xi Jinping's Eager-to-Please Bureaucrats Snarl His China Plans," *Wall Street Journal*, March 7, 2021, https://www.wsj.com/articles/xi-jinpings-eager-to-please-minions-snarl-his-china-plans-11615141195, accessed August 1, 2021.

53. Dawei Jiang, "My Company Is Pushing Me! My Girlfriend Is Also Pushing Me! Man Broke Down After Being Stopped for Riding His Bike the Wrong Way. Netizens: I See Myself" [Gongsi zai cui wo! nüpengyou ye zai cui wo! Hangzhou xiaohuo qiche nixing

bei lan hou dangchang bengkui! Wangyou: fangfu kandao le ziji], *Dushi Kuaibao*, April 1, 2019, https://hznews.hangzhou.com.cn/shehui/content/2019-04/01/content_7170351.htm, accessed June 8, 2020.

54. "Man Who Broke Down after Being Stopped for Riding His Bike in the Wrong Way Responded [Hangzhou qiche nixing beilan benkui de xiaohuozi huiyingle]," *Metropolitan Express* [*Dushi Kuaibao*], April 4, 2019, https://hznews.hangzhou.com.cn/shehui/content/2019-04/04/content_7172124.htm, accessed June 8, 2020.

55. Karl Marx, "Critique of Hegel's 'Philosophy of Right,'" in David McLellan, ed., *Karl Marx: Selected Writings* (Oxford: Oxford University Press, 2000), 37.

56. E.g., Richard McGregor, *The Party: The Secret World of China's Communist Rulers* (London: Penguin UK, 2010).

Bibliography

Abrami, Regina M., Edmund Malesky, and Yu Zheng. "Vietnam through Chinese Eyes: Divergent Accountability in Single-Party Regimes." In *Why Communism Did Not Collapse: Understanding Authoritarian Regime Resilience in Asia and Europe*, edited by Martin K. Dimitrov, 237–75. Cambridge: Cambridge University Press, 2013.

Adkins, Lisa, and Beverley Skeggs, eds. *Feminism After Bourdieu*. Oxford: Blackwell, 2004.

Ahlers, Anna L., Mette Halskov Hansen, and Rune Svarverud. *The Great Smog of China: A Short Event History of Air Pollution*. Ann Arbor: Association for Asian Studies, 2020.

Aklin, Michaël, and Johannes Urpelainen. *Renewables: The Politics of a Global Energy Transition*. Cambridge, MA: MIT Press, 2018.

Alexander, Jeffrey C. *The Performance of Politics: Obama's Victory and the Democratic Struggle for Power*. New York: Oxford University Press, 2010.

Alexander, Jeffrey C. "Seizing the Stage: Social Performances from Mao Zedong to Martin Luther King Jr., and Black Lives Matter Today." *TDR/The Drama Review* 61, no.1 (2017): 14–42.

Alkon, Meir, and Erik H. Wang. "Pollution Lowers Support for China's Regime: Quasi-Experimental Evidence from Beijing." *Journal of Politics* 80, no.1 (2018): 327–31.

Amsden, Alice Hoffenberg. *Asia's Next Giant: South Korea and Late Industrialization*. Oxford: Oxford University Press, 1989.

Anderson, Elizabeth. *Private Government: How Employers Rule Our Lives (and Why We Don't Talk about It)*. Princeton, NJ: Princeton University Press, 2017.

Andrews, Steven Q. "China's Air Pollution Reporting is Misleading." *China Dialogue*, March 27, 2014. https://chinadialogue.net/en/pollution/6856-china-s-air-pollution-reporting-is-misleading/.

Ang Yuen Yuen. *China's Gilded Age: The Paradox of Economic Boom and Vast Corruption*. Cambridge: Cambridge University Press, 2020.

Ang Yuen Yuen. "Beyond Weber: Conceptualizing an Alternative Ideal Type of Bureaucracy in Developing Contexts." *Regulation & Governance* 11, no. 3 (2017): 282–98.

Ang Yuen Yuen. "Counting Cadres: A Comparative View of the Size of China's Public Employment." *China Quarterly* 211 (2012): 676–96.

Ang Yuen Yuen. *How China Escaped the Poverty Trap*. Ithaca, NY: Cornell University Press, 2016.

Austin, J. L. *How to Do Things with Words*. Originally given as the 1955 William James Lecture. London: Oxford University Press, 1962.

Austin, J. L. "Performative Utterances." In *The Semantics-Pragmatics Boundary in Philosophy*, edited by Maite Ezcurdia and Robert J. Stainton, 21–31. Peterborough, Ontario: Broadview Press, 2013.

Baehr, Peter. *Caesar and the Fading of the Roman World: A Study in Republicanism and Caesarism*. Abingdon-on-Thames, UK: Routledge, 2017.

Baehr, Peter. "The "Iron Cage" and the "Shell as Hard as Steel": Parsons, Weber, and the Stahlhartes Gehäuse Metaphor in the Protestant Ethic and the Spirit of Capitalism." *History and Theory* 38, no. 2 (2001): 153–69.

Bai Ying and Ruixue Jia. "Elite Recruitment and Political Stability: The Impact of the Abolition of China's Civil Service Exam." *Econometrica* 84, no. 2 (2016): 677–733.

Bartels, Brandon L., and Christopher D. Johnston. "On the Ideological Foundations of Supreme Court Legitimacy in the American Public." *American Journal of Political Science* 57, no.1 (2013): 184–99.

Beblawi, Hazem. "The Rentier State in the Arab World." *Arab Studies Quarterly* 9, no. 4 (1987): 383–98.

Bell, Daniel. *The China Model: Political Meritocracy and the Limits of Democracy.* Princeton, NJ: Princeton University Press, 2015.

Bellin, Eva. "The Robustness of Authoritarianism in the Middle East: Exceptionalism in Comparative Perspective." *Comparative Politics* 36, no. 2 (2004): 139–57.

Bermeo, Nancy G. *Ordinary People in Extraordinary Times.* Princeton, NJ: Princeton University Press, 2003.

Bernstein, Thomas P., and Xiaobo Lu. *Taxation without Representation in Contemporary Rural China.* New York: Cambridge University Press, 2003.

Blumenthal, David, and Whiao Hsiao. "Privatization and its Discontents—the Evolving Chinese Health Care System." *New England Journal of Medicine* 353 (2005): 1165–70.

Boone, Catherine. *Political Topographies of the African State: Territorial Authority and Institutional Choice.* New York: Cambridge University Press, 2003.

Bourdieu, Pierre. *Distinction: A Social Critique of the Judgement of Taste.* Translated by Richard Nice. Cambridge, MA: Harvard University Press 1984.

Bourdieu, Pierre. *The Logic of Practice.* Translated by Richard Nice. Stanford, CA: Stanford University Press, 1992.

Bourdieu, Pierre, "Rethinking the State: Genesis and Structure of the Bureaucratic Field." *Sociological Theory* 12, no. 1 (1994): 1–18.

Boyd, Olivia. "A Rise in Confucianism Will Make China's Leaders More Eco-Conscious." China Dialogue, November 8, 2021. https://chinadialogue.net/en/nature/5312-a-rise-in-confucianism-will-make-china-s-leaders-more-eco-conscious/.

Brady, Henry E., and David Collier, eds. *Rethinking Social Inquiry: Diverse Tools, Shared Standards.* Lanham, MD: Rowman & Littlefield, 2010.

Brattoli, Magda, et al., "Odour Detection Methods: Olfactometry and Chemical Sensors." *Sensors* (Basel) 11, no. 5 (2011): 5290–5322. https://www.ncbi.nlm.nih.gov/pmc/articles/PMC3231359/.

Bromley, Patricia, and Walter W. Powell, "From Smoke and Mirrors to Walking the Talk: Decoupling in the Contemporary World." *Academy of Management Annals* 6, no. 1 (2012): 483–530.

Brubaker, Rogers. *The Limits of Rationality: An Essay on the Social and Moral Thought of Max Weber.* Abingdon-on-Thames, UK: Routledge, 2013.

Bueno de Mesquita, Bruce, and George W. Downs. "Development and Democracy." *Foreign Affairs* 84, no. 5 (2005): 77–86.

Bueno de Mesquita, Bruce, and Alastair Smith. *The Dictator's Handbook: Why Bad Behavior Is Almost Always Good Politics.* New York: Public Affairs, 2011.

Burns, John P., and Wang Xiaoqi. "Civil Service Reform in China: Impacts on Civil Servants' Behaviour." *China Quarterly* 201 (2010): 58–78.

Butler, Judith. *Gender Trouble: Feminism and the Subversion of Identity.* New York: Routledge, 1990.

Butler, Judith. "Performative Acts and Gender Constitution: An Essay in Phenomenol-ogy and Feminist Theory." *Theatre Journal* 40, no. 4 (1998): 519–31.

Butler, Judith. "Performative Agency." *Journal of Cultural Economy* 3, no. 2 (2010): 147–61.

Cai Yongshun. "Irresponsible State: Local Cadres and Image-Building in China." *Journal of Communist Studies and Transition Politics* 20, no. 4 (2004): 20–41.

Caixin. "New Coronavirus 'Whistleblower' Li Wenliang: Truth is More Important than Rehabilitation [Xinguanfeiyan "chuishaoren" LiWenliang: zhenxiang bi pingfan geng zhongyao]." January 31, 2020. http://china.caixin.com/2020-01-31/101509761.html.

Callon, Michel ed. *The Laws of the Markets.* Oxford: Blackwell, 1998.

Carpenter, Daniel P. *The Forging of Bureaucratic Autonomy: Reputations, Networks, and Policy Innovation in Executive Agencies, 1862–1928.* Princeton, NJ: Princeton University Press, 2001.

Carpenter, Daniel P. *Reputation and Power: Organizational Image and Pharmaceutical Regulation at the FDA.* Princeton, NJ: Princeton University Press, 2010.

Carson, Rachel. *Silent Spring.* Boston, MA: Houghton Mifflin, 1962.

Central Government of the People's Republic of China. "Li Keqiang: a Modern Gov-ernment Must Respond to People's Expectations and Concerns in a Timely Manner." February 17, 2016. http://www.gov.cn/xinwen/2016-02/17/content_5042673.htm.

Central Government of the People's Republic of China. "Report by Hu Jintao at the 17th National Congress (Excerpts) [Hu Jintao zai dangde shiqici quanguodaibi-aodahui shang zuobaogao (zhaiyao)]." October 15, 2007. http://www.gov.cn/ldhd/2007-10/15/content_776431.htm.

Central Government of the People's Republic of China. "Report by Hu Jintao at the 18th National Congress [Hu Jintao zai zhongguogongchandang di shibaci quan-guo daibiao dahui shang de baogao]." November 17, 2012. http://www.gov.cn/ldhd/2012-11/17/content_2268826.htm.

Central Organization Department [Zhongzubu]. "Notice on Improving the Perfor-mance Evaluation of Local Party-State Leadership and Cadres [Guanyu Gaijin Difang Dangzheng Lingdao Banzi he Lingdao Ganbu Zhengji Kaohe Gongzuo de Tongzhi]." December 10, 2013. http://renshi.people.com.cn/n/2013/1210/c139617-23793409.html.

Chan, Roy. "Formalism." In *Afterlives of Chinese Communism: Political Concepts from Mao to Xi*, edited by Christian Sorace, Ivan Franceschini, and Nicholas Loubere, 77–80. Canberra, Australia: ANU Press.

Charmaz. Kathy. *Constructing Grounded Theory.* Thousand Oaks, CA: Sage, 2014.

Charmaz, Kathy. "Grounded Theory," in *Rethinking Methods in Psychology*, edited by Jonathan Smith, Rom Harre, and Luk Van Langenhove, 27–49. Thousand Oaks, CA: Sage, 1995.

Cheibub, Jose Antonio. "Political Regimes and the Extractive Capacity of Govern-ments: Taxation in Democracies and Dictatorships." *World Politics* 50 (1998): 349–76.

Chen, Geoffrey C., and Charles Lees. "Growing China's Renewables Sector: A Developmental State Approach." *New Political Economy* 21, no. 6 (2016): 574–86.

Chen Guangsheng. *Toward Good Governance [Zouxiang shanzhi].* Zhejiang University Press, 2007.

Chen Jidong, Jennifer Pan, and Yiqing Xu. "Sources of Authoritarian Responsiveness: A Field Experiment in China." *American Journal of Political Science* 60, no. 2 (2016): 383–400.

Chen Jing. "Cadmium Rice Reappears: Why Can't 'Poisonous Rice' be Eradicated? [Gedami Chongxian: 'Dudami' Weihe Lvjinbujue?]." *Xinjingbao.* April 25, 2020. http://www.bjnews.com.cn/opinion/2020/04/25/721079.html.

Chen Jing. *Useful Complaints: How Petitions Assist Decentralized Authoritarianism in China.* Lanham, MD: Rowman & Littlefield, 2016.

Chen Ting and Ji Yeon Hong. "Rivals Within: Political Factions, Loyalty, and Elite Competition under Authoritarianism." *Political Science Research and Methods* 9, no. 3 (2021): 599–614.

Chen, Te-Ping "Living in China Takes 3½ Years Off Your Life." *Wall Street Journal.* September 12, 2017. https://www.wsj.com/articles/living-in-china-takes-3-years-off-your-life-1505209673.

Chen Xi. *Social Protest and Contentious Authoritarianism in China.* New York: Cambridge University Press, 2012.

China Central Television. "Toxic Running Tracks Are Made with Industrial Wastes [Dupaodao Jingshi Gongye Feiliao]." June 21, 2016. http://news.xinhuanet.com/fortune/2016-06/21/c_129080075.htm.

China Economic Weekly [Zhongguo Jingji Zhoukan]. "A Revelation of the Total Number of Chinese Civil Servants: 'Too Many Officials and Too Few Agents' at about 7,167,000 Persons [Zhongguo Gongwuyuan Zongshu Pilu: Guan Duo Bin Shao Yue 716.7 Wan Ren]." June 21, 2016. http://www.chinanews.com/gn/2016/06-21/7911130.shtml.

China Environment Net [Zhongguo Huanjing Wang]. "Whatever the Hundred Names Want, We Do [Baixing xiangshenme women jiuyao ganshenme]." Accessed June 30, 2016. http://www.cenews.com.cn/sylm/talk/201307/t20130703_744189.htm.

China National Radio. "Nanjing EPB Responds to Smog-Locked City: Experts Are off on Weekends and Cannot Answer Questions [Nanjing huanbaoju huiying wumai suocheng: zhoumo zhuanjia xiuxi, wufa zuoda]." November 3, 2013. http://www.chinanews.com/gn/2013/11-03/5456773.shtml.

China National Radio Net [Zhonguo Guangbo Wang]. "Wenzhou Mayor Responds to Invitation to Swim in the River: It Will Be Realized in Five Years [Wenzhou shizhang huiying guanyuan beiyao xiahe: wunianhou shixian shuili youyong]." March 13, 2013. http://china.cnr.cn/yaowen/201303/t20130313_512138016.shtml.

China Net. "China's One Hundred Strong Counties with Investment Potentials in 2013 [2013 zhongguo zui ju touzi qianli zhong xiao chengshi baiqiang xianshi gongbu]." China Net [Zhongguowang]. October 21, 2013. http://news.china.com.cn/2013-10/21/content_30357850.htm.

China News Net [Zhongguo Xinwen Wang]. "Governor of Zhejiang Responds to EPA officials Swim in River: A Lack of Law Enforcement and Supervision [Zhejiang shengzhang huiying huanbao juzhang xiahe: zhifa jiandu budaowei]." March 7, 2013. http://www.chinanews.com/gn/2013/03-07/4625246.shtml.

Chu Tung-Tsu. *Local Government in China Under the Ch'ing.* Cambridge, MA: Harvard University Asia Center, 1962.

Cicero. *On the Orator, Books 1–2.* Translated by E. W. Sutton and H. Rackham. Cambridge, MA: Harvard University Press, 1948.

CNN Library. "Flint Water Crisis Fast Facts." March 4, 2016. https://www.cnn.com/2016/03/04/us/flint-water-crisis-fast-facts/index.html.

Collier, David, and James E. Mahon Jr. "Conceptual 'Stretching' Revisited: Adapting Categories in Comparative Analysis." *American Political Science Review* 87, no. 4 (1993): 845–55.

Cornell, Agnes, Carl Henrik Knutsen, and Jan Teorell. "Bureaucracy and Growth." *Comparative Political Studies* 53, no. 14 (2020): 2246–82.

Crenson, Matthew A. *The Un-Politics of Air Pollution: A Study of Non-Decisionmaking in the Cities*. Baltimore: Johns Hopkins Press, 1971.

Cui Jianxin, Hong Chang, George S. Burr, Xiaolong Zhao, and Baoming Jiang. "Climatic Change and the Rise of the Manchu from Northeast China during AD 1600–1650." *Climatic Change* 156, no. 3 (2019): 405–23.

Dahl, Robert. *Polyarchy: Participation and Opposition*. New Haven, CT: Yale University Press, 1971.

Dastagir, Alia E. "George Floyd, Lea Michele and the Problem with Performative Outrage." *USA Today*, June 4, 2020. https://www.usatoday.com/story/news/nation/2020/06/04/george-floyd-lea-michele-and-problem-performative-outrage/3137994001/.

Davison, Nicola. "Rivers of Blood: The Dead Pigs Rotting in China's Water Supply." *The Guardian*. March 29, 2013. https://www.theguardian.com/world/2013/mar/29/dead-pigs-china-water-supply.

Deng Yanhua and Kevin J. O'Brien. "Relational Repression in China: Using Social Ties to Demobilize Protesters." *China Quarterly* 215 (2013): 533–52.

De Quidt, Jonathan, Johannes Haushofer, and Christopher Roth. "Measuring and Bounding Experimenter Demand." *American Economic Review* 108, no. 11 (2018): 3266–302.

Dewey, John. "Ethics." In *The Middle Works of John Dewey, 1899–1924*, edited by Jo Ann Boydston, 1–20. Carbondale: Southern Illinois University Press.

Dickson, Bruce. *The Dictator's Dilemma: The Chinese Communist Party's Strategy for Survival*. Oxford: Oxford University Press, 2016.

Dietz, Mary G. "Trapping the Prince: Machiavelli and the Politics of Deception." *American Political Science Review* 80, no. 3 (1986): 777–99.

Dimitrov, Martin K. "Internal Government Assessments of the Quality of Governance in China." *Studies in Comparative International Development* 50, no.1 (2015): 50–72.

Dimitrov, Martin K. "What the Party Wanted to Know: Citizen Complaints as a 'Barometer of Public Opinion' in Communist Bulgaria." *East European Politics and Societies* 28, no. 2 (2014): 271–95.

Dincecco, Mark, and Yuhua Wang. "Violent Conflict and Political Development over the Long Run: China versus Europe." *Annual Review of Political Science* 21 (2018): 341–58.

Ding, Iza. "Performative Governance." *World Politics* 72, no.4 (2020): 525–56.

Ding, Iza, and Jeffrey Javed, "The Autocrat's Moral-Legal Dilemma: Popular Morality and Legal Institutions in China." *Comparative Political Studies* 54, no. 6 (2021): 989–1022.

Ding, Iza, and Dan Slater, "Democratic Decoupling." *Democratization* 28, no. 1 (2021): 1–18.

Ding, Iza and Michael Thompson-Brusstar. 2021. "The Anti-Bureaucratic Ghost in China's Bureaucratic Machine." *China Quarterly* 248, no.S1 (2021): 116–40.

Ding, Iza, and Denise van der Kamp. Working Paper. "High Maintenance or Low Maintenance? Environmental Policy Implementation in China."

Distelhorst, Greg, and Diana Fu. "Performing Authoritarian Citizenship: Public Transcripts in China." *Perspectives on Politics* 17, no.1 (2019): 106–21.

Distelhorst, Greg, and Yue Hou. "Constituency Service under Nondemocratic Rule: Evidence from China." *Journal of Politics* 79, no. 3 (2017): 1024–40.

Eaton, Sarah, and Genia Kostka. "Authoritarian Environmentalism Undermined? Local Leaders' Time Horizons and Environmental Policy Implementation in China." *China Quarterly* 218 (2014): 359–80.

Eckstein, Harry. "Case Studies and Theory in Political Science." In *Handbook of Political Science*, edited by Fred Greenstein and Nelson Polsby, 79–138. Reading, MA: Addison Wesley, 1975.

Economy, Elizabeth. "Environmental Governance in China: State Control to Crisis Management." *Daedalus* 143, no. 2 (2014): 184–97.

Economy, Elizabeth. *The River Runs Black: The Environmental Challenge to China's Future.* Ithaca, NY: Cornell University Press, 2004.

Eisenberg, Andrew. "Weberian Patrimonialism and Imperial Chinese History." *Theory and Society* 27, no. 1 (1998): 83–102.

Elstrom, Manfred. *Workers and Change in China: Resistance, Repression, Responsiveness.* Cambridge: Cambridge University Press, 2021.

Elvin, Mark. "The Environmental Legacy of Imperial China." *China Quarterly* 156 (1998): 735–36.

Elvin, Mark. *The Retreat of the Elephants: An Environmental History of China.* 2nd ed. New Haven, CT: Yale University Press, 2006.

Esfandiari, Golnaz. "The Twitter Devolution." *Foreign Policy.* June 8, 2010. https://foreignpolicy.com/2010/06/08/the-twitter-devolution/.

Esherick, Joseph W., and Jeffrey N. Wasserstrom. "Acting Out Democracy: Political Theater in Modern China." *Journal of Asian Studies* 49, no. 4 (1990): 835–65.

Evans, Peter B. *Embedded Autonomy: States and Industrial Transformation.* Princeton, NJ: Princeton University Press, 1995.

Evans, Peter B., and James E. Rauch. "Bureaucracy and Growth: A Cross-National Analysis of the Effects of "Weberian" State Structures on Economic Growth." *American Sociological Review* (1999): 748–65.

Falkner, Robert. "International Sources of Environmental Policy Change in China: The Case of Genetically Modified Food." *Pacific Review* 19, no. 4 (2006): 473–94.

Fang Xin. "Economic Development and Environmental Protection [Jingji fazhan he huanjign baohu]." *People's Daily*, June 16, 1973.

Fang Xiuqi et al. "Transmission of Climate Change Impacts from Temperature Change to Grain Harvests, Famines and Peasant Uprisings in Historical China [Lengnuan fengqian jihuang nongminqiyi: jiyu liangshianquan de lishiqihou bianhua yingxiang zai zhongguo shehuixitong zhong de chuandi]." *Science China Earth Sciences* 58 (2015): 1427–39.

Fearon, James, and David Laitin. "Ethnicity, Insurgency, and Civil War." *American Political Science Review* 97, no.1 (2003): 75–90.

Fleming, Leonard. N. "Covid-19 Compounds Flint's Woes after Contaminated Water Crisis." *Detroit News.* June 2, 2020. https://www.detroitnews.com/story/news/local/michigan/2020/06/02/covid-19-compounds-flints-woes-after-contaminated-water-crisis/5221851002/.

Fleming, Leonard. N. and Karen Bouffard. "Snyder Partly to Blame for Flint Crisis, UM Report Says." *The Detroit News.* February 15, 2018. https://www.detroitnews.com/story/news/michigan/flint-water-crisis/2018/02/15/governor-rick-snyder-flint-water-crisis/110463996/.

Fleming, Sean. "Climate Change Helped Destroy These Four Ancient Civilizations." *World Economic Forum*. March 29, 2019. https://www.weforum.org/agenda/2019/03/our-turn-next-a-brief-history-of-civilizations-that-fell-because-of-climate-change/.

Flyvbjerg, Bent. "Five Misunderstandings about Case-Study Research." *Qualitative Inquiry* 12, no. 2 (2006): 219–45.

Flyvbjerg, Bent. *Making Social Science Matter*. Cambridge: Cambridge University Press, 2001.

Focus Taiwan. "Groups Again Appeal for Compensation in Vietnam Pollution Case." April 17, 2020. https://focustaiwan.tw/society/202004170020.

Franke, Wolfgang. *The Reform and Abolition of the Traditional Chinese Examination System*. Leiden, Netherlands: Brill, 1960.

Fu, Diana. *Mobilizing without the Masses: Control and Contention in China*. Cambridge: Cambridge University Press, 2018.

Fujii, Lee Ann. "The Puzzle of Extra-lethal Violence." *Perspectives on Politics* 11, no. 2 (2013): 410–26.

Fukuyama, Francis. *State Building: Governance and World Order in the 21st Century*. London: Profile Books, 2017.

Fulda, Andreas. "Protests in Ningbo Mark the Birth of a Nationwide Environmental Health Movement." *Asia Dialogue*. October 29, 2012. https://theasiadialogue.com/2012/10/29/px-protests-in-ningbo/.

Fung Yu-lan. *A Short History of Chinese Philosophy*. New York: Simon and Schuster, 1997.

Futrell, Robert. "Performative Governance: Impression Management, Teamwork, and Conflict Containment in City Commission Proceedings." *Journal of Contemporary Ethnography* 27, no. 4 (1999): 494–529.

Gaddis, John Lewis. *The Cold War: A New History*. New York: Penguin, 2006.

Gallagher, Marry E. "Mobilizing the Law in China: 'Informed Disenchantment' and the Development of Legal Consciousness." *Law & Society Review* 40, no. 4 (2006): 783–816.

Gallup, John L., Jeffrey D. Sachs, and Andrew D. Mellinger. "Geography and Economic Development." *International Regional Science Review* 22, no. 2 (1999): 179–232. nber.org/papes/w6849.pdf.

Gangel, Jamie, and Shelby Lin Erdman. "Former Presidents Obama, Bush, and Clinton Volunteer to Get Coronavirus Vaccine Publicly to Prove It's Safe." *CNN*. December 3, 2020. https://edition.cnn.com/2020/12/02/politics/obama-vaccine/index.html.

Gao Xiang. "State-Led Digital Governance in Contemporary China." In *State Capacity Building in Contemporary China*, edited by Hiroko Naito and Vida Macikenaite, 29–45. New York: Springer, 2020.

Gao Xiang and Jie Tan, "From Web to Weber: Understanding the Case of 'One-Go at Most' as ICT-Driven Government Reform in Contemporary China." *China Review* 20, no. 3 (2020): 71–98.

Gardner, Daniel. "China's 'Silent Spring' Moment?" *New York Times*. March 19, 2015. https://www.nytimes.com/2015/03/19/opinion/why-under-the-dome-found-a-ready-audience-in-china.html.

Geddes, Barbara. "How the Cases You Choose Affect the Answers You Get: Selection Bias in Comparative Politics." *Political Analysis* (1990): 131–50.

Geertz, Clifford. *Negara: The Theater State in Nineteenth-Century Bali*. Princeton, NJ: Princeton University Press, 1980.

General Office of the Central Committee of the Communist Party of China. "Notice on Solving the Outstanding Problems of Formalism and Reducing Burdens at the Grassroots Level [Guanyu jiejue xingshizhuyi tuchuwenti wei jiceng jianfu de tongzhi]." March 11, 2019. http://www.gov.cn/zhengce/2019-03/11/content_5372964.htm.

General Office of the Communist Party of China, General Office of the State Council [Zhonggong zhongyang bagongting, guowuyuan bangongting]. "Strengthen the Implementation of Cadre Responsibility System Concerning the Comprehensive Management of Public Security [Jianquan luoshi shehui zhi'an zonghe zhili lingdao zerenzhi guiding]." March 24, 2016.

General Office of the State Council. "Notice on the Establishment of a Coordination Group to Promote the Transformation of Government Functions [Guowuyuan bangongting guanyu chengli tuijin zhineng zhuanbian xietiao xiaozu de tongzhi]." April 21, 2015. http://www.gov.cn/zhengce/content/2015-04/21/content_9648.htm.

General Office of the State Council. "Notice on the Establishment of a Coordination Group to Promote the Transformation of Government Functions as well as 'Fangguanfu' Reforms [Guowuyuan bangongting guanyu chengli guowuyuan tuijin zhengfu zhineng zhuanbian he 'fangguanfu' gaige xietiao xiaozu de tongzhi]." July 25, 2018. http://www.gov.cn/zhengce/content/2018-07/25/content_5309035.htm.

Geping Qu. *Population and the Environment in China.* Translated by Kiang Batching and Go Ran. Boulder, CO: Lynne Reinner, 1994.

Gibson, James L. "Understandings of Justice: Institutional Legitimacy, Procedural Justice, and Political Tolerance." *Law & Society Review* 23, no. 3 (1989): 469–96.

Gibson, James L., and Michael J. Nelson. "Is the U.S. Supreme Court's Legitimacy Grounded in Performance Satisfaction and Ideology?" *American Journal of Political Science* 59, no. 1 (2015): 162–74.

Gilley, Bruce. "Authoritarian Environmentalism and China's Response to Climate Change." *Environmental Politics* 21, no. 2 (2012): 287–307.

Ginsburg, Tom, and Tamir Moustafa. *Rule by Law: The Politics of Courts in Authoritarian Regimes.* Cambridge: Cambridge University Press, 2008.

Girardot, N. J., James Miller, and Liu Xiaogan, eds. *Daoism and Ecology: Ways within a Cosmic Landscape.* Cambridge, MA: Harvard University Press, 2001.

Goffman, Erving. "On Face-Work." In *Interaction Ritual: Essays in Face-to-Face Behavior,* ed. Erving Goffman, 5–45. Chicago: Aldine Transaction, 1967.

Goffman, Erving. *The Presentation of Self in Everyday Life.* Garden City, NY: Doubleday, 1959.

Goldsworthy, Adrian. *Caesar: The Life of a Colossus.* London: Hachette, 2006.

Government of the PRC. "Footprints of the Republic—1973: The Beginning of Environmental Protection [Gongheguo de zuji 1973 nian: huanjing baohu kaishi qibu]." August 31, 2009. http://www.gov.cn/test/2009-08/31/content_1405410.htm.

Government of the PRC. "Situation of Environmental Protection [Huanjing baohu zhuangkuang]." July 27, 2005. http://www.gov.cn/test/2005-07/27/content_17757.htm.

Gramsci, Antonio. *Prison Notebooks,* Vol. 1. New York: Columbia University Press, 2007.

Green, Jeffrey Edward. *The Eyes of the People: Democracy in an Age of Spectatorship.* Oxford: Oxford University Press, 2010.

Greenpeace. "Ranking of Urban *PM2.5* Pollution in 2013 Released; The Country Needs Strong Measures." January 10, 2014. http://www.greenpeace.org.cn/PM25-ranking/.

Greenstone, Michael, Guojun He, Shanjun Li, and Eric Zou. "China's War on Pollution: Evidence from the First Five Years." National Bureau of Economic Research Working Paper no. 28467. February 2021. https://www.nber.org/papers/w28467.

Greitens, Sheena Chestnut. "Rethinking China's Coercive Capacity: An Examination of PRC Domestic Security Spending, 1992–2012." *China Quarterly* 232 (2017): 1002–25, 8.

Grzymala-Busse, Anna. *Rebuilding Leviathan: Party Competition and State Exploitation in Postcommunist Democracies.* Cambridge: Cambridge University Press, 2007.

Guancha. "Without the Conditions for Implementation, How Can There Not Be Formalism?" April 3, 2019. https://www.guancha.cn/FangNing/2019_04_03_496159.shtml.

The Guardian. "Flint Activists Still Waiting as Governor Escapes Fallout of Water Crisis." April 23, 2018. https://www.theguardian.com/us-news/2018/apr/23/flint-water-crisis-governor-rick-snyder-criminal-trials.

Guarino, Mark. "National Guard Called in to Hand Out Water in Flint, Mich." *Washington Post.* January 13, 2016. https://www.washingtonpost.com/national/national-guard-called-in-to-hand-out-water-in-flint-mich/2016/01/13/81a0fd88-b961-11e5-829c-26ffb874a18d_story.html?utm_term=.92a268aff6ba.

Gueorguiev, Dimitar D., and Paul J. Schuler. "Collective Charisma: Elite-Mass Relations in China and Vietnam." *Problems of Post-Communism* 68, no. 3 (2021): 190–201.

Guo Huan. "Attach Importance to Environmental Protection Work [Zhongshi huanjing baohu gongzuo]." *People's Daily,* September 17, 1974.

Haddad, Mary Alice, and Stevan Harrell. "The Evolution of the East Asian Eco-Developmental State." In *Greening East Asia: The Rise of the Eco-Developmental State,* edited by Ashley Esarey, Mary Alice Haddad, Joanna Lewis, and Stevan Harrell, 5–31. Seattle: University of Washington Press, 2020.

Hall, Peter. "Aligning Ontology and Methodology in Comparative Research." In *Comparative Historical Analysis in the Social Sciences,* edited by James Mahoney and Dietrich Rueschemeyer, 373–404. New York: Cambridge University Press, 2003.

Hangzhou Daily. "Environmental Protection Under Pressure as the Price of Glyphosate Climbs [Huanbao chengya kaigong shouxian caoganlin jiage jielian pansheng]." April 4, 2013. http://hzdaily.hangzhou.com.cn/dskb/html/2013-04/04/content_1468870.htm.

Harding, Harry. *Organizing China: The Problem of Bureaucracy, 1949–1976.* Stanford, CA: Stanford University Press, 1981.

Havel, Vaclav. *The Power of the Powerless: Citizens against the State in Central-eastern Europe.* Armonk, NY: M. E. Sharpe, 1985.

Heilmann, Sebastian, and Elizabeth J. Perry. *Mao's Invisible Hand: The Political Foundations of Adaptive Governance in China.* Cambridge, MA: Harvard University Asia Center, 2011.

Helveston, John, and Jonas Nahm. "China's Key Role in Scaling Low-Carbon Energy Technologies." *Science* 366, no. 6467 (2019): 794–96. DOI: 10.1126/science.aaz1014.

Hernandez, Javier C. "Chinese Parents Outraged After Illnesses at School Are Tied to Pollution." *New York Times*, April 19, 2016. http://www.nytimes.com/2016/04/19/world/asia/china-pollution-cancer-changzhou.html?_r=0.

Hertog, Steffen. "The 'Rentier Mentality,' 30 Years On: Evidence from Survey Data." *British Journal of Middle Eastern Studies* 47, no. 1 (2020): 6–23.

Heurlin, Christopher. *Responsive Authoritarianism in China.* Cambridge: Cambridge University Press, 2016.

The Hill. "Michigan Congressman Says Flint's Water Still Not Safe to Drink." https://thehill.com/hilltv/rising/424536-flints-congressman-says-water-is-still-not-safe-to-drink. January 9, 2019.

Hirschman, Albert O. *Exit, Voice, and Loyalty: Responses to Decline in Firms, Organizations, and States.* Cambridge, MA: Harvard University Press, 1970.

Hirschman, Albert O. *The Passions and the Interests: Political Arguments for Capitalism before its Triumph.* Westport, CT: Greenwood, 1997.

Hofheinz, Roy. *The Broken Wave: The Chinese Communist Peasant Movement, 1922–1928.* Vol. 90. Cambridge, MA: Harvard University Press, 1977.

Huaxi Metropolitan News. "From 'Rumormonger' to 'a Respectable Person,' Dr. Li Wenliang's Beginning of Year 2020 [Cong 'zaoyaozhe' bian 'kejin de ren' yisheng Li Wenliang de 2020 kainian]." February 3, 2020. https://m.chinanews.com/wap/detail/zw/sh/2020/02-03/9076631.shtml.

Inglehart, Ronald, and Christian Welzel. *Modernization, Cultural Change, and Democracy: The Human Development Sequence.* Cambridge: Cambridge University Press, 2005.

Irfan, Umair. "The UN Climate Action Summit Was a Disappointment." *VOX.* September 24, 2019. https://www.vox.com/2019/9/24/20880416/un-climate-action-summit-2019-greta-thunberg-trump-china-india.

Ives, Mike. "Outrage Over Fish Kill in Vietnam Simmers 6 Months Later." *New York Times.* October 4, 2016. https://www.nytimes.com/2016/10/04/world/asia/formosa-vietnam-fish.html.

Jahiel, Abigail R. "The Organization of Environmental Protection in China." *China Quarterly* 156 (1998): 757–87.

Jamieson, Alastair. "Beijing Olympics Were the Most Polluted Games Ever, Researchers Say." *The Telegraph.* June 22, 2009. https://www.telegraph.co.uk/sport/olympics/london-2012/5597277/Beijing-Olympics-were-the-most-polluted-games-ever-researchers-say.html.

Jaros, Kyle A. *China's Urban Champions: The Politics of Spatial Development.* Princeton, NJ: Princeton University Press, 2019.

Javed, Jeffrey. *Righteous Revolutionaries: Morality and Violence in the Forging of State Authority after the Chinese Communist Revolution.* Ann Arbor: University of Michigan Press, 2022.

Jiang Dawei. "My Company Is Pushing Me! My Girlfriend Is Also Pushing Me! Man Broke Down After Being Stopped for Riding His Bike the Wrong Way. Netizens: I See Myself [Gongsi zai cui wo! Nüpengyou ye zai cui wo! Hangzhou xiaohuo qiche nixing bei lan hou dangchang bengkui! Wangyou: fangfu kandao le ziji]." *Dushi Kuaibao.* April 1, 2019. https://hznews.hangzhou.com.cn/shehui/content/2019-04/01/content_7170351.htm.

Jiang Jingjing et al. "Research on China's Cap-and-Trade Carbon Emission Trading Scheme: Overview and Outlook." *Applied Energy* 178 (2016): 902–17.

Jiang Junyan. "Making Bureaucracy Work: Patronage Networks, Performance Incentives, and Economic Development in China." *American Journal of Political Science* 62, no. 4 (2018): 982–99.

Johnson, Chalmers. *Peasant Nationalism and Communist Power: The Emergence of Revolutionary China, 1937–1945*. Stanford, CA: Stanford University Press, 1962.

Johnson, Chalmers. *MITI and the Japanese Miracle: The Growth of Industrial Policy, 1925–1975*. Stanford, CA: Stanford University Press, 1982.

Johnson, Thomas R. "Regulatory Dynamism of Environmental Mobilization in Urban China." *Regulation & Governance* 10 (2016): 14–28.

Karplus, Valerie J., and Mengying Wu. "Crackdowns in Hierarchies: Evidence from China's Environmental Inspections." Working Paper (2019). Available at SSRN https://ssrn.com/abstract=3449177.

Keliher, Macabe. *The Board of Rites and the Making of Qing China*. Berkeley: University of California Press, 2019.

Kennedy, Gavin. *Adam Smith's Lost Legacy*. London: Palgrave 2005.

Kennet, Wayland. "The Stockholm Conference on the Human Environment." *International Affairs* 48, no.1 (1972): 33–45.

King, Gary, Jennifer Pan, and Margaret E. Roberts. "How Censorship in China Allows Government Criticism but Silences Collective Expression." *American Political Science Review* 107, no. 2 (2013): 326–43.

Kolbert, Elizabeth. *The Sixth Extinction: An Unnatural History*. London: A&C Black, 2014.

Kopstein, Jeffrey. *The Politics of Economic Decline in East Germany, 1945–1989*. Chapel Hill: University of North Carolina Press, 2000.

Kostka, Genia. "Command without Control: The Case of China's Environmental Target System." *Regulation & Governance* 10 (2016): 58–74.

Kostka, Genia. "Environmental Protection Bureau Leadership at the Provincial Level in China: Examining Diverging Career Backgrounds and Appointment Patterns." *Journal of Environmental Policy & Planning* 15, no.1 (2013), 41–63.

Kuper, Simon. "The Myth of Green Growth." *Financial Time*, October 24, 2019. https://www.ft.com/content/47b0917c-f523-11e9-a79c-bc9acae3b654.

Kuran, Timur. "Now Out of Never: The Element of Surprise in the East European Revolution of 1989." *World Politics* 40, no. 1 (1991): 7–48.

Lampton, David M., ed. *Policy Implementation in Post-Mao China*. Berkeley: University of California Press, 1987.

Landry, Pierre F., Xiaobo Lü, and Haiyan Duan. "Does Performance Matter? Evaluating Political Selection along the Chinese Administrative Ladder." *Comparative Political Studies* 51, no. 8 (2018): 1074–105.

Le, Thu Huong. "Amid Fish Deaths, Social Media Comes Alive in Vietnam." *The Diplomat*. May 4, 2016. https://thediplomat.com/2016/05/amid-fish-deaths-social-media-comes-alive-in-vietnam/.

Lee Ching Kwan, and Yonghong Zhang. "The Power of Instability: Unraveling the Microfoundations of Bargained Authoritarianism in China." *American Journal of Sociology* 118, no. 6 (2013): 1475–1508.

Lei Ya-Wen. *The Contentious Public Sphere: Law, Media, and Authoritarian Rule in China*. Princeton, NJ: Princeton University Press, 2017.

Lei Ya-Wen. "Revisiting China's Social Volcano: Attitudes toward Inequality and Political Trust in China." *Socius* 6 (2020): 1–21.

Leib, Ethan, and He Baogang, ed. *The Search for Deliberative Democracy in China*. New York: Springer, 2006.

Lenin, Vladimir. *The State and Revolution*. Translated by Robert Service. New York: Penguin 1992.

Levitsky, Steven, and Lucan Way. "The Durability of Revolutionary Regimes." *Journal of Democracy* 24, no. 3 (2013): 5–17.

Li He. "The New PM2.5 Standard: Can the Deviation of Perception from Index be Changed? [PM2.5 xin biaozhun: nengfou gaibian ganshou yu zhishu de bei-ligan]." *Science Daily* [*Keji ribao*]. December 1, 2011. http://tech.sina.com.cn/d/2011-12-01/11586409712.shtml.

Li Hongbin and Li-An Zhou. "Political Turnover and Economic Performance: The Incentive Role of Personnel Control in China." *Journal of Public Economics* 89, no. 9–10 (2005): 1743–62.

Li Lianjiang. "Rights Consciousness and Rules Consciousness in Contemporary China." *China Journal* 64 (2010): 47–68.

Li, Tania Murray. "Beyond 'the State' and Failed Schemes." *American Anthropologist* 107, no. 3 (2005): 383–94.

Li Xiaojun. "Access, Institutions and Policy Influence: The Changing Political Economy of Trade Protection in Post-reform China." PhD diss., Stanford University, 2013.

Li Yifei and Judith Shapiro. *China Goes Green: Coercive Environmentalism for a Troubled Planet.* Hoboken, NJ: John Wiley & Sons, 2020.

Lieberthal, Kenneth. "China's Governing System and Its Impact on Environmental Policy Implementation." 1997. https://www.wilsoncenter.org/sites/default/files/Lieberthal%20article.pdf.

Lieberthal, Kenneth. "The Fragmented Authoritarianism Model and Its Limitations." In *Bureaucracy, Politics, and Decision Making in Post-Mao China,* edited by Kenneth Lieberthal and David M. Lampton, 1-30. Berkeley: University of California Press, 1992.

Lieberthal, Kenneth, and David M. Lampton. *Bureaucracy, Politics, and Decision Making in Post-Mao China.* Berkeley: University of California Press, 1992.

Lieberthal, Kenneth, and Michel Oksenberg. *Policy Making in China: Leaders, Structures, and Processes.* Princeton, NJ: Princeton University Press, 1990.

Lim, Louisa. "Beijing's 'Airpocalypse' Spurs Pollution Controls, Public Pressure." *National Public Radio,* 2013. https://www.npr.org/2013/01/14/169305324/beijings-air-quality-reaches-hazardous-levels.

Lin Chun. *The Transformation of Chinese Socialism.* Durham, NC: Duke University Press, 2006.

Lin Dashou. "Smog Is Inhumane, and Thus the Government Cannot Be Inhumane." *BBC China.* November 13, 2013. https://www.bbc.com/zhongwen/simp/comments_on_china/2013/11/131104_coc_nanjingsmog.

Linz, Juan, and Alfred Stepan. *Problems of Democratic Transition and Consolidation: Southern Europe, South America, and Post-Communist Europe.* Baltimore: Johns Hopkins, 1996.

Lipset, Seymour Martin. *Political Man.* New York: Doubleday, 1963.

Lipset, Seymour Martin. "Some Social Requisites of Democracy: Economic Development and Political Legitimacy." *American Political Science Review* 53, no. 1 (1959): 69–105.

Lipsky, Michael. *Street-Level Bureaucracy: Dilemmas of the Individual in Public Service.* New York: Russell Sage Foundation, 2010.

Liu Shaoqi. "How to Be a Good Communist." https://www.marxists.org/reference/archive/liu-shaoqi/1939/how-to-be/ch01.htm.

Looney, Kristen E. *Mobilizing for Development: The Modernization of Rural East Asia.* Ithaca, NY: Cornell University Press, 2020.

Lorentzen, Peter L. "Regularizing Rioting: Permitting Public Protest in an Authoritarian Regime." *Quarterly Journal of Political Science* 8, no. 2 (2013): 127–58.

Lorentzen, Peter, and Suzanne Scoggins. "Understanding China's Rising Rights Consciousness." *China Quarterly* 223 (2015): 638–57.

Lovell, Terry. "Thinking Feminism with and Against Bourdieu." *Feminist Theory* 1, no. 1 (2000): 11–32.

Loveman, Mara. "The Modern State and the Primitive Accumulation of Symbolic Power." *American Journal of Sociology* 110, no. 6 (2005): 1651–83.

Lowith, Karl. *Max Weber and Karl Marx*. Abingdon-on-Thames, UK: Routledge, 2002.

Lozano, Rafael, et al. "Global and Regional Mortality from 235 Causes of Death for 20 Age Groups in 1990 and 2010: A Systematic Analysis for the Global Burden of Disease Study 2010." *Lancet* 380, no. 9859 (2012): 2095–2128.

Lu Jinping. "A Mayor Goes Swimming in the River, So What If He Was Putting on a Show [Shizhang xiahe youyong, zongran zuoxiu you hefang?]." *China Environmental News [Zhongguo huanjingbao]*. August 9, 2017. https://cenews.com.cn/opinion/plxl/201708/t20170809_845892.html.

Lubman, Stanley B. *Bird in a Cage: Legal Reform in China after Mao*. Stanford, CA: Stanford University Press, 1999.

Ludwig, Emil. *Napoleon*. Translated by Eden Paul and Cedar Paul. New York: Modern Library, 1915.

Luong, Dien. "Why Vietnam Can't Hold Back Facebook." *Vnexpress International*. September 10, 2017. https://e.vnexpress.net/news/news/why-vietnam-can-t-hold-back-facebook-3639186.html.

Lynch, Jim. "Whistleblower Del Toral Grew Tired of EPA 'Cesspool.'" *Detroit News*. March 28, 2016. https://www.detroitnews.com/story/news/michigan/flint-water-crisis/2016/03/28/whistle-blower-del-toral-grew-tired-epa-cesspool/82365470/.

Ma Jun. "How China Can Truly Lead the Fight against Climate Change." *TIME*. September 12, 2019. https://time.com/5669061/china-climate-change/.

Ma Liang. "Does Citizen Engagement in Government Performance Measurement Matter: A Multilevel Analysis of Chinese Cities [Gongzhong canyu de zhengfu jixiao pinggu zouxiao: jiyu Zhongguo bufen chengshi de duocen fenxi]." *Comparative Economic and Social Systems [Jingji Shehui Tizhi Bijiao]* 3 (2018): 113–24.

Ma Xiaoying and Leonard Ortolano. 2000. *Environmental Regulations in China: Institutions, Enforcement, and Compliance*. Lanham, MD: Rowman and Littlefield.

MacFarquhar, Roderick, and Michael Schoenhals. *Mao's Last Revolution*. Cambridge, MA: Belknap Press, 2006.

Macgowan, J. *Sidelights on Chinese Life*. Philadelphia: Lippincott, 1908.

Machiavelli, Niccòlo. *Discourses on Livy, Book III Chapter 40*. Translated by Harvey C. Mansfield and Nathan Tarcov. Chicago: University of Chicago Press, 1996.

Machiavelli, Niccòlo. *The Prince*. Translated by James B. Atkinson. Indianapolis, IN: Hackett, 1998.

MacKenzie, Donald, Fabian Muniesa, and Lucia Siu, eds. *Do Economists Make Markets? On the Performativity of Economics*. Princeton NJ: Princeton University Press, 2008).

Malesky, Edmund, and Paul Schuler. "Nodding or Needling: Analyzing Delegate Responsiveness in an Authoritarian Parliament." *American Political Science Review* 104, no. 3 (2010): 482–502.

Mallapaty, Smriti. "How China Could be Carbon Neutral by Mid-Century." *Nature* 586, no. 7830 (2020): 482–84. https://www.nature.com/articles/d41586-020-02927-9.

Manion, Melanie. "Policy Implementation in the People's Republic of China: Authoritative Decisions versus Individual Interests." *Journal of Asian Studies* 50, no. 2 (1991): 253–79.

Mann, Michael. "The Autonomous Power of the State: Its Origins, Mechanisms and Results." *European Journal of Sociology* 25 (1985): 185–213.

Mann, Michael. "Infrastructural Power Revisited." *Studies in Comparative International Development* 43, no. 3 (2008): 355–65.

Mann, Michael. *The Sources of Social Power.* Vol. 3. *Global Empires and Revolution, 1890–1945.* Cambridge: Cambridge University Press, 2012.

Marks, Robert. *China: Its Environment and History.* Lanham, MD: Rowman & Littlefield, 2012.

Marks, Robert. *The Origins of the Modern World: A Global and Ecological Narrative from the Fifteenth to the Twenty-first Century.* Lanham, MD: Rowman & Littlefield, 2006.

Martens, Susan. "Public Participation with Chinese Characteristics: Citizen Consumers in China's Environmental Management." *Environmental Politics* 15 (2006): 211–30.

Marx, Karl, and Friedrich Engels. "The Communist Manifesto." In *Karl Marx: Selected Writings,* edited by David McLellan, 245–72. Oxford: Oxford University Press, 2000.

Marx, Karl. "Critique of Hegel's 'Philosophy of Right.'" In *Karl Marx: Selected Writings,* edited by David McLellan, 32–42. Oxford: Oxford University Press, 2000.

Mattingly, Daniel C. *The Art of Political Control in China.* New York: Cambridge University Press, 2019.

Matynia, Elzbieta. *Performative Democracy.* Abingdon-on-Thames, UK: Routledge, 2015.

McGregor, Richard. *The Party: The Secret World of China's Communist Rulers.* London: Penguin UK, 2010.

Mearsheimer, John J., *Why Leaders Lie: The Truth about Lying in International Politics.* Oxford: Oxford University Press, 2013.

Merchant, Carolyn. *The Death of Nature: Women, Ecology, and the Scientific Revolution.* New York: Harper & Row, 1980.

Mertha, Andrew. *China's Water Warriors.* Ithaca, NY: Cornell University Press, 2008.

Mertha, Andrew. "'Fragmented Authoritarianism 2.0': Political Pluralization in the Chinese Policy Process." *China Quarterly* 200 (2009): 995–1012.

Mertha Andrew, and William R. Lowry. "Unbuilt Dams: Seminal Events and Policy Change in China, Australia, and the United States." *Comparative Politics* 39, no.1 (2006): 1–20.

Metropolitan Express [*Dushi kuaibao*]. "CEO of Mao Yuanchang Glasses Pays 200,000 and Invites EPA Director to Go Swimming in a River [Mao Yuanchang dongshizhang chu 20 wan qing huanbao juzhang xiahe youyong]." February 18, 2013.

Metropolitan Express [*Dushi kuaibao*]. "Man Who Broke Down after Being Stopped for Riding His Bike in the Wrong Way Responded [Hangzhou qiche nixing beilan benkui de xiaohuozi huiyingleg]." April 4, 2019. https://hznews.hangzhou.com.cn/shehui/content/2019-04/04/content_7172124.htm.

Michels, Robert. *Political Parties: A Sociological Study of the Oligarchial Tendencies of Modern Democracy.* Translated by Eden Paul. Eastford, CT: Martino Fine Books, 2016.

Minh, Ho Binh, and Mai Nguyen. "Vietnam Says No Proof Formosa Steel Plant Linked to Mass Fish Deaths." *Reuters*. April 27, 2016. https://www.reuters.com/article/us-vietnam-formosa-plastics-environment/vietnam-says-no-proof-formosa-steel-plant-linked-to-mass-fish-deaths-idUSKCN0XO18L.

Ministry of Ecology and Environment of the People's Republic of China. "Emission Standards for Odorous Pollutants." 2007. http://english.mee.gov.cn/Resources/standards/Air_Environment/Emission_standard1/200710/t20071024_111822.shtml.

Ministry of Ecology and Environment of the People's Republic of China. "Environmental Air, Waste Air, and Odorous Air Measurement: Three-Point Comparative Method of Odor Bags (Consultation Draft) [Huanjing feiqi he kongqi, chouqi de ceding: sandianshi bijiao choudaifa]." 2019. http://www.mee.gov.cn/xxgk2018/xxgk/xxgk06/201906/W020190621485478072697.pdf.

Ministry of Ecology and Environment of the People's Republic of China. "Main Responsibilities of the Ministry of Ecology and Environment [Shengtai huanjing zhize]." October 2018. http://www.mee.gov.cn/zjhb/zyzz/201810/t20181011_660310.shtml.

Ministry of Ecology and Environment of the People's Republic of China. "On-Site Fast Measurement of Environmental Air: The Chemosensor Method (Consultation Draft)." 2011. http://www.mee.gov.cn/gkml/hbb/bgth/201105/W020110511535029519957.pdf.

Moed, Jonathan. "This Vietnamese Browser and Search Engine Is Daring Google to Step-Up Its Game." *Forbes*. June 6, 2018. https://www.forbes.com/sites/jonathanmoed/2018/06/06/this-vietnamese-browser-search-engine-is-daring-google-to-step-up-its-game/?sh=77822aae48cb.

Mol, Arthur P., and Neil T. Carter. "China's Environmental Governance in Transition." *Environmental Politics* 15, no. 2 (2006): 159–70.

Montinola, Gabriella, Yingyi Qian, and Barry R. Weingast. "Federalism, Chinese Style: The Political Basis for Economic Success in China." *World Politics* 48, no. 1 (1995): 50–81.

Morgan, Kimberly J., and Ann Shola Orloff, ed., *The Many Hands of the State: Theorizing Political Authority and Social Control*. New York: Cambridge University Press, 2017.

Mummolo, Jonathan, and Erik Peterson. "Demand Effects in Survey Experiments: An Empirical Assessment." *American Political Science Review* 113, no. 2 (2019): 517–29.

Murtazashvili, Jennifer. "Pathologies of Centralized State-Building." *PRISM* 8, no. 2 (2019): 54–67.

Myers, Steven Lee. "In China's Coal Country, a Ban Brings Blue Skies and Cold Homes." *New York Times*, February 10, 2018, https://www.nytimes.com/2018/02/10/world/asia/china-coal-smog-pollution.html.

Nathan, Andrew J. "Authoritarian Resilience." *Journal of Democracy* 14, no.1 (2003): 6–17.

Nathan, Andrew J. *Chinese Democracy*. Berkeley: University of California Press, 1986.

Naughton, Barry. "The Third Front: Defense Industrialization in the Chinese Interior." *China Quarterly* 115 (1988): 351–86.

NDRC. "Construction Standard for Office Space of Party and State Organizations [Dangzhen jiguan bangong yongfang jianshe biaozhun]." December 21, 1999.

NDRC [2014] 2674. "Construction Standard for Office Space of Party and State Organizations" [Dangzhen jiguan bangong yongfang jianshe biaozhun]."

November 27, 2014. https://www.ndrc.gov.cn/fggz/gdzctz/tzfg/201411/
t20141127_1197595.html.

Nee, Victor, Sonja Opper, and Sonia Wong. "Developmental State and Corporate
Governance in China." *Management and Organization Review* 3, no. 1 (2007):
19–53.

Newey, Glen. "Political Lying: A Defense." *Public Affairs Quarterly* 11, no. 2 (1997):
93–116.

Ngo, John. "Choosing Fish over Steel: Ample Protests and the Large-Scale Death of
Fish in Central Vietnam." University of London School of Oriental and African
Studies Dissertation. September 2017.

Ngô, Tuấn. "Thị Xã Kỳ Anh: Cá Chết Hàng Loạt, Thiệt Hại Tiền Tỷ [Kỳ Anh Commune: Mass Fish Death, Damage in Billions]." *Báo Hà Tĩnh*. April 7, 2016.
http://baohatinh.vn/nong-nghiep/thi-xa-ky-anh-ca-chet-hang-loat-thiet-hai-
tien-ty/111853.htm.

Ngoc, Chau Mai, and Sun Yu-Huay. "Fish Death Crisis Prompts Vietnam Waste
Water Probe." *Bloomberg*. May 4, 2016. https://www.bloomberg.com/news/
articles/2016-05-04/fish-death-crisis-prompts-vietnam-to-probe-waste-water-
pipes.

Nietzsche, Friedrich. *On the Genealogy of Morals*. Oxford: Oxford University Press,
1996.

Nietzsche, Friedrich. *Human, All Too Human*. 1878; reprint Cambridge: Cambridge
University Press, 1986.

Nietzsche, Friedrich. *The Joyous Science*. Translated by R. Kevin Hill. Penguin Classics,
2019.

NPR. "Beijing's 'Airpocalypse' Spurs Pollution Controls, Public Pressure." January 14,
2013. https://www.npr.org/2013/01/14/169305324/beijings-air-quality-reaches-
hazardous-levels.

NPR. "Who's to Blame for Flint's Water Problem?" January 17, 2016. https://www.npr.
org/2016/01/17/463405757/whos-to-blame-for-flints-water-problem#:~:
text=For%20many%20people%2C%20the%20blame%20for%20the%20tap%20
water%20contamination,his%20resignation%20have%20been%20growing.

O'Brien, Kevin J., ed. *Popular Protest in China*. Cambridge, MA: Harvard University
Press, 2009.

O'Brien, Kevin J., and Lianjiang Li. *Rightful Resistance in Rural China*. Cambridge:
Cambridge University Press, 2006.

O'Brien, Kevin J., and Lianjiang Li. "Selective Policy Implementation in Rural China."
Comparative Politics 31, no. 2 (1999): 167–86.

Oi, Jean C. 1995. "The Role of the Local State in China's Transitional Economy." *China
Quarterly* 144 (1995): 1132–49.

Olson, Mancur. "Dictatorship, Democracy, and Development." *American Political Science Review* 87, no. 3 (1993): 567–76.

OpenNet Initiative. "Country Report: China." August 9, 2012. https://opennet.net/
research/profiles/china-including-hong-kong.

OpenNet Initiative. "Country Report: Vietnam." August 7, 2012. https://opennet.net/
research/profiles/vietnam.

Paddock, Richard. "Toxic Fish in Vietnam Idle a Local Industry and Challenge the
State." *New York Times*. June 9, 2016. https://www.nytimes.com/2016/06/09/
world/asia/vietnam-fish-kill.html.

Pan, Jennifer. "How Chinese Officials Use the Internet to Construct Their Public
Image." *Political Science Research and Methods* 7, no. 2 (2019): 197–213.

Pan, Jennifer. *Welfare for Autocrats: How Social Assistance in China Cares for its Rulers.* Oxford: Oxford University Press, 2020.

Pan Jiahua. *China's Environmental Governance and Ecological Civilization [Zhongguo de huanjing zhili yu shengtai jianshe].* Beijing: China Social Science Press, 2015.

Pan Yue and Zhou Jigang. "The Rich Consume and the Poor Suffer the Pollution." *China Dialogue.* October 27, 2006. https://www.chinadialogue.net/article/show/single/en/493--The-rich-consume-and-the-poor-suffer-the-pollution-.

PBS. "Coronavirus Pandemic Threatens Flint, Michigan, with 2nd Major Health Crisis." May 12, 2020. https://www.pbs.org/newshour/show/coronavirus-pandemic-threatens-flint-michigan-with-2nd-major-health-crisis.

Peerenboom, Randall. *China's Long March Toward Rule of Law.* New York: Cambridge University Press, 2002.

People.cn. "A Revolutionary Party Is Most Afraid of Not Hearing People's Voices [Yige geming zhengdang, jiupa tingbudao renmin de shengyin]." October 25, 2016. http://cpc.people.com.cn/n1/2016/1025/c69113-28805875.html.

People.cn. "6 Billion People Earning 1000 Yuan a Month? The National Statistics Bureau Responds." June 15, 2020. http://politics.people.com.cn/n1/2020/0615/c1001-31747507.html.

People.cn. "The 2019 National Exam Opens Today: 1,380,000 Applicants Compete For A 95:1 Chance of Passing [2019 nian guokao jin kaikao: jin 138 wan ren baoming guoshen, jingzhen bi 95:1]." December 2, 2018. http://politics.people.com.cn/n1/2018/1202/c1024-30436595.html.

People.cn. "What is Formalism and Bureaucratism? Do You Really Understand? [Shenme shi xingshizhuyi, guanliaozhuyi? ni zhende liaojie ma?]." May 7, 2020. http://fanfu.people.com.cn/n1/2020/0507/c64371-31700033.html.

People's Daily. "Central 'Remain True to Our Original Aspiration and Keep Our Mission Firmly in Mind' Education Work Team Issues 'Notice on Rectifying the Excessiveness of 'Performance Projects' and 'Face Projects' such as 'Landscape Lighting Projects [Zhongyang buwangchuxin laojishiming zhuti jiaoyu xiaozu yinfa tongzhi zhengzhi jingguan lianghua gongcheng guoduhua deng zhengji gongcheng mianzi gongcheng wenti]." December 2, 2019.http://www.gov.cn/xinwen/2019-12/02/content_5457679.htm.

People's Daily. "People's Capital Does Not Allow Living Sparrows, 3 Million People Mobilized, 83,000 Sparrows Annihilated in a Day [Renmin shoudu burong maque shengcun, sanbaiwanren zongdongyuan diyitian jianmie bawansan]." April 20, 1958, translated by the author.

People's Daily. "State Council Notice to Vigorously Launch the Periotic Hygiene Campaign [Guowuyuan guanyu dali kaizhan aiguo weisheng yundong de tongzhi]." April 5, 1977.

People's Daily. "State Council Sends Notice to Revolution Committees in Various Provinces, Cities and Autonomous Regions, Raises Six Demands to Persistently Launch the Periotic Hygiene Campaign [Guowuyuan tongzhi ge sheng shi zizhiqu geweihui he guowuyuan gebuwei, tichu jianchi kaizhan aiguo weisheng yundong liuxiang yaoqiu]." April 8, 1978.

People's Daily. "Tang Ke Spoke on Behalf of Chinese Delegate about Our Country's Stance on the Protection and Improvement of Human Environment at the United Nations Conference on the Environment [Woguo daibiaotuan tuanzhang Tang Ke zai lianheguo renlei huanjing huiyi shang fayan chanshu woguo dui weihu he gaishan renlei huanjing wenti de zhuzhang]." June 11, 1972.

People's Net [renminwang]. "EPA Directors in Zhejiang Swam in Rivers and Earned Trust from People [Zhejiang huanbao juzhang xiahe youyong quxinyumin]." September 11, 2013. http://yuqing.people.com.cn/n/2013/0911/c212785-22880928.html.

Pepper, Suzanne. *Civil War in China: The Political Struggle, 1945–1949.* Lanham, MD: Rowman & Littlefield, 1999.

Perry, Elizabeth J. *Anyuan: Mining China's Revolutionary Tradition.* Berkeley: University of California Press, 2012.

Perry, Elizabeth J. "Casting a Chinese 'Democracy' Movement: The Role of Students, Workers, and Entrepreneurs." In *Popular Protest and Political Culture in Modern China,* edited by Elizabeth Perry and Jeffrey N. Wasserstrom. Boulder, CO: Westview Press, 1989: 74–92.

Perry, Elizabeth J. "Challenging the Mandate of Heaven: Popular Protest in Modern China." *Critical Asian Studies* 33, no. 2 (2001): 163–80.

Perry, Elizabeth J. "Chinese Conceptions of 'Rights': From Mencius to Mao-and Now." *Perspectives on Politics* 6, no. 1 (2008): 37–50.

Perry, Elizabeth J. "Making Communism Work: Sinicizing a Soviet Governance Practice." *Comparative Studies in Society and History* 61, no. 3 (2019): 535–62.

Perry, Elizabeth J. "From Mass Campaigns to Managed Campaigns: 'Constructing a New Socialist Countryside.'" In *Mao's Invisible Hand: The Political Foundations of Adaptive Governance in China,* edited by Sebastian Heilmann and Elizabeth Perry, 30–61. Cambridge, MA: Harvard University Press, 2011.

Perry, Elizabeth J. "Moving the Masses: Emotion Work in the Chinese Revolution." *Mobilization: An International Quarterly* 7, no. 2 (2002): 111–28.

Perry, Elizabeth J. "The Populist Dream of Chinese Democracy." *Journal of Asian Studies* 74, no. 4 (2015): 903–15.

Perry, Elizabeth J. *Rebels and Revolutionaries in North China, 1845–1945.* Stanford, CA: Stanford University Press, 1980.

Perry, Elizabeth J., and Sebastian Heilmann. *Mao's Invisible Hand: The Political Foundations of Adaptive Governance in China.* Cambridge, MA: Harvard University Asia Center, 2011.

Pham, My. "Vietnam Says Facebook Commits to Preventing Offensive Content." *Reuters.* 2017. https://www.reuters.com/article/us-facebook-vietnam/vietnam-says-facebook-commits-to-preventing-offensive-content-idUSKBN17T0A0.

Phoenix Weekly [*Fenghuang zhoukan*]. "China's 100 Cancer Villages [Zhongguo baichu zhiai weidi]." April 2009.

Pomeranz, Kenneth. *The Great Divergence: China, Europe, and the Making of the Modern Economy.* Princeton, NJ: Princeton University Press, 2009.

Prasad, Pushkala. "Symbolic Processes in the Implementation of Technological Change: A Symbolic Interactionist Study of Work Computerization." *Academy of Management Journal* 36, no. 6 (1993): 1400–29.

Pu Xiaoyu. *Rebranding China: Contested Status Signaling in the Changing Global Order.* Stanford, CA: Stanford University Press, 2019.

Putnam, Hilary. *The Collapse of the Fact/Value Dichotomy and Other Essays.* Cambridge, MA: Harvard University Press, 2004.

Putnam, Robert D. *Making Democracy Work.* Princeton, NJ: Princeton University Press, 1993.

Qi Ye. *Research on China's Environmental Management System* [Zhongguo huanjing jianguan tizhi yanjiu]. Shanghai: Shanghai Sanlian Press, 2008.

Qianjiang Evening News [*Qianjiang wanbao*]. "15 EPA Directors in Zhejiang Went Swimming in a River, Vice Mayor and Municipal Party Secretary were the

First to Go [Zhejiang 15 ge huanbao juzhang xiahe youyong, fushizhang shiweishuji daitou]." September 8, 2013. http://news.xinhuanet.com/2013-09/08/c_117273400.htm.

Ramesh, M., Xun Wu, and Alex Jingwei He. "Health Governance and Healthcare Reforms in China." *Health Policy and Planning* 29, no. 6 (2013): 663–72.

Ran Ran. *China's Local Environmental Politics* [Zhongguo difang huanjing zhengzhi: zhengce yu zhixing zhijian de juli]. Beijing: Central Compilation and Translation Press, 2015.

Rankin, Mary Backus. *Elite Activism and Political Transformation in China: Zhejiang Province, 1865–1911*. Stanford, CA: Stanford University Press, 1986.

Reed, Isaac Ariail. "Performative State-formation in the Early American Republic." *American Sociological Review* 84, no. 2 (2019): 334–67.

Reilly, James. *Strong Society, Smart State: The Rise of Public Opinion in China's Japan Policy*. New York: Columbia University Press, 2012.

Repnikova, Maria. *Media Politics in China: Improvising Power under Authoritarianism*. Cambridge: Cambridge University Press, 2017.

Roberts, Andrew. *Napoleon: A Life*. Viking, 2014.

Roberts, Dexter. "China: Choking on Pollution's Effects." *Bloomberg*. November 28, 2005. https://www.bloomberg.com/news/articles/2005-11-28/china-choking-on-pollutions-effects.

Roberts, Luke. *Performing the Great Peace: Political Space and Open Secrets in Tokugawa Japan*. Honolulu: University of Hawaii Press, 2012.

Roberts, Margaret E. *Censored: Distraction and Diversion inside China's Great Firewall*. Princeton, NJ: Princeton University Press, 2018.

Ross, Michael L. "Does Oil Hinder Democracy?" *World Politics* 53, no. 3 (2001): 325–61.

Rostow, Walt Whitman. *The Stages of Economic Growth: A Non-Communist Manifesto*. 1959; reprint Cambridge: Cambridge University Press, 1990.

Rothstein, Bo. "The Chinese Paradox of High Growth and Low Quality of Government: The Cadre Organization Meets Max Weber." *Governance* 28, no. 4 (2015): 533–48.

Rothstein, Bo. "Creating Political Legitimacy: Electoral Democracy versus Quality of Government." *American Behavioral Scientist* 53, no. 3 (2009): 311–30.

Saich, Anthony. "The Quality of Governance in China: The Citizen's View." HKS Faculty Research Working Paper Series RWP 12-051. John F. Kennedy School of Government, Harvard University. http://nrs.harvard.edu/urn-3:HUL.InstRe pos:9924084.

Sands, Gary. "Vietnam's Growing Environmental Activism." *The Diplomat*. October 29, 2016.

Sartori, Giovanni. "Comparing and Miscomparing." *Journal of Theoretical Politics* 3, no. 3 (1991).

Sartori, Giovanni. "Concept Misformation in Comparative Politics." *American Political Science Review* 64, no. 4 (1970): 1033–53.

Schmidt, Vivien A. "Democracy and Legitimacy in the European Union Revisited: Input, Output and 'Throughput.'" *Political Studies* 61, no. 1 (2013): 2–22.

Schwartz, Benjamin I. *Chinese Communism and the Rise of Mao*. Cambridge, MA: Harvard University Press, 2014.

Schwartz, Benjamin I. *The World of Thought in Ancient China*. Cambridge, MA: Harvard University Press, 1985.

Scott, James C. *Seeing Like a State: How Certain Schemes to Improve the Human Condition Have Failed*. New Haven, CT: Yale University Press, 2008.

Scott, James C. *Weapons of the Weak: Everyday Forms of Peasant Resistance.* New Haven, CT: Yale University Press, 1987.

Selden, Mark. *The Yenan Way in Revolutionary China.* Cambridge, MA: Harvard University Press, 1971, 62.

Shapiro, Judith. *Mao's War Against Nature: Politics and the Environment in Revolutionary China.* New York: Cambridge University Press, 2001.

Shaw, Tony. "'Some Writers are More Equal than Others': George Orwell, the State and Cold War Privilege." *Cold War History* 4, no. 1 (2003): 143–70.

Shi Han and Lei Zhang. "China's Environmental Governance of Rapid Industrialisation." *Environmental Politics* 15, no. 2 (2006): 271–92.

Shi Tianjian, and Jie Lu. "The Meaning of Democracy: The Shadow of Confucianism." *Journal of Democracy* 21, no. 4 (2010): 123–30.

Shih, Victor, Christopher Adolph, and Mingxing Liu. "Getting Ahead in the Communist Party: Explaining the Advancement of Central Committee Members in China." *American Political Science Review* 106, no. 1 (2012): 166–87.

Shleifer, Andrei, and Robert W. Vishny. *The Grabbing Hand: Government Pathologies and Their Cures.* Cambridge, MA: Harvard University Press, 1998.

Shue, Vivienne. "Legitimacy Crisis in China?" In *State and Society in 21st Century China: Crisis, Contention, and Legitimation,* edited by Peter Hays Gries and Stanley Rosen. New York: Routledge, 2004.

Sinkule, Barbara J., and Leonard Ortolano. *Implementing Environmental Policy in China.* Westport, CT: Greenwood, 1995.

Skocpol, Theda. "Bringing the State Back In: Strategies of Analysis in Current Research." In *Bringing the State Back In,* edited by Peter B. Evans, Dietrich Rueschemeyer, and Theda Skocpol. New York: Cambridge University Press, 1985: 3–43.

Slater, Dan. *Ordering Power: Contentious Politics and Authoritarian Leviathans in Southeast Asia.* New York: Cambridge University Press, 2010.

Slater, Dan, Benjamin Smith, and Gautam Nair. "Economic Origins of Democratic Breakdown? The Redistributive Model and the Postcolonial State." *Perspectives on Politics* 12, no. 2 (2014): 353–74.

Slater, Dan and Daniel Ziblatt. "The Enduring Indispensability of the Controlled Comparison." *Comparative Political Studies* 46, no. 10 (2013): 1301–27.

Small, Mario Luis. "How Many Cases Do I Need? On Science and the Logic of Case Selection in Field-based Research." *Ethnography* 10, no. 1 (2009): 5–38.

Smith, Adam. *The Theory of Moral Sentiments.* New York: Penguin 2010.

Smith, Lindsay. "After Blowing the Whistle on Flint's Water, EPA "Rogue Employee" Has Been Silent. Until now." *Michigan Radio.* January 21, 2016. https:// www.michiganradio.org/post/after-blowing-whistle-flints-water-epa-rogue-employee-has-been-silent-until-now.

Smith, Lindsay. "Leaked Internal Memo Shows Federal Regulator's Concerns about Lead in Flint's Water." *Michigan Radio.* July 13, 2015. michiganradio.org/post/leaked-internal-memo-shows-federal-regulator-s-concerns-about-lead-flint-s-water.

Solinger, Dorothy J., and Yiyang Hu. "Welfare, Wealth and Poverty in Urban China: The *Dibao* and Its Differential Disbursement." *China Quarterly* 211 (2012): 741–64. doi:10.1017/S0305741012000835.

Sorace, Christian P. *Shaken Authority: China's Communist Party and the 2008 Sichuan Earthquake.* Ithaca, NY: Cornell University Press, 2017.

Southern Metropolitan News. "Directors Went into River to Seal the Mouths of Doubters [Juzhang xiashui duzhu zhiyizhe de zui]." September 10, 2013.

Southern Weekend. "15 EPB Directors Unwelcomed Interviews after Swimming in a River." January 9, 2014. http://www.infzm.com/content/97379.

State Council Leading Group on Environmental Protection. "Key Points on Environmental Protection Work [Huangjing baohu gongzuo huibao yaodian]." No. 79, December 31, 1978.

State Council of The People's Republic of China. "Premier Li Urges Responding to People's Concerns in Time." February 18, 2016. http://english.www.gov.cn/premier/news/2016/02/18/content_281475291965095.htm.

State Council of The People's Republic of China. "Regulations on Rigorous Enforcement of Economy and Anti-Waste for the Party and Government Organs [Dangzheng jiguan lixing jieyue fandui langfei tiaoli]." November 26, 2013. http://www.gov.cn/jrzg/2013-11/26/content_2534611.htm.

Stern, Rachel. *Environmental Litigation in China: A Study in Political Ambivalence.* Cambridge: Cambridge University Press, 2013.

Stockmann, Daniela. *Media Commercialization and Authoritarian Rule in China.* Cambridge: Cambridge University Press, 2014.

Strauss, Julia C. "Morality, Coercion, and State Building by Campaign in the Early PRC: Regime Consolidation and After, 1949–1956." *China Quarterly* 188 (2006): 891–912.

Strauss, Julia C. *State Formation in China and Taiwan: Bureaucracy, Campaign, and Performance.* Cambridge: Cambridge University Press, 2019.

Stromseth, Jonathan, Edmund Malesky, and Dimitar D. Gueorguiev. *China's Governance Puzzle: Enabling Transparency and Participation in a Single-Party State.* New York: Cambridge University Press, 2017.

Su Zheng, and Tianguang Meng. "Selective Responsiveness: Online Public Demands and Government Responsiveness in Authoritarian China." *Social Science Research* 59 (2016): 52–67.

Subramanian, Meera. "Anthropocene Now: Influential Panel Votes to Recognize Earth's New Epoch." *Nature.* May 21, 2019. https://www.nature.com/articles/d41586-019-01641-5.

Sunshine, Jason, and Tom R. Tyler. "The Role of Procedural Justice and Legitimacy in Shaping Public Support for Policing." *Law & Society Review* 37, no. 3 (2003): 513–48.

Tang Wenfang. *Populist Authoritarianism: Chinese Political Culture and Regime Sustainability.* New York: Oxford University Press, 2016.

Tao Jiaqing and Xueyong Ai. "Must Speed Up Environmental Protection Work [Huanjing baohu gongzuo yao zhuajin]." *People's Daily*, October 15, 1973.

Taplin, Nathaniel. "How China's SOEs Squeeze Private Firms." *Wall Street Journal.* February 7, 2019. https://www.wsj.com/articles/how-chinas-soes-squeeze-private-firms-11549530183.

Tian Xingchun and Rong Liu. "The Past and Present of Urban Management: Where Did Urban Management Institutions Come From? [Chengguan de qianshi jinsheng, chengshi guanli zhidu conghe erlai?]." People.cn. October 19, 2011. http://legal.people.com.cn/GB/15940234.html.

Tiezzi, Shannon. "It's Official: Formosa Subsidiary Caused Mass Fish Deaths in Vietnam." *The Diplomat.* July 1, 2016. https://thediplomat.com/2016/07/its-official-formosa-subsidiary-caused-mass-fish-deaths-in-vietnam/.

Tilly, Charles. "War Making and State Making as Organized Crime." In *Bringing the State Back In*, edited by Peter B. Evans, Dietrich Rueschemeyer, and Theda Skocpol, 169–91. Cambridge: Cambridge University Press, 1985.

Tilt, Bryan. "The Political Ecology of Pollution Enforcement in China: A Case from Sichuan's Rural Industrial Sector." *China Quarterly* 192 (2007): 915–32.

Tong, Linh. "Vietnam Fish Deaths Cast Suspicion on Formosa Steel Plant." *The Diplomat*. April 30, 2016. https://thediplomat.com/2016/04/vietnam-fish-deaths-cast-suspicion-on-formosa-steel-plant/.

Trotsky, Leon. *1905*. New York: Random House, 1971.

Truex, Rory. *Making Autocracy Work: Representation and Responsiveness in Modern China*. New York: Cambridge University Press, 2016.

Tsai, Kellee S. "Adaptive Informal Institutions and Endogenous Institutional Change in China." *World Politics* 59, no. 1 (2006): 116–41.

Tsai, Lily L. *Accountability without Democracy: Solidary Groups and Public Goods Provision in Rural China*. Cambridge: Cambridge University Press, 2007.

Turiel, Jesse, Iza Ding, and John Chung-En Liu. "Environmental Governance in China: State, Society, and Market." *Brill Research Perspectives in Governance and Public Policy in China* 1, no. 2 (2017): 1–67.

Turner, Victor. *The Anthropology of Performance*. Cambridge, MA: PAJ Publications: 1988.

Turner, Victor. *From Ritual to Theater: The Human Seriousness of Play*. Cambridge, MA: PAJ Publications, 1982.

United Nations. "Report of the United Nations Conference on the Human Environment." 1972. https://www.un.org/ga/search/view_doc.asp?symbol=A/CONF.48/14/REV.1.

Van der Blom, Henriette. *Oratory and Political Career in the Late Roman Republic*. Cambridge: Cambridge University Press, 2016.

Van der Kamp, Denise S. "Blunt Force Regulation and Bureaucratic Control: Understanding China's War on Pollution." *Governance* 34, no.1 (2021): 191–209.

Van der Kamp, Denise S. "Can Police Patrols Prevent Pollution? The Limits of Authoritarian Environmental Governance in China." *Comparative Politics* 53, no. 3 (2021): 403–33.

Van der Kamp, Denise S. "Clean Air at What Cost? The Rise of Blunt Force Pollution Regulation in China." PhD diss., UC Berkeley, 2017.

Van Rooij, Benjamin, Rachel E. Stern, and Kathinka Furst. "The Authoritarian Logic of Regulatory Pluralism: Understanding China's New Environmental Actors." *Regulation & Governance* 10 (2016): 3–13.

Venkatesh, Sudhir. *Gang Leader for a Day: A Rogue Sociologist Takes to the Streets*. New York: Penguin Press, 2008.

VnExpress. "Minister Trần Hồng Hà: 'I Just Experienced 84 days of Heavy Stress' [Bộ trưởng Trần Hồng Hà: 'Tôi vừa trải qua 84 ngày căng thẳng nặng trĩu']." June 30, 2016. https://vnexpress.net/tin-tuc/thoi-su/bo-truong-tran-hong-ha-toi-vua-trai-qua-84-ngay-cang-thang-nang-triu-3428300.html.

VnExpress. "Vietnam's Top Officials Eat Fish to Calm the Public on Toxic Waters Phobia." April 30, 2016. https://e.vnexpress.net/photo/news/vietnams-top-officials-eat-fish-to-calm-the-public-on-toxic-waters-phobia-3396174.html.

Vogel, Ezra. *The Four Little Dragons: The Spread of Industrialization in East Asia*. Cambridge, MA: Harvard University Press, 1991.

Vogel, Ezra. 1970. "Politicized Bureaucracy: Communist China." In *Frontiers of Development Administration*, edited by A. Doak Barnett and Fred W. Riggs. Durham, NC: Duke University Press, 556–68.

Wakeman, Frederic. *The Great Enterprise: The Manchu Reconstruction of Imperial Order in Seventeenth-Century China*. Berkeley: University of California Press, 1985, 48–58.

Walder, Andrew. *Communist Neo-Traditionalism: Work and Authority in Chinese Industry*. Berkeley: University of California Press, 1986.

Walder, Andrew, and Yang Su. "The Cultural Revolution in the Countryside: Scope, Timing and Human Impact." *China Quarterly* 173 (2003): 74–99.

Wan Ya. "Both Smog and Bureaucratic Attitudes Need Treatment [Wumai yu guanfang de taidu dou jixu zhili]." *Guangzhou Daily*, November 4, 2013.

Wang, Alex L. "Symbolic Legitimacy and Chinese Environmental Reform." *Environmental Law* 48, no. 4 (2018): 699–760.

Wang, Mark, Michael Webber, Brian Finlayson, and Jon Barnett. "Rural Industries and Water Pollution in China." *Journal of Environmental Management* 86, no. 4 (2008): 648–59.

Wang Qing et al. "Estimation of PM2.5-Associated Disease Burden in China in 2020 and 2030 using Population and Air Quality Scenarios: A Modelling Study." *Lancet Planetary Health* 3, no. 2 (2019): e71–e80, https://doi.org/10.1016/S2542-5196(18)30277-8.

Wang Shaoguang. "State Policy Orientation, Extractive Capacity, and the Equality of Healthcare in Urban China [J]." *Social Sciences in China* 6 (2005): 101–20.

Wang Xue'en. "Grassroots Fatigue: An Urgent Problem after the 19th Party Congress [Jicen pipei: shijiuda hou jixu zhongshi de wenti]." December 8, 2017. *Financial Times* (Chinese). https://www.ftchinese.com/story/001075391?archive.

Wang Yangming. *Complete Works of Wang Yangming* [*Wang Yangming quanji*]. Beijing: Hong Qi Chu Ban She, 1996.

Wang Yuhua. *Tying the Autocrat's Hands: The Rise of the Rule of Law in China*. Cambridge: Cambridge University Press, 2015.

Weatherford, Stephen M. "How Does Government Performance Influence Political Support?" *Political Behavior* 9, no. 1 (1987): 5–28.

Weber, Max. "Bureaucracy." In *From Max Weber*, edited and translated by H. H. Gerth and C. Wright Mills, 196–244. New York: Oxford University Press, 1946.

Weber, Max. *Economy and Society: An Outline of Interpretive Sociology* Translated by Guenther Roth and Claus Witt. Berkeley: University of California Press, 1978.

Weber, Max. *From Max Weber: Essays in Sociology*. Translated by Hans Gerth and C. Wright Mills. New York: Oxford University Press, 1946.

Weber, Max. "Politics as a Vocation." In *From Max Weber: Essays in Sociology*, edited and translated by H. H. Gerth and C. Wright Mills, 77–128. New York: Oxford University Press, 1946.

Weber, Max. "The Protestant Ethic and the Spirit of Capitalism." In *The Protestant Ethic and the Spirit of Capitalism and Other Writings*, edited by Peter Baehr and Gordon C. Wells. New York: Penguin Books, 2002.

Wedeen, Lisa. *Ambiguities of Domination: Politics, Rhetoric, and Symbols in Contemporary Syria*. Chicago: University of Chicago Press, 1999.

Wedeen, Lisa. *Peripheral Visions: Publics, Power, and Performance in Yemen*. Chicago: University of Chicago Press, 2009.

Weinberg, Steven. *Dreams of a Final Theory*. New York: Vintage, 1994.

Weiss, Jessica Chen. *Powerful Patriots: Nationalist Protest in China's Foreign Relations*. New York: Oxford University Press, 2014.

Wenzhou Daily. "An Open Letter that Rewards Petitions [Yifeng xuanshang xinfang de gongkaixin]." May 27, 2013.

Westcott, Ben. "How Chinese Doctor Li Wenliang Died Twice in China's State Media." CNN. February 6, 2020, https://www.cnn.com/2020/02/06/asia/china-li-wenliang-whistleblower-death-timeline-intl-hnk/index.html.

White, Stephen. "Economic Performance and Communist Legitimacy." *World Politics* 38, no. 3 (1986): 462–82.

The White House. "President Obama Signs Michigan Emergency Declaration." January 16, 2016. https://obamawhitehouse.archives.gov/the-press-office/2016/01/16/president-obama-signs-michigan-emergency-declaration.

The White House. "U.S.-China Joint Presidential Statement on Climate Change." September 25, 2015. https://obamawhitehouse.archives.gov/the-press-office/2015/09/25/us-china-joint-presidential-statement-climate-change.

Whyte, Martin. *Myth of the Social Volcano: Perceptions of Inequality and Distributive Injustice in Contemporary China.* Stanford, CA: Stanford University Press, 2010.

Wilson, Andrew. *Virtual Politics: Faking Democracy in the Post-Soviet World.* New Haven, CT: Yale University Press, 2005.

Wong Chun Han. "Xi Jinping's Eager-to-Please Bureaucrats Snarl His China Plans." *Wall Street Journal.* March 7, 2021. https://www.wsj.com/articles/xi-jinpings-eager-to-please-minions-snarl-his-china-plans-11615141195.

Wong, Stan Hok-Wui, and Yu Zeng. "Getting Ahead by Getting on the Right Track: Horizontal Mobility in China's Political Selection Process." *Journal of Contemporary China* 27, no. 109 (2018): 61–84.

Wu Jing, Yongheng Deng, Jun Huang, Randall Morck, and Bernard Yeung. "Incentives and Outcomes: China's Environmental Policy." National Bureau of Economic Research Working Paper no. 18754 (2013). https://www.nber.org/papers/w18754.

Xi Jinping. *The Governance of China* [Xi Jinping tan zhiguo lizheng]. Beijing: Beijing Books, 2018.

Xiandai Kuaibao. "Nanjing Covered in Smog on New Year's Eve, the EPB Issues Tickets [Nanjing Xinnian Zao 'Maifu', Huanbaoju Lian Kai Tinggong Da Fadan]." *Xiandai Kuaibao.* January 4, 2017. https://m.nbd.com.cn/articles/2017-01-04/1067057.html.

Xie Yichun, Mei Yu, Yongfei Bai, Xuerong Xing. "Ecological Analysis of an Emerging Urban Landscape Pattern—Desakota: A Case Study in Suzhou, China." *Landscape Ecology* 21, no. 8 (2006): 1297–309.

Xinjingbao. "Multiple Environmental Protection Directors Are Reposted to Become Local First-hands [Duowei huanbao tingzhang zhuangang defang yibashou]." April 30, 2019. http://www.xinhuanet.com/politics/2019-04/30/c_1124435572.htm.

Xinhua Daily News. "Responding to Invitations, Fifteen EPA Directors in Zhejiang Went Swimming in a River [Huiying yaoyue, Zhejiang 15 wei huanbao juzhang xiahe youyong]." September 9, 2013. http://news.xinhuanet.com/mrdx/2013-09/09/c_132703577.htm.

Xinhuanet. "Beijing Releases Latest Analysis of PM 2.5 Sources, Main Source Is Vehicles [Beijing fabu zuixin yilun PM2.5 yuan jiexi, zhuyao laizi jidongche]." May 15, 2018. http://www.xinhuanet.com/politics/2018-05/15/c_1122832062.htm.

Xinhuanet. "Businessman Offers 200 Thousand Yuan to Watch EPA Director to Swim in a River, EPA Director Laughs it Off [Shangren chu 20 wan yuan yaoqing huanbao juzhang xiahe youyong, juzhang yixiaozhizhi]." February 18, 2013. http://news.xinhuanet.com/local/2013-02/18/c_124357770.htm.

Xinhua News. "1973: First Step of Environmental Protection [1973 nian: huanjing baohu kaishi qibu]." *Xinhua News.* August 30, 2009. http://www.gov.cn/jrzg/2009-08/30/content_1404821.htm.

Xu Bin. *The Politics of Compassion: The Sichuan Earthquake and Civic Engagement in China.* Stanford, CA: Stanford University Press, 2017.

Yan Jirong. "Build a Service-oriented Government Based on Public Satisfaction [Jianshe renmin manyi de fuwuxing zhengfu]." *Guangming Daily*. January 21, 2020. http://theory.people.com.cn/n1/2020/0121/c40531-31557829.html.

Yang Dali. "China's Early Warning System Didn't Work on Covid-19. Here's the Story." *The Washington Post*. February 24, 2020. https://www.washingtonpost.com/politics/2020/02/24/china-early-warning-system-didnt-work-covid-19-heres-story/.

Yang Hongxing and Dingxin Zhao. "Performance Legitimacy, State Autonomy and China's Economic Miracle." *Journal of Contemporary China* 24, no. 91 (2015): 64–82.

Yang Jie. *Unknotting the Heart: Unemployment and Therapeutic Governance in China*. Ithaca, NY: Cornell University Press, 2015.

Yang Jisheng. *Tombstone: The Great Chinese Famine, 1958–1962*. New York: Farrer, Straus and Giroux, 2013.

Yu Keping. "Incremental Democracy [Zengliang minzhu]," in *Understanding Chinese Politics [Lijie Zhongguo zhengzhi]*, edited by Jing Yuejin, Zhang Xiaojin, Yu Xunda, 74–82. Beijing: Chinese Academy of Social Science Press, 2011.

Yu Keping. "Incremental Democratization and Political Reform [Zengliang minzhu yu zhengzhi gaige]." In *Reform Consensus and China's Future* [Gaige gongshi yu Zhongguo weilai], edited by Central Compilation and Translation Bureau, 88–100. Beijing: Central Compilation and Translation Press, 2013.

Yuezhi Zhao. *Communication in China: Political Economy, Power, and Conflict*. Lanham, MD: Rowman & Littlefield, 2008.

Yurchak, Alexei. *Everything Was Forever, Until It Was No More: The Last Soviet Generation*. Princeton, NJ: Princeton University Press, 2013.

Zacka, Bernardo. *When the State Meets the Street: Public Service and Moral Agency*. Cambridge, MA: Harvard University Press, 2018.

Zaller, John. *The Nature and Origins of Mass Opinion*. New York: Cambridge University Press, 1992.

Zhang Ling. *The River, the Plain, and the State: An Environmental Drama in Northern Song China, 1048–1128*. Cambridge: Cambridge University Press, 2016.

Zhang Shanhong, Yujun Yi, Yan Liu, and Xinghui Wang. "Hydraulic Principles of the 2,268-Year-Old Dujiangyan Project in China." *Journal of Hydraulic Engineering* 139, no. 5 (2013): 538–46.

Zhang Yang. "Allies in Action: Institutional Actors and Grassroots Environmental Activism in China." *Research in Social Movements, Conflicts and Change* 42 (2018): 9–38.

Zhao Dingxin. "The Mandate of Heaven and Performance Legitimation in Historical and Contemporary China." *American Behavioral Scientist* 53, no. 3 (2009): 416–33.

Zhao Lingyun, Lianhui Zhang, Xinghua Yi and Jianzhong Zhu. *The Construction of Ecological Civilization with Chinese Characteristics [Zhongguo tese shengtai wenming jianshe daolu]*. Beijing: China Financial and Economic Publishing House, 2014.

Zhejiang Daily [Zhejiang Ribao]. "Fifteen EPA Directors in Zhejiang Went Swimming in a River in Response to the Invitation [Zhejiang 15ge huanbao juzhang yingyao xiahe youyong]." September 9, 2013.

Zhejiang Online. "The Culprit of Strange-tasting Tab Water Uncovered—2-tert-butylphenol [Hangzhou zilaishui yiwei yuanxiong chaming linshuidingjibenfen]." *Zhejiang Online [Zhejiang Zaixian]*, January 17, 2014. http://zjnews.zjol.com.cn/system/2014/01/17/019816103.shtml.

Zhou Li'an. "Governing China's Local Officials: An Analysis of the Promotion Tourna-
ment Model [Zhongguo difang guanyuan de jinsheng jinbiaosai moshi yanjiu]."
Economic Research Journal [Jingji yanjiu] 7 (2007): 36–50.
Zhou Xueguang, Hong Lian, Leonard Ortolano, and Yinyu Ye. "A Behavioral Model of
"Muddling Through" in the Chinese Bureaucracy: The Case of Environmental
Protection." *China Journal* 70 (2013): 120–47.
Zhu Yuchao. ""Performance Legitimacy" and China's Political Adaptation Strategy."
Journal of Chinese Political Science 16, no. 2 (2011): 123–40.

Index

996 system, 68, 192n26

accountability, 75, 126
activist citizen, 109
actors
  cynicism of, 135 (*see also* performer
    cynicism)
  of performative governance, 21
  politicians as, 2, 154
  sincere and cynical, 96–97
admonition, 138–39
agricultural development, 47
air pollution
  bureaucrats' rationalization of, 97
  causes of, 54–55, 57
  in China, 4
  citizens' rationalization of, 130
  and Foul Air Law Enforcement Operation,
    82–92, 101, 109, 121
  gaps between issue, knowledge, and
    grievance on, 127–30
  in Lakeville, 65, 73
  in Nanjing, 116–18
  public outcry over, 4–5, 73–75, 82–84
  and public scrutiny, 112–15
  survey findings on scrutiny and, 112–14
air quality
  citizens' perceptions of, 112–14, 129–32
  data, 4, 173n27
  expectations for improvement in, 131–32
  in Lakeville, 65
  and public approval of environmental
    governance, 124–25
Ananich, Jim, 138
Ang Yuen Yuen, 41, 68
Anthropocene, 48, 185n22
appearance, separation of substance and,
  153–54
architecture, and state image, 80
audience, of performance, 3
audience cynicism, 23, 136. *See also*
    destructive information; information
    control
Austin, J. L., 7, 8, 10
authoritarianism

and bureaucracy, 3–4
  fragmented, 30, 56–57
  and performance legitimacy, 13, 188n67
authority
  charismatic, 2
  EPB's growing, 59, 93
  EPB's lack of, 5, 6, 71–72
  hierarchical, 5, 32
  political, 25
  relations, 67, 70

back stage
  in Goffman, 9
  at Lakeville EPB, 71–72
Bell, Daniel, 51
benevolence, 15, 80–81, 130–31
Bermeo, Nancy, 108–9, 197n5
Bonaparte, Napoleon, 24, 107
Bonney, Richard, 21
Boone, Catherine, 34
Bourdieu, Pierre, 8
Bo Xilai, 40
Brady, Henry, 102, 196n97
bribery, 58
Buddhism, and making sense of "sixth
  extinction," 50
budget, as measurement of bureaucratic
  power, 37–38
bureaucracy
  and authoritarianism, 3–4
  versus charismatic politicians, 2–3,
    155–56
  China's environmental, 5, 30–31, 56–60
  Chinese, 36–43, 67–68, 157, 172n20
  and the decoupling of formal and
    substantive rationality, 155–59
  discretion of street-level, 177n90
  hierarchy in, 3, 16, 31–32
  inert, 34
  from inward-looking to outward-facing,
    162
  under Mao, 67, 157
  and mass democracy, 172n19
  paternalistic, 34–35
  performative, 35

CPSIA information can be obtained
at www.ICGtesting.com
Printed in the USA
LVHW032300080323
741244LV00013B/175/J